DERIVATIVES AND ALTERNATIVE INVESTMENTS

CFA® PROGRAM CURRICULUM
2013 • Level I • Volume 6

CFA Institute

WILEY
John Wiley & Sons, Inc.

Please visit our website at
www.WileyGlobalFinance.com.

Contents

[O] indicates an optional segment

O indicates an optional segment

Contents

indicates an optional segment

🔘 indicates an optional segment

How to Use the CFA Program Curriculum

Congratulations on your decision to enter the Chartered Financial Analyst (CFA®) Program. This exciting and rewarding program of study reflects your desire to become a serious investment professional. You are embarking on a program noted for its high ethical standards and the breadth of knowledge, skills, and abilities it develops. Your commitment to the CFA Program should be educationally and professionally rewarding.

The credential you seek is respected around the world as a mark of accomplishment and dedication. Each level of the program represents a distinct achievement in professional development. Successful completion of the program is rewarded with membership in a prestigious global community of investment professionals. CFA charterholders are dedicated to life-long learning and maintaining currency with the ever-changing dynamics of a challenging profession. The CFA Program represents the first step towards a career-long commitment to professional education.

The CFA examination measures your mastery of the core skills required to succeed as an investment professional. These core skills are the basis for the Candidate Body of Knowledge (CBOK™). The CBOK consists of four components:

- A broad topic outline that lists the major top-level topic areas (CBOK Topic Outline)
- Topic area weights that indicate the relative exam weightings of the top-level topic areas
- Learning outcome statements (LOS) that advise candidates about the specific knowledge, skills, and abilities they should acquire from readings covering a topic area (LOS are provided in candidate study sessions and at the beginning of each reading)
- The CFA Program curriculum, readings, and end-of-reading questions, which candidates receive upon exam registration

Therefore, the keys to your success on the CFA exam is studying and understanding the CBOK™. The following sections provide background on the CBOK, the organization of the curriculum, and tips for developing an effective study program.

CURRICULUM DEVELOPMENT PROCESS

The CFA Program is grounded in the practice of the investment profession. Using the Global Body of Investment Knowledge (GBIK) collaborative website, CFA Institute performs a continuous practice analysis with investment professionals around the world to determine the knowledge, skills, and abilities (competencies) that are relevant to the profession. Regional expert panels and targeted surveys are conducted annually to verify and reinforce the continuous feedback from the GBIK collaborative website. The practice analysis process ultimately defines the CBOK. The CBOK contains the competencies that are generally accepted and applied by investment professionals. These competencies are used in practice in a generalist context and are expected to be demonstrated by a recently qualified CFA charterholder.

A committee consisting of practicing charterholders, in conjunction with CFA Institute staff, designs the CFA Program curriculum in order to deliver the CBOK to candidates. The examinations, also written by practicing charterholders, are designed to allow you to demonstrate your mastery of the CBOK as set forth in the CFA Program curriculum. As you structure your personal study program, you should emphasize mastery of the CBOK and the practical application of that knowledge. For more information on the practice analysis, CBOK, and development of the CFA Program curriculum, please visit www.cfainstitute.org.

ORGANIZATION OF THE CURRICULUM

The Level I CFA Program curriculum is organized into 10 topic areas. Each topic area begins with a brief statement of the material and the depth of knowledge expected.

Each topic area is then divided into one or more study sessions. These study sessions—18 sessions in the Level I curriculum—should form the basic structure of your reading and preparation.

Each study session includes a statement of its structure and objective, and is further divided into specific reading assignments. An outline illustrating the organization of these 18 study sessions can be found at the front of each volume.

The reading assignments are the basis for all examination questions, and are selected or developed specifically to teach the knowledge, skills, and abilities reflected in the CBOK. These readings are drawn from CFA Institute-commissioned content, textbook chapters, professional journal articles, research analyst reports, and cases. All readings include problems and solutions to help you understand and master the topic areas.

Reading-specific Learning Outcome Statements (LOS) are listed at the beginning of each reading. These LOS indicate what you should be able to accomplish after studying the reading. The LOS, the reading, and the end-of-reading questions are dependent on each other, with the reading and questions providing context for understanding the scope of the LOS.

You should use the LOS to guide and focus your study, as each examination question is based on an assigned reading and one or more LOS. The readings provide context for the LOS and enable you to apply a principle or concept in a variety of scenarios. The candidate is responsible for the entirety of all of the required material in a study session, the assigned readings as well as the end-of-reading questions and problems.

We encourage you to review the material on LOS (http://www.cfainstitute.org/cfaprogram/courseofstudy/Pages/cfa_los.aspx), including the descriptions of LOS "command words," (www.cfainstitute.org/Documents/cfa_and_cipm_los_command_words.pdf).

FEATURES OF THE CURRICULUM

OPTIONAL
SEGMENT

- **Required vs. Optional Segments** - You should read all of an assigned reading. In some cases, however, we have reprinted an entire chapter or article and marked certain parts of the reading as "optional." The CFA examination is based only on the required segments, and the optional segments are included only when they might help you to better understand the required segments (by seeing the required material in its full context). When an optional segment begins, you will see text and a dashed vertical bar in the outside margin that will continue until the optional segment ends, accompanied by another icon. *Unless the material is specifically marked as optional, you should assume it is required.* You should rely on the required segments and the reading-specific LOS in preparing for the examination.

END OPTIONAL
SEGMENT

- **Problems/Solutions** - *All questions and problems in the readings as well as their solutions (which are provided directly following the problems) are part of the curriculum and are required material for the exam.* When appropriate, we have included problems within and after the readings to demonstrate practical application and reinforce your understanding of the concepts presented. The questions and problems are designed to help you learn these concepts and may serve as a basis for exam questions. Many of these questions are adapted from past CFA examinations.

- **Margins** - The wide margins in each volume provide space for your note-taking.

- **Six-Volume Structure** - For portability of the curriculum, the material is spread over six volumes.

- **Glossary and Index** - For your convenience, we have printed a comprehensive glossary and index in each volume. Throughout the curriculum, a **bolded blue** word in a reading denotes a term defined in the glossary.

- **Source Material** - The authorship, publisher, and copyright owners are given for each reading for your reference. We recommend that you use this CFA Institute curriculum rather than the original source materials because the curriculum may include only selected pages from outside readings, updated sections within the readings, and contains problems and solutions tailored to the CFA Program.

- **LOS Self-Check** - We have inserted checkboxes next to each LOS that you can use to track your progress in mastering the concepts in each reading.

DESIGNING YOUR PERSONAL STUDY PROGRAM

Create a Schedule - An orderly, systematic approach to examination preparation is critical. You should dedicate a consistent block of time every week to reading and studying. Complete all reading assignments and the associated problems and solutions in each study session. Review the LOS both before and after you study each reading to ensure that you have mastered the applicable content and can demonstrate the knowledge, skill, or ability described by the LOS and the assigned reading. Use the LOS self-check to track your progress and highlight areas of weakness for later review.

As you prepare for your exam, we will e-mail you important exam updates, testing policies, and study tips. Be sure to read these carefully. Curriculum errata are periodically updated and posted on the study session page at www.cfainstitute.org. You may also sign up for an RSS feed to alert you to the latest errata update.

Successful candidates report an average of over 300 hours preparing for each exam. Your preparation time will vary based on your prior education and experience. For each level of the curriculum, there are 18 study sessions, so a good plan is to devote 15–20 hours per week, for 18 weeks, to studying the material. Use the final four to six weeks before the exam to review what you've learned and practice with sample and mock exams. This recommendation, however, may underestimate the hours needed for appropriate examination preparation depending on your individual circumstances, relevant experience, and academic background. You will undoubtedly adjust your study time to conform to your own strengths and weaknesses, and your educational and professional background.

You will probably spend more time on some study sessions than on others, but on average you should plan on devoting 15-20 hours per study session. You should allow ample time for both in-depth study of all topic areas and additional concentration on those topic areas for which you feel least prepared.

Online Sample Examinations - CFA Institute online sample examinations are intended to assess your exam preparation as you progress toward the end of your study. After each question, you will receive immediate feedback noting the correct response and indicating the relevant assigned reading, so you will be able to identify areas of weakness for further study. The 120-minute sample examinations reflect the question formats, topics, and level of difficulty of the actual CFA examinations. Aggregate data indicate that the CFA examination pass rate was higher among candidates who took one or more online sample examinations than among candidates who did not take the online sample examinations. For more information on the online sample examinations, please visit www.cfainstitute.org.

Online Mock Examinations - In response to candidate requests, CFA Institute has developed mock examinations that mimic the actual CFA examinations not only in question format and level of difficulty, but also in length and topic weight. The three-hour online mock exams simulate the morning and afternoon sessions of the actual CFA exam, and are intended to be taken after you complete your study of the full curriculum, so you can test your understanding of the CBOK and your readiness for the exam. The mock exams are available in a printable PDF format with feedback provided at the end of the exam, rather than after each question as with the sample exams. CFA Institute recommends that you take these mock exams at the final stage of your preparation toward the actual CFA examination. For more information on the online mock examinations, please visit www.cfainstitute.org.

Preparatory Providers - After you enroll in the CFA Program, you may receive numerous solicitations for preparatory courses and review materials. When considering a prep course make sure the provider is in compliance with the CFA Institute Prep Provider Guidelines Program (www.cfainstitute.org/partners/examprep/Pages/cfa_prep_provider_guidelines.aspx). Just remember, there are no shortcuts to success on the CFA examinations; reading and studying the CFA curriculum is the key to success on the examination. The CFA examinations reference only the CFA Institute assigned curriculum—no preparatory course or review course materials are consulted or referenced.

SUMMARY

Every question on the CFA examination is based on the content contained in the required readings and on one or more LOS. Frequently, an examination question is based on a specific example highlighted within a reading or on a specific end-of-reading question and/or problem and its solution. To make effective use of the CFA Program curriculum, please remember these key points:

1. All pages printed in the curriculum are required reading for the examination except for occasional sections marked as optional. You may read optional pages as background, but you will not be tested on them.

2. All questions, problems, and their solutions - printed at the end of readings - are part of the curriculum and are required study material for the examination.

3. You should make appropriate use of the online sample/mock examinations and other resources available at www.cfainstitute.org.

4. You should schedule and commit sufficient study time to cover the 18 study sessions, review the materials, and take sample/mock examinations.

5. **Note:** Some of the concepts in the study sessions may be superseded by updated rulings and/or pronouncements issued after a reading was published. Candidates are expected to be familiar with the overall analytical framework contained in the assigned readings. Candidates are not responsible for changes that occur after the material was written.

FEEDBACK

At CFA Institute, we are committed to delivering a comprehensive and rigorous curriculum for the development of competent, ethically grounded investment professionals. We rely on candidate and member feedback as we work to incorporate content, design, and packaging improvements. You can be assured that we will continue to listen to your suggestions. Please send any comments or feedback to curriculum@cfainstitute.org. Ongoing improvements in the curriculum will help you prepare for success on the upcoming examinations, and for a lifetime of learning as a serious investment professional.

Derivatives

TOPIC LEVEL LEARNING OUTCOME

The candidate should be able to demonstrate a working knowledge of the analysis of derivative investments, including forwards, futures, options, and swaps.

17

Derivatives

Derivatives—financial instruments that derive their value from the value of some underlying asset—have become increasingly important and fundamental in effectively managing financial risk and creating synthetic exposures to asset classes. As in other security markets, arbitrage and market efficiency play a critical role in establishing prices.

This study session builds the conceptual framework for understanding the basic derivative securities (forwards, futures, options, and swaps), derivative markets, and the use of options in risk management.

READING ASSIGNMENTS

Reading 60 *Derivative Markets and Instruments*

*Analysis of Derivatives for the Chartered Financial Analyst®
Program*, by Don M. Chance, CFA

Reading 61 *Forward Markets and Contracts*

*Analysis of Derivatives for the Chartered Financial Analyst®
Program*, by Don M. Chance, CFA

Reading 62 *Futures Markets and Contracts*

*Analysis of Derivatives for the Chartered Financial Analyst®
Program*, by Don M. Chance, CFA

60

Derivative Markets and Instruments

by Don M. Chance, CFA

LEARNING OUTCOMES

Mastery	The candidate should be able to:
☐	**a** define a derivative and distinguish between exchange-traded and over-the-counter derivatives;
☐	**b** contrast forward commitments and contingent claims;
☐	**c** define forward contracts, futures contracts, options (calls and puts), and swaps and compare their basic characteristics;
☐	**d** describe purposes of and controversies related to derivative markets;
☐	**e** explain arbitrage and the role it plays in determining prices and promoting market efficiency.

INTRODUCTION

1

The concept of risk is at the heart of investment management. Financial analysts and portfolio managers continually identify, measure, and manage risk. In a simple world where only stocks and bonds exist, the only risks are the fluctuations associated with market values and the potential for a creditor to default. Measuring risk often takes the form of standard deviations, betas, and probabilities of default. In the above simple setting, managing risk is limited to engaging in stock and bond transactions that reduce or increase risk. For example, a portfolio manager may hold a combination of a risky stock portfolio and a risk-free bond, with the relative allocations determined by the investor's tolerance for risk. If for some reason the manager desires a lower level of risk, the only transactions available to adjust the risk downward are to reduce the allocation to the risky stock portfolio and increase the allocation to the risk-free bond.

But we do not live in a simple world of only stocks and bonds, and in fact investors can adjust the level of risk in a variety of ways. For example, one way to reduce risk is to use insurance, which can be described as the act of paying someone to assume a risk for you. The financial markets have created their own way of offering insurance against financial loss in the form of contracts called **derivatives**. *A derivative is a financial instrument that offers a return based on the return of some other underlying asset.* In this sense, its return is *derived* from another instrument—hence, the name.

Analysis of Derivatives for the Chartered Financial Analyst® Program, by Don M. Chance, CFA. Copyright © 2003 by CFA Institute.

As the definition states, a derivative's performance is based on the performance of an underlying asset. This underlying asset is often referred to simply as the **underlying**.[1] It trades in a market in which buyers and sellers meet and decide on a price; the seller then delivers the asset to the buyer and receives payment. The price for immediate purchase of the underlying asset is called the **cash price** or **spot price** (in this volume, we will use the latter term). A derivative also has a defined and limited life: A derivative contract initiates on a certain date and terminates on a later date. Often the derivative's payoff is determined and/or made on the expiration date, although that is not always the case. In accordance with the usual rules of law, a derivative contract is an agreement between two parties in which each does something for the other. In some cases, as in the simple insurance analogy, a derivative contract involves one party paying the other some money and receiving coverage against potential losses. In other cases, the parties simply agree that each will do something for the other at a later date. In other words, no money need change hands up front.

We have alluded to several general characteristics of derivative contracts. Let us now turn to the specific types of derivatives that we will cover in this volume.

2 TYPES OF DERIVATIVES

In this section, we take a brief look at the different types of derivative contracts. This brief treatment serves only as a short introduction to familiarize you with the general ideas behind the contracts. We shall examine these derivatives in considerable detail in later readings.

Let us start by noting that derivative contracts are created on and traded in two distinct but related types of markets: exchange traded and over the counter. Exchange-traded contracts have standard terms and features and are traded on an organized derivatives trading facility, usually referred to as a futures exchange or an options exchange. Over-the-counter contracts are any transactions created by two parties anywhere else. We shall examine the other distinctive features of these two types of contracts as we proceed.

Derivative contracts can be classified into two general categories: forward commitments and contingent claims. In the following section, we examine forward commitments, which are contracts in which the two parties enter into an agreement to engage in a transaction at a later date at a price established at the start. Within the category of forward commitments, two major classifications exist: exchanged-traded contracts, specifically futures, and over-the-counter contracts, which consist of forward contracts and swaps.

2.1 Forward Commitments

The **forward contract** is an agreement between two parties in which one party, the buyer, agrees to buy from the other party, the seller, an underlying asset at a future date at a price established at the start. The parties to the transaction specify the forward contract's terms and conditions, such as when and where delivery will take place and the precise identity of the underlying. In this sense, the contract is said to be *customized*. Each party is subject to the possibility that the other party will default.

Many simple, everyday transactions are forms of forward commitments. For example, when you order a pizza for delivery to your home, you are entering into an agreement for a transaction to take place later ("30 minutes or less," as some

---

1 On behalf of the financial world, we apologize to all English teachers. "Underlying" is not a noun, but in the world of derivatives it is commonly used as such. To be consistent with that terminology, we use it in that manner here.

advertise) at a price agreed on at the outset. Although default is not likely, it could occur—for instance, if the party ordering the pizza decided to go out to eat, leaving the delivery person wondering where the customer went. Or perhaps the delivery person had a wreck on the way to delivery and the pizza was destroyed. But such events are extremely rare.

Forward contracts in the financial world take place in a large and private market consisting of banks, investment banking firms, governments, and corporations. These contracts call for the purchase and sale of an underlying asset at a later date. The underlying asset could be a security (i.e., a stock or bond), a foreign currency, a commodity, or combinations thereof, or sometimes an interest rate. In the case of an interest rate, the contract is not on a bond from which the interest rate is derived but rather on the interest rate itself. Such a contract calls for the exchange of a single interest payment for another at a later date, where at least one of the payments is determined at the later date.[2]

As an example of someone who might use a forward contract in the financial world, consider a pension fund manager. The manager, anticipating a future inflow of cash, could engage in a forward contract to purchase a portfolio equivalent to the S&P 500 at a future date—timed to coincide with the future cash inflow date—at a price agreed on at the start. When that date arrives, the cash is received and used to settle the obligation on the forward contract.[3] In this manner, the pension fund manager commits to the position in the S&P 500 without having to worry about the risk that the market will rise during that period. Other common forward contracts include commitments to buy and sell a foreign currency or a commodity at a future date, locking in the exchange rate or commodity price at the start.

The forward market is a private and largely unregulated market. Any transaction involving a commitment between two parties for the future purchase/sale of an asset is a forward contract. Although pizza deliveries are generally not considered forward contracts, similar transactions occur commonly in the financial world. Yet we cannot simply pick up the *Wall Street Journal* or the *Financial Times* and read about them or determine how many contracts were created the previous day.[4] They are private transactions for a reason: The parties want to keep them private and want little government interference. This need for privacy and the absence of regulation does not imply anything illegal or corrupt but simply reflects a desire to maintain a prudent level of business secrecy.

Recall that we described a forward contract as an agreement between two parties in which one party, the buyer, agrees to buy from the other party, the seller, an underlying asset at a future date at a price agreed upon at the start. A **futures contract** is a variation of a forward contract that has essentially the same basic definition but some additional features that clearly distinguish it from a forward contract. For one, a futures contract is not a private and customized transaction. Instead, it is a public, standardized transaction that takes place on a futures exchange. A futures exchange, like a stock exchange, is an organization that provides a facility for engaging in futures transactions and establishes a mechanism through which parties can buy and sell these contracts. The contracts are standardized, which means that the exchange determines the expiration dates, the underlying, how many units of the underlying are included in one contract, and various other terms and conditions.

---

2 These instruments are called forward rate agreements and will be studied in detail in the reading on forward markets and contracts.

3 The settling of the forward contract can occur through delivery, in which case the buyer pays the agreed-upon price and receives the asset from the seller, or through an equivalent cash settlement. In the latter case, the seller pays the buyer the difference between the market price and the agreed-upon price if the market price is higher. The buyer pays the seller the difference between the agreed-upon price and the market price if the agreed-upon price is higher.

4 In Section 4 of this reading, we will look at some ways to measure the amount of this type of trading.

Probably the most important distinction between a futures contract and a forward contract, however, lies in the default risk associated with the contracts. As noted above, in a forward contract, the risk of default is a concern. Specifically, the party with a loss on the contract could default. Although the legal consequences of default are severe, parties nonetheless sometimes fall into financial trouble and are forced to default. For that reason, only solid, credit-worthy parties can generally engage in forward contracts. In a futures contract, however, the futures exchange guarantees to each party that if the other fails to pay, the exchange will pay. In fact, the exchange actually writes itself into the middle of the contract so that each party effectively has a contract with the exchange and not with the other party. The exchange collects payment from one party and disburses payment to the other.

The futures exchange implements this performance guarantee through an organization called the clearinghouse. For some futures exchanges, the clearinghouse is a separate corporate entity. For others, it is a division or subsidiary of the exchange. In either case, however, the clearinghouse protects itself by requiring that the parties settle their gains and losses to the exchange on a daily basis. This process, referred to as the daily settlement or marking to market, is a critical distinction between futures and forward contracts. With futures contracts, profits and losses are charged and credited to participants' accounts each day. This practice prevents losses from accumulating without being collected. For forward contracts, losses accumulate until the end of the contract.[5]

One should not get the impression that forward contracts are rife with credit losses and futures contracts never involve default. Credit losses on forward contracts are extremely rare, owing to the excellent risk management practices of participants. In the case of futures contracts, parties do default on occasion. In fact, it is likely that there are more defaults on futures contracts than on forward contracts.[6] Nonetheless, the exchange guarantee has never failed for the party on the other side of the transaction. Although the possibility of the clearinghouse defaulting does exist, the probability of such a default happening is extremely small. Thus, we can generally assume that futures contracts are default-free. In contrast, the possibility of default, although relatively small, exists for forward contracts.

Another important distinction between forward contracts and futures contracts lies in the ability to engage in offsetting transactions. Forward contracts are generally designed to be held until expiration. It is possible, however, for a party to engage in the opposite transaction prior to expiration. For example, a party might commit to purchase one million euros at a future date at an exchange rate of $0.85/€. Suppose that later the euro has a forward price of $0.90/€. The party might then choose to engage in a new forward contract to sell the euro at the new price of $0.90/€. The party then has a commitment to buy the euro at $0.85 and sell it at $0.90. The risk associated with changes in exchange rates is eliminated, but both transactions remain in place and are subject to default.[7]

---

5 Although this process of losses accumulating on forward contracts until the expiration day is the standard format for a contract, modern risk management procedures include the possibility of forcing a party in debt to periodically pay losses accrued prior to expiration. In addition, a variety of risk-reducing techniques, such as the use of collateral, are used to mitigate the risk of loss. We discuss these points in more detail in the reading on forward markets and contracts.

6 Defaults are more likely for futures contracts than for forward contracts because participants in the forward markets must meet higher credit-worthiness standards than those in the futures markets. Indeed, many individuals participate in the futures markets; forward market participants are usually large, creditworthy companies. But the forward markets have no guarantor of performance, whereas the futures markets do. Therefore, participants in the forward markets have incurred credit losses in the past, while participants in the futures markets have not.

7 It is possible for the party engaging in the first transaction to engage in the second transaction with the same party. The two parties agree to cancel their transactions, settling the difference in value in cash and thereby eliminating the risk associated with exchange rates as well as the possibility of default.

In futures markets, the contracts have standardized terms and trade in a market that provides sufficient liquidity to permit the parties to enter the market and offset transactions previously created. The use of contracts with standardized terms results in relatively widespread acceptance of these terms as homogeneous agreed-upon standards for trading these contracts. For example, a U.S. Treasury bond futures contract covering $100,000 face value of Treasury bonds, with an expiration date in March, June, September, or December, is a standard contract. In contrast, if a party wanted a contract covering $120,000 of Treasury bonds, he would not find any such instrument in the futures markets and would have to create a nonstandard instrument in the forward market. The acceptance of standardized terms makes parties more willing to trade futures contracts. Consequently, futures markets offer the parties liquidity, which gives them a means of buying and selling the contracts. Because of this liquidity, a party can enter into a contract and later, before the contract expires, enter into the opposite transaction and offset the position, much the same way one might buy or sell a stock or bond and then reverse the transaction later. This reversal of a futures position completely eliminates any further financial consequences of the original transaction.[8]

A **swap** is a variation of a forward contract that is essentially equivalent to a series of forward contracts. Specifically, a swap is an agreement between two parties to exchange a series of future cash flows. Typically at least one of the two series of cash flows is determined by a later outcome. In other words, one party agrees to pay the other a series of cash flows whose value will be determined by the unknown future course of some underlying factor, such as an interest rate, exchange rate, stock price, or commodity price. The other party promises to make a series of payments that could also be determined by a second unknown factor or, alternatively, could be preset. We commonly refer to swap payments as being "fixed" or "floating" (sometimes "variable").

We noted that a forward contract is an agreement to buy or sell an underlying asset at a future date at a price agreed on today. A swap in which one party makes a single fixed payment and the other makes a single floating payment amounts to a forward contract. One party agrees to make known payments to the other and receive something unknown in return. This type of contract is like an agreement to buy at a future date, paying a fixed amount and receiving something of unknown future value. That the swap is a *series* of such payments distinguishes it from a forward contract, which is only a single payment.[9]

Swaps, like forward contracts, are private transactions and thus not subject to direct regulation.[10] Swaps are arguably the most successful of all derivative transactions. Probably the most common use of a swap is a situation in which a corporation, currently borrowing at a floating rate, enters into a swap that commits it to making a series of interest payments to the swap counterparty at a fixed rate, while receiving payments from the swap counterparty at a rate related to the floating rate at which it is making its loan payments. The floating components cancel, resulting in the effective conversion of the original floating-rate loan to a fixed-rate loan.

Forward commitments (whether forwards, futures, or swaps) are firm and binding agreements to engage in a transaction at a future date. They obligate each party to complete the transaction, or alternatively, to offset the transaction by engaging in another transaction that settles each party's financial obligation to the other. Contingent claims, on the other hand, allow one party the flexibility to not engage in the future transaction, depending on market conditions.

---

8 A common misconception is that, as a result of their standardized terms, futures contracts are liquid but nonstandardized forward contracts are illiquid. This is not always the case; many futures contracts have low liquidity, and many forward contracts have high liquidity.

9 A few other distinctions exist between swaps and forward contracts, such as the fact that swaps can involve both parties paying a variable amount.

10 Like all over-the-counter derivatives transactions, swaps are subject to indirect regulatory oversight in that the companies using them could be regulated by securities or banking authorities. In addition, swaps, like all contracts, are subject to normal contract and civil law.

2.2 Contingent Claims

Contingent claims are derivatives in which the payoffs occur if a specific event happens. We generally refer to these types of derivatives as options. Specifically, an **option** is a financial instrument that gives one party the right, but not the obligation, to buy or sell an underlying asset from or to another party at a fixed price over a specific period of time. An option that gives the right to buy is referred to as a call; an option that gives the right to sell is referred to as a put. The fixed price at which the underlying can be bought or sold is called the exercise price, strike price, striking price, or strike, and is determined at the outset of the transaction. In this book, we refer to it as the exercise price, and the action of buying or selling the underlying at the exercise price is called exercising the option. The holder of the option has the right to exercise it and will do so if conditions are advantageous; otherwise, the option will expire unexercised. Thus, the payoff of the option is contingent on an event taking place, so options are sometimes referred to as contingent claims.

In contrast to participating in a forward or futures contract, which represents a *commitment* to buy or sell, owning an option represents the *right* to buy or sell. To acquire this right, the buyer of the option must pay a price at the start to the option seller. This price is called the option premium or sometimes just the option price. In this volume, we usually refer to it as the option price.

Because the option buyer has the right to buy or sell an asset, the seller of the option has the potential commitment to sell or buy this asset. If the option buyer has the right to buy, the option seller may be obligated to sell. If the option buyer has the right to sell, the option seller may be obligated to buy. As noted above, the option seller receives the amount of the option price from the option buyer for his willingness to bear this risk.

An important distinction we made between forward and futures contracts was that the former are customized private transactions between two parties without a guarantee against losses from default. The latter are standardized contracts that take place on futures exchanges and are guaranteed by the exchange against losses from default. For options, both types of contracts—over-the-counter customized and exchange-listed standardized—exist. In other words, the buyer and seller of an option can arrange their own terms and create an option contract. Alternatively, the buyer and seller can meet directly, or through their brokers, on an options exchange and trade standardized options. In the case of customized options, the buyer is subject to the possibility of the seller defaulting when and if the buyer decides to exercise the option. Because the option buyer is not obligated to do anything beyond paying the original price, the seller of any type of option is not subject to the buyer defaulting. In the case of a standardized option, the buyer does not face the risk of the seller defaulting. The exchange, through its clearinghouse, guarantees the seller's performance to the buyer.

A variety of other instruments contain options and thus are forms of contingent claims. For instance, many corporations issue convertible bonds offering the holder an optionlike feature that enables the holder to participate in gains on the market price of the corporation's stock without having to participate in losses on the stock. Callable bonds are another example of a common financial instrument that contains an option, in this case the option of the issuer to pay off the bond before its maturity. Options themselves are often characterized in terms of standard or fairly basic options and more advanced options, often referred to as exotic options. There are also options that are not even based on assets but rather on futures contracts or other derivatives. A very widely used group of options is based on interest rates.

Another common type of option is contained in asset-backed securities. An asset-backed security is a claim on a pool of securities. The pool, which might be mortgages, loans, or bonds, is a portfolio assembled by a financial institution that then sells claims on the portfolio. Often, the borrowers who issued the mortgages, loans, or bonds have the right to pay off their debts early, and many choose to do so when interest rates fall significantly. They then refinance their loans by taking out a new loan at a lower interest rate. This right, called a prepayment feature, is a valuable option owned by the borrower. Holders of asset-backed securities bear the risk associated with prepayment options and hence are sellers of those options. The holders, or option sellers, receive a higher promised yield on their bond investment than they would have received on an otherwise equivalent bond without the option.

With an understanding of derivatives, there are no limits to the types of financial instruments that can be constructed, analyzed, and applied to achieve investment objectives. What you learn from this volume and the CFA Program will help you recognize and understand the variety of derivatives that appear in many forms in the financial world.

Exhibit 1 presents a classification of the types of derivative contracts as we have described them. Note that we have partitioned derivatives into those that are exchange-traded and those that trade in the over-the-counter market. The exhibit also notes some other categories not specifically mentioned above. These instruments are included for completeness, but they are relatively advanced and not covered in this reading.

Exhibit 1	**A Classification of Derivatives**

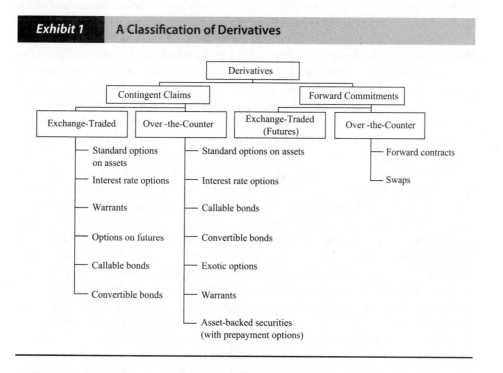

We have now looked at the basic characteristics of derivative contracts. In order to better understand and appreciate derivatives, we should take a quick look at where they came from and where they are now. Accordingly, we take a brief look at the history and current state of derivative markets.

DERIVATIVE MARKETS: PAST AND PRESENT

Derivative markets have an exciting and colorful history. Examining that history gives insights that help us understand the structure of these markets as they exist today.

The basic characteristics of derivative contracts can be found throughout the history of humankind. Agreements to engage in a commercial transaction as well as agreements that provide the right to engage in a commercial transaction date back hundreds of years. In medieval times, contracts for the future delivery of an asset with the price fixed at the time of the contract initiation were frequent. Early indications of futures markets were seen in Japan many hundreds of years ago. The futures markets generally trace their roots, however, to the 1848 creation of the Chicago Board of Trade, the first organized futures market. Its origins resulted from the burgeoning grain markets in Chicago, which created a need for a farmer to secure a price at one point in time, store the grain, and deliver it at a later point in time. At around the same time, customized option transactions were being offered, including some by the well-known financier Russell Sage, who found a clever way to offer combinations of customized options that replicated a loan at a rate that exceeded the maximum allowable rate under the then-existing usury laws.[11]

In the century that followed, the futures industry grew rapidly. Institutions such as the Chicago Board of Trade, the Chicago Mercantile Exchange, and later, the New York Mercantile Exchange and the Chicago Board Options Exchange became the primary forces in the global derivatives industry. These exchanges created and successfully marketed many innovative derivative contracts.[12] Although the first 100 years of futures exchanges were dominated by trading in futures on agricultural commodities, the 1970s saw the introduction of futures on financial instruments such as currencies, bonds, and stock indices. These "financial futures," as well as newly introduced options on individual stocks, currencies, bonds, and stock indices, ushered in a new era in which financial derivatives dominated agricultural derivatives—a situation that continues today. Although the commodity derivatives market includes very active contracts in oil and precious metals, financial derivatives have remained the primary force in the worldwide derivatives market.

Exchange-listed standardized derivatives, however, have hardly been the only instruments in the derivatives world. As noted, customized options have been around since at least the 19th century. The customized-options market flourished until the early 1970s, largely as a retail product. With the introduction of standardized options in 1973, however, the customized options market effectively died. But something else was going on at the time that would later revive this market. In the early 1970s, foreign exchange rates were deregulated and allowed to float freely. This deregulation led not only to the development of a futures, and later options, market for currencies but also to a market for customized forward contracts in foreign currencies. This market became known as the interbank market because it was largely operated within the global banking community, and it grew rapidly. Most importantly, it set the stage for the banking industry to engage in other customized derivative transactions.

Spurred by deregulation of their permitted activities during the 1980s, banks discovered that they could create derivatives of all forms and sell them to corporations and institutions that had risks that could best be managed with products specifically tailored for a given situation. These banks make markets in derivative products by assuming the risks that the corporations want to eliminate. But banks are not in the business of assuming unwanted risks. They use their vast resources and global networks to transfer or lay off the risk elsewhere, often in the futures markets. If they successfully lay off these risks, they can profit by buying and selling the derivatives at a suitable bid-ask spread. In addition to banks, investment banking firms also engage in derivatives transactions of this sort. The commercial and investment banks that make markets in derivatives are called **derivatives dealers**. Buying and selling derivatives is a natural extension of the activity these banks normally undertake in financial markets. This market for customized derivatives is what we refer to as the over-the-counter derivatives market.

By the end of the 20th century, the derivatives market reached a mature stage, growing at only a slow pace but providing a steady offering of existing products and a continuing slate of new products. Derivatives exchanges underwent numerous changes,

---

11 Sage was perhaps the first options arbitrageur. Of course, usury laws are rare these days and most investors understand **put–call parity**, so do not expect to make any money copying Sage's scheme.
12 It is probably also important to note that the futures and options exchanges have introduced many unsuccessful contracts as well.

often spurred by growing competition from the over-the-counter market. Some merged; others that were formerly nonprofit corporations have since become profit making. Some derivatives exchanges have even experimented with offering somewhat customized transactions. Nearly all have lobbied heavily for a reduction in the level or structure of the regulations imposed on them. Some derivatives exchanges have altered the manner in which trading takes place, from the old system of face-to-face on a trading floor (in sections called pits) to off-floor electronic trading in which participants communicate through computer screens. This type of transacting, called electronic trading, has even been extended to the internet and, not surprisingly, is called e-trading. Pit trading is still the primary format for derivatives exchanges in the United States, but electronic trading is clearly the wave of the future. As the dominant form of trading outside the United States, it will likely replace pit trading in the United States in coming years.

Exhibit 2 lists all global derivatives exchanges as of January 2002. Note that almost every country with a reasonably advanced financial market system has a derivatives exchange.

Exhibit 2	**Global Derivatives Exchanges**

North America
American Stock Exchange
Bourse de Montreal
BrokerTec Futures Exchange
Chicago Board Options Exchange
Chicago Board of Trade
Chicago Mercantile Exchange
International Securities Exchange
(New York)
Kansas City Board of Trade
Minneapolis Grain Exchange
New York Board of Trade
New York Mercantile Exchange
Pacific Exchange (San Francisco)
Philadelphia Stock Exchange
Winnipeg Commodity Exchange

Asia
Central Japan Commodity Exchange
Dalian Commodity Exchange
Hong Kong Exchanges & Clearing
Kansai Commodities Exchange (Osaka)
Korea Futures Exchange
Korea Stock Exchange
Malaysia Derivatives Exchange
New Zealand Futures & Options Exchange
Osaka Mercantile Exchange
Shanghai Futures Exchange
Singapore Commodity Exchange
Singapore Exchange
Tokyo Commodity Exchange
Tokyo Grain Exchange
Tokyo International Financial Futures
Exchange
Tokyo Stock Exchange
Zhengzhou Commodity Exchange

Europe
Bolsa de Valores de Lisboa e Porto
Borsa Italiana
Budapest Commodity Exchange
Eurex Frankfurt
Eurex Zurich
Euronext Amsterdam
Euronext Brussels
Euronext Paris
FUTOP Market (Copenhagen)
Helsinki Exchanges Group
International Petroleum Exchange
of London
London International Financial
Futures and Options Exchange
London Metal Exchange
MEFF Renta Fija (Barcelona)
MEFF Renta Variable (Madrid)
OM London Exchange
OM Stockholm Exchange
Romanian Commodity Exchange
Sibiu–Monetary-Financial and
Commodities Exchange (Romania)
Tel Aviv Stock Exchange
Wiener Borse AG (Vienna)

South America
Bolsa de Mercadorias & Futuros
(Sao Paulo)
Mercado a Termino de Buenos
Aires
Santiago Stock Exchange

Africa
South African Futures Exchange

Australia
Australian Stock Exchange
Sydney Futures Exchange

Source: Futures [magazine] *2002 Sourcebook.*

We cannot technically identify where over-the-counter derivatives markets exist. These types of transactions can conceivably occur anywhere two parties can agree to engage in a transaction. It is generally conceded, however, that London and New York are the primary markets for over-the-counter derivatives; considerable activity also takes place in Tokyo, Paris, Frankfurt, Chicago, Amsterdam, and many other major world cities.

Now we know where the derivative markets are, but are they big enough for us to care about? We examine this question in Section 4.

4 HOW BIG IS THE DERIVATIVES MARKET?

Good question. And the answer is: We really do not know. Because trading in exchange-listed contracts, such as futures and some options, is recorded, volume figures for those types of contracts are available. Exhibit 3 presents summary statistics for contract volume of global futures and options for 2000 and 2001. Note that in 2001, the largest category is equity indices. In 2000, the largest category was individual equities, followed by interest rates. In prior years, the largest category had been interest rates.

Currently, the United States accounts for approximately 35 percent of global futures and options volume. The largest exchange in the world, however, is the Korea Stock Exchange, which trades an exceptionally large volume of options on a Korean stock index. The second-largest exchange (and the largest exchange in terms of futures volume only) is the combined German–Swiss exchange called Eurex. The other largest exchanges (in order of 2001 volume) are the Chicago Mercantile Exchange, the Chicago Board of Trade, the London International Financial Futures and Options Exchange, the Paris Bourse, the New York Mercantile Exchange, the Bolsa de Mercadorias & Futuros of Brazil, and the Chicago Board Options Exchange. All of these exchanges traded at least 70 million contracts in 2001.[13]

Exhibit 3	Global Exchange-Traded Futures and Options Contract Volume (in Millions of Contracts)	

Contract Type	2000	2001
Equity indices	674.8	1,470.3
Interest rates	844.3	1,216.1
Individual equities	969.7	1,112.7
Energy	154.8	166.9
Agricultural	185.7	156.5
Nonprecious metals	75.7	70.2
Currencies	47.0	49.2
Precious metals	36.2	39.1
Other	1.3	0.8
Overall Total	2,989.5	4,281.8

Source: Futures Industry (January/February 2002).

---

[13] *Futures Industry* (January/February 2002).

One important factor that must be considered, however, in looking at trading volume as a measure of activity is that the futures and options exchanges influence their own volume by designating a contract's size. For example, a standard option in the United States covers 100 shares of the underlying stock. If an investor takes a position in options on 1,000 shares of stock, the investor would trade 10 options. If the options exchange had designated that the contract size be 200 shares, then the investor would trade only five contracts. Although there are often good reasons for setting a contract size at a certain level, volume comparisons must be taken with a degree of skepticism.[14]

The over-the-counter derivatives market is much more difficult to measure. Because the transactions are private, unregulated, and can take place virtually anywhere two parties can enter into an agreement, no official tabulation exists that allows us to identify the size of the market. Information is available, however, from semiannual surveys conducted by the Bank for International Settlements (BIS) of Basel, Switzerland, an international organization of central banks. The BIS publishes this data in its semiannual report "Regular OTC Derivatives Market Statistics," available on its website at www.bis.org/publ/regpubl.htm.

Exhibit 4 presents two charts constructed from the 30 June 2001 BIS survey and shows figures for foreign exchange, interest rate, equity, and commodity derivatives transactions. The "other" category, however, does include transactions of these types and reflects the BIS's estimates of positions taken by parties that do not report in this survey. It is used primarily to obtain an estimate for the overall size of the market and is not broken down by category.

For over-the-counter derivatives, notional principal is the most widely used measure of market size. Notional principal measures the amount of the underlying asset covered by a derivative contract. For example, a swap involving interest payments on ¥500 million has a notional principal of ¥500 million. The actual payments made in the swap, however, are merely interest payments on ¥500 million and do not come close to ¥500 million.[15] Thus, although notional principal is a commonly used measure of the size of the market, it can give a misleading impression by suggesting that it reflects the amount of money involved.[16]

Nonetheless, we would be remiss if we failed to note the market size as measured by notional principal. Based on Exhibit 4A, the total notional principal summing over these five categories is almost $100 trillion. Also note that interest rate derivatives are the most widely used category by far.

Exhibit 4B gives another picture of the size of the market by indicating the market value of over-the-counter derivatives. Market value indicates the economic worth of a derivative contract and represents the amount of money that would change hands if these transactions were terminated at the time of the report. The total market

---

14 For example, in 1999 the volume of Treasury bond futures on the Chicago Board of Trade was about 90 million contracts while the volume of Eurodollar futures on the Chicago Mercantile Exchange was about 93 million contracts. Consequently, at that time these two contracts appeared to have about the same amount of activity. But the Treasury bond contract covers Treasury bonds with a face value of $100,000, while the Eurodollar contract covers Eurodollars with a face value of $1,000,000. Thus, the Eurodollar futures market was arguably 10 times the size of the Treasury bond futures market. In 2002, about three Eurodollar futures contracts were traded for every Treasury bond futures contract traded.
15 In fact, the payments on a swap are even smaller than the interest payments on the notional principal. Swap interest payments usually equal only the difference between the interest payments owed by the two parties.
16 The over-the-counter derivatives industry originally began the practice of measuring its size by notional principal. This was a deliberate tactic designed to make the industry look larger so it would be more noticed and viewed as a significant and legitimate force. As it turns out, this tactic backfired, resulting in fears that more money was involved and at risk of loss than really was. Calls for increased scrutiny of the industry by government authorities resulted in the industry backpedaling on its use of notional principal and focusing more on market value as a measure of its size. Nonetheless, notional principal continues to be used as one, if not the primary, measure of the industry's size.

value for all categories is about $3 trillion. Market value is a better indication of the size of the market because it more accurately represents the actual money involved. Nonetheless, market value is subject to greater errors in estimation and thus is a less reliable measure than notional principal.

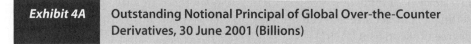

| Exhibit 4A | Outstanding Notional Principal of Global Over-the-Counter Derivatives, 30 June 2001 (Billions) |

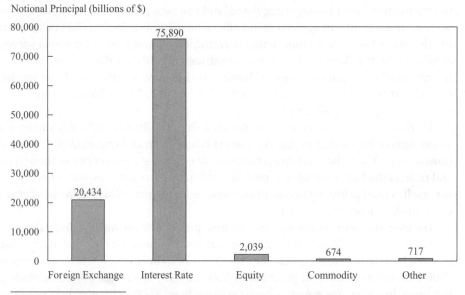

Source: Bank for International Settlements, www.bis.org/publ/regpubl.htm.

 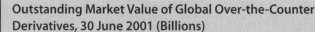

| Exhibit 4B | Outstanding Market Value of Global Over-the-Counter Derivatives, 30 June 2001 (Billions) |

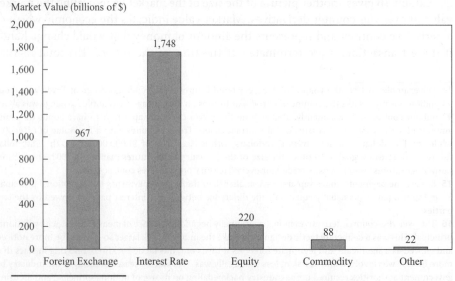

Source: Bank for International Settlements, www.bis.org/publ/regpubl.htm.

Although it is impossible to determine where these contracts originate, dollar-denominated derivatives represented about 34 percent of the global interest rate derivatives market in 2001, with euro-denominated derivatives accounting for about 27 percent and yen-denominated derivatives representing 17 percent.

Whether notional principal or market value is used, it is clear that the derivatives industry is large by any standard. Derivatives are widely available in global asset markets, and consequently, understanding derivatives is essential to operating in these markets, whether one chooses to use them or not.

Because derivative markets have been created around the world, there must be a reason for their continued existence. Let us now look at why derivative markets exist.

THE PURPOSES OF DERIVATIVE MARKETS

5

Derivative markets serve a variety of purposes in global social and economic systems. One of the primary functions of futures markets is **price discovery**. Futures markets provide valuable information about the prices of the underlying assets on which futures contracts are based. They provide this information in two ways. First, many of these assets are traded in geographically dispersed markets. Recall that the current price of the underlying asset is called the spot price. With geographically dispersed markets, many different spot prices could exist. In the futures markets, the price of the contract with the shortest time to expiration often serves as a proxy for the price of the underlying asset. Second, the prices of all futures contracts serve as prices that can be accepted by those who trade contracts in lieu of facing the risk of uncertain future prices. For example, a company that mines gold can hedge by selling a futures contract on gold expiring in two months, which locks in the price of gold two months later. In this manner, the two-month futures price substitutes for the uncertainty of the price of gold over the next two months.[17]

Futures contracts are not, however, the only derivatives that serve this purpose. In fact, forward contracts and swaps allow users to substitute a single locked-in price for the uncertainty of future spot prices and thereby permit the same form of price discovery as do futures.

Options work in a slightly different manner. They are used in a different form of hedging, one that permits the holder to protect against loss while allowing participation in gains if prices move favorably. Options do not so much reveal *prices* as they reveal *volatility*. As we shall see in the reading on option markets and contracts, the volatility of the underlying asset is a critical factor in the pricing of options. It is possible, therefore, to infer what investors feel about volatility from the prices of options.

Perhaps the most important purpose of derivative markets is **risk management**. We define risk management as the process of identifying the desired level of risk, identifying the actual level of risk, and altering the latter to equal the former. Often this process is described as hedging, which generally refers to the reduction, and in some cases the elimination, of risk. On the other side is the process called speculation. Traditional discussions of derivatives refer to hedging and speculation as complementary activities. In general, hedgers seek to eliminate risk and need speculators to assume risk, but such is not always the case. Hedgers often trade with other hedgers, and speculators often trade with other speculators. All one needs to hedge or speculate

---

17 Some people view futures prices as revealing expectations of future spot prices of the underlying asset, and in that sense, leading to price discovery. This view, however, is incorrect. Futures prices are not necessarily expectations of future spot prices. As we discussed above, they allow a substitution of the futures price for the uncertainty of future spot prices of the asset. In that sense they permit the acceptance of a sure price and the avoidance of risk.

is a party with opposite beliefs or opposite risk exposure. For example, a corporation that mines gold could hedge the future sale of gold by entering into a derivative transaction with a company that manufactures jewelry. Both of these companies are hedgers, seeking to avoid the uncertainty of future gold prices by locking in a price for a future transaction. The mining corporation has concerns about a price decrease, and the jewelry manufacturer is worried about a price increase.

An unfortunate consequence of the use of the terms "hedging" and "speculating" is that hedgers are somehow seen as on the high moral ground and speculators are sometimes seen as evil—a distortion of the role of speculators. In fact, there need be very little difference between hedgers and speculators. To restate an example we used when discussing swaps, consider a corporation that currently borrows at a floating rate. A common response to a fear of rising interest rates is for the corporation to use an interest rate swap in which it will make payments at a fixed rate and receive payments at a floating rate. The floating-rate payments it receives from the swap offset the floating-rate payments on the loan, thereby effectively converting the loan to a fixed-rate loan. The company is now borrowing at a fixed rate and, in the eyes of many, hedging.

But is the company really hedging? Or is it simply making a bet that interest rates will increase? If interest rates decrease, the company will be losing money in the sense of the lost opportunity to borrow at a lower rate. From a budgeting and cash flow standpoint, however, its fixed interest payments are set in stone. Moreover, the market value of a fixed-rate loan is considerably more volatile than that of a floating-rate loan. Thus, our "hedging" corporation can be viewed as taking more risk than it originally had.

The more modern view of the reason for using derivatives does not refer to hedging or speculation. Although we shall sometimes use those terms, we shall use them carefully and make our intentions clear. In the grander scheme of things, derivatives are tools that enable companies to more easily practice risk management. In the context of our corporation borrowing at the floating rate, it made a conscious decision to borrow at a fixed rate. Engaging in the swap is simply an activity designed to align its risk with the risk it wants, given its outlook for interest rates. Whether one calls this activity hedging or speculation is not even very important. The company is simply managing risk.

Derivative markets serve several other useful purposes. As we show later when exploring the pricing of derivative contracts, they improve market efficiency for the underlying assets. Efficient markets are fair and competitive and do not allow one party to easily take money from another. As a simple example, buying a stock index fund can be replicated by buying a futures on the fund and investing in risk-free bonds with the money that otherwise would have been spent on the fund. In other words, the fund and the combination of the futures and risk-free bond will have the same performance. But if the fund costs more than the combination of the futures and risk-free bond, investors have the opportunity to avoid the overpriced fund and take the combination.[18] This decreased demand for the fund will lower its price. The benefits to investors who do not even use derivatives should be clear: They can now invest in the fund at a more attractive price, because the derivatives market forced the price back to its appropriate level.

Derivative markets are also characterized by relatively low transaction costs. For example, the cost of investing in a stock index portfolio is as much as 20 times the cost of buying a futures contract on the index and a risk-free bond as described above. One might reasonably ask why derivatives are so much less expensive in terms of

---

18 Some investors, called arbitrageurs, will even find ways to sell the fund short to eliminate the risk of holding the futures and the bond, earning a profit from any discrepancy in their prices. We shall cover this type of transaction later in this reading.

transaction costs. The answer is that derivatives are designed to provide a means of managing risk. As we have previously described, they serve as a form of insurance. Insurance cannot be a viable product if its cost is too high relative to the value of the insured asset. In other words, derivatives must have low transaction costs; otherwise, they would not exist.

It would be remiss to overlook the fact that derivative markets have been subject to many criticisms. We next present some of these complaints and the reasons behind them.

CRITICISMS OF DERIVATIVE MARKETS

Derivatives have been highly controversial for a number of reasons. For one, they are very complex. Much of the criticism has stemmed from a failure to understand derivatives. When derivatives fail to do their job, it is often the derivatives themselves, rather than the users of derivatives, that take the blame. Yet, in many cases, the critics of derivatives simply do not understand them well enough. As described in Section 2, when homeowners take out mortgages, they usually receive a valuable option: the right to prepay their mortgages. When interest rates fall, homeowners often pay off their mortgages, refinancing them at lower rates. The holders of these mortgages usually sell them to other parties, which can include small organizations and individuals. Thus, we often find unsophisticated investors holding securities based on the payments from mortgages. When homeowners refinance, they capture huge interest savings. Where does this money come from? It comes from the pockets of the holders of mortgage securities. When these unsophisticated investors lose a lot of money, derivatives usually get the blame. Yet these losses went into the pockets of homeowners in the form of interest savings. Who is to blame? Probably the brokers, who sold the securities to investors who did not know what they were buying—which leads us to the next common criticism of derivatives.

The complexity of derivatives means that sometimes the parties that use them do not understand them well. As a result, they are often used improperly, leading to potentially large losses. Such an argument can, however, be used to describe fire, electricity, and chemicals. Used improperly, perhaps in the hands of a child or someone who does not know how to use them, all of these can be extremely dangerous. Yet, we know that sufficient knowledge of fire, electricity, and chemicals to use them properly is not very difficult to obtain. The same is true for derivatives; treat them with respect and healthy doses of knowledge.

Derivatives are also mistakenly characterized as a form of legalized gambling. Although gambling is certainly legal in many parts of the world, derivatives are often viewed as a government's sanction of gambling via the financial markets. But there is an important distinction between gambling and derivatives: The benefits of derivatives extend much further across society. By providing a means of managing risk along with the other benefits discussed above, derivatives make financial markets work better. The organized gambling industry affects the participants, the owners of casinos, and perhaps some citizens who benefit from state lotteries. Organized gambling does not, however, make society function better, and it arguably incurs social costs.

We have taken a look at what derivatives are, where they come from, where they are now, why we have them, and what people think of them. Understanding derivatives, however, requires a basic understanding of the market forces that govern derivative prices. Although we shall cover derivative pricing in more detail in later readings, here we take a brief look at the process of pricing derivatives by examining some important fundamental principles.

7   ELEMENTARY PRINCIPLES OF DERIVATIVE PRICING

In this section, we take a preliminary glance at how derivative contracts are priced. First, we introduce the concept of **arbitrage**. Arbitrage occurs when equivalent assets or combinations of assets sell for two different prices. This situation creates an opportunity to profit at no risk with no commitment of money. Let us start with the simplest (and least likely) opportunity for arbitrage: the case of a stock selling for more than one price at a given time. Assume that a stock is trading in two markets simultaneously. Suppose the stock is trading at $100 in one market and $98 in the other market. We simply buy a share for $98 in one market and immediately sell it for $100 in the other. We have no net position in the stock, so it does not matter what price the stock moves to. We make an easy $2 at no risk and we did not have to put up any funds of our own. The sale of the stock at $100 was more than adequate to finance the purchase of the stock at $98. Naturally, many market participants would do this, which would create downward pressure on the price of the stock in the market where it trades for $100 and upward pressure on the price of the stock in the market where it trades for $98. Eventually the two prices must come together so that there is but a single price for the stock. Accordingly, the principle that no arbitrage opportunities should be available is often referred to as the **law of one price**.

Recall that we mentioned in Section 5 that an asset can potentially trade in different geographic markets and, therefore, have several spot prices. This potential would appear to violate the law of one price, but in reality, the law is still upheld. A given asset selling in two different locations is not necessarily the same asset. If a buyer in one location discovered that it is possible to buy the asset more cheaply in another location, the buyer would still have to incur the cost of moving the asset to the buyer's location. Transportation costs could offset any such price differences.[19]

Now suppose we face the situation illustrated in Exhibit 5. In Exhibit 5A, observe that we have one stock, AXE Electronics, which today is worth $50 and which, one period later, will be worth either $75 or $40. We shall denote these prices as AXE = 50, $AXE^+ = 75$, and $AXE^- = 40$. Another stock, BYF Technology, is today worth $38 and one period later will be worth $60 or $32. Thus, BYF = 38, $BYF^+ = 60$, and $BYF^- = 32$. Let us assume the risk-free borrowing and lending rate is 4 percent. We assume no dividends on either stock during the period covered by this example.

Exhibit 5A	Arbitrage Opportunity with Stock AXE, Stock BYF, and a Risk-Free Bond

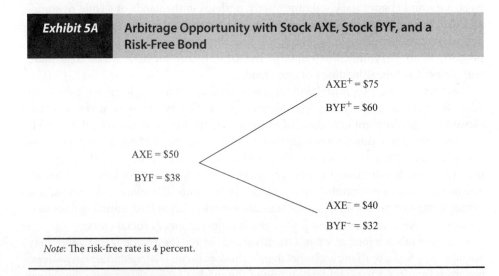

Note: The risk-free rate is 4 percent.

---

19 One might reasonably wonder if finding a consumer article selling in Wal-Mart at a lower price than in Target is not a violation of the law of one price. It certainly is, but we make no claim that the market for consumer products is efficient. Our focus is on the financial markets where, for example, Goldman Sachs can hardly offer shares of IBM at one price while Merrill Lynch offers them at another.

Exhibit 5B	Execution of Arbitrage Transaction with Stock AXE, Stock BYF, and a Risk-Free Bond

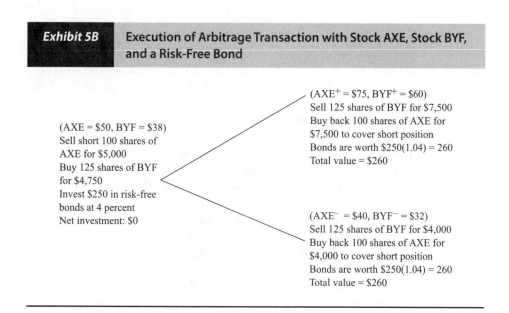

(AXE$^+$ = \$75, BYF$^+$ = \$60)
Sell 125 shares of BYF for \$7,500
Buy back 100 shares of AXE for
\$7,500 to cover short position
Bonds are worth \$250(1.04) = 260
Total value = \$260

(AXE = \$50, BYF = \$38)
Sell short 100 shares of
AXE for \$5,000
Buy 125 shares of BYF
for \$4,750
Invest \$250 in risk-free
bonds at 4 percent
Net investment: \$0

(AXE$^-$ = \$40, BYF$^-$ = \$32)
Sell 125 shares of BYF for \$4,000
Buy back 100 shares of AXE for
\$4,000 to cover short position
Bonds are worth \$250(1.04) = 260
Total value = \$260

The opportunity exists to make a profit at no risk without committing any of our funds, as demonstrated in Exhibit 5B. Suppose we borrow 100 shares of stock AXE, which is selling for \$50, and sell short, thereby receiving \$5,000. We take \$4,750 and purchase 125 shares of stock BYF. We invest the remaining \$250 in risk-free bonds at 4 percent. This transaction will not require us to put up any funds of our own: The short sale will be sufficient to fund the investment in BYF and leave money to invest in risk-free bonds.

If the top outcome in Exhibit 5 occurs, we sell the 125 shares of BYF for 125 × \$60 = \$7,500. This amount is sufficient to buy back the 100 shares of AXE, which is selling for \$75. But we will also have the bonds, which are worth \$250 × 1.04 = \$260. If the bottom outcome occurs, we sell the 125 shares of BYF for 125 × \$32 = \$4,000—enough money to buy back the 100 shares of AXE, which is selling for \$40. Again, we will have the risk-free bonds, worth \$260. Regardless of the outcome, we end up with \$260.

Recall that we put up no money of our own and ended up with a sure \$260. It should be apparent that this is an extremely attractive transaction, so everyone would do it. The combined actions of multiple investors would drive down the price of AXE and/or drive up the price of BYF until an equilibrium was reached at which this transaction would not be profitable. Assuming stock BYF's price remained constant, stock AXE would fall to \$47.50. Or assuming stock AXE's price remained constant, stock BYF would rise to \$40.

Of course, this example is extremely simplified. Clearly a stock price can change to more than two other prices. Also, if a given stock is at one price, another stock may be at any other price. We have created a simple case here to illustrate a point. When derivatives are involved, the simplification here is relatively safe. In fact, it is quite appropriate.

Now we look at another type of arbitrage opportunity, which involves a forward contract and will establish an appropriate price for the forward contract. Let stock AXE sell for \$50. We borrow \$50 at 4 percent interest by issuing a risk-free bond, use the money to buy one share of stock AXE, and simultaneously enter into a forward contract to sell this share at a price of \$54 one period later. The stock will then move to either \$75 or \$40 in the next period; the forward contract will require that we deliver the stock and accept \$54 for it; and we shall owe \$50 × 1.04 = \$52 on the loan.

Let us look at the two outcomes. Suppose stock AXE goes to \$75. We deliver the stock to settle the obligation on the forward contract and receive \$54 for it. We use \$52 of the \$54 to pay back the loan, leaving a gain of \$2. Now suppose AXE goes to \$40. We deliver the stock, fulfilling the obligation of the forward contract, and receive \$54. Again, we use \$52 of the \$54 to pay back the loan, leaving a gain of \$2.

In either case we made $2, free and clear. In fact, we can even accommodate the possibility of more than two future prices for AXE. The key point is that we faced no risk and did not have to put up any of our own money, but we ended up with $2—clearly a good deal. In fact, this is what we would call an arbitrage profit. But from where did it originate?

It turns out that the forward price we received, $54, was an inappropriate price given current market conditions. In fact, it was just an arbitrary price, made up to illustrate the point. To eliminate the opportunity to earn the $2 profit, the forward price should be $52—equal, not coincidentally, to the amount owed on the loan. It is also no coincidence that $52 is the price of the asset increased by the rate of interest.

In this example, many market participants would do this transaction as long as it generates an arbitrage profit. These forces of arbitrage would either force the forward price down or force the price of the stock up until an equilibrium is reached that eliminates the opportunity to profit at no risk with no commitment of one's own funds.

We have just had a taste of not only the powerful forces of arbitrage but also a pricing model for one derivative, the forward contract. In this simple example, according to the pricing model, the forward price should be the spot price increased by the interest rate. Although there is a lot more to derivative pricing than shown here, the basic principle remains the same regardless of the type of instrument or the complexity of the setting: *Prices are set to eliminate the opportunity to profit at no risk with no commitment of one's own funds.* There are no opportunities for arbitrage profits.

Lest we be too naive, however, we must acknowledge that there is a large industry of arbitrageurs. So how can such an industry exist if there are no opportunities for riskless profit? One explanation is that most of the arbitrage transactions are more complex than this simple example and involve estimating information, which can result in differing opinions. Arbitrage involving options, for example, usually requires estimates of a stock's volatility. Different participants have different opinions about this volatility. It is quite possible that two counterparties trading with each other can believe that each is arbitraging against the other.

But more importantly, the absence of arbitrage opportunities is upheld, ironically, only if participants believe that arbitrage opportunities *do* exist. If market traders believe that no opportunities exist to earn arbitrage profits, then they will not follow market prices and compare these prices with what they ought to be, as in the forward contract example given above. Without participants watching closely, prices would surely get out of line and offer arbitrage opportunities. Thus, eliminating arbitrage opportunities requires that participants be vigilant to arbitrage opportunities. In other words, strange as it may sound, disbelief and skepticism concerning the absence of arbitrage opportunities are required in order that it hold as a legitimate principle.

Markets in which arbitrage opportunities are either nonexistent or are quickly eliminated are relatively efficient markets. Recall from your study of portfolio theory and investment analysis that efficient markets are those in which it is not possible, except by chance, to earn returns in excess of those that would be fair compensation for the risk assumed. Although abnormal returns can be earned in a variety of ways, arbitrage profits are definitely examples of abnormal returns, relatively obvious to identify and easy to capture. Thus, they are the most egregious violations of the principle of market efficiency. A market in which arbitrage profits do not exist is one in which the most obvious violations of market efficiency have been eliminated.

Throughout this study session, we shall study derivatives by using the principle of arbitrage as a guide. We will assume that arbitrage opportunities cannot exist for any significant length of time. Thus, prices must conform to models that assume no arbitrage. On the other hand, we do not want to take the absence of arbitrage opportunities so seriously that we give up and believe that arbitrage opportunities never exist. Otherwise, they will arise, and someone else will take them from us.

SUMMARY

- A derivative contract is a financial instrument with a return that is obtained from or "derived" from the return of another underlying financial instrument.

- Exchange-traded derivatives are created, authorized, and traded on a derivatives exchange, an organized facility for trading derivatives. Exchange-traded derivatives are standardized instruments with respect to certain terms and conditions of the contract. They trade in accordance with rules and specifications prescribed by the derivatives exchange and are usually subject to governmental regulation. Exchange-traded derivatives are guaranteed by the exchange against loss resulting from the default of one of the parties. Over-the-counter derivatives are transactions created by any two parties off of a derivatives exchange. The parties set all of their own terms and conditions, and each assumes the credit risk of the other party.

- A forward commitment is an agreement between two parties in which one party agrees to buy and the other agrees to sell an asset at a future date at a price agreed on today. The three types of forward commitments are forward contracts, futures contracts, and swaps.

- A forward contract is a forward commitment created in the over-the-counter market. A futures contract is a forward commitment created and traded on a futures exchange. A swap is an over-the-counter transaction consisting of a series of forward commitments.

- A contingent claim is a derivative contract with a payoff dependent on the occurrence of a future event. The primary types of contingent claims are options, but other types involve variations of options, often combined with other financial instruments or derivatives.

- An option is a derivative contract giving one party the right to buy or sell an underlying asset at a fixed price over a period of time or at a specific point in time. The party obtaining the right pays a premium (the option price) at the start and receives the right to buy or sell, as prescribed by the contract. The two types of options are a call (the right to buy) and a put (the right to sell).

- The size of the global derivatives market can be measured by notional principal, which is the amount of the underlying on which a derivative is based, and by market value, which is the economic worth of the derivative.

- Derivative markets serve many useful purposes such as providing price discovery, facilitating risk management, making markets more efficient, and lowering transaction costs. Derivatives are often criticized as being excessively dangerous for unknowledgeable investors and have been inappropriately likened to gambling.

- Arbitrage is a process through which an investor can buy an asset or combination of assets at one price and concurrently sell at a higher price, thereby earning a profit without investing any money or being exposed to any risk. The combined actions of many investors engaging in arbitrage results in rapid price adjustments that eliminate these opportunities, thereby bringing prices back in line and making markets more efficient.

PRACTICE PROBLEMS FOR READING 60

1. For all parties involved, which of the following financial instruments is *not* an example of a forward commitment?

   A. Swap.

   B. Call option.

   C. Futures contract.

2. The main risk faced by an individual who enters into a forward contract to buy the S&P 500 Index is that:

   A. the market may rise.

   B. the market may fall.

   C. market volatility may rise.

3. Which of the following statements is *most* accurate?

   A. Forward contracts are marked to market daily.

   B. Futures contracts have more default risk than forward contracts.

   C. Forward contracts require that both parties to the transaction have a high degree of credit-worthiness.

4. Which of the following statements is *least* accurate?

   A. Futures contracts are easier to offset than forward contracts.

   B. Forward contracts are generally more liquid than futures contracts.

   C. Forward contracts are easier to tailor to specific needs than futures contracts.

5. A swap is *best* characterized as a:

   A. series of forward contracts.

   B. derivative contract that has not gained widespread popularity.

   C. single fixed payment in exchange for a single floating payment.

6. Which of the following is *most* representative of forward contracts and contingent claims?

	Forward Contracts	Contingent Claims
A.	Premium paid at inception	Premium paid at inception
B.	Premium paid at inception	No premium paid at incept
C.	No premium paid at inception	Premium paid at inception

7. For the long position, the *most likely* advantage of contingent claims over forward commitments is that contingent claims:

   A. are easier to offset than forward commitments.

   B. have lower default risk than forward commitments.

   C. permit gains while protecting against losses.

8. For derivative contracts, the notional principal is *best* described as:

   A. the amount of the underlying asset covered by the contract.

   B. a measure of the actual payments made and received in the contract.

   C. tending to underestimate the actual payments made and received in the contract.

9. By volume, the most widely used group of derivatives is the one with contracts written on which of the following types of underlying assets?

   A. Financial.

   B. Commodities.

   C. Energy-related.

10. Which of the following is *least* likely to be a purpose served by derivative markets?

    A. Arbitrage.

    B. Price discovery.

    C. Risk management.

11. The *most likely* reason derivative markets have flourished is that:

    A. derivatives are easy to understand and use.

    B. derivatives have relatively low transaction costs.

    C. the pricing of derivatives is relatively straightforward.

12. A private transaction in which one party agrees to make a single fixed payment in the future and another party agrees to make a single floating payment in the future is *best* characterized as a(n):

    A. futures contract.

    B. forward contract.

    C. over-the-counter contingent claim.

13. A public, standardized transaction that constitutes a commitment between two parties to transfer the underlying asset at a future date at a price agreed upon now is *best* characterized as a(n):

    A. swap.

    B. futures contract.

    C. exchange-traded contingent claim.

SOLUTIONS FOR READING 60

1. B is correct. A call option is not binding on *both* parties in the same sense that the other financial instruments are. The call option gives the holder a right but does not impose an obligation.

2. B is correct. If the market falls, the buyer of a forward contract could pay more for the index, as determined by the price that was contracted for at the inception of the contract, than the index is worth when the contract matures.

3. C is correct. Forward contracts are usually private transactions that do not have an intermediary such as a clearinghouse to guarantee performance by both parties. This type of transaction requires a high degree of credit-worthiness for both parties.

4. B is correct. Forward contracts are usually less liquid than futures contracts because they are typically private transactions tailored to suit both parties, unlike futures contracts, which are usually for standardized amounts and are exchange traded.

5. A is correct. A swap is most like a series of forward contracts. An example is a swap in which one party makes a set of fixed-rate payments over time in exchange for a set of floating-rate payments based on some notional amount.

6. C is correct. Unlike a contingent claim, a forward commitment typically requires no premium to be paid up front. An intuitive way to look at this is to realize that a forward commitment is binding on both parties, so any up-front fees would cancel, while a contingent claim is binding only on the party in the short position. For this, the party in the short position demands (and receives) compensation.

7. C is correct. Because the holder of a contingent claim (the party in the long position) has a right but not an obligation, she will only exercise when it is in her best interest to do so and not otherwise. This will happen only when she stands to gain and never when she stands to lose.

8. A is correct. The notional principal is the amount of the underlying asset covered by the derivative contract.

9. A is correct. The most widely used derivative contracts are written on underlying assets that are financial, such as Treasury instruments and stock indices.

10. A is correct. Arbitrage, or the absence of it, is the basis for pricing most derivative contracts. Consequently, it is relatively unusual, although certainly not impossible, for derivative markets to be used to generate arbitrage profits.

11. B is correct. One reason derivative markets have flourished is that they have relatively low transaction costs. For example, buying a risk-free Treasury security and a futures contract on the S&P 500 Index to replicate payoffs to the index is cheaper than buying the 500 stocks in the index in their proper proportions to get the same payoff.

12. B is correct. The clues that guide the response are 1) the transaction is private, which eliminates the futures contract answer, and 2) the transaction is a commitment ("agrees to make"), thus eliminating the contingent claims answers. A swap with a single payment is equivalent to a forward contract.

13. B is correct. The transaction is a commitment, which eliminates the contingent claim answer; the transaction is standardized, which is a characteristic of futures contracts; and the transaction is for single delivery at a future date, which is, in general, not a characteristic of a newly-initiated swap contract.

61

Forward Markets and Contracts

by Don M. Chance, CFA

LEARNING OUTCOMES

Mastery	The candidate should be able to:
☐	**a** explain delivery/settlement and default risk for both long and short positions in a forward contract;
☐	**b** describe the procedures for settling a forward contract at expiration, and how termination prior to expiration can affect credit risk;
☐	**c** distinguish between a dealer and an end user of a forward contract;
☐	**d** describe the characteristics of equity forward contracts and forward contracts on zero-coupon and coupon bonds;
☐	**e** describe the characteristics of the Eurodollar time deposit market, and define LIBOR and Euribor;
☐	**f** describe forward rate agreements (FRAs) and calculate the gain/loss on a FRA;
☐	**g** calculate and interpret the payoff of a FRA and explain each of the component terms of the payoff formula;
☐	**h** describe the characteristics of currency forward contracts.

INTRODUCTION

1

In the reading on derivative markets and instruments, we gave a general overview of global derivative markets. We identified those markets as forward markets, futures markets, options markets, and swap markets. The following series of readings focuses individually on those markets. We begin with forward markets.

First recall our definition of a forward contract: *A forward contract is an agreement between two parties in which one party, the buyer, agrees to buy from the other party, the seller, an underlying asset or other derivative, at a future date at a price established at the start of the contract.* Therefore, it is a commitment by two parties to engage in a transaction at a later date with the price set in advance. The buyer is often called the **long** and the seller is often called the **short**.[1] Although any two parties can agree on

---

1 As pointed out in the reading on derivative markets and instruments with respect to the word *underlying*, the derivatives industry often uses nouns, verbs, adjectives, and adverbs as parts of speech other than what they are. Hence, words like *long* and *short* are used not as adjectives but as nouns.

such a contract, in this book we are interested only in forward contracts that involve large corporations, financial institutions, nonprofit organizations, or governments.

Recalling an example from the reading on derivative markets and instruments, a pension fund manager, anticipating the receipt of cash at a future date, might enter into a commitment to purchase a stock portfolio at a later date at a price agreed on today. By doing so, the manager's position is unaffected by any changes in the value of the stock portfolio between today and the date of the actual investment in the stock portfolio. In this sense, the manager is hedged against an increase in stock prices until the cash is received and invested. The disadvantage of such a transaction is that the manager is also hedged against any decreases in stock prices. If stock prices fall between the time the commitment is established and the time the cash is received, the manager will regret having entered into the forward contract because the stock could have been acquired at a lower price. But that is the nature of a forward contract hedge: It locks in a price.

An important feature of a forward contract is that neither party pays any money at the start. The parties might require some collateral to minimize the risk of default, but for most of this reading, we shall ignore this point. So keep in mind this very important aspect of forward contracts: *No money changes hands at the start.*

1.1 Delivery and Settlement of a Forward Contract

When a forward contract expires, there are two possible arrangements that can be used to settle the obligations of the parties. A deliverable forward contract stipulates that the long will pay the agreed-upon price to the short, who in turn will deliver the underlying asset to the long, a process called **delivery**. An alternative procedure, called **cash settlement**, permits the long and short to pay the net cash value of the position on the delivery date. For example, suppose two parties agree to a forward contract to deliver a zero-coupon bond at a price of $98 per $100 par. At the contract's expiration, suppose the underlying zero-coupon bond is selling at a price of $98.25. The long is due to receive from the short an asset worth $98.25, for which a payment to the short of $98.00 is required. In a cash-settled forward contract, the short simply pays the long $0.25. If the zero-coupon bond were selling for $97.50, the long would pay the short $0.50. Delivery of a zero-coupon bond is not a difficult thing to do, however, and cash-settled contracts are more commonly used in situations where delivery is impractical.[2] For example, if the underlying is the Russell 3000 Index, the short would have to deliver to the long a portfolio containing each of the Russell 3000 stocks proportionate to its weighting in the index. Consequently, cash settlement is much more practical. Cash-settled forward contracts are sometimes called **NDFs**, for **nondeliverable forwards**, although this term is used predominately with respect to foreign exchange forwards.

1.2 Default Risk and Forward Contracts

An important characteristic of forward contracts is that they are subject to default. Regardless of whether the contract is for delivery or cash settlement, the potential exists for a party to default. In the zero-coupon bond example above, the long might be unable to pay the $98 or the short might be unable to buy the zero-coupon bond and make delivery of the bond to the long. Generally speaking, however, forward contracts are structured so that only the party owing the greater amount can default. In other words, if the short is obligated to deliver a zero-coupon bond selling for more than $98, then the long would not be obligated to make payment unless the

---

2 Be aware, however, that the choice of delivery or cash settlement is not an option available at expiration. It is negotiated between the parties at the start.

short makes delivery. Likewise, in a cash settled contract, only one party—the one owing the greater amount—can default. We discuss the nature of this credit risk in the following section.

1.3 Termination of a Forward Contract

Let us note that a forward contract is nearly always constructed with the idea that the participants will hold on to their positions until the contract expires and either engage in delivery of the asset or settle the cash equivalent, as required in the specific contract. The possibility exists, however, that at least one of the participants might wish to terminate the position prior to expiration. For example, suppose a party goes long, meaning that she agrees to buy the asset at the expiration date at the price agreed on at the start, but she subsequently decides to terminate the contract before expiration. We shall assume that the contract calls for delivery rather than cash settlement at expiration.

To see the details of the contract termination, suppose it is part of the way through the life of the contract, and the long decides that she no longer wishes to buy the asset at expiration. She can then re-enter the market and create a new forward contract expiring at the same time as the original forward contract, taking the position of the seller instead. Because of price changes in the market during the period since the original contract was created, this new contract would likely have a different price at which she would have to commit to sell. She would then be long a contract to buy the asset at expiration at one price and short a contract to sell the asset at expiration at a different price. It should be apparent that she has no further exposure to the price of the asset.

For example, suppose she is long to buy at $40 and short to deliver at $42. Depending on the characteristics of the contract, one of several possibilities could occur at expiration. Everything could go as planned—the party holding the short position of the contract on which she is long at $40 delivers the asset to her, and she pays him $40. She then delivers the asset to the party who is long the contract on which she is short at $42. That party pays her $42. She nets $2. The transaction is over.

There is always a possibility that her counterparty on the long contract could default. She is still obligated to deliver the asset on the short contract, for which she will receive $42. But if her counterparty on the long contract defaults, she has to buy the asset in the market and could suffer a significant loss. There is also a possibility that the counterparty on her short contract could fail to pay her the $42. Of course, she would then not deliver the asset but would be exposed to the risk of changes in the asset's price. This type of problem illustrates the credit risk in a forward contract.

To avoid the credit risk, when she re-enters the market to go short the forward contract, she could contact the same counterparty with whom she engaged in the long forward contract. They could agree to cancel both contracts. Because she would be owed $2 at expiration, cancellation of the contract would result in the counterparty paying her the present value of $2. This termination or offset of the original forward position is clearly desirable for both counterparties because it eliminates the credit risk.[3] It is always possible, however, that she might receive a better price from another counterparty. If that price is sufficiently attractive and she does not perceive the credit risk to be too high, she may choose to deal with the other counterparty and leave the credit risk in the picture.

---

3 This statement is made under the assumption that the parties do not want the credit risk. Credit risk, like other risks, however, can be a risk that some parties want because of the potential for earning attractive returns by using their expertise in measuring the actual credit risk relative to the credit risk as perceived by the market. In addition, credit risk offers diversification benefits.

THE STRUCTURE OF GLOBAL FORWARD MARKETS

The global market for forward contracts is part of a vast network of financial institutions that make markets in these instruments as well as in other related derivatives, such as swaps and options. Some dealers specialize in certain markets and contracts, such as forward contracts on the euro or forward contracts on Japanese equity products. These dealers are mainly large global banking institutions, but many large non-banking institutions, such as Goldman Sachs and Merrill Lynch, are also big players in this market.

Dealers engage in transactions with two types of parties: end users and other dealers. An end user is typically a corporation, nonprofit organization, or government.[4] An end user is generally a party with a risk management problem that is searching for a dealer to provide it with a financial transaction to solve that problem. Although the problem could simply be that the party wants to take a position in anticipation of a market move, more commonly the end user has a risk it wants to reduce or eliminate.

As an example, Hoffman-LaRoche, the large Swiss pharmaceutical company, sells its products globally. Anticipating the receipt of a large amount of cash in U.S. dollars and worried about a decrease in the value of the dollar relative to the Swiss franc, it could buy a forward contract to sell the dollar and buy Swiss francs. It might seek out a dealer such as UBS Warburg, the investment firm affiliated with the large Swiss bank UBS, or it might approach any of the other large multinational banks with which it does business. Or it might end up dealing with a non-bank entity, like Merrill Lynch. Assume that Hoffman-LaRoche enters into this contract with UBS Warburg. Hoffman-LaRoche is the end user; UBS Warburg is the dealer.

Transactions in forward contracts typically are conducted over the phone. Each dealer has a quote desk, whose phone number is well known to the major participants in the market. If a party wishes to conduct a transaction, it simply phones the dealer for a quote. The dealer stands ready to take either side of the transaction, quoting a bid and an ask price or rate. The bid is the price at which the dealer is willing to pay for the future purchase of the asset, and the ask is the price at which the dealer is willing to sell. When a dealer engages in a forward transaction, it has then taken on risk from the other party. For example, in the aforementioned transaction of Hoffman-LaRoche and UBS Warburg, by entering into the contract, UBS Warburg takes on a risk that Hoffman-LaRoche has eliminated. Specifically, UBS Warburg has now committed to buying dollars and selling Swiss francs at a future date. Thus, UBS Warburg is effectively long the dollar and stands to gain from a strengthening dollar/weakening Swiss franc. Typically dealers do not want to hold this exposure. Rather, they find another party to offset the exposure with another derivative or spot transaction. Thus, UBS Warburg is a wholesaler of risk—buying it, selling it, and trying to earn a profit off the spread between its buying price and selling price.

One might reasonably wonder why Hoffman-LaRoche could not avoid the cost of dealing with UBS Warburg. In some cases, it might be able to. It might be aware of another party with the exact opposite needs, but such a situation is rare. The market for financial products such as forward contracts is made up of wholesalers of risk management products who use their technical expertise, their vast network of contacts, and their access to critical financial market information to provide a more efficient means for end users to engage in such risk management transactions.

Dealers such as UBS Warburg lay off the risk they do not wish to assume by transacting with other dealers and potentially other end users. If they do this carefully, quickly, and at accurate prices, they can earn a profit from this market-making

---

4 The U.S. government does not transact in forward contracts or other derivatives, but some foreign governments and central banks do. Within the United States, however, some state and local governments do engage in forward contracts and other derivatives.

activity. One should not get the impression, however, that market making is a highly profitable activity. The competition is fierce, which keeps bid-ask spreads very low and makes it difficult to earn much money on a given transaction. Indeed, many market makers do not make much money on individual transactions—they typically make a small amount of money on each transaction and do a large number of transactions. They may even lose money on some standard transactions, hoping to make up losses on more-complicated, nonstandard transactions, which occur less frequently but have higher bid-ask spreads.

Risk magazine conducts annual surveys to identify the top dealers in various derivative products. Exhibit 1 presents the results of those surveys for two of the forward products we cover here, currency and interest rate forwards. Interest rate forwards are called forward rate agreements (FRAs). In the next section, we shall study the different types of forward contracts and note that there are some others not covered in the *Risk* surveys.

One of these surveys was sent to banks and investment banks that are active dealers in over-the-counter derivatives. The other survey was sent to end users. The tabulations are based on respondents' simple rankings of who they think are the best dealers. Although the identities of the specific dealer firms are not critical, it is interesting and helpful to be aware of the major players in these types of contracts. Most of the world's leading global financial institutions are listed, but many other big names are not. It is also interesting to observe that the perceptions of the users of these dealer firms' services differ somewhat from the dealers' self-perceptions. Be aware, however, that the rankings change, sometimes drastically, each year.

Exhibit 1	*Risk* Magazine Surveys of Banks, Investment Banks, and Corporate End Users to Determine the Top Three Dealers in Currency and Interest Rate Forwards

	Respondents	
Currencies	**Banks and Investment Banks**	**Corporate End Users**
Currency Forwards		
$/€	UBS Warburg	Citigroup
	Deutsche Bank	Royal Bank of Scotland
	JP Morgan Chase	JP Morgan Chase/Bank of America
$/¥	UBS Warburg	Citigroup
	Citigroup	Bank of America
	JP Morgan Chase	JP Morgan Chase/UBS Warburg
$/£	UBS Warburg	Royal Bank of Scotland
	Royal Bank of Scotland	Citigroup
	Hong Kong Shanghai Banking Corporation	UBS Warburg
$/SF	UBS Warburg	UBS Warburg
	Credit Suisse First Boston	Citigroup
	BNP Paribas	Credit Suisse First Boston
Interest Rate Forwards (FRAs)		
$	JP Morgan Chase	JP Morgan Chase
	Bank of America	Royal Bank of Scotland

(continued)

Exhibit 1	Continued

	Respondents	
Currencies	Banks and Investment Banks	Corporate End Users
	Deutsche Bank	Bank of America
€	Deutsche Bank	Royal Bank of Scotland
	Intesa BCI	JP Morgan Chase
	Royal Bank of Scotland	Deutsche Bank
¥	Mizuho Securities	Citigroup
	JP Morgan Chase	Merrill Lynch
	BNP Paribas	Hong Kong Shanghai Banking Corporation
£	Royal Bank of Scotland	Royal Bank of Scotland
	Commerzbank	Bank of America/ING Barings
	Deutsche Bank	
SF	Credit Suisse First Boston	UBS Warburg
	UBS Warburg	Credit Suisse First Boston
	Deutsche Bank	Citigroup/ING Barings

Note: $ = U.S. dollar, € = euro, ¥ = Japanese yen, £ = U.K. pound sterling, SF = Swiss franc.
Source: *Risk*, September 2002, pp. 30–67 for banks and investment banking dealer respondents, and June 2002, pp. 24–34 for end user respondents. The end user survey provides responses from corporations and asset managers. The above results are for corporate respondents only.

3   TYPES OF FORWARD CONTRACTS

In this section, we examine the types of forward contracts that fall within the scope of this book. By the word "types," we mean the underlying asset groups on which these forward contracts are created. Because the CFA Program focuses on the asset management industry, our primary interest is in equity, interest rate and fixed-income, and currency forwards.

3.1 Equity Forwards

An **equity forward** is a contract calling for the purchase of an individual stock, a stock portfolio, or a stock index at a later date. For the most part, the differences in types of equity forward contracts are only slight, depending on whether the contract is on an individual stock, a portfolio of stocks, or a stock index.

3.1.1 *Forward Contracts on Individual Stocks*

Consider an asset manager responsible for the portfolio of a high-net-worth individual. As is sometimes the case, such portfolios may be concentrated in a small number of stocks, sometimes stocks that have been in the family for years. In many cases, the individual may be part of the founding family of a particular company. Let us say that the stock is called Gregorian Industries, Inc., or GII, and the client is so heavily invested in this stock that her portfolio is not diversified. The client notifies the portfolio manager of her need for $2 million in cash in six months. This cash can be raised by selling

16,000 shares at the current price of $125 per share. Thus, the risk exposure concerns the market value of $2 million of stock. For whatever reason, it is considered best not to sell the stock any earlier than necessary. The portfolio manager realizes that a forward contract to sell GII in six months will accomplish the client's desired objective. The manager contacts a forward contract dealer and obtains a quote of $128.13 as the price at which a forward contract to sell the stock in six months could be constructed. In other words, the portfolio manager could enter into a contract to sell the stock to the dealer in six months at $128.13. We assume that this contract is deliverable, meaning that when the sale is actually made, the shares will be delivered to the dealer. Assuming that the client has some flexibility in the amount of money needed, let us say that the contract is signed for the sale of 15,600 shares at $128.13, which will raise $1,998,828. Of course when the contract expires, the stock could be selling for any price. The client can gain or lose on the transaction. If the stock rises to a price above $128.13 during the six-month period, the client will still have to deliver the stock for $128.13. But if the price falls, the client will still get $128.13 per share for the stock.

3.1.2 *Forward Contracts on Stock Portfolios*

Because modern portfolio theory and good common sense dictate that investors should hold diversified portfolios, it is reasonable to assume that forward contracts on specific stock portfolios would be useful. Suppose a pension fund manager knows that in three months he will need to sell about $20 million of stock to make payments to retirees. The manager has analyzed the portfolio and determined the precise identities of the stocks he wants to sell and the number of shares of each that he would like to sell. Thus the manager has designated a specific subportfolio to be sold. The problem is that the prices of these stocks in three months are uncertain. The manager can, however, lock in the sale prices by entering into a forward contract to sell the portfolio. This can be done one of two ways.

The manager can enter into a forward contract on each stock that he wants to sell. Alternatively, he can enter into a forward contract on the overall portfolio. The first way would be more costly, as each contract would incur administrative costs, whereas the second way would incur only one set of costs.[5] Assume that the manager chooses the second method. He provides a list of the stocks and number of shares of each he wishes to sell to the dealer and obtains a quote. The dealer gives him a quote of $20,200,000. So, in three months, the manager will sell the stock to the dealer and receive $20,200,000. The transaction can be structured to call for either actual delivery or cash settlement, but in either case, the client will effectively receive $20,200,000 for the stock.[6]

3.1.3 *Forward Contracts on Stock Indices*

Many equity forward contracts are based on a stock index. For example, consider a U.K. asset manager who wants to protect the value of her portfolio that is a Financial Times Stock Exchange 100 index fund, or who wants to eliminate a risk for which the FTSE 100 Index is a sufficiently accurate representation of the risk she wishes

---

5 Ignoring those costs, there would be no difference in doing forward contracts on individual stocks or a single forward contract on a portfolio. Because of the non-linearity of their payoffs, this is not true for options. A portfolio of options is not the same as an option on a portfolio, but a portfolio of forward contracts is the same as a forward contract on a portfolio, ignoring the aforementioned costs.

6 If, for example, the stock is worth $20,500,000 and the transaction calls for delivery, the manager will transfer the stocks to the dealer and receive $20,200,000. The client effectively takes an opportunity loss of $300,000. If the transaction is structured as a cash settlement, the client will pay the dealer $300,000. The client would then sell the stock in the market, receiving $20,500,000 and netting $20,200,000 after settling the forward contract with the dealer. Similarly, if the stock is selling for less than the amount guaranteed by the forward contract, the client will deliver the stock and receive $20,200,000 or, if the transaction is cash settled, the client will sell the stock in the market and receive a cash payment from the dealer, making the effective sale price still $20,200,000.

to eliminate. For example, the manager may be anticipating the sale of a number of U.K. blue chip shares at a future date. The manager could, as in our stock portfolio example, take a specific portfolio of stocks to a forward contract dealer and obtain a forward contract on that portfolio. She realizes, however, that a forward contract on a widely accepted benchmark would result in a better price quote, because the dealer can more easily hedge the risk with other transactions. Moreover, the manager is not even sure which stocks she will still be holding at the later date. She simply knows that she will sell a certain amount of stock at a later date and believes that the FTSE 100 is representative of the stock that she will sell. The manager is concerned with the systematic risk associated with the U.K. stock market, and accordingly, she decides that selling a forward contract on the FTSE 100 would be a good way to manage the risk.

Assume that the portfolio manager decides to protect £15,000,000 of stock. The dealer quotes a price of £6,000 on a forward contract covering £15,000,000. We assume that the contract will be cash settled because such index contracts are nearly always done that way. When the contract expiration date arrives, let us say that the index is at £5,925—a decrease of 1.25 percent from the forward price. Because the manager is short the contract and its price went down, the transaction makes money. But how much did it make on a notional principal of £15,000,000?

The index declined by 1.25 percent. Thus, the transaction should make $0.0125 \times £15,000,000 = £187,500$. In other words, the dealer would have to pay £187,500 in cash. If the portfolio were a FTSE 100 index fund, then it would be viewed as a portfolio initially worth £15,000,000 that declined by 1.25 percent, a loss of £187,500. The forward contract offsets this loss. Of course, in reality, the portfolio is not an index fund and such a hedge is not perfect, but as noted above, there are sometimes reasons for preferring that the forward contract be based on an index.

3.1.4 *The Effect of Dividends*

It is important to note the effect of dividends in equity forward contracts. Any equity portfolio nearly always has at least a few stocks that pay dividends, and it is inconceivable that any well-known equity index would not have some component stocks that pay dividends. Equity forward contracts typically have payoffs based only on the price of the equity, value of the portfolio, or level of the index. They do not ordinarily pay off any dividends paid by the component stocks. An exception, however, is that some equity forwards on stock indices are based on total return indices. For example, there are two versions of the well-known S&P 500 Index. One represents only the market value of the stocks. The other, called the S&P 500 Total Return Index, is structured so that daily dividends paid by the stocks are reinvested in additional units of the index, as though it were a portfolio. In this manner, the rate of return on the index, and the payoff of any forward contract based on it, reflects the payment and reinvestment of dividends into the underlying index. Although this feature might appear attractive, it is not necessarily of much importance in risk management problems. The variability of prices is so much greater than the variability of dividends that managing price risk is considered much more important than worrying about the uncertainty of dividends.

In summary, equity forwards can be based on individual stocks, specific stock portfolios, or stock indices. Moreover, these underlying equities often pay dividends, which can affect forward contracts on equities. Let us now look at bond and **interest rate forward** contracts.

3.2 Bond and Interest Rate Forward Contracts

Forward contracts on bonds are similar to forward contracts on interest rates, but the two are different instruments. Forward contracts on bonds, in fact, are no more difficult to understand than those on equities. Drawing on our experience of Section 3.1, we simply extend the notion of a forward contract on an individual stock, a specific stock portfolio, or a stock index to that of a forward contract on an individual bond, a specific bond portfolio, or a bond index.[7]

3.2.1 *Forward Contracts on Individual Bonds and Bond Portfolios*

Although a forward contract on a bond and one on a stock are similar, some basic differences nonetheless exist between the two. For example, the bond may pay a coupon, which corresponds somewhat to the dividend that a stock might pay. But unlike a stock, a bond matures, and a forward contract on a bond must expire prior to the bond's maturity date. In addition, bonds often have many special features such as calls and convertibility. Finally, we should note that unlike a stock, a bond carries the risk of default. A forward contract written on a bond must contain a provision to recognize how default is defined, what it means for the bond to default, and how default would affect the parties to the contract.

In addition to forward contracts on individual bonds, there are also forward contracts on portfolios of bonds as well as on bond indices. The technical distinctions between forward contracts on individual bonds and collections of bonds, however, are relatively minor.

The primary bonds for which we shall consider forward contracts are default-free zero-coupon bonds, typically called Treasury bills or T-bills in the United States, which serve as a proxy for the risk-free rate.[8] In a forward contract on a T-bill, one party agrees to buy the T-bill at a later date, prior to the bill's maturity, at a price agreed on today. T-bills are typically sold at a discount from par value and the price is quoted in terms of the discount rate. Thus, if a 180-day T-bill is selling at a discount of 4 percent, its price per $1 par will be $1 − 0.04(180/360) = $0.98. The use of 360 days is the convention in calculating the discount. So the bill will sell for $0.98. If purchased and held to maturity, it will pay off $1. This procedure means that the interest is deducted from the face value in advance, which is called **discount interest**.

The T-bill is usually traded by quoting the discount rate, not the price. It is understood that the discount rate can be easily converted to the price by the above procedure. A forward contract might be constructed that would call for delivery of a 90-day T-bill in 60 days. Such a contract might sell for $0.9895, which would imply a discount rate of 4.2 percent because $1 − 0.042(90/360) = $0.9895.

In addition to forward contracts on zero-coupon bonds/T-bills, there are also forward contracts on default-free coupon-bearing bonds, also called Treasury bonds in the United States. These instruments pay interest, typically in semiannual installments, and can sell for more (less) than par value if the yield is lower (higher) than the coupon rate. Prices are typically quoted without the interest that has accrued since the last coupon date, but with a few exceptions, we shall always work with the full price—that is, the price including accrued interest. Prices are often quoted by stating the yield. Forward contracts call for delivery of such a bond at a date prior to the bond's maturity, for which the long pays the short the agreed-upon price.

3.2.2 *Forward Contracts on Interest Rates: Forward Rate Agreements*

So far in Section 3.2 we have discussed forward contracts on actual fixed-income securities. Fixed-income security prices are driven by interest rates. A more common type of forward contract is the interest rate forward contract, more commonly called a **forward rate agreement** or **FRA**. Before we can begin to understand FRAs, however, we must examine the instruments on which they are based.

---

[7] It may be useful to review Chapters 1 and 3 of *Fixed Income Analysis for the Chartered Financial Analyst Program* by Frank J. Fabozzi, New Hope, PA: Frank J. Fabozzi Associates (2000).

[8] A government-issued zero-coupon bond is typically used as a proxy for a risk-free asset because it is assumed to be free of default risk. It can be purchased and held to maturity, thereby eliminating any market value risk, and it has no reinvestment risk because it has no coupons. If the bond is liquidated before maturity, however, some market value risk exists in addition to the risk associated with reinvesting the market price.

There is a large global market for time deposits in various currencies issued by large creditworthy banks. This market is primarily centered in London but also exists elsewhere, though not in the United States. The primary time deposit instrument is called the **Eurodollar**, which is a dollar deposited outside the United States. Banks borrow dollars from other banks by issuing Eurodollar time deposits, which are essentially short-term unsecured loans. In London, the rate on such dollar loans is called the London Interbank Rate. Although there are rates for both borrowing and lending, in the financial markets the lending rate, called the **London Interbank Offer Rate** or **LIBOR**, is more commonly used in derivative contracts. LIBOR is the rate at which London banks lend dollars to other London banks. Even though it represents a loan outside of the United States, LIBOR is considered to be the best representative rate on a dollar borrowed by a private, i.e., nongovernmental, high-quality borrower. It should be noted, however, that the London market includes many branches of banks from outside the United Kingdom, and these banks are also active participants in the Eurodollar market.

A Eurodollar time deposit is structured as follows. Let us say a London bank such as NatWest needs to borrow $10 million for 30 days. It obtains a quote from the Royal Bank of Scotland for a rate of 5.25 percent. Thus, 30-day LIBOR is 5.25 percent. If NatWest takes the deal, it will owe $10,000,000 \times [1 + 0.0525(30/360)] = \$10,043,750$ in 30 days. Note that, like the Treasury bill market, the convention in the Eurodollar market is to prorate the quoted interest rate over 360 days. In contrast to the Treasury bill market, the interest is not deducted from the principal. Rather, it is added on to the face value, a procedure appropriately called **add-on interest**. The market for Eurodollar time deposits is quite large, and the rates on these instruments are assembled by a central organization and quoted in financial newspapers. The British Bankers Association publishes a semi-official Eurodollar rate, compiled from an average of the quotes of London banks.

The U.S. dollar is not the only instrument for which such time deposits exist. Eurosterling, for example, trades in Tokyo, and Euroyen trades in London. You may be wondering about Euroeuro. Actually, there is no such entity as Euroeuro, at least not by that name. The Eurodollar instrument described here has nothing to do with the European currency known as the euro. Eurodollars, Euroyen, Eurosterling, etc. have been around longer than the euro currency and, despite the confusion, have retained their nomenclature. An analogous instrument does exist, however—a euro-denominated loan in which one bank borrows euros from another. Trading in euros and euro deposits occurs in most major world cities, and two similar rates on such euro deposits are commonly quoted. One, called EuroLIBOR, is compiled in London by the British Bankers Association, and the other, called Euribor, is compiled in Frankfurt and published by the European Central Bank. Euribor is more widely used and is the rate we shall refer to in this book.

Now let us return to the world of FRAs. FRAs are contracts in which the underlying is neither a bond nor a Eurodollar or Euribor deposit but simply an interest payment made in dollars, Euribor, or any other currency at a rate appropriate for that currency. Our primary focus will be on dollar LIBOR and Euribor, so we shall henceforth adopt the terminology LIBOR to represent dollar LIBOR and Euribor to represent the euro deposit rate.

Because the mechanics of FRAs are the same for all currencies, for illustrative purposes we shall use LIBOR. Consider an FRA expiring in 90 days for which the underlying is 180-day LIBOR. Suppose the dealer quotes this instrument at a rate of 5.5 percent. Suppose the end user goes long and the dealer goes short. The end user is essentially long the rate and will benefit if rates increase. The dealer is essentially short the rate and will benefit if rates decrease. The contract covers a given notional principal, which we shall assume is $10 million.

The contract stipulates that at expiration, the parties identify the rate on new 180-day LIBOR time deposits. This rate is called 180-day LIBOR. It is, thus, the underlying rate on which the contract is based. Suppose that at expiration in 90 days, the rate on 180-day LIBOR is 6 percent. That 6 percent interest will be paid 180 days later. Therefore, the present value of a Eurodollar time deposit at that point in time would be

$$\frac{\$10,000,000}{1 + 0.06\left(\frac{180}{360}\right)}$$

At expiration, then, the end user, the party going long the FRA in our example, receives the following payment from the dealer, which is the party going short:

$$\$10,000,000\left[\frac{(0.06 - 0.055)\left(\frac{180}{360}\right)}{1 + 0.06\left(\frac{180}{360}\right)}\right] = \$24,272$$

If the underlying rate is less than 5.5 percent, the payment is calculated based on the difference between the 5.5 percent rate and the underlying rate and is paid by the long to the short. It is important to note that even though the contract expires in 90 days, the rate is on a 180-day LIBOR instrument; therefore, the rate calculation adjusts by the factor 180/360. The fact that 90 days have elapsed at expiration is not relevant to the calculation of the payoff.

Before presenting the general formula, let us review the calculations in the numerator and denominator. In the numerator, we see that the contract is obviously paying the difference between the actual rate that exists in the market on the contract expiration date and the agreed-upon rate, adjusted for the fact that the rate applies to a 180-day instrument, multiplied by the notional principal. The divisor appears because when Eurodollar rates are quoted in the market, they are based on the assumption that the rate applies to an instrument that accrues interest at that rate with the interest paid a certain number of days (here 180) later. When participants determine this rate in the London Eurodollar market, it is understood to apply to a Eurodollar time deposit that begins now and matures 180 days later. So the interest on an actual Eurodollar deposit would not be paid until 180 days later. Thus, it is necessary to adjust the FRA payoff to reflect the fact that the rate implies a payment that would occur 180 days later on a standard Eurodollar deposit. This adjustment is easily done by simply discounting the payment at the current LIBOR, which here is 6 percent, prorated over 180 days. These conventions are also followed in the market for FRAs with other underlying rates.

In general, the FRA payoff formula (from the perspective of the party going long) is

$$\text{Notional principal}\left[\frac{(\text{Underlying rate at expiration} - \text{Forward contract rate})\left(\frac{\text{Days in underlying rate}}{360}\right)}{1 + \text{Underlying rate at expiration}\left(\frac{\text{Days in underlying rate}}{360}\right)}\right]$$

where *forward contract rate* represents the rate the two parties agree will be paid and *days in underlying rate* refers to the number of days to maturity of the instrument on which the underlying rate is based.

One somewhat confusing feature of FRAs is the fact that they mature in a certain number of days and are based on a rate that applies to an instrument maturing in a certain number of days measured from the maturity of the FRA. Thus, there are two day figures associated with each contract. Our example was a 90-day contract on 180-day LIBOR. To avoid confusion, the FRA markets use a special type of terminology that converts the number of days to months. Specifically, our example FRA is referred to as a 3 × 9, reflecting the fact that the contract expires in three months and that six months later, or nine months from the contract initiation date, the interest is paid on the underlying Eurodollar time deposit on whose rate the contract is based.[9]

Exhibit 2	**FRA Descriptive Notation and Interpretation**	
Notation	**Contract Expires in**	**Underlying Rate**
1 × 3	1 month	60-day LIBOR
1 × 4	1 month	90-day LIBOR
1 × 7	1 month	180-day LIBOR
3 × 6	3 months	90-day LIBOR
3 × 9	3 months	180-day LIBOR
6 × 12	6 months	180-day LIBOR
12 × 18	12 months	180-day LIBOR

Note: This list is not exhaustive and represents only the most commonly traded FRAs.

FRAs are available in the market for a variety of maturities that are considered somewhat standard. Exhibit 2 presents the most common maturities. Most dealers follow the convention that contracts should expire in a given number of exact months and should be on the most commonly traded Eurodollar rates such as 30-day LIBOR, 60-day LIBOR, 90-day LIBOR, 180-day LIBOR, and so on. If a party wants a contract expiring in 37 days on 122-day LIBOR, it would be considered an exception to the standard, but most dealers would be willing to make a market in such an instrument. Such nonstandard instruments are called *off the run*. Of course, FRAs are available in all of the leading currencies.

The FRA market is large, but not as large as the swaps market. It is important, however, to understand FRAs before trying to understand swaps. As we will show in the reading on swap markets and contracts, a swap is a special combination of FRAs. But let us now turn to another large forward market, the market for currency forwards.

3.3 Currency Forward Contracts

Spurred by the relaxation of government controls over the exchange rates of most major currencies in the early 1970s, a currency forward market developed and grew extremely large. Currency forwards are widely used by banks and corporations to manage foreign exchange risk. For example, suppose Microsoft has a European subsidiary that expects to send it €12 million in three months. When Microsoft receives the euros, it will then convert them to dollars. Thus, Microsoft is essentially long euros because it will have to sell euros, or equivalently, it is short dollars because it will have to buy dollars. A currency forward contract is especially useful in this situation, because it enables Microsoft to lock in the rate at which it will sell euros and buy dollars in three months. It can do this by going short the forward contract, meaning that it goes short the euro and long the dollar. This arrangement serves to offset its otherwise long-euro, short-dollar position. In other words, it needs a forward contract to sell euros and buy dollars.

For example, say Microsoft goes to JP Morgan Chase and asks for a quote on a currency forward for €12 million in three months. JP Morgan Chase quotes a rate of $0.925, which would enable Microsoft to sell euros and buy dollars at a rate of

---

9 The notation "3 × 9" is pronounced "three by nine."

$0.925 in three months. Under this contract, Microsoft would know it could convert its €12 million to 12,000,000 × $0.925 = $11,100,000. The contract would also stipulate whether it will settle in cash or will call for Microsoft to actually deliver the euros to the dealer and be paid $11,100,000. This simplified example is a currency forward hedge.

Now let us say that three months later, the spot rate for euros is $0.920. Microsoft is quite pleased that it locked in a rate of $0.925. It simply delivers the euros and receives $11,100,000 at an exchange rate of $0.925.[10] Had rates risen, however, Microsoft would still have had to deliver the euros and accept a rate of $0.925.

A few variations of currency forward contracts exist, but most of them are somewhat specialized and beyond the objectives of this reading. Let us now take a very brief look at a few other types of forward contracts.

3.4 Other Types of Forward Contracts

Although the focus is primarily on the financial derivatives used by asset managers, we should mention here some of the other types. Commodity forwards—in which the underlying asset is oil, a precious metal, or some other commodity—are widely used. In addition, the derivatives industry has created forward contracts and other derivatives on various sources of energy (electricity, gas, etc.) and even weather, in which the underlying is a measure of the temperature or the amount of disaster damage from hurricanes, earthquakes, or tornados.

Many of these instruments are particularly difficult to understand, price, and trade. Nonetheless, through the use of derivatives and indirect investments, such as hedge funds, they can be useful for managing risk and investing in general. They are not, however, the focus here.

In the examples and illustrations used, we have made reference to certain prices. Determining appropriate prices and fair values of financial instruments is a central objective of much of the process of asset management. Accordingly, pricing and valuation occupies a major portion of the CFA Program.

SUMMARY

- The holder of a long forward contract (the "long") is obligated to take delivery of the underlying asset and pay the forward price at expiration. The holder of a short forward contract (the "short") is obligated to deliver the underlying asset and accept payment of the forward price at expiration.

- At expiration, a forward contract can be terminated by having the short make delivery of the underlying asset to the long or having the long and short exchange the equivalent cash value. If the asset is worth more (less) than the forward price, the short (long) pays the long (short) the cash difference between the market price or rate and the price or rate agreed on in the contract.

- A party can terminate a forward contract prior to expiration by entering into an opposite transaction with the same or a different counterparty. It is possible to leave both the original and new transactions in place, thereby leaving both transactions subject to credit risk, or to have the two transactions cancel each other. In the latter case, the party owing the greater amount pays the market

---

10 Had the contract been structured to settle in cash, the dealer would have paid Microsoft 12,000,000 × ($0.925 – $0.920) = $60,000. Microsoft would have converted the euros to dollars at the current spot exchange rate of $0.920, receiving 12,000,000 × $0.920 = $11,040,000. Adding the $60,000 payment from the dealer, Microsoft would have received $11,100,000, an effective rate of $0.925.

value to the other party, resulting in the elimination of the remaining credit risk. This elimination can be achieved, however, only if the counterparty to the second transaction is the same counterparty as in the first.

■ A dealer is a financial institution that makes a market in forward contracts and other derivatives. A dealer stands ready to take either side of a transaction. An end user is a party that comes to a dealer needing a transaction, usually for the purpose of managing a particular risk.

■ Equity forward contracts can be written on individual stocks, specific stock portfolios, or stock indices. Equity forward contract prices and values must take into account the fact that the underlying stock, portfolio, or index could pay dividends.

■ Forward contracts on bonds can be based on zero-coupon bonds or on coupon bonds, as well as portfolios or indices based on zero-coupon bonds or coupon bonds. Zero-coupon bonds pay their return by discounting the face value, often using a 360-day year assumption. Forward contracts on bonds must expire before the bond's maturity. In addition, a forward contract on a bond can be affected by special features of bonds, such as callability and convertibility.

■ Eurodollar time deposits are dollar loans made by one bank to another. Although the term "Eurodollars" refers to dollar-denominated loans, similar loans exist in other currencies. Eurodollar deposits accrue interest by adding it on to the principal, using a 360-day year assumption. The primary Eurodollar rate is called LIBOR.

■ LIBOR stands for London Interbank Offer Rate, the rate at which London banks are willing to lend to other London banks. Euribor is the rate on a euro time deposit, a loan made by banks to other banks in Frankfurt in which the currency is the euro.

■ An FRA is a forward contract in which one party, the long, agrees to pay a fixed interest payment at a future date and receive an interest payment at a rate to be determined at expiration. FRAs are described by a special notation. For example, a 3 × 6 FRA expires in three months; the underlying is a Eurodollar deposit that begins in three months and ends three months later, or six months from now.

■ The payment of an FRA at expiration is based on the net difference between the underlying rate and the agreed-upon rate, adjusted by the notional principal and the number of days in the instrument on which the underlying rate is based. The payoff is also discounted, however, to reflect the fact that the underlying rate on which the instrument is based assumes that payment will occur at a later date.

■ A currency forward contract is a commitment for one party, the long, to buy a currency at a fixed price from the other party, the short, at a specific date. The contract can be settled by actual delivery, or the two parties can choose to settle in cash on the expiration day.

PRACTICE PROBLEMS FOR READING 61

1. The treasurer of Company A expects to receive a cash inflow of $15,000,000 in 90 days. The treasurer expects short-term interest rates to fall during the next 90 days. In order to hedge against this risk, the treasurer decides to use an FRA that expires in 90 days and is based on 90-day LIBOR. The FRA is quoted at 5 percent. At expiration, LIBOR is 4.5 percent. Assume that the notional principal on the contract is $15,000,000.

    A. Indicate whether the treasurer should take a long or short position to hedge interest rate risk.

    B. Using the appropriate terminology, identify the type of FRA used here.

    C. Calculate the gain or loss to Company A as a consequence of entering the FRA.

2. Suppose that a party wanted to enter into an FRA that expires in 42 days and is based on 137-day LIBOR. The dealer quotes a rate of 4.75 percent on this FRA. Assume that at expiration, the 137-day LIBOR is 4 percent and the notional principal is $20,000,000.

    A. What is the term used to describe such nonstandard instruments?

    B. Calculate the FRA payoff on a long position.

3. Assume Sun Microsystems expects to receive €20,000,000 in 90 days. A dealer provides a quote of $0.875 for a currency forward contract to expire in 90 days. Suppose that at the end of 90 days, the rate is $0.90. Assume that settlement is in cash. Calculate the cash flow at expiration if Sun Microsystems enters into a forward contract expiring in 90 days to buy dollars at $0.875.

SOLUTIONS FOR READING 61

1. **A.** Taking a short position will hedge the interest rate risk for Company A. The gain on the contract will offset the reduced interest rate that can be earned when rates fall.

   B. This is a 3 × 6 FRA.

   C. $\$15,000,000 \left[\dfrac{(0.045 - 0.05)(90/360)}{1 + 0.045(90/360)} \right] = -\$18,541.41$

   The negative sign indicates a gain to the short position, which Company A holds.

2. **A.** These instruments are called off-the-run FRAs.

   B. $\$20,000,000 \left[\dfrac{(0.04 - 0.0475)(137/360)}{1 + 0.04(137/360)} \right] = -\$56,227.43$

   Because the party is long, this amount represents a loss.

3. The contract is settled in cash, so the settlement would be €20,000,000(0.875 − 0.90) = −$500,000. This amount would be paid by Sun Microsystems to the dealer. Sun would convert euros to dollars at the spot rate of $0.90, receiving €20,000,000 × (0.90) = $18,000,000. The net cash receipt is $17,500,000, which results in an effective rate of $0.875.

62

Futures Markets and Contracts

by Don M. Chance, CFA

LEARNING OUTCOMES

Mastery	The candidate should be able to:
☐	**a** describe the characteristics of futures contracts;
☐	**b** compare futures contracts and forward contracts;
☐	**c** distinguish between margin in the securities markets and margin in the futures markets, and explain the role of initial margin, maintenance margin, variation margin, and settlement in futures trading;
☐	**d** describe price limits and the process of marking to market, and calculate and interpret the margin balance, given the previous day's balance and the change in the futures price;
☐	**e** describe how a futures contract can be terminated at or prior to expiration;
☐	**f** describe the characteristics of the following types of futures contracts: Treasury bill, Eurodollar, Treasury bond, stock index, and currency.

INTRODUCTION

1

In the reading on derivative markets and instruments, we undertook a general overview of derivative markets. In the reading on forward markets and contracts, we focused on forward markets. Now we explore futures markets in a similar fashion. Although we shall see a clear similarity between forward and futures contracts, critical distinctions nonetheless exist between the two.

In the reading on derivative markets and instruments we learned that, like a forward contract, *a futures contract is an agreement between two parties in which one party, the buyer, agrees to buy from the other party, the seller, an underlying asset or other derivative, at a future date at a price agreed on today.* Unlike a forward contract, however, a futures contract is not a private and customized transaction but rather a public transaction that takes place on an organized futures exchange. In addition, a futures contract is standardized—the exchange, rather than the individual parties, sets the terms and conditions, with the exception of price. As a result, futures contracts have a secondary market, meaning that previously created contracts can be traded. Also, parties to futures contracts are guaranteed against credit losses resulting from the counterparty's inability to pay. A clearinghouse provides this guarantee via a procedure in which it converts gains and losses that accrue on a daily basis into actual cash gains and losses. Futures contracts are regulated at the federal government level; as we noted in the reading on forward markets and contracts, forward contracts are essentially unregulated. Futures contracts are created on organized trading facilities referred to as futures exchanges, whereas forward contracts are not created in any specific location but rather initiated between any two parties who wish to enter into such a contract. Finally, each futures exchange has a division or subsidiary called a clearinghouse that performs the specific responsibilities of paying and collecting daily gains and losses as well as guaranteeing to each party the performance of the other.

In a futures transaction, one party, the long, is the buyer and the other party, the short, is the seller. The buyer agrees to buy the underlying at a later date, the expiration, at a price agreed on at the start of the contract. The seller agrees to sell the underlying to the buyer at the expiration, at the price agreed on at the start of the contract. Every day, the futures contract trades in the market and its price changes in response to new information. Buyers benefit from price increases, and sellers benefit from price decreases. On the expiration day, the contract terminates and no further trading takes place. Then, either the buyer takes delivery of the underlying from the seller, or the two parties make an equivalent cash settlement. We shall explore each of these characteristics of futures contracts in more detail. First, however, it is important to take a brief look at how futures markets came into being.

1.1 A Brief History of Futures Markets

Although vestiges of futures markets appear in the Japanese rice markets of the 18th century and perhaps even earlier, the mid-1800s marked the first clear origins of modern futures markets. For example, in the United States in the 1840s, Chicago was becoming a major transportation and distribution center for agricultural commodities. Its central location and access to the Great Lakes gave Chicago a competitive advantage over other U.S. cities. Farmers from the Midwest would harvest their grain and take it to Chicago for sale. Grain production, however, is seasonal. As a result, grain prices would rise sharply just prior to the harvest but then plunge when the grain was brought to the market. Too much grain at one time and too little at another resulted in severe problems. Grain storage facilities in Chicago were inadequate to accommodate the oversupply. Some farmers even dumped their grain in the Chicago River because prices were so low that they could not afford to take their grain to another city to sell.

To address this problem, in 1848 a group of businessmen formed an organization later named the Chicago Board of Trade (CBOT) and created an arrangement called a "to-arrive" contract. These contracts permitted farmers to sell their grain before delivering it. In other words, farmers could harvest the grain and enter into a contract to deliver it at a much later date at a price already agreed on. This transaction allowed the farmer to hold the grain in storage at some other location besides Chicago. On the other side of these contracts were the businessmen who had formed the Chicago Board of Trade.

It soon became apparent that trading in these to-arrive contracts was more important and useful than trading in the grain itself. Soon the contracts began trading in a type of secondary market, which allowed buyers and sellers to discharge their obligations by passing them on, for a price, to other parties. With the addition of the clearinghouse in the 1920s, which provided a guarantee against default, modern futures markets firmly established their place in the financial world. It was left to other exchanges, such as today's Chicago Mercantile Exchange, the New York Mercantile Exchange, Eurex, and the London International Financial Futures Exchange, to develop and become, along with the Chicago Board of Trade, the global leaders in futures markets.

We shall now explore the important features of futures contracts in more detail.

1.2 Public Standardized Transactions

A private transaction is not generally reported in the news or to any price reporting service. Forward contracts are private contracts. Just as in most legal contracts, the parties do not publicly report that they have engaged in a contract. In contrast, a futures transaction is reported to the futures exchange, the clearinghouse, and at least one regulatory agency. The price is recorded and available from price reporting services and even on the internet.[1]

We noted that a futures transaction is not customized. Recall from the reading on forward markets and contracts that in a forward contract, the two parties establish all of the terms of the contract, including the identity of the underlying, the expiration date, and the manner in which the contract is settled (cash or actual delivery) as well as the price. The terms are customized to meet the needs of both parties. In a futures contract, the price is the only term established by the two parties; the exchange establishes all other terms. Moreover, the terms that are established by the exchange are standardized, meaning that the exchange selects a number of choices for underlyings, expiration dates, and a variety of other contract-specific items. These standardized terms are well known to all parties. If a party wishes to trade a futures contract, it must accept these terms. The only alternative would be to create a similar but customized contract on the forward market.

With respect to the underlying, for example, a given asset has a variety of specifications and grades. Consider a futures contract on U.S. Treasury bonds. There are many different Treasury bonds with a variety of characteristics. The futures exchange must decide which Treasury bond or group of bonds the contract covers. One of the most actively traded commodity futures contracts is oil, but there are many different types of oil.[2] To which type of oil does the contract apply? The exchange decides at the time it designs the contract.

The parties to a forward contract set its expiration at whatever date they want. For a futures contract, the exchange establishes a set of expiration dates. The first specification of the expiration is the month. An exchange might establish that a given futures contract expires only in the months of March, June, September, and December. The second specification determines how far the expirations go out into the future. For example, in January of a given year, there may be expirations of March, June, September, and December. Expirations might also be available for March, June, September, and December of the following year, and perhaps some months of the year after that. The exchange decides which expiration months are appropriate for trading, based on which expirations they believe would be actively traded. Treasury bond futures have expirations going out only about a year. Eurodollar futures, however, have expirations that go out about 10 years.[3] The third specification of the expiration is the specific day of expiration. Many, but not all, contracts expire some time during the third week of the expiration month.

The exchange determines a number of other contract characteristics, including the contract size. For example, one Eurodollar futures contract covers $1 million of a Eurodollar time deposit. One U.S. Treasury bond futures contract covers $100,000 face value of Treasury bonds. One futures contract on crude oil covers 1,000 barrels. The exchange also decides on the price quotation unit. For example, Treasury bond futures are quoted in points and 32nds of par of 100. Hence, you will see a price like 104 21/32, which means 104.65625. With a contract size of $100,000, the actual price is $104,656.25.

---

1 The information reported to the general public does not disclose the identity of the parties to transactions but only that a transaction took place at a particular price.

2 Some of the main types are Saudi Arabian light crude, Brent crude, and West Texas intermediate crude.

3 You may be wondering why some Eurodollar futures contracts have such long expirations. Dealers in swaps and forward rate agreements use Eurodollar futures to hedge their positions. Many of those over-the-counter contracts have very long expirations.

The exchange also determines what hours of the day trading takes place and at what physical location on the exchange the contract will be traded. Many futures exchanges have a trading floor, which contains octagonal-shaped pits. A contract is assigned to a certain pit. Traders enter the pits and express their willingness to buy and sell by calling out and/or indicating by hand signals their bids and offers. Some exchanges have electronic trading, which means that trading takes place on computer terminals, generally located in companies' offices. Some exchanges have both floor trading and electronic trading; some have only one or the other.

1.3 Homogenization and Liquidity

By creating contracts with generally accepted terms, the exchange standardizes the instrument. In contrast, forward contracts are quite heterogeneous because they are customized. Standardizing the instrument makes it more acceptable to a broader group of participants, with the advantage being that the instrument can then more easily trade in a type of secondary market. Indeed, the ability to sell a previously purchased contract or purchase a previously sold contract is one of the important features of futures contracts. A futures contract is therefore said to have liquidity in contrast to a forward contract, which does not generally trade after it has been created.[4] This ability to trade a previously opened contract allows participants in this market to offset the position before expiration, thereby obtaining exposure to price movements in the underlying without the actual requirement of holding the position to expiration. We shall discuss this characteristic further when we describe futures trading in Section 2.

1.4 The Clearinghouse, Daily Settlement, and Performance Guarantee

Another important distinction between futures and forwards is that the futures exchange guarantees to each party the performance of the other party, through a mechanism known as the clearinghouse. This guarantee means that if one party makes money on the transaction, it does not have to worry about whether it will collect the money from the other party because the clearinghouse ensures it will be paid. In contrast, each party to a forward contract assumes the risk that the other party will default.

An important and distinguishing feature of futures contracts is that the gains and losses on each party's position are credited and charged on a daily basis. This procedure, called **daily settlement** or **marking to market**, essentially results in paper gains and losses being converted to cash gains and losses each day. It is also equivalent to terminating a contract at the end of each day and reopening it the next day at that settlement price. In some sense, a futures contract is like a strategy of opening up a forward contract, closing it one day later, opening up a new contract, closing it one day later, and continuing in that manner until expiration. The exact manner in which the daily settlement works will be covered in more detail later in Section 3.

1.5 Regulation

In most countries, futures contracts are regulated at the federal government level. State and regional laws may also apply. In the United States, the Commodity Futures Trading Commission regulates the futures market. In the United Kingdom, the Financial Services Authority regulates both the securities and futures markets.

---

4 The notion of liquidity here is only that a market exists for futures contracts, but this does not imply a high degree of liquidity. There may be little trading in a given contract, and the bid–ask spread can be high. In contrast, some forward markets can be very liquid, allowing forward contracts to be offset.

Federal regulation of futures markets generally arises out of a concern to protect the general public and other futures market participants, as well as through a recognition that futures markets affect all financial markets and the economy. Regulations cover such matters as ensuring that prices are reported accurately and in a timely manner, that markets are not manipulated, that professionals who offer their services to the public are qualified and honest, and that disputes are resolved. In the United States, the government has delegated some of these responsibilities to an organization called the National Futures Association (NFA). An industry self-regulatory body, the NFA was created with the objective of having the industry regulate itself and reduce the federal government's burden.

FUTURES TRADING

In this section, we look more closely at how futures contracts are traded. As noted above, futures contracts trade on a futures exchange either in a pit or on a screen or electronic terminal.

We briefly mentioned pit trading, also known as floor-based trading, in Section 1.2. Pit trading is a very physical activity. Traders stand in the pit and shout out their orders in the form of prices they are willing to pay or accept. They also use hand signals to indicate their bids and offers.[5] They engage in transactions with other traders in the pits by simply agreeing on a price and number of contracts to trade. The activity is fast, furious, exciting, and stressful. The average pit trader is quite young, owing to the physical demands of the job and the toll it takes on body and mind. In recent years, more trading has come off of the exchange floor to electronic screens or terminals. In electronic or screen-based trading, exchange members enter their bids and offers into a computer system, which then displays this information and allows a trader to consummate a trade electronically. In the United States, pit trading is dominant, owing to its long history and tradition. Exchange members who trade on the floor enjoy pit trading and have resisted heavily the advent of electronic trading. Nonetheless, the exchanges have had to respond to market demands to offer electronic trading. In the United States, both pit trading and electronic trading are used, but in other countries, electronic trading is beginning to drive pit trading out of business.[6]

A person who enters into a futures contract establishes either a long position or a short position. Similar to forward contracts, long positions are agreements to buy the underlying at the expiration at a price agreed on at the start. Short positions are agreements to sell the underlying at a future date at a price agreed on at the start. When the position is established, each party deposits a small amount of money, typically called the margin, with the clearinghouse. Then, as briefly described in Section 1.4, the contract is marked to market, whereby the gains are distributed to and the losses collected from each party. We cover this marking-to-market process in more detail in the next section. For now, however, we focus only on the opening and closing of the position.

A party that has opened a long position collects profits or incurs losses on a daily basis. At some point in the life of the contract prior to expiration, that party may wish to re-enter the market and close out the position. This process, called **offsetting**, is the same as selling a previously purchased stock or buying back a stock to close a short position. The holder of a long futures position simply goes back into the market and offers the identical contract for sale. The holder of a short position goes back into the market and offers to buy the identical contract. It should be noted that when a party offsets a position, it does not necessarily do so with the same counterparty to

---

5 Hand signals facilitate trading with someone who is too far away in the pit for verbal communication.
6 For example, in France electronic trading was introduced while pit trading continued. Within two weeks, all of the volume had migrated to electronic trading and pit trading was terminated.

the original contract. In fact, rarely would a contract be offset with the same counterparty. Because of the ability to offset, futures contracts are said to be fungible, which means that any futures contract with any counterparty can be offset by an equivalent futures contract with another counterparty. Fungibility is assured by the fact that the clearinghouse inserts itself in the middle of each contract and, therefore, becomes the counterparty to each party.

For example, suppose in early January a futures trader purchases an S&P 500 stock index futures contract expiring in March. Through 15 February, the trader has incurred some gains and losses from the daily settlement and decides that she wants to close the position out. She then goes back into the market and offers for sale the March S&P 500 futures. Once she finds a buyer to take the position, she has a long and short position in the same contract. The clearinghouse considers that she no longer has a position in that contract and has no remaining exposure, nor any obligation to make or take delivery at expiration. Had she initially gone short the March futures, she might re-enter the market in February offering to buy it. Once she finds a seller to take the opposite position, she becomes long and short the same contract and is considered to have offset the contract and therefore have no net position.

3 THE CLEARINGHOUSE, MARGINS, AND PRICE LIMITS

As briefly noted in the previous section, when a trader takes a long or short position in a futures, he must first deposit sufficient funds in a margin account. This amount of money is traditionally called the margin, a term derived from the stock market practice in which an investor borrows a portion of the money required to purchase a certain amount of stock.

Margin in the stock market is quite different from margin in the futures market. In the stock market, "margin" means that a loan is made. The loan enables the investor to reduce the amount of his own money required to purchase the securities, thereby generating leverage or gearing, as it is sometimes known. If the stock goes up, the percentage gain to the investor is amplified. If the stock goes down, however, the percentage loss is also amplified. The borrowed money must eventually be repaid with interest. The margin percentage equals the market value of the stock minus the market value of the debt divided by the market value of the stock—in other words, the investor's own equity as a percentage of the value of the stock. For example, in the United States, regulations permit an investor to borrow up to 50 percent of the initial value of the stock. This percentage is called the initial margin requirement. On any day thereafter, the equity or percentage ownership in the account, measured as the market value of the securities minus the amount borrowed, can be less than 50 percent but must be at least a percentage known as the maintenance margin requirement. A typical maintenance margin requirement is 25 to 30 percent.

In the futures market, by contrast, the word **margin** is commonly used to describe the amount of money that must be put into an account by a party opening up a futures position, but the term is misleading. When a transaction is initiated, a futures trader puts up a certain amount of money to meet the **initial margin requirement**; however, the remaining money is not borrowed. The amount of money deposited is more like a down payment for the commitment to purchase the underlying at a later date. Alternatively, one can view this deposit as a form of good faith money, collateral, or a performance bond: The money helps ensure that the party fulfills his or her obligation.[7] Moreover, both the buyer and the seller of a futures contract must deposit margin.

---

[7] In fact, the Chicago Mercantile Exchange uses the term "performance bond" instead of "margin." Most other exchanges use the term "margin."

In securities markets, margin requirements are normally set by federal regulators. In the United States, maintenance margin requirements are set by the securities exchanges and the FINRA. In futures markets, margin requirements are set by
the clearinghouses. In further contrast to margin practices in securities markets,
futures margins are traditionally expressed in dollar terms and not as a percentage of the futures price. For ease of comparison, however, we often speak of the
futures margin in terms of its relationship to the futures price. In futures markets,
the initial margin requirement is typically much lower than the initial margin
requirement in the stock market. In fact, futures margins are usually less than 10
percent of the futures price.[8] Futures clearinghouses set their margin requirements
by studying historical price movements. They then establish minimum margin
levels by taking into account normal price movements and the fact that accounts
are marked to market daily. The clearinghouses thus collect and disburse margin
money every day. Moreover, they are permitted to do so more often than daily,
and on some occasions they have used that privilege. By carefully setting margin
requirements and collecting margin money every day, clearinghouses are able to
control the risk of default.

In spite of the differences in margin practices for futures and securities markets,
the effect of leverage is similar for both. By putting up a small amount of money, the
trader's gains and losses are magnified. Given the tremendously low margin requirements of futures markets, however, the magnitude of the leverage effect is much
greater in futures markets. We shall see how this works as we examine the process
of the daily settlement.

As previously noted, each day the clearinghouse conducts an activity known as the
daily settlement, also called marking to market. This practice results in the conversion
of gains and losses on paper into actual gains and losses. As margin account balances
change, holders of futures positions must maintain balances above a level called the
maintenance margin requirement. The maintenance margin requirement is lower
than the initial margin requirement. On any day in which the amount of money in
the margin account at the end of the day falls below the maintenance margin requirement, the trader must deposit sufficient funds to bring the balance back up to the
initial margin requirement. Alternatively, the trader can simply close out the position
but is responsible for any further losses incurred if the price changes before a closing
transaction can be made.

To provide a fair mark-to-market process, the clearinghouse must designate
the official price for determining daily gains and losses. This price is called the
settlement price and represents an average of the final few trades of the day. It
would appear that the closing price of the day would serve as the settlement price,
but the closing price is a single value that can potentially be biased high or low or
perhaps even manipulated by an unscrupulous trader. Hence, the clearinghouse takes
an average of all trades during the closing period (as defined by each exchange).

Exhibit 1 provides an example of the marking-to-market process that occurs
over a period of six trading days. We start with the assumption that the futures
price is $100 when the transaction opens, the initial margin requirement is $5, and
the maintenance margin requirement is $3. In Panel A, the trader takes a long posi-
tion of 10 contracts on Day 0, depositing $50 ($5 times 10 contracts) as indicated
in Column 3. At the end of the day, his ending balance is $50.[9] Although the trader

---

8 For example, the margin requirement of the Eurodollar futures contract at the Chicago Mercantile
Exchange has been less than one-tenth of one percent of the futures price. An exception to this requirement,
however, is individual stock futures, which in the United States have margin requirements comparable to
those of the stock market.

9 Technically, we are assuming that the position was opened at the settlement price on Day 0. If the position
is opened earlier during the day, it would be marked to the settlement price at the end of the day.

can withdraw any funds in excess of the initial margin requirement, we shall assume that he does not do so.[10]

The ending balance on Day 0 is then carried forward to the beginning balance on Day 1. On Day 1, the futures price moves down to 99.20, as indicated in Column 4 of Panel A. The futures price change, Column 5, is −0.80 (99.20 − 100). This amount is then multiplied by the number of contracts to obtain the number in Column 6 of −0.80 × 10 = −$8. The ending balance, Column 7, is the beginning balance plus the gain or loss. The ending balance on Day 1 of $42 is above the maintenance margin requirement of $30, so no funds need to be deposited on Day 2.

Exhibit 1	Mark-to-Market Example

Initial futures price = $100, Initial margin requirement = $5, Maintenance margin requirement = $3

Panel A. Holder of Long Position of 10 Contracts

Day (1)	Beginning Balance (2)	Funds Deposited (3)	Settlement Price (4)	Futures Price Change (5)	Gain/Loss (6)	Ending Balance (7)
0	0	50	100.00			50
1	50	0	99.20	−0.80	−8	42
2	42	0	96.00	−3.20	−32	10
3	10	40	101.00	5.00	50	100
4	100	0	103.50	2.50	25	125
5	125	0	103.00	−0.50	−5	120
6	120	0	104.00	1.00	10	130

Panel B. Holder of Short Position of 10 Contracts

Day (1)	Beginning Balance (2)	Funds Deposited (3)	Settlement Price (4)	Futures Price Change (5)	Gain/Loss (6)	Ending Balance (7)
0	0	50	100.00			50
1	50	0	99.20	−0.80	8	58
2	58	0	96.00	−3.20	32	90
3	90	0	101.00	5.00	−50	40
4	40	0	103.50	2.50	−25	15
5	15	35	103.00	−0.50	5	55
6	55	0	104.00	1.00	−10	45

On Day 2 the settlement price goes down to $96. Based on a price decrease of $3.20 per contract and 10 contracts, the loss is $32, lowering the ending balance to $10. This amount is $20 below the maintenance margin requirement. Thus, the trader will get a margin call the following morning and must deposit $40 to bring the balance up to the initial margin level of $50. This deposit is shown in Column 3 on Day 3.

---

10 Virtually all professional traders are able to deposit interest-earning assets, although many other account holders are required to deposit cash. If the deposit earns interest, there is no opportunity cost and no obvious necessity to withdraw the money to invest elsewhere.

Here, we must emphasize two important points. First, additional margin that must be deposited is the amount sufficient to bring the ending balance up to the initial margin requirement, not the maintenance margin requirement.[11] This additional margin is called the **variation margin**. In addition, the amount that must be deposited the following day is determined regardless of the price change the following day, which might bring the ending balance well above the initial margin requirement, as it does here, or even well below the maintenance margin requirement. Thus, another margin call could occur. Also note that when the trader closes the position, the account is marked to market to the final price at which the transaction occurs, not the settlement price that day.

Over the six-day period, the trader in this example deposited $90. The account balance at the end of the sixth day is $130—nearly a 50 percent return over six days; not bad. But look at Panel B, which shows the position of a holder of 10 short contracts over that same period. Note that the short gains when prices decrease and loses when prices increase. Here the ending balance falls below the maintenance margin requirement on Day 4, and the short must deposit $35 on Day 5. At the end of Day 6, the short has deposited $85 and the balance is $45, a loss of $40 or nearly 50 percent, which is the same $40 the long made. Both cases illustrate the leverage effect that magnifies gains and losses.

When establishing a futures position, it is important to know the price level that would trigger a margin call. In this case, it does not matter how many contracts one has. The price change would need to fall for a long position (or rise for a short position) by the difference between the initial and maintenance margin requirements. In this example, the difference between the initial and maintenance margin requirements is $5 − $3 = $2. Thus, the price would need to fall from $100 to $98 for a long position (or rise from $100 to $102 for a short position) to trigger a margin call.

As described here, when a trader receives a margin call, he is required to deposit funds sufficient to bring the account balance back up to the initial margin level. Alternatively, the trader can choose to simply close out the position as soon as possible. For example, consider the position of the long at the end of the second day when the margin balance is $10. This amount is $20 below the maintenance level, and he is required to deposit $40 to bring the balance up to the initial margin level. If he would prefer not to deposit the additional funds, he can close out the position as soon as possible the following day. Suppose, however, that the price is moving quickly at the opening on Day 3. If the price falls from $96 to $95, he has lost $10 more, wiping out the margin account balance. In fact, if it fell any further, he would have a negative margin account balance. He is still responsible for these losses. Thus, the trader could lose more than the amount of money he has placed in the margin account. The total amount of money he could lose is limited to the price per contract at which he bought, $100, times the number of contracts, 10, or $1,000. Such a loss would occur if the price fell to zero, although this is not likely. This potential loss may not seem like a lot, but it is certainly large relative to the initial margin requirement of $50. For the holder of the short position, there is no upper limit on the price and the potential loss is theoretically infinite.

Example 1

Consider a futures contract in which the current futures price is $82. The initial margin requirement is $5, and the maintenance margin requirement is $2. You go long 20 contracts and meet all margin calls but do not withdraw any excess margin. Assume that on the first day, the contract is established at the settlement price, so there is no mark-to-market gain or loss on that day.

---

[11] In the stock market, one must deposit only the amount necessary to bring the balance up to the maintenance margin requirement.

A. Complete the following table and provide an explanation of any funds deposited.

Day	Beginning Balance	Funds Deposited	Futures Price	Price Change	Gain/Loss	Ending Balance
0			82			
1			84			
2			78			
3			73			
4			79			
5			82			
6			84			

B. Determine the price level that would trigger a margin call.

Solution to A:

Day	Beginning Balance	Funds Deposited	Futures Price	Price Change	Gain/Loss	Ending Balance
0	0	100	82			100
1	100	0	84	2	40	140
2	140	0	78	-6	-120	20
3	20	80	73	-5	-100	0
4	0	100	79	6	120	220
5	220	0	82	3	60	280
6	280	0	84	2	40	320

On Day 0, you deposit $100 because the initial margin requirement is $5 per contract and you go long 20 contracts. At the end of Day 2, the balance is down to $20, which is $20 below the $40 maintenance margin requirement ($2 per contract times 20 contracts). You must deposit enough money to bring the balance up to the initial margin requirement of $100 ($5 per contract times 20 contracts). So on Day 3, you deposit $80. The price change on Day 3 causes a gain/loss of -$100, leaving you with a balance of $0 at the end of Day 3. On Day 4, you must deposit $100 to return the balance to the initial margin level.

Solution to B:

A price decrease to $79 would trigger a margin call. This calculation is based on the fact that the difference between the initial margin requirement and the maintenance margin requirement is $3. If the futures price starts at $82, it can fall by $3 to $79 before it triggers a margin call.

Some futures contracts impose limits on the price change that can occur from one day to the next. Appropriately, these are called **price limits**. These limits are usually set as an absolute change over the previous day. Using the example above, suppose the price limit was $4. This would mean that each day, no transaction could take place higher than the previous settlement price plus $4 or lower than the previous settlement price minus $4. So the next day's settlement price cannot go beyond the price limit and thus no transaction can take place beyond the limits.

If the price at which a transaction would be made exceeds the limits, then price essentially freezes at one of the limits, which is called a **limit move**. If the price is stuck at the upper limit, it is called **limit up**; if stuck at the lower limit, it is called **limit down**. If a transaction cannot take place because the price would be beyond the limits, this situation is called **locked limit**. By the end of the day, unless the price has moved back within the limits, the settlement price will then be at one of the limits. The following day, the new range of acceptable prices is based on the settlement price plus or minus limits. The exchanges have different rules that provide for expansion or contraction of price limits under some circumstances. In addition, not all contracts have price limits.

Finally, we note that the exchanges have the power to mark contracts to market whenever they deem it necessary. Thus, they can do so during the trading day rather than wait until the end of the day. They sometimes do so when abnormally large market moves occur.

The daily settlement procedure is designed to collect losses and distribute gains in such a manner that losses are paid before becoming large enough to impose a serious risk of default. Recall that the clearinghouse guarantees to each party that it need not worry about collecting from the counterparty. The clearinghouse essentially positions itself in the middle of each contract, becoming the short counterparty to the long and the long counterparty to the short. The clearinghouse collects funds from the parties incurring losses in this daily settlement procedure and distributes them to the parties incurring gains. By doing so each day, the clearinghouse ensures that losses cannot build up. Of course, this process offers no guarantee that counterparties will not default. Some defaults do occur, but the counterparty is defaulting to the clearinghouse, which has never failed to pay off the opposite party. In the unlikely event that the clearinghouse were unable to pay, it would turn to a reserve fund or to the exchange, or it would levy a tax on exchange members to cover losses.

DELIVERY AND CASH SETTLEMENT

As previously described, a futures trader can close out a position before expiration. If the trader holds a long position, she can simply enter into a position to go short the same futures contract. From the clearinghouse's perspective, the trader holds both a long and short position in the same contract. These positions are considered to offset and, therefore, there is no open position in place. Most futures contracts are offset before expiration. Those that remain in place are subject to either delivery or a final cash settlement. Here we explore this process, which determines how a futures contract terminates at expiration.

When the exchange designs a futures contract, it specifies whether the contract will terminate with delivery or cash settlement. If the contract terminates in delivery, the clearinghouse selects a counterparty, usually the holder of the oldest long contract, to accept delivery. The holder of the short position then delivers the underlying to the holder of the long position, who pays the short the necessary cash for the underlying. Suppose, for example, that two days before expiration, a party goes long one futures contract at a price of $50. The following day (the day before expiration), the settlement price is $52. The trader's margin account is then marked to market by crediting it with a gain of $2. Then suppose that the next day the contract expires with the settlement price at $53. As the end of the trading day draws near, the trader has two choices. She can attempt to close out the position by selling the futures contract. The margin account would then be marked to market at the price at which she sells. If she sells close enough to the expiration, the price she sold at would be very close to the final settlement price of $53. Doing so would add $1 to her margin account balance.

The other choice is to leave the position open at the end of the trading day. Then she would have to take delivery. If that occurred, she would be required to take possession of the asset and pay the short the settlement price of the previous day. Doing so would be equivalent to paying $52 and receiving the asset. She could then sell the asset for its price of $53, netting a $1 gain, which is equivalent to the final $1 credited to her margin account if she had terminated the position at the settlement price of $53, as described above.[12]

An alternative settlement procedure, which we described in the reading on forward markets and contracts, is cash settlement. The exchange designates certain futures contracts as cash-settled contracts. If the contract used in this example were cash settled, then the trader would not need to close out the position close to the end of the expiration day. She could simply leave the position open. When the contract expires, her margin account would be marked to market for a gain on the final day of $1. Cash settlement contracts have some advantages over delivery contracts, particularly with respect to significant savings in transaction costs.[13]

Exhibit 2 illustrates the equivalence of these three forms of delivery. Note, however, that because of the transaction costs of delivery, parties clearly prefer a closeout or cash settlement over physical delivery, particularly when the underlying asset is a physical commodity.

Exhibit 2	Closeout versus Physical Delivery versus Cash Settlement

```
                                                              Closeout:
                                                          Sell contract at 53
                                                      Mark to market profit/loss:
                                                             53 – 52 = 1
                                                                  or
                                                          Physical Delivery:
                                                       Pay 52, receive asset worth 53
                                       Mark to market                  or
                                        profit/loss:              Cash Settlement:
       Buy futures at 50:                52 – 50 = 2             Receive 53 – 52 = 1
          Pay nothing

          └────────────────────────────┴────────────────────────────┘

     2 days before expiration        1 day before expiration          Expiration
       (futures price = 50)          (settlement price = 52)      (settlement price = 53)
```

Contracts designated for delivery have a variety of features that can complicate delivery. In most cases, delivery does not occur immediately after expiration but takes place over several days. In addition, many contracts permit the short to choose when delivery takes place. For many contracts, delivery can be made any business day of the month. The delivery period usually includes the days following the last trading day of the month, which is usually in the third week of the month.

In addition, the short often has other choices regarding delivery, a major one being exactly which underlying asset is delivered. For example, a futures contract on U.S.

---

12 The reason she pays the settlement price of the previous day is because on the previous day when her account was marked to market, she essentially created a new futures position at a price of $52. Thus, she committed to purchase the asset at expiration, just one day later, at a price of $52. The next day when the contract expires, it is then appropriate that she buy the underlying for $52.

13 Nonetheless, cash settlement has been somewhat controversial in the United States. If a contract is designated as cash settlement, it implies that the buyer of the contract never intended to actually take possession of the underlying asset. Some legislators and regulators feel that this design is against the spirit of the law, which views a futures contract as a commitment to buy the asset at a later date. Even though parties often offset futures contracts prior to expiration, the possibility of actual delivery is still present in contracts other than those settled by cash. This controversy, however, is relatively minor and has caused no serious problems or debates in recent years.

Treasury bonds trading at the Chicago Board of Trade permits the short to deliver any of a number of U.S. Treasury bonds.[14] The wheat futures contract at the Chicago Board of Trade permits delivery of any of several types of wheat. Futures contracts calling for physical delivery of commodities often permit delivery at different locations. A given commodity delivered to one location is not the same as that commodity delivered to another because of the costs involved in transporting the commodity. The short holds the sole right to make decisions about what, when, and where to deliver, and the right to make these decisions can be extremely valuable. The right to make a decision concerning these aspects of delivery is called a **delivery option**.

Some futures contracts that call for delivery require delivery of the actual asset, and some use only a book entry. For example, in this day and age, no one physically handles U.S. Treasury bonds in the form of pieces of paper. Bonds are transferred electronically over the Federal Reserve's wire system. Other contracts, such as oil or wheat, do actually involve the physical transfer of the asset. Physical delivery is more common when the underlying is a physical commodity, whereas book entry is more common when the underlying is a financial asset.

Futures market participants use one additional delivery procedure, which is called **exchange for physicals (EFP)**. In an EFP transaction, the long and short arrange an alternative delivery procedure. For example, the Chicago Board of Trade's wheat futures contracts require delivery on certain dates at certain locations either in Chicago or in a few other specified locations in the Midwest. If the long and short agree, they could effect delivery by having the short deliver the wheat to the long in, for example, Omaha. The two parties would then report to the Chicago Board of Trade that they had settled their contract outside of the exchange's normal delivery procedures, which would be satisfactory to the exchange.

FUTURES EXCHANGES

A futures exchange is a legal corporate entity whose shareholders are its members. The members own memberships, more commonly called **seats**. Exchange members have the privilege of executing transactions on the exchange. Each member acts as either a **floor trader** or a **broker**. Floor traders are typically called **locals**; brokers are typically called **futures commission merchants (FCMs)**. Locals are market makers, standing ready to buy and sell by quoting a bid and an ask price. They are the primary providers of liquidity to the market. FCMs execute transactions for other parties off the exchange.

The locals on the exchange floor typically trade according to one of several distinct styles. The most common is called scalping. A **scalper** offers to buy or sell futures contracts, holding the position for only a brief period of time, perhaps just seconds. Scalpers attempt to profit by buying at the bid price and selling at the higher ask price. A **day trader** holds a position open somewhat longer but closes all positions at the end of the day.[15] A **position trader** holds positions open overnight. Day traders and position traders are quite distinct from scalpers in that they attempt to profit from the anticipated direction of the market; scalpers are trying simply to buy at the bid and sell at the ask.

---

14 We shall cover this feature in more detail in Section 6.2.

15 The term "day trader" has been around the futures market for a long time but has recently acquired a new meaning in the broader financial markets. The term is now used to describe individual investors who trade stocks, often over the internet, during the day for a living or as a hobby. In fact, the term has even been used in a somewhat pejorative manner, in that day traders are often thought of as naïve investors speculating wildly with money they can ill afford to lose.

Recall that futures exchanges have trading either on the floor or off the floor on electronic terminals, or in some cases, both. As previously described, floor trading in the United States takes place in pits, which are octagonal, multitiered areas where floor traders stand and conduct transactions. Traders wear jackets of specific colors and badges to indicate such information as what type of trader (FCM or local) they are and whom they represent.[16] As noted, to indicate a willingness to trade, a trader shouts and uses a set of standard hand signals. A trade is consummated by two traders agreeing on a price and a number of contracts. These traders might not actually say anything to each other; they may simply use a combination of hand signals and/or eye contact to agree on a transaction. When a transaction is agreed on, the traders fill out small paper forms and turn them over to clerks, who then see that the transactions are entered into the system and reported.

Each trader is required to have an account at a clearing firm. The clearing firms are the actual members of the clearinghouse. The clearinghouse deals only with the clearing firms, which then deal with their individual and institutional customers.

In electronic trading, the principles remain essentially the same but the traders do not stand in the pits. In fact, they do not see each other at all. They sit at computer terminals, which enable them to see the bids and offers of other traders. Transactions are executed by the click of a computer mouse or an entry from a keyboard.

Exhibit 3 lists the world's 20 leading futures exchanges in 2001, ranked by trading volume. Recall from the reading on derivative markets and instruments that trading volume can be a misleading measure of the size of futures markets; nonetheless, it is the measure primarily used. The structure of global futures exchanges has changed considerably in recent years. Exchanges in the United States, primarily the Chicago Board of Trade and the Chicago Mercantile Exchange, were clearly the world leaders in the past. Note that the volume leader now, however, is Eurex, the combined German–Swiss exchange. Eurex has been so successful partly because of its decision to be an all-electronic futures exchange, whereas the Chicago exchanges are still primarily pit-trading exchanges. Note the popularity of futures trading in Japan; four of the 20 leading exchanges are Japanese.

Exhibit 3	The World's 20 Leading Futures Exchanges
Exchange and Location	**Volume in 2001 (Number of Contracts)**
Eurex (Germany and Switzerland)	435,141,707
Chicago Mercantile Exchange (United States)	315,971,885
Chicago Board of Trade (United States)	209,988,002
London International Financial Futures and Options Exchange (United Kingdom)	161,522,775
Bolsa de Mercadorias & Futuros (Brazil)	94,174,452
New York Mercantile Exchange (United States)	85,039,984
Tokyo Commodity Exchange (Japan)	56,538,245
London Metal Exchange (United Kingdom)	56,224,495
Paris Bourse SA (France)	42,042,673
Sydney Futures Exchange (Australia)	34,075,508
Korea Stock Exchange (Korea)	31,502,184

---

16 For example, an FCM or local could be trading for himself or could represent a company.

Exhibit 3	Continued

Exchange and Location	Volume in 2001 (Number of Contracts)
Singapore Exchange (Singapore)	30,606,546
Central Japan Commodity Exchange (Japan)	27,846,712
International Petroleum Exchange (United Kingdom)	26,098,207
OM Stockholm Exchange (Sweden)	23,408,198
Tokyo Grain Exchange (Japan)	22,707,808
New York Board of Trade (United States)	14,034,168
MEFF Renta Variable (Spain)	13,108,293
Tokyo Stock Exchange (Japan)	12,465,433
South African Futures Exchange (South Africa)	11,868,242

Source: Futures Industry, January/February 2002.

TYPES OF FUTURES CONTRACTS

The different types of futures contracts are generally divided into two main groups: commodity futures and financial futures. Commodity futures cover traditional agricultural, metal, and petroleum products. Financial futures include stocks, bonds, and currencies. Exhibit 4 gives a broad overview of the most active types of futures contracts traded on global futures exchanges. These contracts are those covered by the *Wall Street Journal* on the date indicated.

Our primary focus here is on financial and currency futures contracts. Within the financials group, our main interest is on interest rate and bond futures, stock index futures, and currency futures. We may occasionally make reference to a commodity futures contract, but that will primarily be for illustrative purposes. In the following subsections, we introduce the primary contracts we shall focus on. These are U.S. contracts, but they resemble most types of futures contracts found on exchanges throughout the world. Full contract specifications for these and other contracts are available on the websites of the futures exchanges, which are easy to locate with most internet search engines.

Exhibit 4	Most-Active Global Futures Contracts as Covered by the *Wall Street Journal,* 18 June 2002

Commodity Futures		Financial Futures
Corn (CBOT)	Treasury Bonds (CBOT)	Euro (CME)
Oats (CBOT)	Treasury Notes (CBOT)	Euro–Sterling (NYBOT)
Soybeans (CBOT)	10-Year Agency Notes (CBOT)	Euro–U.S. Dollar (NYBOT)
Soybean Meal (CBOT)	10-Year Interest Rate Swaps (CBOT)	Euro–Yen (NYBOT)
Soybean Oil (CBOT)	2-Year Agency Notes (CBOT)	Dow Jones Industrial Average (CBOT)
Wheat (CBOT, KCBT, MGE)	5-Year Treasury Notes (CBOT)	Mini Dow Jones Industrial Average (CBOT)
Canola (WPG)	2-Year Treasury Notes (CBOT)	S&P 500 Index (CME)
Barley (WPG)	Federal Funds (CBOT)	Mini S&P 500 Index (CME)

(continued)

| Exhibit 4 | Continued |

Commodity Futures		Financial Futures
Feeder Cattle (CME)	Municipal Bond Index (CBOT)	S&P Midcap 400 Index (CME)
Live Cattle (CME)	Treasury Bills (CME)	Nikkei 225 (CME)
Lean Hogs (CME)	1-Month LIBOR (CME)	NASDAQ 100 Index (CME)
Pork Bellies (CME)	Eurodollar (CME)	Mini NASDAQ Index (CME)
Milk (CME)	Euroyen (CME, SGX)	Goldman Sachs Commodity Index (CME)
Lumber (CME)	Short Sterling (LIFFE)	Russell 1000 Index (CME)
Cocoa (NYBOT)	Long Gilt (LIFFE)	Russell 2000 Index (CME)
Coffee (NYBOT)	3-Month Euribor (LIFFE)	NYSE Composite Index (NYBOT)
World Sugar (NYBOT)	3-Month Euroswiss (LIFFE)	U.S. Dollar Index (NYBOT)
Domestic Sugar (NYBOT)	Canadian Bankers Acceptance (ME)	Share Price Index (SFE)
Cotton (NYBOT)	10-Year Canadian Government Bond (ME)	CAC 40 Stock Index (MATIF)
Orange Juice (NYBOT)	10-Year Euro Notional Bond (MATIF)	Xetra Dax (EUREX)
Copper (NYMEX)	3-Month Euribor (MATIF)	FTSE 200 Index (LIFFE)
Gold (NYMEX)	3-Year Commonwealth T-Bonds (SFE)	Dow Jones Euro Stoxx 50 Index (EUREX)
Platinum (NYMEX)	5-Year German Euro Government Bond (EUREX)	Dow Jones Stoxx 50 Index (EUREX)
Palladium (NYMEX)	10-Year German Euro Government Bond (EUREX)	
Silver (NYMEX)	2-Year German Euro Government Bond (EUREX)	
Crude Oil (NYMEX)	Japanese Yen (CME)	
No. 2 Heating Oil (NYMEX)	Canadian Dollar (CME)	
Unleaded Gasoline (NYMEX)	British Pound (CME)	
Natural Gas (NYMEX)	Swiss Franc (CME)	
Brent Crude Oil (IPEX)	Australian Dollar (CME)	
Gas Oil (IPEX)	Mexican Peso (CME)	

Exchange codes: CBOT (Chicago Board of Trade), CME (Chicago Mercantile Exchange), LIFFE (London International Financial Futures Exchange), WPG (Winnipeg Grain Exchange), EUREX (Eurex), NYBOT (New York Board of Trade), IPEX (International Petroleum Exchange), MATIF (Marché a Terme International de France), ME (Montreal Exchange), MGE (Minneapolis Grain Exchange), SFE (Sydney Futures Exchange), SGX (Singapore Exchange), KCBT (Kansas City Board of Trade), NYMEX (New York Mercantile Exchange).
Note: These are not the only global futures contracts but are those covered in the *Wall Street Journal* on the date given and represent the most active contracts at that time.

6.1 Short-Term Interest Rate Futures Contracts

The primary short-term interest rate futures contracts are those on U.S. Treasury bills and Eurodollars on the Chicago Mercantile Exchange.

6.1.1 Treasury Bill Futures

The Treasury bill contract, launched in 1976, was the first interest rate futures contract. It is based on a 90-day U.S. Treasury bill, one of the most important U.S. government debt instruments (described in Section 3.2.1 of the reading on forward markets and contracts). The Treasury bill, or T-bill, is a discount instrument, meaning that its price equals the face value minus a discount representing interest. The discount equals the face value multiplied by the quoted rate times the days to maturity divided by 360. Thus, using the example from the reading on forward markets and contracts, if a 180-day T-bill is selling at a discount of 4 percent, its price per $1 par is $1 - 0.04(180/360) = \$0.98$. An investor who buys the bill and holds it to maturity would receive $1 at maturity, netting a gain of $0.02.

The futures contract is based on a 90-day $1,000,000 U.S. Treasury bill. Thus, on any given day, the contract trades with the understanding that a 90-day T-bill will be delivered at expiration. While the contract is trading, its price is quoted as 100 minus the rate quoted as a percent priced into the contract by the futures market. This value, 100 – Rate, is known as the IMM Index; IMM stands for International Monetary Market, a division of the Chicago Mercantile Exchange. The IMM Index is a reported and publicly available price; however, it is not the actual futures price, which is

$$100\big[1 - (\text{Rate}/100)(90/360)\big]$$

For example, suppose on a given day the rate priced into the contract is 6.25 percent. Then the quoted price will be 100 – 6.25 = 93.75. The actual futures price would be

$$\$1,000,000\big[1 - 0.0625(90/360)\big] = \$984,375$$

Recall, however, that except for the small margin deposit, a futures transaction does not require any cash to be paid up front. As trading takes place, the rate fluctuates with market interest rates and the associated IMM Index price changes accordingly. The actual futures price, as calculated above, also fluctuates according to the above formula, but interestingly, that price is not very important. The same information can be captured more easily by referencing the IMM Index than by calculating the actual price.

Suppose, for example, that a trader had his account marked to market to the above price, 6.25 in terms of the rate, 93.75 in terms of the IMM Index, and $984,375 in terms of the actual futures price. Now suppose the rate goes to 6.50, an increase of 0.25 or 25 basis points. The IMM Index declines to 93.50, and the actual futures price drops to

$$\$1,000,000\big[1 - 0.065(90/360)\big] = \$983,750$$

Thus, the actual futures price decreased by $984,375 – $983,750 = $625. A trader who is long would have a loss of $625; a trader who is short would have a gain of $625.

This $625 gain or loss can be arrived at more directly, however, by simply noting that each basis point move is equivalent to $25.[17] This special design of the contract makes it easy for floor traders to do the necessary arithmetic in their heads. For example, if floor traders observe the IMM Index move from 93.75 to 93.50, they immediately know that it has moved down 25 basis points and that 25 basis points times $25 per basis point is a loss of $625. The minimum tick size is one-half basis point or $12.50.

T-bill futures contracts have expirations of the current month, the next month, and the next four months of March, June, September, and December. Because of the small trading volume, however, only the closest expiration has much trading volume, and even that one is only lightly traded. T-bill futures expire specifically on the Monday of the week of the third Wednesday each month and settle in cash rather than physical delivery of the T-bill, as described in Section 4.

As important as Treasury bills are in U.S. financial markets, however, today this futures contract is barely active. The Eurodollar contract is considered much more important because it reflects the interest rate on a dollar borrowed by a high-quality private borrower. The rates on T-bills are considered too heavily influenced by U.S. government policies, budget deficits, government funding plans, politics, and Federal Reserve monetary policy. Although unquestionably Eurodollar rates are affected by those factors, market participants consider them much less directly influenced. But in spite of this relative inactivity, T-bill futures are useful instruments for illustrating

---

17 Expressed mathematically, $\$1,000,000[0.0001(90/360)] = \$25$. In other words, any move in the last digit of the rate (a basis point) affects the actual futures price by $25.

certain principles of futures market pricing and trading. Accordingly, we shall use them on some occasions. For now, however, we turn to the Eurodollar futures contract.

6.1.2 *Eurodollar Futures*

Recall that in the reading on forward markets and contracts, we devoted a good bit of effort to understanding Eurodollar forward contracts, known as FRAs. These contracts pay off based on LIBOR on a given day. The Eurodollar futures contract of the Chicago Mercantile Exchange is based on $1 million notional principal of 90-day Eurodollars. Specifically, the underlying is the rate on a 90-day dollar-denominated time deposit issued by a bank in London. As we described in the reading on forward markets and contracts, this deposit is called a Eurodollar time deposit, and the rate is referred to as LIBOR (London Interbank Offer Rate). On a given day, the futures contract trades based on the understanding that at expiration, the official Eurodollar rate, as compiled by the British Bankers Association (BBA), will be the rate at which the final settlement of the contract is made. While the contract is trading, its price is quoted as 100 minus the rate priced into the contract by futures traders. Like its counterpart in the T-bill futures market, this value, 100 − Rate, is also known as the IMM Index.

As in the T-bill futures market, on a given day, if the rate priced into the contract is 5.25 percent, the quoted price will be 100 − 5.25 = 94.75. With each contract based on $1 million notional principal of Eurodollars, the actual futures price is

$$\$1,000,000\big[1 - 0.0525(90/360)\big] = \$986,875$$

Like the T-bill contract, the actual futures price moves $25 for every basis point move in the rate or IMM Index price.

As with all futures contracts, the price fluctuates on a daily basis and margin accounts are marked to market according to the exchange's official settlement price. At expiration, the final settlement price is the official rate quoted on a 90-day Eurodollar time deposit by the BBA. That rate determines the final settlement. Eurodollar futures contracts do not permit actual delivery of a Eurodollar time deposit; rather, they settle in cash, as described in Section 4.

The Eurodollar futures contract is one of the most active in the world. Because its rate is based on LIBOR, it is widely used by dealers in swaps, FRAs, and interest rate options to hedge their positions taken in dollar-denominated over-the-counter interest rate derivatives. Such derivatives usually use LIBOR as the underlying rate.

It is important to note, however, that there is a critical distinction between the manner in which the interest calculation is built into the Eurodollar futures contract and the manner in which interest is imputed on actual Eurodollar time deposits. Recall from the reading on forward markets and contracts that when a bank borrows $1 million at a rate of 5 percent for 90 days, the amount it will owe in 90 days is

$$\$1,000,000\big[1 + 0.05(90/360)\big] = \$1,012,500$$

Interest on Eurodollar time deposits is computed on an add-on basis to the principal. As described in this section, however, it appears that in computing the futures price, interest is deducted from the principal so that a bank borrowing $1,000,000 at a rate of 5 percent would receive

$$\$1,000,000\big[1 - 0.05(90/360)\big] = \$987,500$$

and would pay back $1,000,000. This procedure is referred to as discount interest and is used in the T-bill market.

The discount interest computation associated with Eurodollar futures is merely a convenience contrived by the futures exchange to facilitate quoting prices in a manner already familiar to its traders, who were previously trading T-bill futures.

The minimum tick size for Eurodollar futures is 1 basis point or $25. The available expirations are the next two months plus March, June, September, and December. The expirations go out about 10 years, a reflection of their use by over-the-counter derivatives dealers to hedge their positions in long-term interest rate derivatives. Eurodollar futures expire on the second business day on which London banks are open before the third Wednesday of the month and terminate with a cash settlement.

6.2 Intermediate- and Long-Term Interest Rate Futures Contracts

In U.S. markets, the primary interest-rate-related instruments of intermediate and long maturities are U.S. Treasury notes and bonds. The U.S. government issues both instruments: Treasury notes have an original maturity of 2 to 10 years, and Treasury bonds have an original maturity of more than 10 years. Futures contracts on these instruments are very actively traded on the Chicago Board of Trade. For the most part, there are no real differences in the contract characteristics for Treasury note and Treasury bond futures; the underlying bonds differ slightly, but the futures contracts are qualitatively the same. We shall focus here on one of the most active instruments, the U.S. Treasury bond futures contract.

The contract is based on the delivery of a U.S. Treasury bond with any coupon but with a maturity of at least 15 years. If the deliverable bond is callable, it cannot be callable for at least 15 years from the delivery date.[18] These specifications mean that there are potentially a large number of deliverable bonds, which is exactly the way the Chicago Board of Trade, the Federal Reserve, and the U.S. Treasury want it. They do not want a potential run on a single issue that might distort prices. By having multiple deliverable issues, however, the contract must be structured with some fairly complicated procedures to adjust for the fact that the short can deliver whatever bond he chooses from among the eligible bonds. This choice gives the short a potentially valuable option and puts the long at a disadvantage. Moreover, it complicates pricing the contract, because the identity of the underlying bond is not clear. Although when referring to a futures contract on a 90-day Eurodollar time deposit we are relatively clear about the underlying instrument, a futures contract on a long-term Treasury bond does not allow us the same clarity.

To reduce the confusion, the exchange declares a standard or hypothetical version of the deliverable bond. This hypothetical deliverable bond has a 6 percent coupon. When a trader holding a short position at expiration delivers a bond with a coupon greater (less) than 6 percent, she receives an upward (a downward) adjustment to the price paid for the bond by the long. The adjustment is done by means of a device called the **conversion factor**. In brief, the conversion factor is the price of a $1.00 par bond with a coupon and maturity equal to those of the deliverable bond and a yield of 6 percent. Thus, if the short delivers a bond with a coupon greater (less) than 6 percent, the conversion factor exceeds (is less than) 1.0.[19] The amount the long pays the short is the futures price at expiration multiplied by the conversion factor. Thus, delivery of a bond with coupon greater (less) than the standard amount, 6 percent, results in the short receiving an upward (a downward) adjustment to the amount received. A number of other technical considerations are also involved in determining the delivery price.[20]

---

18 The U.S. government no longer issues callable bonds but has done so in the past.

19 This statement is true regardless of the maturity of the deliverable bond. Any bond with a coupon in excess of its yield is worth more than its par value.

20 For example, the actual procedure for delivery of U.S. Treasury bonds is a three-day process starting with the short notifying the exchange of intention to make delivery. Delivery actually occurs several days later. In addition, as is the custom in U.S. bond markets, the quoted price does not include the accrued interest. Accordingly, an adjustment must be made.

The conversion factor system is designed to put all bonds on equal footing. Ideally, application of the conversion factor would result in the short finding no preference for delivery of any one bond over any other. That is not the case, however, because the complex relationships between bond prices cannot be reduced to a simple linear adjustment, such as the conversion factor method. As a result, some bonds are cheaper to deliver than others. When making the delivery decision, the short compares the cost of buying a given bond on the open market with the amount she would receive upon delivery of that bond. The former will always exceed the latter; otherwise, a clear arbitrage opportunity would be available. The most attractive bond for delivery would be the one in which the amount received for delivering the bond is largest relative to the amount paid on the open market for the bond. The bond that minimizes this loss is referred to as the **cheapest-to-deliver bond**.

At any time during the life of a Treasury bond futures contract, traders can identify the cheapest-to-deliver bond. Determining the amount received at delivery is straightforward; it equals the current futures price times the conversion factor for a given bond. To determine the amount the bond would cost at expiration, one calculates the forward price of the bond, positioned at the delivery date. Of course, this is just a forward computation; circumstances could change by the expiration date. But this forward calculation gives a picture of circumstances as they currently stand and identifies which bond is currently the cheapest to deliver. That bond is then considered the bond most likely to be delivered. Recall that one problem with this futures contract is that the identity of the underlying bond is unclear. Traders traditionally treat the cheapest to deliver as the bond that underlies the contract. As time passes and interest rates change, however, the cheapest-to-deliver bond can change. Thus, the bond underlying the futures contract can change, adding an element of uncertainty to the pricing and trading of this contract.

With this complexity associated with the U.S. Treasury bond futures contract, one might suspect that it is less actively traded. In fact, the opposite is true: Complexity creates extraordinary opportunities for gain for those who understand what is going on and can identify the cheapest bond to deliver.

The Chicago Board of Trade's U.S. Treasury bond futures contract covers $100,000 par value of U.S. Treasury bonds. The expiration months are March, June, September, and December. They expire on the seventh business day preceding the last business day of the month and call for actual delivery, through the Federal Reserve's wire system, of the Treasury bond. Prices are quoted in points and 32nds, meaning that you will see prices like 98 18/32, which equals 98.5625. For a contract covering $100,000 par value, for example, the price is $98,562.50. The minimum tick size is 1/32, which is $31.25.

In addition to the futures contract on the long-term government bond, there are also very similar futures contracts on intermediate-term government bonds. The Chicago Board of Trade's contracts on 2-, 5-, and 10-year Treasury notes are very actively traded and are almost identical to its long-term bond contract, except for the exact specification of the underlying instrument. Intermediate and long-term government bonds are important instruments in every country's financial markets. They give the best indication of the long-term default-free interest rate and are often viewed as a benchmark bond for various comparisons in financial markets.[21] Accordingly, futures contracts on such bonds play an important role in a country's financial markets and are almost always among the most actively traded contracts in futures markets around the world.

If the underlying instrument is not widely available and not actively traded, the viability of a futures contract on it becomes questionable. The reduction seen in U.S.

---

21 For example, the default risk of a corporate bond is often measured as the difference between the corporate bond yield and the yield on a Treasury bond or note of comparable maturity. Fixed rates on interest rate swaps are usually quoted as a spread over the rate on a Treasury bond or note of comparable maturity.

government debt in the late 1990s has led to a reduction in the supply of intermediate and long-term government bonds, and some concern has arisen over this fact. In the United States, some efforts have been made to promote the long-term debt of Fannie Mae and Freddie Mac as substitute benchmark bonds.[22] It remains to be seen whether such efforts will be necessary and, if so, whether they will succeed.

6.3 Stock Index Futures Contracts

One of the most successful types of futures contracts of all time is the class of futures on stock indices. Probably the most successful has been the Chicago Mercantile Exchange's contract on the Standard and Poor's 500 Stock Index. Called the S&P 500 Stock Index futures, this contract premiered in 1982 and has benefited from the widespread acceptance of the S&P 500 Index as a stock market benchmark. The contract is quoted in terms of a price on the same order of magnitude as the S&P 500 itself. For example, if the S&P 500 Index is at 1183, a two-month futures contract might be quoted at a price of, say, 1187.

The contract implicitly contains a multiplier, which is (appropriately) multiplied by the quoted futures price to produce the actual futures price. The multiplier for the S&P 500 futures is $250. Thus, when you hear of a futures price of 1187, the actual price is 1187($250) = $296,750.

S&P 500 futures expirations are March, June, September, and December and go out about two years, although trading is active only in the nearest two to three expirations. With occasional exceptions, the contracts expire on the Thursday preceding the third Friday of the month. Given the impracticality of delivering a portfolio of the 500 stocks in the index combined according to their relative weights in the index, the contract is structured to provide for cash settlement at expiration.

The S&P 500 is not the only active stock index futures contract. In fact, the Chicago Mercantile Exchange has a smaller version of the S&P 500 contract, called the Mini S&P 500, which has a multiplier of $50 and trades only electronically. Other widely traded contracts in the United States are on the Dow Jones Industrials, the S&P Midcap 400, and the NASDAQ 100. Virtually every developed country has a stock index futures contract based on the leading equities of that country. Well-known stock index futures contracts around the world include the United Kingdom's FTSE 100 (pronounced "Footsie 100"), Japan's Nikkei 225, France's CAC 40, and Germany's DAX 30.

6.4 Currency Futures Contracts

In the reading on forward markets and contracts, we described forward contracts on foreign currencies. There are also futures contracts on foreign currencies. Although the forward market for foreign currencies is much more widely used, the futures market is still quite active. In fact, currency futures were the first futures contracts not based on physical commodities. Thus, they are sometimes referred to as the first financial futures contracts, and their initial success paved the way for the later introduction of interest rate and stock index futures.

Compared with forward contracts on currencies, currency futures contracts are much smaller in size. In the United States, these contracts trade at the Chicago

---

22 Fannie Mae is the Federal National Mortgage Association, and Freddie Mac is the Federal Home Loan Mortgage Corporation. These institutions were formerly U.S. government agencies that issued debt to raise funds to buy and sell mortgages and mortgage-backed securities. These institutions are now publicly traded corporations but are considered to have extremely low default risk because of their critical importance in U.S. mortgage markets. It is believed that an implicit Federal government guarantee is associated with their debt. Nonetheless, it seems unlikely that the debt of these institutions could take over that of the U.S. government as a benchmark. The Chicago Board of Trade has offered futures contracts on the bonds of these organizations, but the contracts have not traded actively.

Mercantile Exchange with a small amount of trading at the New York Board of Trade. In addition there is some trading on exchanges outside the United States. The characteristics we describe below refer to the Chicago Mercantile Exchange's contract.

In the United States, the primary currencies on which trading occurs are the euro, Canadian dollar, Swiss franc, Japanese yen, British pound, Mexican peso, and Australian dollar. Each contract has a designated size and a quotation unit. For example, the euro contract covers €125,000 and is quoted in dollars per euro. A futures price such as $0.8555 is stated in dollars and converts to a contract price of

$$125,000(\$0.8555) = \$106,937.50$$

The Japanese yen futures price is structured somewhat differently. Because of the large number of yen per dollar, the contract covers ¥12,500,000 and is quoted without two zeroes that ordinarily precede the price. For example, a price might be stated as 0.8205, but this actually represents a price of 0.008205, which converts to a contract price of

$$12,500,000(0.008205) = \$102,562.50$$

Alternatively, a quoted price of 0.8205 can be viewed as $1/0.008205 = ¥121.88$ per dollar.

Currency futures contracts expire in the months of March, June, September, and December. The specific expiration is the second business day before the third Wednesday of the month. Currency futures contracts call for actual delivery, through book entry, of the underlying currency.

We have briefly examined the different types of futures contracts of interest to us. Of course there are a variety of similar instruments trading on futures exchanges around the world. Our purpose, however, is not to provide institutional details, which can be obtained at the websites of the world's futures exchanges, but rather to enhance your understanding of the important principles necessary to function in the world of derivatives.

SUMMARY

- Futures contracts are standardized instruments that trade on a futures exchange, have a secondary market, and are guaranteed against default by means of a daily settling of gains and losses. Forward contracts are customized instruments that are not guaranteed against default and are created anywhere off of an exchange.

- Modern futures markets primarily originated in Chicago out of a need for grain farmers and buyers to be able to transact for delivery at future dates for grain that would, in the interim, be placed in storage.

- Futures transactions are standardized and conducted in a public market, are homogeneous, have a secondary market giving them an element of liquidity, and have a clearinghouse, which collects margins and settles gains and losses daily to provide a guarantee against default. Futures markets are also regulated at the federal government level.

- Margin in the securities markets is the deposit of money, the margin, and a loan for the remainder of the funds required to purchase a stock or bond. Margin in the futures markets is much smaller and does not involve a loan. Futures margin is more like a performance bond or down payment.

- Futures trading occurs on a futures exchange, which involves trading either in a physical location called a pit or via a computer terminal off of the floor of the futures exchange as part of an electronic trading system. In either case, a party to a futures contract goes long, committing to buy the underlying asset at an agreed-upon price, or short, committing to sell the underlying asset at an agreed-upon price.

■ A futures trader who has established a position can re-enter the market and close out the position by doing the opposite transaction (sell if the original position was long or buy if the original position was short). The party has offset the position, no longer has a contract outstanding, and has no further obligation.

■ Initial margin is the amount of money in a margin account on the day of a transaction or when a margin call is made. Maintenance margin is the amount of money in a margin account on any day other than when the initial margin applies. Minimum requirements exist for the initial and maintenance margins, with the initial margin requirement normally being less than 10 percent of the futures price and the maintenance margin requirement being smaller than the initial margin requirement. Variation margin is the amount of money that must be deposited into the account to bring the balance up to the required level. The settlement price is an average of the last few trades of the day and is used to determine the gains and losses marked to the parties' accounts.

■ The futures clearinghouse engages in a practice called marking to market, also known as the daily settlement, in which gains and losses on a futures position are credited and charged to the trader's margin account on a daily basis. Thus, profits are available for withdrawal and losses must be paid quickly before they build up and pose a risk that the party will be unable to cover large losses.

■ The margin balance at the end of the day is determined by taking the previous balance and accounting for any gains or losses from the day's activity, based on the settlement price, as well as any money added or withdrawn.

■ Price limits are restrictions on the price of a futures trade and are based on a range relative to the previous day's settlement price. No trade can take place outside of the price limits. A limit move is when the price at which two parties would like to trade is at or beyond the price limit. Limit up is when the market price would be at or above the upper limit. Limit down is when the market price would be at or below the lower limit. Locked limit occurs when a trade cannot take place because the price would be above the limit up or below the limit down prices.

■ A futures contract can be terminated by entering into an offsetting position very shortly before the end of the expiration day. If the position is still open when the contract expires, the trader must take delivery (if long) or make delivery (if short), unless the contract requires that an equivalent cash settlement be used in lieu of delivery. In addition, two participants can agree to alternative delivery terms, an arrangement called exchange for physicals.

■ Delivery options are features associated with a futures contract that permit the short some flexibility in what to deliver, where to deliver it, and when in the expiration month to make delivery.

■ Scalpers are futures traders who take positions for very short periods of time and attempt to profit by buying at the bid price and selling at the ask price. Day traders close out all positions by the end of the day. Position traders leave their positions open overnight and potentially longer.

■ Treasury bill futures are contracts in which the underlying is $1,000,000 of a U.S. Treasury bill. Eurodollar futures are contracts in which the underlying is $1,000,000 of a Eurodollar time deposit. Treasury bond futures are contracts in which the underlying is $100,000 of a U.S. Treasury bond with a minimum 15-year maturity. Stock index futures are contracts in which the underlying is a well-known stock index, such as the S&P 500 or FTSE 100. Currency futures are contracts in which the underlying is a foreign currency.

PRACTICE PROBLEMS FOR READING 62

1. **A.** In February, Dave Parsons purchased a June futures contract on the NASDAQ 100 Index. He decides to close out his position in April. Describe how he would do so.

    B. Peggy Smith is a futures trader. In early August, she took a short position in an S&P 500 Index futures contract expiring in September. After a week, she decides to close out her position. Describe how she would do so.

2. A gold futures contract requires the long trader to buy 100 troy ounces of gold. The initial margin requirement is $2,000, and the maintenance margin requirement is $1,500.

    A. Matthew Evans goes long one June gold futures contract at the futures price of $320 per troy ounce. When could Evans receive a maintenance margin call?

    B. Chris Tosca sells one August gold futures contract at a futures price of $323 per ounce. When could Tosca receive a maintenance margin call?

3. A copper futures contract requires the long trader to buy 25,000 lbs of copper. A trader buys one November copper futures contract at a price of $0.75/lb. Theoretically, what is the maximum loss this trader could have? Another trader sells one November copper futures contract. Theoretically, what is the maximum loss this trader with a short position could have?

4. Consider a hypothetical futures contract in which the current price is $212. The initial margin requirement is $10, and the maintenance margin requirement is $8. You go long 20 contracts and meet all margin calls but do not withdraw any excess margin.

    A. When could there be a margin call?

    B. Complete the table below and explain any funds deposited. Assume that the contract is purchased at the settlement price of that day so there is no mark-to-market profit or loss on the day of purchase.

Day	Beginning Balance	Funds Deposited	Futures Price	Price Change	Gain/Loss	Ending Balance
0			212			
1			211			
2			214			
3			209			
4			210			
5			204			
6			202			

    C. How much are your total gains or losses by the end of Day 6?

5. Sarah Moore has taken a short position in one Chicago Board of Trade Treasury bond futures contract with a face value of $100,000 at the price of 96 6/32. The initial margin requirement is $2,700, and the maintenance margin requirement is $2,000. Moore would meet all margin calls but would not withdraw any excess margin.

Practice Problems and Solutions: 1–6 taken from *Analysis of Derivatives for the Chartered Financial Analyst® Program*, by Don M. Chance, CFA. Copyright © 2003 by CFA Institute. All other problems and solutions copyright © CFA Institute.

A. Complete the table below and provide an explanation of any funds deposited. Assume that the contract is purchased at the settlement price of that day, so there is no mark-to-market profit or loss on the day of purchase.

Day	Beginning Balance	Funds Deposited	Futures Price	Price Change	Gain/Loss	Ending Balance
0			96-06			
1			96-31			
2			97-22			
3			97-18			
4			97-24			
5			98-04			
6			97-31			

B. How much are Moore's total gains or losses by the end of Day 6?

6. A. The IMM index price in yesterday's newspaper for a September Eurodollar futures contract is 95.23. What is the actual price of this contract?

B. The IMM index price in today's newspaper for the contract mentioned above is 95.25. How much is the change in the actual futures price of the contract since the previous day?

7. Consider the following statements about a futures clearinghouse:

Statement 1   "A clearinghouse in futures contracts allows for the offsetting of contracts prior to delivery."

Statement 2   "A clearinghouse in futures contracts collects initial margin (performance bonds) from both the long and short sides in the contract."

Are the statements *most likely* correct or incorrect?

A. Both statements are correct.

B. Statement 1 is incorrect, but Statement 2 is correct.

C. Statement 1 is correct, but Statement 2 is incorrect.

8. A trader enters into a short position of 20 futures contracts at an initial futures price of $85.00. Initial margin, per contract, is $7.50. Maintenance margin, per contract, is $7.00. Each contract is for one unit of the underlying asset. Over the next three days, the contract settles at $86.00, $84.25, and $85.50, respectively. Assuming the trader does not withdraw any funds from his/her margin account during the period, but does post variation margin sufficient to meet any maintenance margin calls, the balance in the margin account will be:

A. $140.00 at initiation and $150.00 at settlement on Day 3.

B. $150.00 at initiation and $150.00 at settlement on Day 3.

C. $150.00 at initiation and $160.00 at settlement on Day 3.

9. Consider the following statements regarding futures contracts that may be settled by delivery:

Statement 1   "The long initiates the delivery process."

Statement 2   "For many such contracts, delivery can take place any business day during the delivery month."

Are the statements *most likely* correct or incorrect?

A. Both statements are correct.

B. Statement 1 is incorrect, but Statement 2 is correct.

C. Statement 1 is correct, but Statement 2 is incorrect.

SOLUTIONS FOR READING 62

1. **A.** Parsons would close out his position in April by offsetting his long position with a short position. To do so, he would re-enter the market and offer for sale a June futures contract on the NASDAQ 100 index. When he has a buyer, he has both a long and a short position in the June futures contract on the NASDAQ 100 index. From the point of view of the clearinghouse, he no longer has a position in the contract.

    B. Smith would close out her position in August by offsetting her short position with a long position. To do so, she would re-enter the market and purchase a September futures contract on the S&P 500. She then has both a short and a long position in the September futures contract on the S&P 500. From the point of view of the clearinghouse, she no longer has a position in the contract.

2. The difference between initial and maintenance margin requirements for one gold futures contract is $2,000 – $1,500 = $500. Because one gold futures contract is for 100 troy ounces, the difference between initial and maintenance margin requirements per troy ounce is $500/100, or $5.

    A. Because Evans has a long position, he would receive a maintenance margin call if the price were to *fall* below $320 – $5, or $315 per troy ounce.

    B. Because Tosca has a short position, he would receive a maintenance margin call if the price were to *rise* above $323 + $5, or $328 per troy ounce.

3. *Trader with a long position*: This trader loses if the price falls. The maximum loss would be incurred if the futures price falls to zero, and this loss would be $0.75/lb × 25,000 lbs, or $18,750. Of course, this scenario is only theoretical, not realistic.

    Trader with a short position: This trader loses if the price increases. Because there is no limit on the price increase, there is no theoretical upper limit on the loss that the trader with a short position could incur.

4. **A.** The difference between the initial margin requirement and the maintenance margin requirement is $2. Because the initial futures price was $212, a margin call would be triggered if the price falls below $210.

    B.

Day	Beginning Balance	Funds Deposited	Futures Price	Price Change	Gain/Loss	Ending Balance
0	0	200	212			200
1	200	0	211	–1	–20	180
2	180	0	214	3	60	240
3	240	0	209	–5	–100	140
4	140	60	210	1	20	220
5	220	0	204	–6	–120	100
6	100	100	202	–2	–40	160

On Day 0, you deposit $200 because the initial margin requirement is $10 per contract and you go long 20 contracts ($10 per contract times 20 contracts equals $200). At the end of Day 3, the balance is down to $140, $20 below the $160 maintenance margin requirement ($8 per contract times 20 contracts). You must deposit enough money to bring the balance up to the initial margin requirement of $200. So, the next day (Day 4), you deposit $60. The price change on Day 5 causes a gain/loss of –$120, leaving you with a balance of $100 at the end of Day 5. Again, this amount is less than the $160 maintenance margin requirement. You must deposit enough money to bring the balance up to the initial margin requirement of $200. So on Day 6, you deposit $100.

C. By the end of Day 6, the price is $202, a decrease of $10 from your purchase price of $212. Your loss so far is $10 per contract times 20 contracts, or $200.

You could also look at your loss so far as follows. You initially deposited $200, followed by margin calls of $60 and $100. Thus, you have deposited a total of $360 so far and have not withdrawn any excess margin. The ending balance, however, is only $160. Thus, the total loss incurred by you so far is $360 – $160, or $200.

5. A.

Day	Beginning Balance	Funds Deposited	Futures Price	Price Change	Gain/Loss	Ending Balance
0	0	2,700.00	96-06			2,700.00
1	2,700.00	0	96-31	25/32	–781.25	1,918.75
2	1,918.75	781.25	97-22	23/32	–718.75	1,981.25
3	1,981.25	718.75	97-18	–4/32	125.00	2,825.00
4	2,825.00	0	97-24	6/32	–187.50	2,637.50
5	2,637.50	0	98-04	12/32	–375.00	2,262.50
6	2,262.50	0	97-31	–5/32	156.25	2,418.75

On Day 0, Moore deposits $2,700 because the initial margin requirement is $2,700 per contract and she has gone short one contract. At the end of Day 1, the price has increased from 96-06 to 96-31—that is, the price has increased from $96,187.50 to $96,968.75. Because Moore has taken a short position, this increase of $781.25 is an adverse price movement for her, and the balance is down by $781.25 to $1,918.75. Because this amount is less than the $2,000 maintenance margin requirement, she must deposit additional funds to bring her account back to the initial margin requirement of $2,700. So, the next day (Day 2), she deposits $781.25. Another adverse price movement takes place on Day 2 as the price further increases by $718.75 to $97,687.50. Her ending balance is again below the maintenance margin requirement of $2,000, and she must deposit enough money to bring her account back to the initial margin requirement of $2,700. So, the next day (Day 3), she deposits $718.75. Subsequently, even though her balance falls below the initial margin requirement, it does not go below the maintenance margin requirement, and she does not need to deposit any more funds.

B. Moore bought the contract at a futures price of 96-06. By the end of Day 6, the price is 97-31, an increase of 1 25/32. Therefore, her loss so far is 1.78125 percent of $100,000, which is $1,781.25.

You could also look at her loss so far as follows: She initially deposited $2,700, followed by margin calls of $781.25 and $718.75. Thus, she has deposited a total of $4,200 so far, and has not withdrawn any excess margin. Her ending balance is $2,418.75. Thus, the total loss so far is $4,200 – $2,418.75, or $1,781.25.

6. **A.** Because the IMM index price is 95.23, the annualized LIBOR rate priced into the contract is 100 − 95.23 = 4.77 percent. With each contract based on $1 million notional principal of 90-day Eurodollars, the actual futures price is $1,000,000[1 − 0.0477(90/360)] = $988,075.

    B. Because the IMM index price is 95.25, the annualized LIBOR rate priced into the contract is 100 − 95.25 = 4.75 percent. The actual futures price is $1,000,000[1 − 0.0475(90/360)] = $988,125. So, the change in actual futures price is $988,125 − $988,075 = $50.

    You could also compute the change in price directly by noting that the IMM index price increased by 2 basis points. Because each basis point move in the rate moves the actual futures price by $25, the increase in the actual futures price is 2 × $25, or $50.

7. A is correct. Both statements describe functions of a clearinghouse.

8. C is correct. Initial margin is 20 contracts × $7.50 margin per contract = $150. At the end of Day 1, the short position has lost $20 ((85 − 86) × 20 contracts) leaving a margin balance of $130. Because this violates the required maintenance margin of $140, the short must deposit $20 variation margin to bring the margin account back to the initial margin balance of $150. On Day 2, the short position has a daily gain of $35 ((86 − 84.25) × 20) bringing the margin account to a balance of $185. The short position loses $25 on Day 3 ((84.25 − 85.50) × 20) leaving a margin balance of $160.

9. B is correct. The short initiates the delivery process and actual delivery typically can occur on any business day of the delivery month.

63

Option Markets and Contracts

by Don M. Chance, CFA

LEARNING OUTCOMES

Mastery	The candidate should be able to:
☐	**a** describe call and put options;
☐	**b** distinguish between European and American options;
☐	**c** define the concept of moneyness of an option;
☐	**d** compare exchange-traded options and over-the-counter options;
☐	**e** identify the types of options in terms of the underlying instruments;
☐	**f** compare interest rate options with forward rate agreements (FRAs);
☐	**g** define interest rate caps, floors, and collars;
☐	**h** calculate and interpret option payoffs and explain how interest rate options differ from other types of options;
☐	**i** define intrinsic value and time value, and explain their relationship;
☐	**j** determine the minimum and maximum values of European options and American options;
☐	**k** calculate and interpret the lowest prices of European and American calls and puts based on the rules for minimum values and lower bounds;
☐	**l** explain how option prices are affected by the exercise price and the time to expiration;
☐	**m** explain put–call parity for European options, and explain how put–call parity is related to arbitrage and the construction of synthetic options;
☐	**n** explain how cash flows on the underlying asset affect put–call parity and the lower bounds of option prices;
☐	**o** determine the directional effect of an interest rate change or volatility change on an option's price.

Analysis of Derivatives for the Chartered Financial Analyst® Program, by Don M. Chance, CFA. Copyright © 2003 by CFA Institute.

INTRODUCTION

Prior readings provided a general introduction to derivative markets and examined forward contracts and futures contracts. We noted how similar forward and futures contracts are: Both are commitments to buy an underlying asset at a fixed price at a later date. Forward contracts, however, are privately created, over-the-counter customized instruments that carry credit risk. Futures contracts are publicly traded, exchange-listed standardized instruments that effectively have no credit risk. Now we turn to options. Like forwards and futures, they are derivative instruments that provide the opportunity to buy or sell an underlying asset with a specific expiration date. But in contrast, buying an option gives the *right*, not the obligation, to buy or sell an underlying asset. And whereas forward and futures contracts involve no exchange of cash up front, options require a cash payment from the option buyer to the option seller.

Yet options contain several features common to forward and futures contracts. For one, options can be created by any two parties with any set of terms they desire. In this sense, options can be privately created, over-the-counter, customized instruments that are subject to credit risk. In addition, however, there is a large market for publicly traded, exchange-listed, standardized options, for which credit risk is essentially eliminated by the clearinghouse.

Just as we examined the pricing of forwards and futures in the last two readings, we shall examine option pricing in this reading. We shall also see that options can be created out of forward contracts, and that forward contracts can be created out of options. With some simplifying assumptions, options can be created out of futures contracts and futures contracts can be created out of options.

Finally, note that options also exist that have a futures or forward contract as the underlying. These instruments blend some of the features of both options and forwards/futures.

As background, we discuss the definitions and characteristics of options.

BASIC DEFINITIONS AND ILLUSTRATIONS OF OPTIONS CONTRACTS

In the reading on derivative markets and instruments, we defined an option as a financial derivative contract that provides a party the right to buy or sell an underlying at a fixed price by a certain time in the future. The party holding the right is the option buyer; the party granting the right is the option seller. There are two types of options, a **call** and a **put**. A call is an option granting the right to buy the underlying; a put is an option granting the right to sell the underlying. With the exception of some advanced types of options, a given option contract is either a call, granting the right to buy, or a put, granting the right to sell, but not both.[1] We emphasize that this right to buy or sell is held by the option buyer, also called the long or option holder, and granted by the option seller, also called the short or option writer.

To obtain this right, the option buyer pays the seller a sum of money, commonly referred to as the **option price**. On occasion, this option price is called the **option premium** or just the **premium**. This money is paid when the option contract is initiated.

2.1 Basic Characteristics of Options

The fixed price at which the option holder can buy or sell the underlying is called the **exercise price**, **strike price**, **striking price**, or **strike**. The use of this right to buy

---

1 Of course, a party could buy both a call and a put, thereby holding the right to buy *and* sell the underlying.

or sell the underlying is referred to as **exercise** or **exercising the option**. Like all derivative contracts, an option has an expiration date, giving rise to the notion of an option's **time to expiration**. When the expiration date arrives, an option that is not exercised simply expires.

What happens at exercise depends on whether the option is a call or a put. If the buyer is exercising a call, she pays the exercise price and receives either the underlying or an equivalent cash settlement. On the opposite side of the transaction is the seller, who receives the exercise price from the buyer and delivers the underlying, or alternatively, pays an equivalent cash settlement. If the buyer is exercising a put, she delivers the stock and receives the exercise price or an equivalent cash settlement. The seller, therefore, receives the underlying and must pay the exercise price or the equivalent cash settlement.

As noted in the above paragraph, cash settlement is possible. In that case, the option holder exercising a call receives the difference between the market value of the underlying and the exercise price from the seller in cash. If the option holder exercises a put, she receives the difference between the exercise price and the market value of the underlying in cash.

There are two primary exercise styles associated with options. One type of option has European-style exercise, which means that the option can be exercised only on its expiration day. In some cases, exercise could occur during that day; in others, exercise can occur only when the option has expired. In either case, such an option is called a **European option**. The other style of exercise is American-style exercise. Such an option can be exercised on any day through the expiration day and is generally called an **American option**.[2]

Option contracts specify a designated number of units of the underlying. For exchange-listed, standardized options, the exchange establishes each term, with the exception of the price. The price is negotiated by the two parties. For an over-the-counter option, the two parties decide each of the terms through negotiation.

In an over-the-counter option—one created off of an exchange by any two parties who agree to trade—the buyer is subject to the possibility of the writer defaulting. When the buyer exercises, the writer must either deliver the stock or cash if a call, or pay for the stock or pay cash if a put. If the writer cannot do so for financial reasons, the option holder faces a credit loss. Because the option holder paid the price up front and is not required to do anything else, the seller does not face any credit risk. Thus, although credit risk is bilateral in forward contracts—the long assumes the risk of the short defaulting, and the short assumes the risk of the long defaulting—the credit risk in an option is unilateral. Only the buyer faces credit risk because only the seller can default. As we discuss later, in exchange-listed options, the clearinghouse guarantees payment to the buyer.

2.2 Some Examples of Options

Consider some call and put options on Sun Microsystems (SUNW). The date is 13 June and Sun is selling for $16.25. Exhibit 1 gives information on the closing prices of four options, ones expiring in July and October and ones with exercise prices of 15.00 and 17.50. The July options expire on 20 July and the October options expire on 18 October. In the parlance of the profession, these are referred to as the July 15 calls, July 17.50 calls, October 15 calls, and October 17.50 calls, with similar terminology for the puts. These particular options are American style.

---

2 It is worthwhile to be aware that these terms have nothing to do with Europe or America. Both types of options are found in Europe and America. The names are part of the folklore of options markets, and there is no definitive history to explain how they came into use.

| Exhibit 1 | Closing Prices of Selected Options on SUNW, 13 June | | | |

Exercise Price	July Calls	October Calls	July Puts	October Puts
15.00	2.35	3.30	0.90	1.85
17.50	1.00	2.15	2.15	3.20

Note: Stock price is $16.25; July options expire on 20 July; October options expire on 18 October.

Consider the July 15 call. This option permits the holder to buy SUNW at a price of $15 a share any time through 20 July. To obtain this option, one would pay a price of $2.35. Therefore, a writer received $2.35 on 13 June and must be ready to sell SUNW to the buyer for $15 during the period through 20 July. Currently, SUNW trades above $15 a share, but as we shall see in more detail later, the option holder has no reason to exercise the option right now.[3] To justify purchase of the call, the buyer must be anticipating that SUNW will increase in price before the option expires. The seller of the call must be anticipating that SUNW will not rise sufficiently in price before the option expires.

Note that the option buyer could purchase a call expiring in July but permitting the purchase of SUNW at a price of $17.50. This price is more than the $15.00 exercise price, but as a result, the option, which sells for $1.00, is considerably cheaper. The cheaper price comes from the fact that the July 17.50 call is less likely to be exercised, because the stock has a higher hurdle to clear. A buyer is not willing to pay as much and a seller is more willing to take less for an option that is less likely to be exercised.

Alternatively, the option buyer could choose to purchase an October call instead of a July call. For any exercise price, however, the October calls would be more expensive than the July calls because they allow a longer period for the stock to make the move that the buyer wants. October options are more likely to be exercised than July options; therefore, a buyer would be willing to pay more and the seller would demand more for the October calls.

Suppose the buyer expects the stock price to go down. In that case, he might buy a put. Consider the October 17.50 put, which would cost the buyer $3.20. This option would allow the holder to sell SUNW at a price of $17.50 any time up through 18 October.[4] He has no reason to exercise the option right now, because it would mean he would be buying the option for $3.20 and selling a stock worth $16.25 for $17.50. In effect, the option holder would part with $19.45 (the cost of the option of $3.20 plus the value of the stock of $16.25) and obtain only $17.50.[5] The buyer of a put obviously must be anticipating that the stock will fall before the expiration day.

If he wanted a cheaper option than the October 17.50 put, he could buy the October 15 put, which would cost only $1.85 but would allow him to sell the stock for only $15.00 a share. The October 15 put is less likely to be exercised than the October 17.50, because the stock price must fall below a lower hurdle. Thus, the buyer is not willing to pay as much and the seller is willing to take less.

---

3 The buyer paid $2.35 for the option. If he exercised it right now, he would pay $15.00 for the stock, which is worth only $16.25. Thus, he would have effectively paid $17.35 (the cost of the option of $2.35 plus the exercise price of $15) for a stock worth $16.25. Even if he had purchased the option previously at a much lower price, the current option price of $2.35 is the opportunity cost of exercising the option—that is, he can always sell the option for $2.35. Therefore, if he exercised the option, he would be throwing away the $2.35 he could receive if he sold it.

4 Even if the option holder did not own the stock, he could use the option to sell the stock short.

5 Again, even if the option were purchased in the past at a much lower price, the $3.20 current value of the option is an opportunity cost. Exercise of the option is equivalent to throwing away the opportunity cost.

For either exercise price, purchase of a July put instead of an October put would be much cheaper but would allow less time for the stock to make the downward move necessary for the transaction to be worthwhile. The July put is cheaper than the October put; the buyer is not willing to pay as much and the seller is willing to take less because the option is less likely to be exercised.

In observing these option prices, we have obtained our first taste of some principles involved in pricing options.

Call options have a lower premium the higher the exercise price.

Put options have a lower premium the lower the exercise price.

Both call and put options are cheaper the shorter the time to expiration.[6]

These results should be intuitive, but later in this reading we show unequivocally why they must be true.

2.3 The Concept of Moneyness of an Option

An important concept in the study of options is the notion of an option's **money-ness**, which refers to the relationship between the price of the underlying and the exercise price.

We use the terms **in-the-money**, **out-of-the-money**, and **at-the-money**. We explain the concept in Exhibit 2 with examples from the SUNW options. Note that in-the-money options are those in which exercising the option would produce a cash inflow that exceeds the cash outflow. Thus, calls are in-the-money when the value of the underlying exceeds the exercise price. Puts are in-the-money when the exercise price exceeds the value of the underlying. In our example, there are no at-the-money SUNW options, which would require that the stock value equal the exercise price; however, an at-the-money option can effectively be viewed as an out-of-the-money option, because its exercise would not bring in more money than is paid out.

Exhibit 2	Moneyness of an Option		
In-the-Money		**Out-of-the-Money**	
Option	**Justification**	**Option**	**Justification**
July 15 call	16.25 > 15.00	July 17.50 call	16.25 < 17.50
October 15 call	16.25 > 15.00	October 17.50 call	16.25 < 17.50
July 17.50 put	17.50 > 16.25	July 15 put	15.00 < 16.25
October 17.50 put	17.50 > 16.25	October 15 put	15.00 < 16.25

Notes: Sun Microsystems options on 13 June; stock price is 16.25. See Exhibit 1 for more details. There are no options with an exercise price of 16.25, so no options are at-the-money.

As explained above, *one would not necessarily exercise an in-the-money option, but one would never exercise an out-of-the-money option.*

We now move on to explore how options markets are organized.

---

6 There is an exception to the rule that put options are cheaper the shorter the time to expiration. This statement is always true for American options but not always for European options. We explore this point later.

THE STRUCTURE OF GLOBAL OPTIONS MARKETS

Although no one knows exactly how options first got started, contracts similar to options have been around for thousands of years. In fact, insurance is a form of an option. The insurance buyer pays the insurance writer a premium and receives a type of guarantee that covers losses. This transaction is similar to a put option, which provides coverage of a portion of losses on the underlying and is often used by holders of the underlying. The first true options markets were over-the-counter options markets in the United States in the 19th century.

3.1 Over-the-Counter Options Markets

In the United States, customized over-the-counter options markets were in existence in the early part of the 20th century and lasted well into the 1970s. An organization called the Put and Call Brokers and Dealers Association consisted of a group of firms that served as brokers and dealers. As brokers, they attempted to match buyers of options with sellers, thereby earning a commission. As dealers, they offered to take either side of the option transaction, usually laying off (hedging) the risk in another transaction. Most of these transactions were retail, meaning that the general public were their customers.

As we discuss in Section 3.2, the creation of the Chicago Board Options Exchange was a revolutionary event, but it effectively killed the Put and Call Brokers and Dealers Association. Subsequently, the increasing use of swaps facilitated a rebirth of the customized over-the-counter options market. Currency options, a natural extension to currency swaps, were in much demand. Later, interest rate options emerged as a natural outgrowth of interest rate swaps. Soon bond, equity, and index options were trading in a vibrant over-the-counter market. In contrast to the previous over-the-counter options market, however, the current one emerged as a largely wholesale market. Transactions are usually made with institutions and corporations and are rarely conducted directly with individuals. This market is much like the forward market described in the reading on forward markets and contracts, with dealers offering to take either the long or short position in options and hedging that risk with transactions in other options or derivatives. There are no guarantees that the seller will perform; hence, the buyer faces credit risk. As such, option buyers must scrutinize sellers' credit risk and may require some risk reduction measures, such as collateral.

As previously noted, customized options have *all* of their terms—such as price, exercise price, time to expiration, identification of the underlying, settlement or delivery terms, size of the contract, and so on—determined by the two parties.

Like forward markets, over-the-counter options markets are essentially unregulated. In most countries, participating firms, such as banks and securities firms, are regulated by the appropriate authorities, but there is usually no particular regulatory body for the over-the-counter options markets. In some countries, however, there are regulatory bodies for these markets.

Exhibit 3 provides information on the leading dealers in over-the-counter currency and interest rate options as determined by *Risk* magazine in its annual surveys of banks and investment banks and also end users.

Exhibit 3	*Risk* Magazine Surveys of Banks, Investment Banks, and Corporate End Users to Determine the Top Three Dealers in Over-the-Counter Currency and Interest Rate Options

	Respondents	
Currencies	**Banks and Investment Banks**	**Corporate End Users**
Currency Options		
$/€	UBS Warburg	Citigroup
	Citigroup/Deutsche Bank	Royal Bank of Scotland
		Deutsche Bank
$/¥	UBS Warburg	Citigroup
	Credit Suisse First Boston	JP Morgan Chase
	JP Morgan Chase/Royal Bank of Scotland	UBS Warburg
$/£	Royal Bank of Scotland	Royal Bank of Scotland
	UBS Warburg	Citigroup
	Citigroup	Hong Kong Shanghai Banking Corp.
$/SF	UBS Warburg	UBS Warburg
	Credit Suisse First Boston	Credit Suisse First Boston
	Citigroup	Citigroup
Interest Rate Options		
$	JP Morgan Chase	JP Morgan Chase
	Deutsche Bank	Citigroup
	Bank of America	Deutsche Bank/ Lehman Brothers*
€	JP Morgan Chase	JP Morgan Chase
	Credit Suisse First Boston/ Morgan Stanley	Citigroup
		UBS Warburg
¥	JP Morgan Chase/Deutsche Bank	UBS Warburg
	Bank of America	Barclays Capital
		Citigroup
£	Barclays Capital	Royal Bank of Scotland
	Societe Generale Groupe	Citigroup
	Bank of America/Royal Bank of Scotland	Hong Kong Shanghai Banking Corp.
SF	UBS Warburg	UBS Warburg
	JP Morgan Chase	JP Morgan Chase
	Credit Suisse First Boston	Goldman Sachs

Notes: $ = U.S. dollar, € = euro, ¥ = Japanese yen, £ = U.K. pound sterling, SF = Swiss franc.
*Barclays has acquired Lehman Brothers and will maintain the family of Lehman Brothers indices and the associated index calculation, publication, and analytical infrastructure and tools.
Source: Risk, September 2002, pp. 30–67 for Banks and Investment Banking dealer respondents, and June 2002, pp. 24–34 for Corporate End User respondents.
Results for Corporate End Users for Interest Rate Options are from *Risk*, July 2001, pp. 38–46. *Risk* omitted this category from its 2002 survey.

3.2 Exchange Listed Options Markets

As briefly noted above, the Chicago Board Options Exchange was formed in 1973. Created as an extension of the Chicago Board of Trade, it became the first organization to offer a market for standardized options. In the United States, standardized options also trade on the AMEX–NASDAQ, the Philadelphia Stock Exchange, and the Pacific Stock Exchange.[7] On a worldwide basis, standardized options are widely traded on such exchanges as LIFFE (the London International Financial Futures and Options Exchange) in London, Eurex in Frankfurt, and most other foreign exchanges. Exhibit 4 shows the 20 largest options exchanges in the world. Note, perhaps surprisingly, that the leading options exchange is in Korea.

Exhibit 4	World's 20 Largest Options Exchanges
Exchange and Location	**Volume in 2001**
Korea Stock Exchange (Korea)	854,791,792
Chicago Board Options Exchange (United States)	306,667,851
MONEP (France)	285,667,686
Eurex (Germany and Switzerland)	239,016,516
American Stock Exchange (United States)	205,103,884
Pacific Stock Exchange (United States)	102,701,752
Philadelphia Stock Exchange (United States)	101,373,433
Chicago Mercantile Exchange (United States)	95,740,352
Amsterdam Exchange (Netherlands)	66,400,654
LIFFE (United Kingdom)	54,225,652
Chicago Board of Trade (United States)	50,345,068
OM Stockholm (Sweden)	39,327,619
South African Futures Exchange (South Africa)	24,307,477
MEFF Renta Variable (Spain)	23,628,446
New York Mercantile Exchange (United States)	17,985,109
Korea Futures Exchange (Korea)	11,468,991
Italian Derivatives Exchange (Italy)	11,045,804
Osaka Securities Exchange (Japan)	6,991,908
Bourse de Montreal (Canada)	5,372,930
Hong Kong Futures Exchange (China)	4,718,880

Note: Volume given is in number of contracts.
Source: Data supplied by *Futures Industry* magazine.

As described in the reading on futures markets and contracts, the exchange fixes all terms of standardized instruments except the price. Thus, the exchange establishes the expiration dates and exercise prices as well as the minimum price quotation unit. The exchange also determines whether the option is European or American, whether the exercise is cash settlement or delivery of the underlying, and the contract size. In the United States, an option contract on an individual stock covers 100 shares of

---

7 You may wonder why the New York Stock Exchange is not mentioned. Standardized options did trade on the NYSE at one time but were not successful, and the right to trade these options was sold to another exchange.

stock. Terminology such as "one option" is often used to refer to one option contract, which is really a set of options on 100 shares of stock. Index option sizes are stated in terms of a multiplier, indicating that the contract covers a hypothetical number of shares, as though the index were an individual stock. Similar specifications apply for options on other types of underlyings.

The exchange generally allows trading in exercise prices that surround the current stock price. As the stock price moves, options with exercise prices around the new stock price are usually added. The majority of trading occurs in options that are close to being at-the-money. Options that are far in-the-money or far out-of-the-money, called **deep-in-the-money** and **deep-out-of-the-money** options, are usually not very actively traded and are often not even listed for trading.

Most exchange-listed options have fairly short-term expirations, usually the current month, the next month, and perhaps one or two other months. Most of the trading takes place for the two shortest expirations. Some exchanges list options with expirations of several years, which have come to be called LEAPS, for **long-term equity anticipatory securities**. These options are fairly actively purchased, but most investors tend to buy and hold them and do not trade them as often as they do the shorter-term options.

The exchanges also determine on which companies they will list options for trading. Although specific requirements do exist, generally the exchange will list the options of any company for which it feels the options would be actively traded. The company has no voice in the matter. Options of a company can be listed on more than one exchange in a given country.

In the reading on futures markets and contracts, we described the manner in which futures are traded. The procedure is very similar for exchange-listed options. Some exchanges have pit trading, whereby parties meet in the pit and arrange a transaction. Some exchanges use electronic trading, in which transactions are conducted through computers. In either case, the transactions are guaranteed by the clearinghouse. In the United States, the clearinghouse is an independent company called the Options Clearing Corporation or OCC. The OCC guarantees to the buyer that the clearinghouse will step in and fulfill the obligation if the seller reneges at exercise.

When the buyer purchases the option, the premium, which one might think would go to the seller, instead goes to the clearinghouse, which maintains it in a margin account. In addition, the seller must post some margin money, which is based on a formula that reflects whether the seller has a position that hedges the risk and whether the option is in- or out-of-the-money. If the price moves against the seller, the clearinghouse will force the seller to put up additional margin money. Although defaults are rare, the clearinghouse has always been successful in paying when the seller defaults. Thus, exchange-listed options are effectively free of credit risk.

Because of the standardization of option terms and participants' general acceptance of these terms, exchange-listed options can be bought and sold at any time prior to expiration. Thus, a party who buys or sells an option can re-enter the market before the option expires and offset the position with a sale or a purchase of the identical option. From the clearinghouse's perspective, the positions cancel.

As in futures markets, traders on the options exchange are generally either market makers or brokers. Some slight technical distinctions exist between different types of market makers in different options markets, but the differences are minor and do not concern us here. Like futures traders, option market makers attempt to profit by scalping (holding positions very short term) to earn the bid–ask spread and sometimes holding positions longer, perhaps closing them overnight or leaving them open for days or more.

When an option expires, the holder decides whether or not to exercise it. When the option is expiring, there are no further gains to waiting, so in-the-money options are always exercised, assuming they are in-the-money by more than the transaction cost of buying or selling the underlying or arranging a cash settlement when exercising. Using our example of the SUNW options, if at expiration the stock is at 16, the calls with an exercise price of 15 would be exercised. Most exchange-listed stock options call for actual delivery of the stock. Thus, the seller delivers the stock and the buyer pays the seller, through the clearinghouse, $15 per share. If the exchange specifies that the contract is cash settled, the seller simply pays the buyer $1. For puts requiring delivery, the buyer tenders the stock and receives the exercise price from the seller. If the option is out-of-the-money, it simply expires unexercised and is removed from the books. If the put is cash settled, the writer pays the buyer the equivalent cash amount.

Some nonstandardized exchange-traded options exist in the United States. In an attempt to compete with the over-the-counter options market, some exchanges permit some options to be individually customized and traded on the exchange, thereby benefiting from the advantages of the clearinghouse's credit guarantee. These options are primarily available only in large sizes and tend to be traded only by large institutional investors.

Like futures markets, exchange-listed options markets are typically regulated at the federal level. In the United States, federal regulation of options markets is the responsibility of the Securities and Exchange Commission; similar regulatory structures exist in other countries.

TYPES OF OPTIONS

Almost anything with a random outcome can have an option on it. Note that by using the word *anything*, we are implying that the underlying does not even need to be an asset. In this section, we shall discover the different types of options, identified by the nature of the underlying. Our focus is on financial options, but it is important, nonetheless, to gain some awareness of other types of options.

4.1 Financial Options

Financial options are options in which the underlying is a financial asset, interest rate, or a currency.

4.1.1 *Stock Options*

Options on individual stocks, also called **equity options**, are among the most popular. Exchange-listed options are available on most widely traded stocks and an option on any stock can potentially be created on the over-the-counter market. We have already given examples of stock options in an earlier section; we now move on to index options.

4.1.2 *Index Options*

Stock market indices are well known, not only in the investment community but also among many individuals who are not even directly investing in the market. Because a stock index is just an artificial portfolio of stocks, it is reasonable to expect that one could create an option on a stock index. Indeed, we have already covered forward and futures contracts on stock indices; options are no more difficult in structure.

For example, consider options on the S&P 500 Index, which trade on the Chicago Board Options Exchange and have a designated index contract multiplier of 100. On 13 June of a given year, the S&P 500 closed at 1241.60. A call option with an exercise price of $1,250 expiring on 20 July was selling for $28. The option is European style and settles in cash. The underlying, the S&P 500, is treated as though it were a share of stock worth $1,241.60, which can be bought, using the call option, for $1,250 on

20 July. At expiration, if the option is in-the-money, the buyer exercises it and the writer pays the buyer the $100 contract multiplier times the difference between the index value at expiration and $1,250.

In the United States, there are also options on the Dow Jones Industrial Average, the NASDAQ, and various other indices. There are nearly always options on the best-known stock indices in most countries.

Just as there are options on stocks, there are also options on bonds.

4.1.3 *Bond Options*

Options on bonds, usually called **bond options**, are primarily traded in the over-the-counter markets. Options exchanges have attempted to generate interest in options on bonds, but have not been very successful. Corporate bonds are not very actively traded; most are purchased and held to expiration. Government bonds, however, are very actively traded; nevertheless, options on them have not gained widespread acceptance on options exchanges. Options exchanges generate much of their trading volume from individual investors, who have far more interest in and understanding of stocks than bonds.

Thus, bond options are found almost exclusively in the over-the-counter market and are almost always options on government bonds. Consider, for example, a U.S. Treasury bond maturing in 27 years. The bond has a coupon of 5.50 percent, a yield of 5.75 percent, and is selling for $0.9659 per $1 par. An over-the-counter options dealer might sell a put or call option on the bond with an exercise price of $0.98 per $1.00 par. The option could be European or American. Its expiration day must be significantly before the maturity date of the bond. Otherwise, as the bond approaches maturity, its price will move toward par, thereby removing much of the uncertainty in its price. The option could be specified to settle with actual delivery of the bond or with a cash settlement. The parties would also specify that the contract cover a given notional principal, expressed in terms of a face value of the underlying bond.

Continuing our example, let us assume that the contract covers $5 million face value of bonds and is cash settled. Suppose the buyer exercises a call option when the bond price is at $0.995. Then the option is in-the-money by $0.995 − $0.98 = $0.015 per $1 par. The seller pays the buyer 0.015($5,000,000) = $75,000. If instead the contract called for delivery, the seller would deliver $5 million face value of bonds, which would be worth $5,000,000($0.995) = $4,975,000. The buyer would pay $5,000,000($0.98) = $4,900,000. Because the option is created in the over-the-counter market, the option buyer would assume the risk of the seller defaulting.

Even though bond options are not very widely traded, another type of related option is widely used, especially by corporations. This family of options is called **interest rate options**. These are quite different from the options we have previously discussed, because the underlying is not a particular financial instrument.

4.1.4 *Interest Rate Options*

In the reading on futures markets and contracts, we devoted considerable effort to understanding the Eurodollar spot market and forward contracts on the Eurodollar rate or LIBOR, called FRAs. In this reading, we cover options on LIBOR. Although these are not the only interest rate options, their characteristics are sufficiently general to capture most of what we need to know about options on other interest rates. First recall that a Eurodollar is a dollar deposited outside of the United States. The primary Eurodollar rate is LIBOR, and it is considered the best measure of an interest rate paid in dollars on a nongovernmental borrower. These Eurodollars represent dollar-denominated time deposits issued by banks in London borrowing from other banks in London.

Before looking at the characteristics of interest rate options, let us set the perspective by recalling that FRAs are forward contracts that pay off based on the difference between the underlying rate and the fixed rate embedded in the contract when it is constructed. For example, consider a 3 × 9 FRA. This contract expires in three months. The underlying rate is six-month LIBOR. Hence, when the contract is constructed, the underlying Eurodollar instrument matures in nine months. *When the contract expires, the payoff is made immediately,* but the rate on which it is based, 180-day LIBOR, is set in the spot market, where it is assumed that interest will be paid 180 days later. Hence, the payoff on an FRA is discounted by the spot rate on 180-day LIBOR to give a present value for the payoff as of the expiration date.

Just as an FRA is a forward contract in which the underlying is an interest rate, an **interest rate option** is an option in which the underlying is an interest rate. Instead of an exercise price, it has an **exercise rate** (or **strike rate**), which is expressed on an order of magnitude of an interest rate. At expiration, the option payoff is based on the difference between the underlying rate in the market and the exercise rate. Whereas an FRA is a *commitment* to make one interest payment and receive another at a future date, an interest rate option is the *right* to make one interest payment and receive another. And just as there are call and put options, there is also an **interest rate call** and an **interest rate put**.

An interest rate call is an option in which the holder has the right to make a known interest payment and receive an unknown interest payment. The underlying is the unknown interest rate. If the unknown underlying rate turns out to be higher than the exercise rate at expiration, the option is in-the-money and is exercised; otherwise, the option simply expires. *An interest rate put is an option in which the holder has the right to make an unknown interest payment and receive a known interest payment.* If the unknown underlying rate turns out to be lower than the exercise rate at expiration, the option is in-the-money and is exercised; otherwise, the option simply expires. All interest rate option contracts have a specified size, which, as in FRAs, is called the notional principal. An interest rate option can be European or American style, but most tend to be European style. Interest rate options are settled in cash.

As with FRAs, these options are offered for purchase and sale by dealers, which are financial institutions, usually the same ones who offer FRAs. These dealers quote rates for options of various exercise prices and expirations. When a dealer takes an option position, it usually then offsets the risk with other transactions, often Eurodollar futures.

To use the same example we used in introducing FRAs, consider options expiring in 90 days on 180-day LIBOR. The option buyer specifies whatever exercise rate he desires. Let us say he chooses an exercise rate of 5.5 percent and a notional principal of $10 million.

Now let us move to the expiration day. Suppose that 180-day LIBOR is 6 percent. Then the call option is in-the-money. The payoff to the holder of the option is

$$(\$10,000,000)(0.06 - 0.055)\left(\frac{180}{360}\right) = \$25,000$$

This money is not paid at expiration, however; it is paid 180 days later. There is no reason why the payoff could not be made at expiration, as is done with an FRA. The delay of payment associated with interest rate options actually makes more sense, because these instruments are commonly used to hedge floating-rate loans in which the rate is set on a given day but the interest is paid later. We shall see examples of the convenience of this type of structure in the reading on risk management applications of option strategies.

Note that the difference between the underlying rate and the exercise rate is multiplied by 180/360 to reflect the fact that the rate quoted is a 180-day rate but is stated as an annual rate. Also, the interest calculation is multiplied by the notional principal.

In general, the payoff of an interest rate call is

$$
\text{(Notional Principal)}\,\text{Max}\left(0,\text{Underlying rate at expiration}\right.
$$

$$
\left. - \text{Exercise rate}\right)\left(\frac{\text{Days in underlying rate}}{360}\right) \tag{1}
$$

The expression Max(0,Underlying rate at expiration − Exercise rate) is similar to a form that we shall commonly see throughout this reading for all options. The payoff of a call option at expiration is based on the maximum of zero or the underlying minus the exercise rate. If the option expires out-of-the-money, then "Underlying rate at expiration − Exercise rate" is negative; consequently, zero is greater. Thus, the option expires with no value. If the option expires in-the-money, "Underlying rate at expiration − Exercise rate" is positive. Thus, the option expires worth this difference (multiplied by the notional principal and the Days/360 adjustment). The expression "Days in underlying rate," which we used in the reading on forward markets and contracts, refers to the fact that the rate is specified as the rate on an instrument of a specific number of days to maturity, such as a 90-day or 180-day rate, thereby requiring that we multiply by 90/360 or 180/360 or some similar adjustment.

For an interest rate put option, the general formula is

$$
\text{(Notional Principal)}\,\text{Max}\left(0,\text{Exercise rate}\right.
$$

$$
\left. - \text{Underlying rate at expiration}\right)\left(\frac{\text{Days in underlying rate}}{360}\right) \tag{2}
$$

For an exercise rate of 5.5 percent and an underlying rate at expiration of 6 percent, an interest rate put expires out-of-the-money. Only if the underlying rate is less than the exercise rate does the put option expire in-the-money.

As noted above, borrowers often use interest rate call options to hedge the risk of rising rates on floating-rate loans. Lenders often use interest rate put options to hedge the risk of falling rates on floating-rate loans. The form we have seen here, in which the option expires with a single payoff, is not the more commonly used variety of interest rate option. Floating-rate loans usually involve multiple interest payments. Each of those payments is set on a given date. To hedge the risk of interest rates increasing, the borrower would need options expiring on each rate reset date. Thus, the borrower would require a combination of interest rate call options. Likewise, a lender needing to hedge the risk of falling rates on a multiple-payment floating-rate loan would need a combination of interest rate put options.

A combination of interest rate calls is referred to as an **interest rate cap** or sometimes just a **cap**. A combination of interest rate puts is called an **interest rate floor** or sometimes just a **floor**.[8] Specifically, *an interest rate cap is a series of call options on an interest rate, with each option expiring at the date on which the floating loan rate will be reset, and with each option having the same exercise rate.*[9] Each option is independent of the others; thus, exercise of one option does not affect the right to exercise any of the others. Each component call option is called a **caplet**. *An interest rate floor is a series of put options on an interest rate, with each option expiring at the date on which the floating loan rate will be reset, and with each option having the same exercise rate.* Each component put option is called a **floorlet**. The price of an interest rate cap or floor is the sum of the prices of the options that make up the cap or floor.

A special combination of caps and floors is called an **interest rate collar**. *An interest rate collar is a combination of a long cap and a short floor or a short cap and a long floor.* Consider a borrower in a floating rate loan who wants to hedge the risk

---

8 It is possible to construct caps and floors with options on any other type of underlying, but they are very often used when the underlying is an interest rate.

9 Technically, each option need not have the same exercise rate, but they generally do.

of rising interest rates but is concerned about the requirement that this hedge must have a cash outlay up front: the option premium. A collar, which adds a short floor to a long cap, is a way of reducing and even eliminating the up-front cost of the cap. The sale of the floor brings in cash that reduces the cost of the cap. It is possible to set the exercise rates such that the price received for the sale of the floor precisely offsets the price paid for the cap, thereby completely eliminating the up-front cost. This transaction is sometimes called a **zero-cost collar**. The term is a bit misleading, however, and brings to mind the importance of noting the true cost of a collar. Although the cap allows the borrower to be paid from the call options when rates are high, the sale of the floor requires the borrower to pay the counterparty when rates are low. Thus, the cost of protection against rising rates is the loss of the advantage of falling rates. Caps, floors, and collars are popular instruments in the interest rate markets. We shall explore strategies using them in the reading on risk management applications of option strategies.

Although interest rate options are primarily written on such rates as LIBOR, Euribor, and Euroyen, the underlying can be any interest rate.

4.1.5 *Currency Options*

As we noted in the reading on forward markets and contracts, the currency forward market is quite large. The same is true for the currency options market. A **currency option** allows the holder to buy (if a call) or sell (if a put) an underlying currency at a fixed exercise rate, expressed as an exchange rate. Many companies, knowing that they will need to convert a currency X at a future date into a currency Y, will buy a call option on currency Y specified in terms of currency X. For example, say that a U.S. company will be needing €50 million for an expansion project in three months. Thus, it will be buying euros and is exposed to the risk of the euro rising against the dollar. Even though it has that concern, it would also like to benefit if the euro weakens against the dollar. Thus, it might buy a call option on the euro. Let us say it specifies an exercise rate of $0.90. So it pays cash up front for the right to buy €50 million at a rate of $0.90 per euro. If the option expires with the euro above $0.90, it can buy euros at $0.90 and avoid any additional cost over $0.90. If the option expires with the euro below $0.90, it does not exercise the option and buys euros at the market rate.

Note closely these two cases:

Euro expires above $0.90

　Company buys €50 million at $0.90

Euro expires at or below $0.90

　Company buys €50 million at the market rate

These outcomes can also be viewed in the following manner:

Dollar expires below €1.1111, that is, €1 > $0.90

　Company sells $45 million (€50 million × $0.90) at €1.1111, equivalent to buying €50 million

Dollar expires above €1.1111, that is, €1 < $0.90

　Company sells sufficient dollars to buy €50 million at the market rate

This transaction looks more like a put in which the underlying is the dollar and the exercise rate is expressed as €1.1111. Thus, the call on the euro can be viewed as a put on the dollar. Specifically, a call to buy €50 million at an exercise price of $0.90 is also a put to sell €50 million × $0.90 = $45 million at an exercise price of 1/$0.90, or €1.1111.

Most foreign currency options activity occurs on the customized over-the-counter markets. Some exchange-listed currency options trade on a few exchanges, but activity is fairly low.

4.2 Options on Futures

In the reading on forward markets and contracts we covered futures markets. One of the important innovations of futures markets is options on futures. These contracts originated in the United States as a result of a regulatory structure that separated exchange-listed options and futures markets. The former are regulated by the Securities and Exchange Commission, and the latter are regulated by the Commodity Futures Trading Commission (CFTC). SEC regulations forbid the trading of options side by side with their underlying instruments. Options on stocks trade on one exchange, and the underlying trades on another or on NASDAQ.

The futures exchanges got the idea that they could offer options in which the underlying is a futures contract; no such prohibitions for side-by-side trading existed under CFTC rules. As a result, the futures exchanges were able to add an attractive instrument to their product lines. The side-by-side trading of the option and its underlying futures made for excellent arbitrage linkages between these instruments. Moreover, some of the options on futures are designed to expire on the same day the underlying futures expires. Thus, the options on the futures are effectively options on the spot asset that underlies the futures.

A call option on a futures gives the holder the right to enter into a long futures contract at a fixed futures price. A put option on a futures gives the holder the right to enter into a short futures contract at a fixed futures price. The fixed futures price is, of course, the exercise price. Consider an option on the Eurodollar futures contract trading at the Chicago Mercantile Exchange. On 13 June of a particular year, an option expiring on 13 July was based on the July Eurodollar futures contract. That futures contract expires on 16 July, a few days after the option expires.[10] The call option with exercise price of 95.75 had a price of $4.60. The underlying futures price was 96.21. Recall that this price is the IMM index value, which means that the price is based on a discount rate of $100 - 96.21 = 3.79$. The contract size is $1 million.

The buyer of this call option on a futures would pay $0.046($1,000,000) = $46,000$ and would obtain the right to buy the July futures contract at a price of 95.75. Thus, at that time, the option was in the money by $96.21 - 95.75 = 0.46$ per $100 face value. Suppose that when the option expires, the futures price is 96.00. Then the holder of the call would exercise it and obtain a long futures position at a price of 95.75. The price of the underlying futures is 96.00, so the margin account is immediately marked to market with a credit of 0.25 or $625.[11] The party on the short side of the contract is immediately set up with a short futures contract at the price of 95.75. That party will be charged the $625 gain that the long made. If the option is a put, exercise of it establishes a short position. The exchange assigns the put writer a long futures position.

4.3 Commodity Options

Options in which the asset underlying the futures is a commodity, such as oil, gold, wheat, or soybeans, are also widely traded. There are exchange-traded as well as over-the-counter versions. Over-the-counter options on oil are widely used.

---

10 Some options on futures expire a month or so before the futures expires. Others expire very close to, if not at, the futures expiration.

11 If the contract is in-the-money by $96 - 95.75 = 0.25$ per $100 par, it is in-the-money by $0.25/100 = 0.0025$, or 0.25 percent of the face value. Because the face value is $1 million, the contract is in the money by $(0.0025)(90/360)($1,000,000) = 625. (Note the adjustment by 90/360.) Another way to look at this calculation is that the futures price at 95.75 is $1 - (0.0425)(90/360) = 0.989375 per $1 par, or $989,375. At 96, the futures price is $1 - 0.04(90/360) = 0.99 per $1 par or $990,000. The difference is $625. So, exercising this option is like entering into a futures contract at a price of $989,375 and having the price immediately go to $990,000, a gain of $625. The call holder must deposit money to meet the Eurodollar futures margin, but the exercise of the option gives him $625. In other words, assuming he meets the minimum initial margin requirement, he is immediately credited with $625 more.

Our focus is on financial instruments so we will not spend any time on commodity options, but readers should be aware of the existence and use of these instruments by companies whose business involves the buying and selling of these commodities.

4.4 Other Types of Options

As derivative markets develop, options (and even some other types of derivatives) have begun to emerge on such underlyings as electricity, various sources of energy, and even weather. These instruments are almost exclusively customized over-the-counter instruments. Perhaps the most notable feature of these instruments is how the underlyings are often instruments that cannot actually be held. For example, electricity is not considered a storable asset because it is produced and almost immediately consumed, but it is nonetheless an asset and certainly has a volatile price. Consequently, it is ideally suited for options and other derivatives trading.

Consider weather. It is hardly an asset at all but simply a random factor that exerts an enormous influence on economic activity. The need to hedge against and speculate on the weather has created a market in which measures of weather activity, such as economic losses from storms or average temperature or rainfall, are structured into a derivative instrument. Option versions of these derivatives are growing in importance and use. For example, consider a company that generates considerable revenue from outdoor summer activities, provided that it does not rain. Obviously a certain amount of rain will occur, but the more rain, the greater the losses for the company. It could buy a call option on the amount of rainfall with the exercise price stated as a quantity of rainfall. If actual rainfall exceeds the exercise price, the company exercises the option and receives an amount of money related to the excess of the rainfall amount over the exercise price.

Another type of option, which is not at all new but is increasingly recognized in practice, is the real option. A real option is an option associated with the flexibility inherent in capital investment projects. For example, companies may invest in new projects that have the option to defer the full investment, expand or contract the project at a later date, or even terminate the project. In fact, most capital investment projects have numerous elements of flexibility that can be viewed as options. Of course, these options do not trade in markets the same way as financial and commodity options, and they must be evaluated much more carefully. They are, nonetheless, options and thus have the potential for generating enormous value.

Again, our emphasis is on financial options, but readers should be aware of the growing role of these other types of options in our economy. Investors who buy shares in companies that have real options are, in effect, buying real options. In addition, commodity and other types of options are sometimes found in investment portfolios in the form of "alternative investments" and can provide significant diversification benefits.

To this point, we have examined characteristics of options markets and contracts. Now we move forward to the all-important topic of how options are priced.

PRINCIPLES OF OPTION PRICING

In the readings on forward markets and contracts and on futures markets and contracts, we discussed the pricing and valuation of forward and futures contracts. Recall that the value of a contract is what someone must pay to buy into it or what someone would receive to sell out of it. A forward or futures contract has zero value at the start of the contract, but the value turns positive or negative as prices or rates change. A contract that has positive value to one party and negative value to the counterparty can turn around and have negative value to the former and positive value to the latter as prices or rates change. The forward or futures price is the price that the parties agree will be paid on the future date to buy and sell the underlying.

With options, these concepts are different. An option has a positive value at the start. The buyer must pay money and the seller receives money to initiate the contract. Prior to expiration, the option always has positive value to the buyer and negative value to the seller. In a forward or futures contract, the two parties agree on the fixed price the buyer will pay the seller. This fixed price is set such that the buyer and seller do not exchange any money. The corresponding fixed price at which a call holder can buy the underlying or a put holder can sell the underlying is the exercise price. It, too, is negotiated between buyer and seller but still results in the buyer paying the seller money up front in the form of an option premium or price.[12]

Thus, what we called the forward or futures price corresponds more to the exercise price of an option. The option price *is* the option value: With a few exceptions that will be clearly noted, in this reading we do not distinguish between the option price and value.

In this section of the reading, we examine the principles of option pricing. These principles are characteristics of option prices that are governed by the rationality of investors.

Before we begin, it is important to remind the reader that we assume all participants in the market behave in a rational manner such that they do not throw away money and that they take advantage of arbitrage opportunities. As such, we assume that markets are sufficiently competitive that no arbitrage opportunities exist.

Let us start by developing the notation, which is very similar to what we have used previously. Note that time 0 is today and time T is the expiration.

S_0, S_T = price of the underlying asset at time 0 (today) and time T (expiration)
  X = exercise price
  r = risk-free rate
  T = time to expiration, equal to number of days to expiration divided by 365
c_0, c_T = price of European call today and at expiration
C_0, C_T = price of American call today and at expiration
p_0, p_T = price of European put today and at expiration
P_0, P_T = price of American put today and at expiration

On occasion, we will introduce some variations of the above as well as some new notation. For example, we start off with no cash flows on the underlying, but we shall discuss the effects of cash flows on the underlying in Section 5.7.

5.1 Payoff Values

The easiest time to determine an option's value is at expiration. At that point, there is no future. Only the present matters. An option's value at expiration is called its **payoff**. We introduced this material briefly in our basic descriptions of types of options; now we cover it in more depth.

At expiration, a call option is worth either zero or the difference between the underlying price and the exercise price, whichever is greater:

$$c_T = \text{Max}(0, S_T - X)$$
$$C_T = \text{Max}(0, S_T - X)$$

(3)

Note that at expiration, a European option and an American option have the same payoff because they are equivalent instruments at that point.

---

12 For a call, there is no finite exercise price that drives the option price to zero. For a put, the unrealistic example of a zero exercise price would make the put price be zero.

The expression $Max(0, S_T - X)$ means to take the greater of zero or $S_T - X$. Suppose the underlying price exceeds the exercise price, $S_T > X$. In this case, the option is expiring in-the-money and the option is worth $S_T - X$. Suppose that at the instant of expiration, it is possible to buy the option for less than $S_T - X$. Then one could buy the option, immediately exercise it, and immediately sell the underlying. Doing so would cost c_T (or C_T) for the option and X to buy the underlying but would bring in S_T for the sale of the underlying. If c_T (or C_T) $< S_T - X$, this transaction would net an immediate risk-free profit. The collective actions of all investors doing this would force the option price up to $S_T - X$. The price could not go higher than $S_T - X$, because all that the option holder would end up with an instant later when the option expires is $S_T - X$. If $S_T < X$, meaning that the call is expiring out-of-the-money, the formula says the option should be worth zero. It cannot sell for less than zero because that would mean that the option seller would have to pay the option buyer. A buyer would not pay more than zero, because the option will expire an instant later with no value.

At expiration, a put option is worth either zero or the difference between the exercise price and the underlying price, whichever is greater:

$$p_T = Max(0, X - S_T)$$
$$P_T = Max(0, X - S_T)$$

(4)

Suppose $S_T < X$, meaning that the put is expiring in-the-money. At the instant of expiration, suppose the put is selling for less than $X - S_T$. Then an investor buys the put for p_T (or P_T) and the underlying for S_T and exercises the put, receiving X. If p_T (or P_T) $< X - S_T$, this transaction will net an immediate risk-free profit. The combined actions of participants doing this will force the put price up to $X - S_T$. It cannot go any higher, because the put buyer will end up an instant later with only $X - S_T$ and would not pay more than this. If $S_T > X$, meaning that the put is expiring out-of the-money, it is worth zero. It cannot be worth less than zero because the option seller would have to pay the option buyer. It cannot be worth more than zero because the buyer would not pay for a position that, an instant later, will be worth nothing.

These important results are summarized along with an example in Exhibit 5. The payoff diagrams for the short positions are also shown and are obtained as the negative of the long positions. For the special case of $S_T = X$, meaning that both call and put are expiring at-the-money, we can effectively treat the option as out-of-the-money because it is worth zero at expiration.

The value $Max(0, S_T - X)$ for calls or $Max(0, X - S_T)$ for puts is also called the option's **intrinsic value** or **exercise value**. We shall use the former terminology. Intrinsic value is what the option is worth to exercise it based on current conditions. In this section, we have talked only about the option at expiration. Prior to expiration, an option will normally sell for more than its intrinsic value.[13] The difference between the market price of the option and its intrinsic value is called its **time value** or **speculative value**. We shall use the former terminology. The time value reflects the potential for the option's intrinsic value at expiration to be greater than its current intrinsic value. At expiration, of course, the time value is zero.

There is no question that everyone agrees on the option's intrinsic value; after all, it is based on the current stock price and exercise price. It is the time value that we have more difficulty estimating. So remembering that Option price = Intrinsic value + Time value, let us move forward and attempt to determine the value of an option today, prior to expiration.

---

[13] We shall later see an exception to this statement for European puts, but for now take it as the truth.

| Exhibit 5 | Option Values at Expiration (Payoffs) | | |

| | | Example (X = 50) | |
Option	Value	$S_T = 52$	$S_T = 48$
European call	$c_T = Max(0, S_T - X)$	$c_T = Max(0, 52 - 50) = 2$	$c_T = Max(0, 48 - 50) = 0$
American call	$C_T = Max(0, S_T - X)$	$C_T = Max(0, 52 - 50) = 2$	$C_T = Max(0, 48 - 50) = 0$
European put	$p_T = Max(0, X - S_T)$	$p_T = Max(0, 50 - 52) = 0$	$p_T = Max(0, 50 - 48) = 2$
American put	$P_T = Max(0, X - S_T)$	$P_T = Max(0, 50 - 52) = 0$	$P_T = Max(0, 50 - 48) = 2$

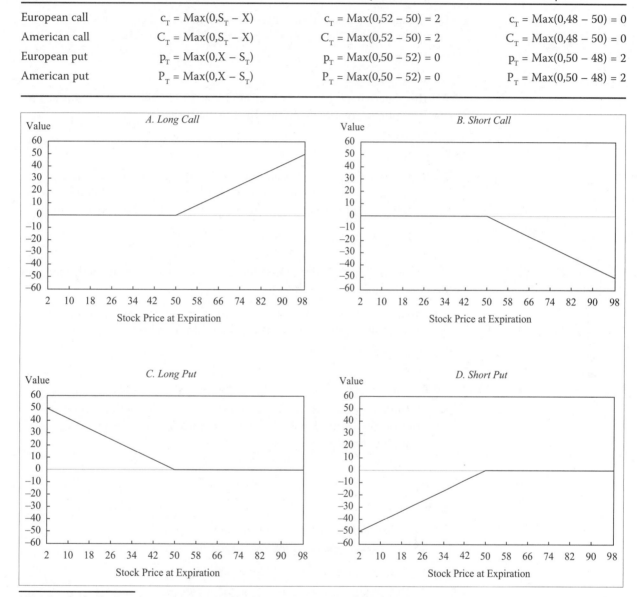

Notes: Results for the European and American calls correspond to Graph A. Results for Graph B are the negative of Graph A. Results for the European and American puts correspond to Graph C, and results for Graph D are the negative of Graph C.

Example 1

For Parts A through E, determine the payoffs of calls and puts under the conditions given.

A. The underlying is a stock index and is at 5,601.19 when the options expire. The multiplier is 500. The exercise price is:

  i. 5,500.

  ii. 6,000.

B. The underlying is a bond and is at $1.035 per $1 par when the options expire. The contract is on $100,000 face value of bonds. The exercise price is:

   i. $1.00.

   ii. $1.05.

C. The underlying is a 90-day interest rate and is at 9 percent when the options expire. The notional principal is $50 million. The exercise rate is:

   i. 8 percent.

   ii. 10.5 percent.

D. The underlying is the Swiss franc and is at $0.775 when the options expire. The options are on SF500,000. The exercise price is:

   i. $0.75.

   ii. $0.81.

E. The underlying is a futures contract and is at 110.5 when the options expire. The options are on a futures contract covering $1 million of the underlying. These prices are percentages of par. The exercise price is:

   i. 110.

   ii. 115.

For Parts F and G, determine the payoffs of the strategies indicated and describe the payoff graph.

F. The underlying is a stock priced at $40. A call option with an exercise price of $40 is selling for $7. You buy the stock and sell the call. At expiration, the stock price is:

   i. $52.

   ii. $38.

G. The underlying is a stock priced at $60. A put option with an exercise price of $60 is priced at $5. You buy the stock and buy the put. At expiration, the stock price is:

   i. $68.

   ii. $50.

Solutions:

A. **i.** Calls: Max(0,5601.19 − 5500) × 500 = 50,595

   Puts: Max(0,5500 − 5601.19) × 500 = 0

   ii. Calls: Max(0,5601.19 − 6000) × 500 = 0

   Puts: Max(0,6000 − 5601.19) × 500 = 199,405

B. **i.** Calls: Max(0,1.035 − 1.00) × $100,000 = $3,500

   Puts: Max(0,1.00 − 1.035) × $100,000 = $0

   ii. Calls: Max(0,1.035 − 1.05) × $100,000 = $0

   Puts: Max(0,1.05 − 1.035) × $100,000 = $1,500

C. **i.** Calls: Max(0,0.09 − 0.08) × (90/360) × $50,000,000 = $125,000

   Puts: Max(0,0.08 − 0.09) × (90/360) × $50,000,000 = $0

   ii. Calls: Max(0,0.09 − 0.105) × (90/360) × $50,000,000 = $0

   Puts: Max(0,0.105 − 0.09) × (90/360) × $50,000,000 = $187,500

D. **i.** Calls: Max(0,0.775 − 0.75) × SF500,000 = $12,500

   Puts: Max(0,0.75 − 0.775) × SF500,000 = $0

ii. Calls: $\text{Max}(0, 0.775 - 0.81) \times \text{SF}500{,}000 = \$0$

Puts: $\text{Max}(0, 0.81 - 0.775) \times \text{SF}500{,}000 = \$17{,}500$

E. **i.** Calls: $\text{Max}(0, 110.5 - 110) \times (1/100) \times \$1{,}000{,}000 = \$5{,}000$

Puts: $\text{Max}(0, 110 - 110.5) \times (1/100) \times \$1{,}000{,}000 = \$0$

ii. Calls: $\text{Max}(0, 110.5 - 115) \times (1/100) \times \$1{,}000{,}000 = \$0$

Puts: $\text{Max}(0, 115 - 110.5) \times (1/100) \times \$1{,}000{,}000 = \$45{,}000$

F. **i.** $52 - \text{Max}(0, 52 - 40) = 40$

ii. $38 - \text{Max}(0, 38 - 40) = 38$

For any value of the stock price at expiration of 40 or above, the payoff is constant at 40. For stock price values below 40 at expiration, the payoff declines with the stock price. The graph would look similar to the short put in Panel D of Exhibit 5. This strategy is known as a covered call and is discussed in the reading on risk management applications of option strategies.

G. **i.** $68 + \text{Max}(0, 60 - 68) = 68$

ii. $50 + \text{Max}(0, 60 - 50) = 60$

For any value of the stock price at expiration of 60 or below, the payoff is constant at 60. For stock price values above 60 at expiration, the payoff increases with the stock price at expiration. The graph will look similar to the long call in Panel A of Exhibit 5. This strategy is known as a protective put and is covered later in this reading and in the reading on risk management applications of option strategies.

5.2 Boundary Conditions

We start by examining some simple results that establish minimum and maximum values for options prior to expiration.

5.2.1 Minimum and Maximum Values

The first and perhaps most obvious result is one we have already alluded to: *The minimum value of any option is zero.* We state this formally as

$$c_0 \geq 0, C_0 \geq 0$$
$$p_0 \geq 0, P_0 \geq 0 \tag{5}$$

No option can sell for less than zero, for in that case the writer would have to pay the buyer.

Now consider the maximum value of an option. It differs somewhat depending on whether the option is a call or a put and whether it is European or American. *The maximum value of a call is the current value of the underlying:*

$$c_0 \leq S_0, C_0 \leq S_0 \tag{6}$$

A call is a means of buying the underlying. It would not make sense to pay more for the right to buy the underlying than the value of the underlying itself.

For a put, it makes a difference whether the put is European or American. One way to see the maximum value for puts is to consider the best possible outcome for the put holder. The best outcome is that the underlying goes to a value of zero. Then the put holder could sell a worthless asset for X. For an American put, the holder could sell it immediately and capture a value of X. For a European put, the holder would have to wait until expiration; consequently, we must discount X from the expiration day to the present. Thus, *the maximum value of a European put is the present value of the exercise price. The maximum value of an American put is the exercise price,*

$$p_0 \leq X/(1+r)^T, P_0 \leq X \qquad (7)$$

where r is the risk-free interest rate and T is the time to expiration. These results for the maximums and minimums for calls and puts are summarized in Exhibit 6, which also includes a numerical example.

Exhibit 6	Minimum and Maximum Values of Options		
Option	**Minimum Value**	**Maximum Value**	**Example ($S_0 = 52$, X = 50, r = 5%, T = 1/2 year)**
European call	$c_0 \geq 0$	$c_0 \leq S_0$	$0 \leq c_0 \leq 52$
American call	$C_0 \geq 0$	$C_0 \leq S_0$	$0 \leq C_0 \leq 52$
European put	$p_0 \geq 0$	$p_0 \leq X/(1+r)^T$	$0 \leq p_0 \leq 48.80$ [$48.80 = 50/(1.05)^{0.5}$]
American put	$P_0 \geq 0$	$P_0 \leq X$	$0 \leq P_0 \leq 50$

5.2.2 Lower Bounds

The results we established in Section 5.2.1 do not put much in the way of restrictions on the option price. They tell us that the price is somewhere between zero and the maximum, which is either the underlying price, the exercise price, or the present value of the exercise price—a fairly wide range of possibilities. Fortunately, we can tighten the range up a little on the low side: We can establish a **lower bound** on the option price.

For American options, which are exercisable immediately, we can state that the lower bound of an American option price is its current intrinsic value:[14]

$$C_0 \geq \text{Max}(0, S_0 - X)$$
$$P_0 \geq \text{Max}(0, X - S_0) \qquad (8)$$

The reason these results hold today is the same reason we have already shown for why they must hold at expiration. If the option is in-the-money and is selling for less than its intrinsic value, it can be bought and exercised to net an immediate risk-free profit.[15] The collective actions of market participants doing this will force the American option price up to at least the intrinsic value.

Unfortunately, we cannot make such a statement about European options—but we can show that the lower bound is either zero or the current underlying price minus the present value of the exercise price, whichever is greater. They cannot be exercised early; thus, there is no way for market participants to exercise an option selling for too little with respect to its intrinsic value. Fortunately, however, there is a way to establish

---

14 Normally we have italicized sentences containing important results. This one, however, is a little different: We are stating it temporarily. We shall soon show that we can override one of these results with a lower bound that is higher and, therefore, is a better lower bound.

15 Consider, for example, an in-the-money call selling for less than $S_0 - X$. One can buy the call for C_0, exercise it, paying X, and sell the underlying netting a gain of $S_0 - X - C_0$. This value is positive and represents an immediate risk-free gain. If the option is an in-the-money put selling for less than $X - S_0$, one can buy the put for P_0, buy the underlying for S_0, and exercise the put to receive X, thereby netting an immediate risk-free gain of $X - S_0 - P_0$.

a lower bound for European options. We can combine options with risk-free bonds and the underlying in such a way that a lower bound for the option price emerges.

First, we need the ability to buy and sell a risk-free bond with a face value equal to the exercise price and current value equal to the present value of the exercise price. This procedure is simple but perhaps not obvious. If the exercise price is X (say, 100), we buy a bond with a face value of X (100) maturing on the option expiration day. The current value of that bond is the present value of X, which is $X/(1 + r)^T$. So we buy the bond today for $X/(1 + r)^T$ and hold it until it matures on the option expiration day, at which time it will pay off X. We assume that we can buy or sell (issue) this type of bond. Note that this transaction involves borrowing or lending an amount of money equal to the present value of the exercise price with repayment of the full exercise price.

Exhibit 7 illustrates the construction of a special combination of instruments. We buy the European call and the risk-free bond and sell short the underlying asset. Recall that short selling involves borrowing the asset and selling it. At expiration, we shall buy back the asset. In order to illustrate the logic behind the lower bound for a European call in the simplest way, we assume that we can sell short without any restrictions.

Exhibit 7	A Lower Bound Combination for European Calls		
		Value at Expiration	
Transaction	**Current Value**	$S_T \leq X$	$S_T > X$
Buy call	c_0	0	$S_T - X$
Sell short underlying	$-S_0$	$-S_T$	$-S_T$
Buy bond	$X/(1 + r)^T$	X	X
Total	$c_0 - S_0 + X/(1 + r)^T$	$X - S_T \geq 0$	0

In Exhibit 7 the two right-hand columns contain the value of each instrument when the option expires. The rightmost column is the case of the call expiring in-the-money, in which case it is worth $S_T - X$. In the other column, the out-of-the-money case, the call is worth zero. The underlying is worth $-S_T$ (the negative of its current value) in either case, reflecting the fact that we buy it back to cover the short position. The bond is worth X in both cases. The sum of all the positions is positive when the option expires out-of-the-money and zero when the option expires in-the-money. Therefore, in no case does this combination of instruments have a negative value. That means that we never have to pay out any money at expiration. We are guaranteed at least no loss at expiration and possibly something positive.

If there is a possibility of a positive outcome from the combination and if we know we shall never have to pay anything out from holding a combination of instruments, the cost of that combination must be positive—it must cost us something to enter into the position. We cannot take in money to enter into the position. In that case, we would be receiving money up front and never having to pay anything out. The cost of entering the position is shown in the second column, labeled the "Current Value." Because that value must be positive, we therefore require that $c_0 - S_0 + X/(1 + r)^T \geq 0$. Rearranging this equation, we obtain $c_0 \geq S_0 - X/(1 + r)^T$. Now we have a statement about the minimum value of the option, which can serve as a lower bound. This result is solid, because if the call is selling for less than $S_0 - X/(1 + r)^T$, an investor can buy the call, sell short the underlying, and buy the bond. Doing so would bring in money up front and, as we see in Exhibit 7, an investor would not have to pay out any money at expiration and might even get a little more money. Because other investors would do the same, the call price would be forced up until it is at least $S_0 - X/(1 + r)^T$.

But we can improve on this result. Suppose $S_0 - X/(1 + r)^T$ is negative. Then we are stating that the call price is greater than a negative number. But we already know that the call price cannot be negative. So we can now say that

$$c_0 \geq \text{Max}\left[0, S_0 - X/(1 + r)^T\right]$$

In other words, *the lower bound on a European call price is either zero or the underlying price minus the present value of the exercise price, whichever is greater.* Notice how this lower bound differs from the minimum value for the American call, $\text{Max}(0, S_0 - X)$. For the European call, we must wait to pay the exercise price and obtain the underlying. Therefore, the expression contains the current underlying value—the present value of its future value—as well as the present value of the exercise price. For the American call, we do not have to wait until expiration; therefore, the expression reflects the potential to immediately receive the underlying price minus the exercise price. We shall have more to say, however, about the relationship between these two values.

To illustrate the lower bound, let $X = 50$, $r = 0.05$, and $T = 0.5$. If the current underlying price is 45, then the lower bound for the European call is

$$\text{Max}\left[0, 45 - 50/(1.05)^{0.5}\right] = \text{Max}(0, 45 - 48.80) = \text{Max}(0, -3.80) = 0$$

All this calculation tells us is that the call must be worth no less than zero, which we already knew. If the current underlying price is 54, however, the lower bound for the European call is

$$\text{Max}(0, 54 - 48.80) = \text{Max}(0, 5.20) = 5.20$$

which tells us that the call must be worth no less than 5.20. With European puts, we can also see that the lower bound differs from the lower bound on American puts in this same use of the present value of the exercise price.

Exhibit 8 constructs a similar type of portfolio for European puts. Here, however, we buy the put and the underlying and borrow by issuing the zero-coupon bond. The payoff of each instrument is indicated in the two rightmost columns.

Exhibit 8	A Lower Bound Combination for European Puts		

		Value at Expiration	
Transaction	Current Value	$S_T < X$	$S_T \geq X$
Buy put	p_0	$X - S_T$	0
Buy underlying	S_0	S_T	S_T
Issue bond	$-X/(1 + r)^T$	$-X$	$-X$
Total	$p_0 + S_0 - X/(1 + r)^T$	0	$S_T - X \geq 0$

Note that the total payoff is never less than zero. Consequently, the initial value of the combination must not be less than zero. Therefore, $p_0 + S_0 - X/(1 + r)^T \geq 0$. Isolating the put price gives us $p_0 \geq X/(1 + r)^T - S_0$. But suppose that $X/(1 + r)^T - S_0$ is negative. Then, the put price must be greater than a negative number. We know that the put price must be no less than zero. So we can now formally say that

$$p_0 \geq \text{Max}\left[0, X/(1 + r)^T - S_0\right]$$

In other words, *the lower bound of a European put is the greater of either zero or the present value of the exercise price minus the underlying price.* For the American put, recall that the expression was $\text{Max}(0, X - S_0)$. So for the European put, we adjust this value to the present value of the exercise price. The present value of the asset price is already adjusted to S_0.

Using the same example we did for calls, let X = 50, r = 0.05, and T = 0.5. If the current underlying price is 45, then the lower bound for the European put is

$$\text{Max}\left(0,50/(1.05)^{0.5} - 45\right) = \text{Max}(0,48.80 - 45) = \text{Max}(0,3.80) = 3.80$$

If the current underlying price is 54, however, the lower bound is

$$\text{Max}(0,48.80 - 54) = \text{Max}(0,-5.20) = 0$$

At this point let us reconsider what we have found. The lower bound for a European call is $\text{Max}[0,S_0 - X/(1 + r)^T]$. We also observed that an American call must be worth at least $\text{Max}(0,S_0 - X)$. But except at expiration, the European lower bound is greater than the minimum value of the American call.[16] We could not, however, expect an American call to be worth less than a European call. Thus the lower bound of the European call holds for American calls as well. Hence, we can conclude that

$$c_0 \geq \text{Max}\left[0,S_0 - X/(1 + r)^T\right]$$
$$C_0 \geq \text{Max}\left[0,S_0 - X/(1 + r)^T\right] \tag{9}$$

For European puts, the lower bound is $\text{Max}[0,X/(1 + r)^T - S_0]$. For American puts, the minimum price is $\text{Max}(0,X - S_0)$. The European lower bound is lower than the minimum price of the American put, so the American put lower bound is not changed to the European lower bound, the way we did for calls. Hence,

$$p_0 \geq \text{Max}\left[0,X/(1 + r)^T - S_0\right]$$
$$P_0 \geq \text{Max}(0,X - S_0) \tag{10}$$

These results tell us the lowest possible price for European and American options.

Recall that we previously referred to an option price as having an intrinsic value and a time value. For American options, the intrinsic value is the value if exercised, $\text{Max}(0,S_0 - X)$ for calls and $\text{Max}(0,X - S_0)$ for puts. The remainder of the option price is the time value. For European options, the notion of a time value is somewhat murky, because it first requires recognition of an intrinsic value. Because a European option cannot be exercised until expiration, in a sense, all of the value of a European option is time value. The notion of an intrinsic value and its complement, a time value, is therefore inappropriate for European options, though the concepts are commonly applied to European options. Fortunately, understanding European options does not require that we separate intrinsic value from time value. We shall include them together as they make up the option price.

Example 2

Consider call and put options expiring in 42 days, in which the underlying is at 72 and the risk-free rate is 4.5 percent. The underlying makes no cash payments during the life of the options.

A. Find the lower bounds for European calls and puts with exercise prices of 70 and 75.

B. Find the lower bounds for American calls and puts with exercise prices of 70 and 75.

---

16 We discuss this point more formally and in the context of whether it is ever worthwhile to exercise an American call early in Section 5.6.

Solutions:

A. 70 call: $\text{Max}\left[0, 72 - 70/(1.045)^{0.1151}\right] = \text{Max}(0, 2.35) = 2.35$

      75 call: $\text{Max}\left[0, 72 - 75/(1.045)^{0.1151}\right] = \text{Max}(0, -2.62) = 0$

      70 put: $\text{Max}\left[0, 70/(1.045)^{0.1151} - 72\right] = \text{Max}(0, -2.35) = 0$

      75 put: $\text{Max}\left[0, 75/(1.045)^{0.1151} - 72\right] = \text{Max}(0, 2.62) = 2.62$

B. 70 call: $\text{Max}\left[0, 72 - 70/(1.045)^{0.1151}\right] = \text{Max}(0, 2.35) = 2.35$

      75 call: $\text{Max}\left[0, 72 - 75/(1.045)^{0.1151}\right] = \text{Max}(0, -2.62) = 0$

      70 put: $\text{Max}(0, 70 - 72) = 0$

      75 put: $\text{Max}(0, 75 - 72) = 3$

5.3 The Effect of a Difference in Exercise Price

Now consider two options on the same underlying with the same expiration day but different exercise prices. Generally, the higher the exercise price, the lower the value of a call and the higher the price of a put. To see this, let the two exercise prices be X_1 and X_2, with X_1 being the smaller. Let $c_0(X_1)$ be the price of a European call with exercise price X_1 and $c_0(X_2)$ be the price of a European call with exercise price X_2. We refer to these as the X_1 call and the X_2 call. In Exhibit 9, we construct a combination in which we buy the X_1 call and sell the X_2 call.

| Exhibit 9 | Portfolio Combination for European Calls Illustrating the Effect of Differences in Exercise Prices | | | |

		Value at Expiration		
Transaction	**Current Value**	$S_T \leq X_1$	$X_1 < S_T < X_2$	$S_T \geq X_2$
Buy call ($X = X_1$)	$c_0(X_1)$	0	$S_T - X_1$	$S_T - X_1$
Sell call ($X = X_2$)	$-c_0(X_2)$	0	0	$-(S_T - X_2)$
Total	$c_0(X_1) - c_0(X_2)$	0	$S_T - X_1 > 0$	$X_2 - X_1 > 0$

Note first that the three outcomes are all non-negative. This fact establishes that the current value of the combination, $c_0(X_1) - c_0(X_2)$ has to be non-negative. We have to pay out at least as much for the X_1 call as we take in for the X_2 call; otherwise, we would get money up front, have the possibility of a positive value at expiration, and never have to pay any money out. Thus, because $c_0(X_1) - c_0(X_2) \geq 0$, we restate this result as

$$c_0(X_1) \geq c_0(X_2)$$

This expression is equivalent to the statement that *a call option with a higher exercise price cannot have a higher value than one with a lower exercise price.* The option with the higher exercise price has a higher hurdle to get over; therefore, the buyer is not willing to pay as much for it. Even though we demonstrated this result with European calls, it is also true for American calls. Thus,[17]

$$C_0(X_1) \geq C_0(X_2)$$

In Exhibit 10 we construct a similar portfolio for puts, except that we buy the X_2 put (the one with the higher exercise price) and sell the X_1 put (the one with the lower exercise price).

Exhibit 10	Portfolio Combination for European Puts Illustrating the Effect of Differences in Exercise Prices

| | | Value at Expiration | | |
Transaction	Current Value	$S_T \leq X_1$	$X_1 < S_T < X_2$	$S_T \geq X_2$
Buy put (X = X_2)	$p_0(X_2)$	$X_2 - S_T$	$X_2 - S_T$	0
Sell put (X = X_1)	$-p_0(X_1)$	$-(X_1 - S_T)$	0	0
Total	$p_0(X_2) - p_0(X_1)$	$X_2 - X_1 > 0$	$X_2 - S_T > 0$	0

Observe that the value of this combination is never negative at expiration; therefore, it must be non-negative today. Hence, $p_0(X_2) - p_0(X_1) \geq 0$. We restate this result as

$$p_0(X_2) \geq p_0(X_1)$$

Thus, *the value of a European put with a higher exercise price must be at least as great as the value of a European put with a lower exercise price.* These results also hold for American puts. Therefore,

$$P_0(X_2) \geq P_0(X_1)$$

Even though it is technically possible for calls and puts with different exercise prices to have the same price, *generally we can say that the higher the exercise price, the lower the price of a call and the higher the price of a put.* For example, refer back to Exhibit 1 and observe how the most expensive calls and least expensive puts have the lower exercise prices.

5.4 The Effect of a Difference in Time to Expiration

Option prices are also affected by the time to expiration of the option. Intuitively, one might expect that the longer the time to expiration, the more valuable the option. A longer-term option has more time for the underlying to make a favorable move. In addition, if the option is in-the-money by the end of a given period of time, it has a better chance of moving even further in-the-money over a longer period of time. If the additional time gives it a better chance of moving out-of-the-money or further out-of-the-money, the limitation of losses to the amount of the option premium means that the disadvantage of the longer time is no greater. In most cases, a longer time to expiration is beneficial for an option. We will see that longer-term American and European calls and longer-term American puts are worth no less than their shorter-term counterparts.

First let us consider each of the four types of options: European calls, American calls, European puts, and American puts. We shall introduce options otherwise identical except that one has a longer time to expiration than the other. The one expiring

---

17 It is possible to use the results from this table to establish a limit on the difference between the prices of these two options, but we shall not do so here.

earlier has an expiration of T_1 and the one expiring later has an expiration of T_2. The prices of the options are $c_0(T_1)$ and $c_0(T_2)$ for the European calls, $C_0(T_1)$ and $C_0(T_2)$ for the American calls, $p_0(T_1)$ and $p_0(T_2)$ for the European puts, and $P_0(T_1)$ and $P_0(T_2)$ for the American puts.

When the shorter-term call expires, the European call is worth $Max(0, S_{T1} - X)$, but we have already shown that the longer-term European call is worth *at least* $Max\left(0, S_{T_1} - X/(1 + r)^{(T_2 - T_1)}\right)$, which is at least as great as this amount.[18] Thus, the longer-term European call is worth at least the value of the shorter-term European call. These results are not altered if the call is American. When the shorter-term American call expires, it is worth $Max(0, S_{T1} - X)$. The longer-term American call must be worth at least the value of the European call, so it is worth *at least* $Max\left[0, S - X/(1 + r)^{T_2 - T_1}\right]$. Thus, the longer-term call, European or American, is worth no less than the shorter-term call when the shorter-term call expires. Because this statement is always true, the longer-term call, European or American, is worth no less than the shorter-term call at any time prior to expiration. Thus,

$$c_0(T_2) \geq c_0(T_1)$$
$$C_0(T_2) \geq C_0(T_1)$$

(11)

Notice that these statements do not mean that the longer-term call is always worth more; it means that the longer-term call can be worth no less. With the exception of the rare case in which both calls are so far out-of-the-money or in-the-money that the additional time is of no value, the longer-term call will be worth more.

For European puts, we have a slight problem. For calls, the longer term gives additional time for a favorable move in the underlying to occur. For puts, this is also true, but there is one disadvantage to waiting the additional time. When a put is exercised, the holder receives money. The lost interest on the money is a disadvantage of the additional time. For calls, there is no lost interest. In fact, a call holder earns additional interest on the money by paying out the exercise price later. Therefore, it is not always true that additional time is beneficial to the holder of a European put. It is true, however, that the additional time is beneficial to the holder of an American put. An American put can always be exercised; there is no penalty for waiting. Thus, we have

$$p_0(T_2) \text{ can be either greater or less than } p_0(T_1)$$
$$P_0(T_2) \geq P_0(T_1)$$

(12)

So for European puts, either the longer-term or the shorter-term option can be worth more. The longer-term European put will tend to be worth more when volatility is greater and interest rates are lower.

Referring back to Exhibit 1, observe that the longer-term put and call options are more expensive than the shorter-term ones. As noted, we might observe an exception to this rule for European puts, but these are all American options.

5.5 Put–Call Parity

So far we have been working with puts and calls separately. To see how their prices must be consistent with each other and to explore common option strategies, let us combine puts and calls with each other or with a risk-free bond. We shall put together some combinations that produce equivalent results.

---

18 Technically, we showed this calculation using a time to expiration of T, but here the time to expiration is $T_2 - T_1$.

5.5.1 *Fiduciary Calls and Protective Puts*

First we consider an option strategy referred to as a **fiduciary call**. It consists of a European call and a risk-free bond, just like the ones we have been using, that matures on the option expiration day and has a face value equal to the exercise price of the call. The upper part of the table in Exhibit 11 shows the payoffs at expiration of the fiduciary call. We see that if the price of the underlying is below X at expiration, the call expires worthless and the bond is worth X. If the price of the underlying is above X at expiration, the call expires and is worth S_T (the underlying price) – X. So at expiration, the fiduciary call will end up worth X or S_T, whichever is greater.

Exhibit 11	Portfolio Combinations for Equivalent Packages of Puts and Calls		

		Value at Expiration	
Transaction	**Current Value**	$S_T \leq X$	$S_T > X$
Fiduciary Call			
Buy call	c_0	0	$S_T - X$
Buy bond	$X/(1 + r)^T$	X	X
Total	$c_0 + X/(1 + r)^T$	X	S_T
Protective Put			
Buy put	p_0	$X - S_T$	0
Buy underlying asset	S_0	S_T	S_T
Total	$p_0 + S_0$	X	S_T

Value of Fiduciary Call and
Protective Put at Expiration

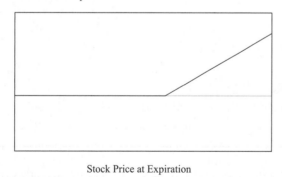

Stock Price at Expiration

This type of combination is called a fiduciary call because it allows protection against downside losses and is thus faithful to the notion of preserving capital.

Now we construct a strategy known as a **protective put**, which consists of a European put and the underlying asset. If the price of the underlying is below X at expiration, the put expires and is worth $X - S_T$ and the underlying is worth S_T. If the price of the underlying is above X at expiration, the put expires with no value and the underlying is worth S_T. So at expiration, the protective put is worth X or S_T, whichever is greater. The lower part of the table in Exhibit 11 shows the payoffs at expiration of the protective put.

Thus, the fiduciary call and protective put end up with the same value. They are, therefore, identical combinations. To avoid arbitrage, their values today must be the same. The value of the fiduciary call is the cost of the call, c_0, and the cost of the bond, $X/(1 + r)^T$. The value of the protective put is the cost of the put, p_0, and the cost of the underlying, S_0. Thus,

$$c_0 + X \big/ (1 + r)^T = p_0 + S_0 \qquad\qquad (13)$$

This equation is called **put–call parity** and is one of the most important results in options. It does not say that puts and calls are equivalent, but it does show an equivalence (parity) of a call/bond portfolio and a put/underlying portfolio.

Put–call parity can be written in a number of other ways. By rearranging the four terms to isolate one term, we can obtain some interesting and important results. For example,

$$c_0 = p_0 + S_0 - X \big/ (1 + r)^T$$

means that a call is equivalent to a long position in the put, a long position in the asset, and a short position in the risk-free bond. The short bond position simply means to borrow by issuing the bond, rather than lend by buying the bond as we did in the fiduciary call portfolio. We can tell from the sign whether we should go long or short. Positive signs mean to go long; negative signs mean to go short.

5.5.2 Synthetics

Because the right-hand side of the above equation is equivalent to a call, we often refer to it as a **synthetic call**. To see that the synthetic call is equivalent to the actual call, look at Exhibit 12:

		Value at Expiration	
Transaction	**Current Value**	$S_T \leq X$	$S_T > X$
Call			
Buy call	c_0	0	$S_T - X$
Synthetic Call			
Buy put	p_0	$X - S_T$	0
Buy underlying asset	S_0	S_T	S_T
Issue bond	$-X/(1 + r)^T$	$-X$	$-X$
Total	$p_0 + S_0 - X/(1 + r)^T$	0	$S_T - X$

Exhibit 12   **Call and Synthetic Call**

The call produces the value of the underlying minus the exercise price or zero, whichever is greater. The synthetic call does the same thing, but in a different way. When the call expires in-the-money, the synthetic call produces the underlying value minus the payoff on the bond, which is X. When the call expires out-of-the-money, the put covers the loss on the underlying and the exercise price on the put matches the amount of money needed to pay off the bond.

Similarly, we can isolate the put as follows:

$$p_0 = c_0 - S_0 + X \big/ (1 + r)^T$$

which says that a put is equivalent to a long call, a short position in the underlying, and a long position in the bond. Because the left-hand side is a put, it follows that the right-hand side is a **synthetic put**. The equivalence of the put and synthetic put is shown in Exhibit 13.

Exhibit 13	Put and Synthetic Put			

		Value at Expiration	
Transaction	**Current Value**	$S_T \leq X$	$S_T > X$
Put			
Buy put	p_0	$X - S_T$	0
Synthetic Put			
Buy call	c_0	0	$S_T - X$
Short underlying asset	$-S_0$	$-S_T$	$-S_T$
Buy bond	$X/(1 + r)^T$	X	X
Total	$c_0 - S_0 + X/(1 + r)^T$	$X - S_T$	0

As you can well imagine, there are numerous other combinations that can be constructed. Exhibit 14 shows a number of the more important combinations. There are two primary reasons that it is important to understand synthetic positions in option pricing. Synthetic positions enable us to price options, because they produce the same results as options and have known prices. Synthetic positions also tell how to exploit mispricing of options relative to their underlying assets. Note that we cannot only synthesize a call or a put, but we can also synthesize the underlying or the bond. As complex as it might seem to do this, it is really quite easy. First, we learn that *a fiduciary call is a call plus a risk-free bond maturing on the option expiration day with a face value equal to the exercise price of the option.* Then we learn that *a protective put is the underlying plus a put.* Then we learn the basic put–call parity equation: *A fiduciary call is equivalent to a protective put:*

$$c_0 + X/(1 + r)^T = p_0 + S_0$$

Exhibit 14	Alternative Equivalent Combinations of Calls, Puts, the Underlying, and Risk-Free Bonds						

Strategy	**Consisting of**	**Worth**	**Equates to**	**Strategy**	**Consisting of**	**Worth**
Fiduciary call	Long call + Long bond	$c_0 + X/(1 + r)^T$	=	Protective put	Long put + Long underlying	$p_0 + S_0$
Long call	Long call	c_0	=	Synthetic call	Long put + Long underlying + Short bond	$p_0 + S_0 - X/(1 + r)^T$
Long put	Long put	p_0	=	Synthetic put	Long call + Short underlying + Long bond	$c_0 - S_0 + X/(1 + r)^T$
Long underlying	Long underlying	S_0	=	Synthetic underlying	Long call + Long bond + Short put	$c_0 + X/(1 + r)^T - p_0$
Long bond	Long bond	$X/(1 + r)^T$	=	Synthetic bond	Long put + Long underlying + Short call	$p_0 + S_0 - c_0$

Learn the put–call parity equation this way, because it is the easiest form to remember and has no minus signs.

Next, we decide which instrument we want to synthesize. We use simple algebra to isolate that instrument, with a plus sign, on one side of the equation, moving all other instruments to the other side. We then see what instruments are on the other side, taking plus signs as long positions and minus signs as short positions. Finally, to check our results, we should construct a table like Exhibits 11 or 12, with the expiration payoffs of the instrument we wish to synthesize compared with the expiration payoffs of the equivalent combination of instruments. We then check to determine that the expiration payoffs are the same.

5.5.3 *An Arbitrage Opportunity*

In this section we examine the arbitrage strategies that will push prices to put–call parity. Suppose that in the market, prices do not conform to put–call parity. This is a situation in which price does not equal value. Recalling our basic equation, $c_0 + X/(1 + r)^T = p_0 + S_0$, we should insert values into the equation and see if the equality holds. If it does not, then obviously one side is greater than the other. We can view one side as overpriced and the other as underpriced, which suggests an arbitrage opportunity. To exploit this mispricing, we buy the underpriced combination and sell the overpriced combination.

Consider the following example involving call options with an exercise price of $100 expiring in half a year (T = 0.5). The risk-free rate is 10 percent. The call is priced at $7.50, and the put is priced at $4.25. The underlying price is $99.

The left-hand side of the basic put–call parity equation is $c_0 + X/(1 + r)^T = 7.50 + 100/(1.10)^{0.5} = 7.50 + 95.35 = 102.85$. The right-hand side is $p_0 + S_0 = 4.25 + 99 = 103.25$. So the right-hand side is greater than the left-hand side. This means that the protective put is overpriced. Equivalently, we could view this as the fiduciary call being underpriced. Either way will lead us to the correct strategy to exploit the mispricing.

We sell the overpriced combination, the protective put. This means that we sell the put and sell short the underlying. Doing so will generate a cash inflow of $103.25. We buy the fiduciary call, paying out $102.85. This series of transactions nets a cash inflow of $103.25 − $102.85 = $0.40. Now, let us see what happens at expiration.

The options expire with the underlying above 100:

> The bond matures, paying $100.
>
> Use the $100 to exercise the call, receiving the underlying.
>
> Deliver the underlying to cover the short sale.
>
> The put expires with no value.
>
> Net effect: No money in or out.

The options expire with the underlying below 100:

> The bond matures, paying $100.
>
> The put expires in-the-money; use the $100 to buy the underlying.
>
> Use the underlying to cover the short sale.
>
> The call expires with no value.
>
> Net effect: No money in or out.

So we receive $0.40 up front and do not have to pay anything out. The position is perfectly hedged and represents an arbitrage profit. The combined effects of other investors performing this transaction will result in the value of the protective put going down and/or the value of the covered call going up until the two strategies are equivalent in value. Of course, it is possible that transaction costs might consume any profit, so small discrepancies will not be exploited.

It is important to note that regardless of which put–call parity equation we use, we will arrive at the same strategy. For example, in the above problem, the synthetic put (a long call, a short position in the underlying, and a long bond) is worth

$7.50 – $99 + $95.35 = $3.85. The actual put is worth $4.25. Thus, we would conclude that we should sell the actual put and buy the synthetic put. To buy the synthetic put, we would buy the call, short the underlying, and buy the bond—precisely the strategy we used to exploit this price discrepancy.

In all of these examples based on put–call parity, we used only European options. Put–call parity using American options is considerably more complicated. The resulting parity equation is a complex combination of inequalities. Thus, we cannot say that a given combination exactly equals another; we can say only that one combination is more valuable than another. Exploitation of any such mispricing is somewhat more complicated, and we shall not explore it here.

Example 3

European put and call options with an exercise price of 45 expire in 115 days. The underlying is priced at 48 and makes no cash payments during the life of the options. The risk-free rate is 4.5 percent. The put is selling for 3.75, and the call is selling for 8.00.

A. Identify the mispricing by comparing the price of the actual call with the price of the synthetic call.

B. Based on your answer in Part A, demonstrate how an arbitrage transaction is executed.

Solution to A:

Using put–call parity, the following formula applies:

$$c_0 = p_0 + S_0 - X/(1 + r)^T$$

The time to expiration is $T = 115/365 = 0.3151$. Substituting values into the right-hand side:

$$c_0 = 3.75 + 48 - 45/(1.045)^{0.3151} = 7.37$$

Hence, the synthetic call is worth 7.37, but the actual call is selling for 8.00 and is, therefore, overpriced.

Solution to B:

Sell the call for 8.00 and buy the synthetic call for 7.37. To buy the synthetic call, buy the put for 3.75, buy the underlying for 48.00, and issue a zero-coupon bond paying 45.00 at expiration. The bond will bring in $45.00/(1.045)^{0.3151} = 44.38$ today. This transaction will bring in $8.00 - 7.37 = 0.63$.

At expiration, the following payoffs will occur:

	$S_T < 45$	$S_T \geq 45$
Short call	0	$-(S_T - 45)$
Long put	$45 - S_T$	0
Underlying	S_T	S_T
Bond	-45	-45
Total	0	0

Thus there will be no cash in or out at expiration. The transaction will net a risk-free gain of $8.00 - 7.37 = 0.63$ up front.

5.6 American Options, Lower Bounds, and Early Exercise

As we have noted, American options can be exercised early and in this section we specify cases in which early exercise can have value. Because early exercise is never mandatory, the right to exercise early may be worth something but could never hurt the option holder. Consequently, the prices of American options must be no less than the prices of European options:

$$C_0 \geq c_0$$
$$P_0 \geq p_0$$

(14)

Recall that we already used this result in establishing the minimum price from the lower bounds and intrinsic value results in Section 5.2.2. Now, however, our concern is understanding the conditions under which early exercise of an American option might occur.

Suppose today, time 0, we are considering exercising early an in-the-money American call. If we exercise, we pay X and receive an asset worth S_0. But we already determined that a European call is worth at least $S_0 - X/(1 + r)^T$—that is, the underlying price minus the present value of the exercise price, which is more than $S_0 - X$. Because we just argued that the American call must be worth no less than the European call, it therefore must also be worth at least $S_0 - X/(1 + r)^T$. This means that the value we could obtain by selling it to someone else is more than the value we could obtain by exercising it. Thus, there is no reason to exercise the call early.

Some people fail to see the logic behind not exercising early. Exercising a call early simply gives the money to the call writer and throws away the right to decide at expiration if you want the underlying. It is like renewing a magazine subscription before the current subscription expires. Not only do you lose the interest on the money, you also lose the right to decide later if you want to renew. Without offering an early exercise incentive, the American call would have a price equal to the European call price. Thus, we must look at another case to see the value of the early exercise option.

If the underlying makes a cash payment, there may be reason to exercise early. If the underlying is a stock and pays a dividend, there may be sufficient reason to exercise just before the stock goes ex-dividend. By exercising, the option holder throws away the time value but captures the dividend. We shall skip the technical details of how this decision is made and conclude by stating that

■ *When the underlying makes no cash payments, $C_0 = c_0$.*
■ *When the underlying makes cash payments during the life of the option, early exercise can be worthwhile and C_0 can thus be higher than c_0.*

We emphasize the word *can*. It is possible that the dividend is not high enough to justify early exercise.

For puts, there is nearly always a possibility of early exercise. Consider the most obvious case, an investor holding an American put on a bankrupt company. The stock is worth zero. It cannot go any lower. Thus, the put holder would exercise immediately. As long as there is a possibility of bankruptcy, the American put will be worth more than the European put. But in fact, bankruptcy is not required for early exercise. The stock price must be very low, although we cannot say exactly how low without resorting to an analysis using option pricing models. Suffice it to say that *the American put is nearly always worth more than the European put: $P_0 > p_0$.*

5.7 The Effect of Cash Flows on the Underlying Asset

Both the lower bounds on puts and calls and the put–call parity relationship must be modified to account for cash flows on the underlying asset. In the readings on forward markets and contracts and on futures markets and contracts, we discussed situations in which the underlying has cash flows. Stocks pay dividends, bonds pay interest, foreign currencies pay interest, and commodities have carrying costs. As we have done in the previous readings, we shall assume that these cash flows are either known or can be expressed as a percentage of the asset price. Moreover, as we did previously, we can remove the present value of those cash flows from the price of the underlying and use this adjusted underlying price in the results we have obtained above.

We can specify these cash flows in the form of the accumulated value at T of all cash flows incurred on the underlying over the life of the derivative contract. When the underlying is a stock, we specify these cash flows more precisely in the form of dividends, using the notation $FV(D,0,T)$ as the future value, or alternatively $PV(D,0,T)$ as the present value, of these dividends. When the underlying is a bond, we use the notation $FV(CI,0,T)$ or $PV(CI,0,T)$, where CI stands for "coupon interest." When the cash flows can be specified in terms of a yield or rate, we use the notation δ where $S_0/(1 + \delta)^T$ is the underlying price reduced by the present value of the cash flows. Using continuous compounding, the rate can be specified as δ^c so that $S_0 e^{-\delta^c T}$ is the underlying price reduced by the present value of the dividends. For our purposes in this reading on options, let us just write this specification as $PV(CF,0,T)$, which represents the present value of the cash flows on the underlying over the life of the options. Therefore, we can restate the lower bounds for European options as

$$c_0 \geq Max\left\{0, \left[S_0 - PV(CF,0,T)\right] - X/(1 + r)^T\right\}$$

$$p_0 \geq Max\left\{0, X/(1 + r)^T - \left[S_0 - PV(CF,0,T)\right]\right\}$$

and put–call parity as

$$c_0 + X/(1 + r)^T = p_0 + \left[S_0 - PV(CF,0,T)\right]$$

which reflects the fact that, as we said, we simply reduce the underlying price by the present value of its cash flows over the life of the option.

5.8 The Effect of Interest Rates and Volatility

It is important to know that interest rates and volatility exert an influence on option prices. *When interest rates are higher, call option prices are higher and put option prices are lower.* This effect is not obvious and strains the intuition somewhat. When investors buy call options instead of the underlying, they are effectively buying an indirect leveraged position in the underlying. When interest rates are higher, buying the call instead of a direct leveraged position in the underlying is more attractive. Moreover, by using call options, investors save more money by not paying for the underlying until a later date. For put options, however, higher interest rates are disadvantageous. When interest rates are higher, investors lose more interest while waiting to sell the underlying when using puts. Thus, the opportunity cost of waiting is higher when interest rates are higher. Although these points may not seem completely clear, fortunately they are not critical. Except when the underlying is a bond or interest rate, interest rates do not have a very strong effect on option prices.

Volatility, however, has an extremely strong effect on option prices. *Higher volatility increases call and put option prices because it increases possible upside values and increases possible downside values of the underlying.* The upside effect helps calls and does not hurt puts. The downside effect does not hurt calls and helps puts. The reason calls are not hurt on the downside and puts are not hurt on the upside is that when options are out-of-the-money, it does not matter if they end up more out-of-the-money. But when options are in-the-money, it does matter if they end up more in-the-money.

Volatility is a critical variable in pricing options. It is the only variable that affects option prices that is not directly observable either in the option contract or in the market. It must be estimated.

5.9 Option Price Sensitivities

Option price sensitivity measures have Greek names:

- *Delta* is the sensitivity of the option price to a change in the price of the underlying.
- *Gamma* is a measure of how well the delta sensitivity measure will approximate the option price's response to a change in the price of the underlying.
- *Rho* is the sensitivity of the option price to the risk-free rate.
- *Theta* is the rate at which the time value decays as the option approaches expiration.
- *Vega* is the sensitivity of the option price to volatility.

SUMMARY

- Options are rights to buy or sell an underlying at a fixed price, the exercise price, for a period of time. The right to buy is a call; the right to sell is a put. Options have a definite expiration date. Using the option to buy or sell is the action of exercising it. The buyer or holder of an option pays a price to the seller or writer for the right to buy (a call) or sell (a put) the underlying instrument. The writer of an option has the corresponding potential obligation to sell or buy the underlying.

- European options can be exercised only at expiration; American options can be exercised at any time prior to expiration. Moneyness refers to the characteristic that an option has positive intrinsic value. The payoff is the value of the option at expiration. An option's intrinsic value is the value that can be captured if the option is exercised. Time value is the component of an option's price that reflects the uncertainty of what will happen in the future to the price of the underlying.

- Options can be traded as standardized instruments on an options exchange, where they are protected from default on the part of the writer, or as customized instruments on the over-the-counter market, where they are subject to the possibility of the writer defaulting. Because the buyer pays a price at the start and does not have to do anything else, the buyer cannot default.

- The underlying instruments for options are individual stocks, stock indices, bonds, interest rates, currencies, futures, commodities, and even such random factors as the weather. In addition, a class of options called real options is associated with the flexibility in capital investment projects.

- Like FRAs, which are forward contracts in which the underlying is an interest rate, interest rate options are options in which the underlying is an interest rate. However, FRAs are commitments to make one interest payment and receive another, whereas interest rate options are rights to make one interest payment and receive another.

- Option payoffs, which are the values of options when they expire, are determined by the greater of zero or the difference between underlying price and exercise price, if a call, or the greater of zero or the difference between exercise price and underlying price, if a put. For interest rate options, the exercise price is a specified rate and the underlying price is a variable interest rate.

- Interest rate options exist in the form of caps, which are call options on interest rates, and floors, which are put options on interest rates. Caps consist of a series of call options, called caplets, on an underlying rate, with each option expiring at a different time. Floors consist of a series of put options, called floorlets, on an underlying rate, with each option expiring at a different time.

- The minimum value of European and American calls and puts is zero. The maximum value of European and American calls is the underlying price. The maximum value of a European put is the present value of the exercise price. The maximum value of an American put is the exercise price.

- The lower bound of a European call is established by constructing a portfolio consisting of a long call and risk-free bond and a short position in the underlying asset. This combination produces a non-negative value at expiration, so its current value must be non-negative. For this situation to occur, the call price has to be worth at least the underlying price minus the present value of the exercise price. The lower bound of a European put is established by constructing a portfolio consisting of a long put, a long position in the underlying, and the issuance of a zero-coupon bond. This combination produces a non-negative value at expiration so its current value must be non-negative. For this to occur, the put price has to be at least as much as the present value of the exercise price minus the underlying price. For both calls and puts, if this lower bound is negative, we invoke the rule that an option price can be no lower than zero.

- The lowest price of a European call is referred to as the lower bound. The lowest price of an American call is also the lower bound of a European call. The lowest price of a European put is also referred to as the lower bound. The lowest price of an American put, however, is its intrinsic value.

- Buying a call with a given exercise price and selling an otherwise identical call with a higher exercise price creates a combination that always pays off with a non-negative value. Therefore, its current value must be non-negative. For this to occur, the call with the lower exercise price must be worth at least as much as the other call. A similar argument holds for puts, except that one would buy the put with the higher exercise price. This line of reasoning shows that the put with the higher exercise price must be worth at least as much as the one with the lower exercise price.

- A longer-term European or American call must be worth at least as much as a corresponding shorter-term European or American call. A longer-term American put must be worth at least as much as a shorter-term American put. A longer-term European put, however, can be worth more or less than a shorter-term European put.

- A fiduciary call, consisting of a European call and a zero-coupon bond, produces the same payoff as a protective put, consisting of the underlying and a European put. Therefore, their current values must be the same. For this equivalence to occur, the call price plus bond price must equal the underlying price plus put price. This relationship is called put–call parity and can be used to identify combinations of instruments that synthesize another instrument by rearranging the equation to isolate the instrument you are trying to create.

Long positions are indicated by positive signs, and short positions are indicated by negative signs. One can create a synthetic call, a synthetic put, a synthetic underlying, and a synthetic bond, as well as synthetic short positions in these instruments for the purpose of exploiting mispricing in these instruments.

■ Put–call parity violations exist when one side of the equation does not equal the other. An arbitrageur buys the lower-priced side and sells the higher-priced side, thereby earning the difference in price, and the positions offset at expiration. The combined actions of many arbitrageurs performing this set of transactions would increase the demand and price for the underpriced instruments and decrease the demand and price for the overpriced instruments, until the put–call parity relationship is upheld.

■ American option prices must always be no less than those of otherwise equivalent European options. American call options, however, are never exercised early unless there is a cash flow on the underlying, so they can sell for the same as their European counterparts in the absence of such a cash flow. American put options nearly always have a possibility of early exercise, so they ordinarily sell for more than their European counterparts.

■ Cash flows on the underlying affect an option's boundary conditions and put–call parity by lowering the underlying price by the present value of the cash flows over the life of the option.

■ A higher interest rate increases a call option's price and decreases a put option's price.

APPENDIX 63

	Cumulative Probabilities for a Standard Normal Distribution $P(X \leq x) = N(x)$ for $x \geq 0$ or $1 - N(-x)$ for $x < 0$								

x	0	0.01	0.02	0.03	0.04	0.05	0.06	0.07	0.08	0.09
0.00	0.5000	0.5040	0.5080	0.5120	0.5160	0.5199	0.5239	0.5279	0.5319	0.5359
0.10	0.5398	0.5438	0.5478	0.5517	0.5557	0.5596	0.5636	0.5675	0.5714	0.5753
0.20	0.5793	0.5832	0.5871	0.5910	0.5948	0.5987	0.6026	0.6064	0.6103	0.6141
0.30	0.6179	0.6217	0.6255	0.6293	0.6331	0.6368	0.6406	0.6443	0.6480	0.6517
0.40	0.6554	0.6591	0.6628	0.6664	0.6700	0.6736	0.6772	0.6808	0.6844	0.6879
0.50	0.6915	0.6950	0.6985	0.7019	0.7054	0.7088	0.7123	0.7157	0.7190	0.7224
0.60	0.7257	0.7291	0.7324	0.7357	0.7389	0.7422	0.7454	0.7486	0.7517	0.7549
0.70	0.7580	0.7611	0.7642	0.7673	0.7704	0.7734	0.7764	0.7794	0.7823	0.7852
0.80	0.7881	0.7910	0.7939	0.7967	0.7995	0.8023	0.8051	0.8078	0.8106	0.8133
0.90	0.8159	0.8186	0.8212	0.8238	0.8264	0.8289	0.8315	0.8340	0.8365	0.8389
1.00	0.8413	0.8438	0.8461	0.8485	0.8508	0.8531	0.8554	0.8577	0.8599	0.8621
1.10	0.8643	0.8665	0.8686	0.8708	0.8729	0.8749	0.8770	0.8790	0.8810	0.8830
1.20	0.8849	0.8869	0.8888	0.8907	0.8925	0.8944	0.8962	0.8980	0.8997	0.9015
1.30	0.9032	0.9049	0.9066	0.9082	0.9099	0.9115	0.9131	0.9147	0.9162	0.9177
1.40	0.9192	0.9207	0.9222	0.9236	0.9251	0.9265	0.9279	0.9292	0.9306	0.9319
1.50	0.9332	0.9345	0.9357	0.9370	0.9382	0.9394	0.9406	0.9418	0.9429	0.9441
1.60	0.9452	0.9463	0.9474	0.9484	0.9495	0.9505	0.9515	0.9525	0.9535	0.9545
1.70	0.9554	0.9564	0.9573	0.9582	0.9591	0.9599	0.9608	0.9616	0.9625	0.9633
1.80	0.9641	0.9649	0.9656	0.9664	0.9671	0.9678	0.9686	0.9693	0.9699	0.9706
1.90	0.9713	0.9719	0.9726	0.9732	0.9738	0.9744	0.9750	0.9756	0.9761	0.9767
2.00	0.9772	0.9778	0.9783	0.9788	0.9793	0.9798	0.9803	0.9808	0.9812	0.9817
2.10	0.9821	0.9826	0.9830	0.9834	0.9838	0.9842	0.9846	0.9850	0.9854	0.9857
2.20	0.9861	0.9864	0.9868	0.9871	0.9875	0.9878	0.9881	0.9884	0.9887	0.9890
2.30	0.9893	0.9896	0.9898	0.9901	0.9904	0.9906	0.9909	0.9911	0.9913	0.9916
2.40	0.9918	0.9920	0.9922	0.9925	0.9927	0.9929	0.9931	0.9932	0.9934	0.9936
2.50	0.9938	0.9940	0.9941	0.9943	0.9945	0.9946	0.9948	0.9949	0.9951	0.9952
2.60	0.9953	0.9955	0.9956	0.9957	0.9959	0.9960	0.9961	0.9962	0.9963	0.9964
2.70	0.9965	0.9966	0.9967	0.9968	0.9969	0.9970	0.9971	0.9972	0.9973	0.9974
2.80	0.9974	0.9975	0.9976	0.9977	0.9977	0.9978	0.9979	0.9979	0.9980	0.9981
2.90	0.9981	0.9982	0.9982	0.9983	0.9984	0.9984	0.9985	0.9985	0.9986	0.9986
3.00	0.9987	0.9987	0.9987	0.9988	0.9988	0.9989	0.9989	0.9989	0.9990	0.9990

PRACTICE PROBLEMS FOR READING 63

1. **A.** Calculate the payoff at expiration for a call option on the S&P 100 stock index in which the underlying price is 579.32 at expiration, the multiplier is 100, and the exercise price is:

   i. 450.

   ii. 650.

   B. Calculate the payoff at expiration for a put option on the S&P 100 in which the underlying is at 579.32 at expiration, the multiplier is 100, and the exercise price is:

   i. 450.

   ii. 650.

2. **A.** Calculate the payoff at expiration for a call option on a bond in which the underlying is at $0.95 per $1 par at expiration, the contract is on $100,000 face value bonds, and the exercise price is:

   i. $0.85.

   ii. $1.15.

   B. Calculate the payoff at expiration for a put option on a bond in which the underlying is at $0.95 per $1 par at expiration, the contract is on $100,000 face value bonds, and the exercise price is:

   i. $0.85.

   ii. $1.15.

3. **A.** Calculate the payoff at expiration for a call option on an interest rate in which the underlying is a 180-day interest rate at 6.53 percent at expiration, the notional principal is $10 million, and the exercise price is:

   i. 5 percent.

   ii. 8 percent.

   B. Calculate the payoff at expiration for a put option on an interest rate in which the underlying is a 180-day interest rate at 6.53 percent at expiration, the notional principal is $10 million, and the exercise price is:

   i. 5 percent.

   ii. 8 percent.

4. **A.** Calculate the payoff at expiration for a call option on the British pound in which the underlying is at $1.438 at expiration, the options are on 125,000 British pounds, and the exercise price is:

   i. $1.35.

   ii. $1.55.

   B. Calculate the payoff at expiration for a put option on the British pound where the underlying is at $1.438 at expiration, the options are on 125,000 British pounds, and the exercise price is:

   i. $1.35.

   ii. $1.55.

5. **A.** Calculate the payoff at expiration for a call option on a futures contract in which the underlying is at 1136.76 at expiration, the options are on a futures contract for $1,000, and the exercise price is:

       i. 1130.

       ii. 1140.

   B. Calculate the payoff at expiration for a put option on a futures contract in which the underlying is at 1136.76 at expiration, the options are on a futures contract for $1,000, and the exercise price is:

       i. 1130.

       ii. 1140.

6. Consider a stock index option that expires in 75 days. The stock index is currently at 1240.89 and makes no cash payments during the life of the option. Assume that the stock index has a multiplier of 1. The risk-free rate is 3 percent.

   A. Calculate the lowest and highest possible prices for European-style call options on the above stock index with exercise prices of:

       i. 1225.

       ii. 1255.

   B. Calculate the lowest and highest possible prices for European-style put options on the above stock index with exercise prices of:

       i. 1225.

       ii. 1255.

7. A. Consider American-style call and put options on a bond. The options expire in 60 days. The bond is currently at $1.05 per $1 par and makes no cash payments during the life of the option. The risk-free rate is 5.5 percent. Assume that the contract is on $1 face value bonds. Calculate the lowest and highest possible prices for the calls and puts with exercise prices of:

       i. $0.95.

       ii. $1.10.

   B. Consider European-style call and put options on a bond. The options expire in 60 days. The bond is currently at $1.05 per $1 par and makes no cash payments during the life of the option. The risk-free rate is 5.5 percent. Assume that the contract is on $1 face value bonds. Calculate the lowest and highest possible prices for the calls and puts with exercise prices of:

       i. $0.95.

       ii. $1.10.

8. You are provided with the following information on put and call options on a stock:

    Call price, $c_0 = \$6.64$

    Put price, $p_0 = \$2.75$

    Exercise price, $X = \$30$

    Days to option expiration = 219

    Current stock price, $S_0 = \$33.19$

  Put–call parity shows the equivalence of a call/bond portfolio (fiduciary call) and a put/underlying portfolio (protective put). Illustrate put–call parity assuming stock prices at expiration (S_T) of $20 and of $40. Assume that the risk-free rate, r, is 4 percent.

9. With respect to put–call parity, a protective put consists of a European:
   A. put option and the underlying asset.
   B. call option and the underlying asset.
   C. put option and a risk-free bond with a face value equal to the exercise price of a European call option on the underlying asset.

10. Unless far out-of-the-money or far in-the-money, for otherwise identical call options, the longer the term to expiration, the lower the price for:
    A. American call options, but not European call options.
    B. both European call options and American call options.
    C. neither European call options nor American call options.

11. A call option with an exercise price of 65 will expire in 73 days. No cash payments will be made by the underlying asset over the life of the option. If the underlying asset price is at 70 and the risk-free rate of return is 5.0 percent, the lower bounds for an American call option and a European call option, respectively, are *closest* to:

	Lower bound for American call option	Lower bound for European call option
A.	5.00	5.63
B.	5.63	5.00
C.	5.63	5.63

12. A put option with an exercise price of 75 will expire in 73 days. No cash payments will be made by the underlying asset over the life of the option. If the underlying asset is at 70 and the risk-free rate of return is 5.0 percent, the lower bounds for an American put option and a European put option, respectively, are *closest* to:

	Lower bound for American put option	Lower bound for European put option
A.	4.27	4.27
B.	4.27	5.00
C.	5.00	4.27

13. Compare an American call with a strike of 50 which expires in 90 days to an American call on the same underlying asset which has a strike of 60 and expires in 120 days. The underlying asset is selling at 55. Consider the following statements:

    Statement 1   "The 50 strike call is in-the-money and the 60 strike call is out-of-the-money."

    Statement 2   "The time value of the 60 strike call, as a proportion of the 60 strike call's premium, exceeds the time value of the 50 strike call as a proportion of the 50 strike call's premium."

    Are the statements *most likely* correct or incorrect?
    A. Both statements are correct.
    B. Statement 1 is incorrect, but Statement 2 is correct.
    C. Statement 1 is correct, but Statement 2 is incorrect.

14. Marla Johnson priced both a put and a call on Alpha Numero using standard option pricing software. To use the program, Johnson entered the strike price of the options, the price of the underlying asset, an estimate of the risk-free rate, the time to expiration of the option, and an estimate of the volatility of the returns of the underlying asset into her computer. Both prices calculated by the software program were substantially above the actual market values observed in that day's exchange trading. Which of the following is the *most likely* explanation? The value Johnson entered into the program for the:

   A. estimate of volatility was too low.

   B. estimate of volatility was too high.

   C. time to expiration of the options was too low.

15. A call with a strike price of $40 is available on a stock currently trading for $35. The call expires in one year and the risk-free rate of return is 10%. The lower bound on this call's value:

   A. is zero.

   B. is $5 if the call is American-style.

   C. is $1.36 if the call is European-style.

16. An investor writes a call option priced at $3 with an exercise price of $100 on a stock that he owns. The investor paid $85 for the stock. If at expiration of the call option the stock price has risen to $110, the profit for the investor's position would be *closest* to:

   A. $3.

   B. $12.

   C. $18.

17. If an investor paid $5 for a put option with an exercise price of $60 that is in-the-money $2, the price of the underlying is *closest* to:

   A. $53.

   B. $58.

   C. $62.

18. An investor paid $10 for an option that is currently in-the-money $5. If the underlying is priced at $90, which of the following *best* describes that option?

   A. Call option with an exercise price of $80.

   B. Put option with an exercise price of $95.

   C. Call option with an exercise price of $95.

19. Assume the probability of bankruptcy for the underlying asset is high. Compared to the price of an American put option on the same underlying asset, the price of an equivalent European put option will *most likely* be:

   A. lower.

   B. higher.

   C. the same because the probability of bankruptcy does not affect pricing.

SOLUTIONS FOR READING 63

1. **A.** $S_T = 579.32$
   - **i.** Call payoff, X = 450: $\text{Max}(0,579.32 - 450) \times 100 = \$12,932$
   - **ii.** Call payoff, X = 650: $\text{Max}(0,579.32 - 650) \times 100 = 0$

   B. $S_T = 579.32$
   - **i.** Put payoff, X = 450: $\text{Max}(0,450 - 579.32) \times 100 = 0$
   - **ii.** Put payoff, X = 650: $\text{Max}(0,650 - 579.32) \times 100 = \$7,068$

2. **A.** $S_T = \$0.95$
   - **i.** Call payoff, X = 0.85: $\text{Max}(0,0.95 - 0.85) \times 100,000 = \$10,000$
   - **ii.** Call payoff, X = 1.15: $\text{Max}(0,0.95 - 1.15) \times 100,000 = \$0$

   B. $S_T = \$0.95$
   - **i.** Put payoff, X = 0.85: $\text{Max}(0,0.85 - 0.95) \times 100,000 = \$0$
   - **ii.** Put payoff, X = 1.15: $\text{Max}(0,1.15 - 0.95) \times 100,000 = \$20,000$

3. **A.** $S_T = 0.0653$
   - **i.** Call payoff, X = 0.05: $\text{Max}(0,0.0653 - 0.05) \times (180/360) \times 10,000,000 = \$76,500$
   - **ii.** Call payoff, X = 0.08: $\text{Max}(0,0.0653 - 0.08) \times (180/360) \times 10,000,000 = 0$

   B. $S_T = 0.0653$
   - **i.** Put payoff, X = 0.05: $\text{Max}(0,0.05 - 0.0653) \times (180/360) \times 10,000,000 = 0$
   - **ii.** Put payoff, X = 0.08: $\text{Max}(0,0.08 - 0.0653) \times (180/360) \times 10,000,000 = \$73,500$

4. **A.** $S_T = \$1.438$
   - **i.** Call payoff, X = 1.35: $\text{Max}(0,1.438 - 1.35) \times 125,000 = \$11,000$
   - **ii.** Call payoff, X = 1.55: $\text{Max}(0,1.438 - 1.55) \times 125,000 = \$0$

   B. $S_T = \$1.438$
   - **i.** Put payoff, X = 1.35: $\text{Max}(0,1.35 - 1.438) \times 125,000 = \$0$
   - **ii.** Put payoff, X = 1.55: $\text{Max}(0,1.55 - 1.438) \times 125,000 = \$14,000$

5. **A.** $S_T = 1136.76$
   - **i.** Call payoff, X = 1130: $\text{Max}(0,1136.76 - 1130) \times 1,000 = \$6,760$
   - **ii.** Call payoff, X = 1140: $\text{Max}(0,1136.76 - 1140) \times 1,000 = 0$

   B. $S_T = 1136.76$
   - **i.** Put payoff, X = 1130: $\text{Max}(0,1130 - 1136.76) \times 1,000 = 0$
   - **ii.** Put payoff, X = 1140: $\text{Max}(0,1140 - 1136.76) \times 1,000 = \$3,240$

6. **A.** $S_0 = 1240.89$, T = 75/365 = 0.2055, X = 1225 or 1255, call options
   - **i.** X = 1225

     Maximum value for the call: $c_0 = S_0 = 1240.89$

     Lower bound for the call: $c_0 = \text{Max}[0,1240.89 - 1225/(1.03)^{0.2055}] = 23.31$
   - **ii.** X = 1255

     Maximum value for the call: $c_0 = S_0 = 1240.89$

     Lower bound for the call: $c_0 = \text{Max}[0,1240.89 - 1255/(1.03)^{0.2055}] = 0$

B. $S_0 = 1240.89$, $T = 75/365 = 0.2055$, $X = 1225$ or 1255, put options

   i. $X = 1225$

      Maximum value for the put: $p_0 = 1225/(1.03)^{0.2055} = 1217.58$

      Lower bound for the put: $p_0 = \text{Max}[0, 1225/(1.03)^{0.2055} - 1240.89] = 0$

   ii. $X = 1255$

      Maximum value for the put: $p_0 = 1255/(1.03)^{0.2055} = 1247.40$

      Lower bound for the put: $p_0 = \text{Max}[0, 1255/(1.03)^{0.2055} - 1240.89] = 6.51$

7. A. $S_0 = 1.05$, $T = 60/365 = 0.1644$, $X = 0.95$ or 1.10, American-style options

   i. $X = \$0.95$

      Maximum value for the call: $C_0 = S_0 = \$1.05$

      Lower bound for the call: $C_0 = \text{Max}[0, 1.05 - 0.95/(1.055)^{0.1644}] = \$0.11$

      Maximum value for the put: $P_0 = X = \$0.95$

      Lower bound for the put: $P_0 = \text{Max}(0, 0.95 - 1.05) = \$0$

   ii. $X = \$1.10$

      Maximum value for the call: $C_0 = S_0 = \$1.05$

      Lower bound for the call: $C_0 = \text{Max}[0, 1.05 - 1.10/(1.055)^{0.1644}] = \$0$

      Maximum value for the put: $P_0 = X = \$1.10$

      Lower bound for the put: $P_0 = \text{Max}(0, 1.10 - 1.05) = \$0.05$

B. $S_0 = 1.05$, $T = 60/365 = 0.1644$, $X = 0.95$ or 1.10, European-style options

   i. $X = \$0.95$

      Maximum value for the call: $c_0 = S_0 = \$1.05$

      Lower bound for the call: $c_0 = \text{Max}[0, 1.05 - 0.95/(1.055)^{0.1644}] = \$0.11$

      Maximum value for the put: $p_0 = 0.95/(1.055)^{0.1644} = \$0.94$

      Lower bound for the put: $p_0 = \text{Max}[0, 0.95/(1.055)^{0.1644} - 1.05] = \$0$

   ii. $X = \$1.10$

      Maximum value for the call: $c_0 = S_0 = \$1.05$

      Lower bound for the call: $c_0 = \text{Max}[0, 1.05 - 1.10/(1.055)^{0.1644}] = \$0$

      Maximum value for the put: $p_0 = 1.10/(1.055)^{0.1644} = \$1.09$

      Lower bound for the put: $p_0 = \text{Max}[0, 1.10/(1.055)^{0.1644} - 1.05] = \$0.04$

8. We can illustrate put–call parity by showing that for the fiduciary call and the protective put, the current values and values at expiration are the same.

    Call price, $c_0 = \$6.64$

    Put price, $p_0 = \$2.75$

    Exercise price, $X = \$30$

    Risk-free rate, $r = 4$ percent

    Time to expiration $= 219/365 = 0.6$

Current stock price, S_0 = \$33.19

Bond price, $X/(1 + r)^T = 30/(1 + 0.04)^{0.6}$ = \$29.30

Transaction	Current Value	Value at Expiration $S_T = 20$	$S_T = 40$
Fiduciary call			
Buy call	6.64	0	40 − 30 = 10
Buy bond	29.30	30	30
Total	35.94	30	40
Protective put			
Buy put	2.75	30 − 20 = 10	0
Buy stock	33.19	20	40
Total	35.94	30	40

The values in the table show that the current values and values at expiration for the fiduciary call and the protective put are the same. That is, $c_0 + X/(1 + r)^T = p_0 + S_0$.

9. A is correct. This is the definition of a protective put.

10. C is correct. Although there are exceptions, in general the longer the time to expiration the more valuable is the option, ceteris paribus. With the exception of the rare case in which [options] are so far out-of-the-money or in-the-money that the additional time is of no value, the longer term [options] will be worth more. In addition, it is not always true that a longer-term is beneficial to the holder of a European put.

11. C is correct. Because time remains until expiration and the problem deals with calls, the lower bound of the European call will exceed the intrinsic value. In concept, one can invest the strike price amount until it is needed at expiration and earn the risk-free rate on this amount for that period of time. The intrinsic value is \$5.00; given the available answers, the lower bound for the European call must be \$5.63. This is confirmed by applying the formula $c_0 \geq \text{Max}[0, S_0 - X/(1 + r)^T]$. In this problem, the lower bound is the greater of 0 or $70 - 65/(1.05)^{0.2}$ = 5.63. Note that the value of the American call cannot be less than the value of the European call.

12. C is correct. When valuing European puts that have time left until expiration, the lower bound must reflect the fact that exercise is delayed until the expiration date. That is, with a European put one can't recognize the current intrinsic value, but must wait until expiration. This delay in receiving payment for selling (putting) the stock to the writer has a cost. The lower bound will therefore be below the intrinsic value (but never negative). This can be confirmed by applying the formula $p_0 \geq \text{Max}[0, X/(1 + r)^T - S_0]$. In this problem, the lower bound is the greater of 0 or $75/(1.05)^{0.2}$ 70 = 4.27. Regarding the American put, as one can recognize the intrinsic value of an American put immediately if one chooses to, the lower bound of an American put, in the absence of intervening cash payments on the underlying asset, will simply be equal to the intrinsic value.

13. A is correct. A call is in-the-money when the underlying asset price exceeds the strike price. The entire premium of the 60 strike call reflects time value; only a part of the 50 strike call's premium is time value, the rest will be intrinsic value.

14. B is correct. If Johnson entered too high an estimate of volatility into the program, both the put and the call values given by the program would be too high.

15. A is correct. For an American- or European-style call, the lower bound is the greater of zero or the difference between the stock price and the present value of the strike price. In this problem, the difference is 35 minus (40 / 1.10) = negative $1.36. Thus, the lower bound is zero.

16. C is correct. The investor collects $3 from writing the call and makes $15 on the stock before it is called, resulting in a profit of $18.

17. B is correct. A put option is in-the-money if the price of the underlying is less than the exercise price. The difference between the exercise price and the underlying equals the amount the put option is in-the-money. $60 − 58 = $2.

18. B is correct. A put option is in-the-money if the stock price is less than the exercise price. The put option with an exercise price of $95 is in-the-money $5. The call option with an exercise price of $80 is in-the-money $10, and the call option with an exercise price of $95 is out-of-the-money $5.

19. A is correct. In bankruptcy, the price of the bankrupt company's stock falls. In the limit it falls to zero. At a price of zero, the price cannot go any lower, and it would be advantageous to exercise the American put at that point in time rather than be forced to wait until the expiration date. Therefore, the American-style put is likely to have a higher price than an equivalent European-style put.

Market		
Seoul		
Johann. (Comp.)		
Mumbai		
Singapore		
Sydney		
Shanghai B	297.0	
Hong Kong	46,441.0	0.9%	-10.5%
Toronto	316.8	0.7%	-6.9%
Stockholm	22,700.9	0.5%	-4.2%
Mexico Ci...	13,524.8	0.1%	4.1%

Swap Markets and Contracts

by Don M. Chance, CFA

LEARNING OUTCOMES

Mastery	The candidate should be able to:
☐	**a** describe the characteristics of swap contracts and explain how swaps are terminated;
☐	**b** describe, calculate, and interpret the payments of currency swaps, plain vanilla interest rate swaps, and equity swaps.

INTRODUCTION

1

This reading completes the survey of the main types of derivative instruments. The three preceding readings covered forward contracts, futures contracts, and options. This reading covers swaps. Although swaps were the last of the main types of derivatives to be invented, they are clearly not the least important. In fact, judging by the size of the swap market, they are probably the most important. In the reading on derivative markets and instruments, we noted that the Bank for International Settlements had estimated the notional principal of the global over-the-counter derivatives market as of 30 June 2001 at $100 trillion. Of that amount, interest rate and currency swaps account for about $61 trillion, with interest rate swaps representing about $57 trillion of that total.[1] Indeed, interest rate swaps have had overwhelming success as a derivative product. They are widely used by corporations, financial institutions, and governments.

In the reading on derivative markets and instruments, we briefly described the characteristics of swaps, but now we explore this subject in more detail. Recall first that *a swap is an agreement between two parties to exchange a series of future cash flows.* For most types of swaps, one party makes payments that are determined by a random outcome, such as an interest rate, a currency rate, an equity return, or a commodity price. These payments are commonly referred to as variable or *floating*. The other party either makes variable or floating payments determined by some other random factor or makes fixed payments. At least one type of swap involves both parties making fixed payments, but the values of those payments vary due to random factors.

In forwards, futures, and options, the terminology of *long* and *short* has been used to describe buyers and sellers. These terms are not used as often in swaps. The preferred terminology usually designates a party as being the floating- (or variable-) rate payer or the fixed-rate payer. Nonetheless, in swaps in which one party receives a floating rate and the other receives a fixed rate, the former is usually said to be long and the latter is

---

1 Equity and commodity swaps account for less than the notional principal of currency swaps.

Analysis of Derivatives for the Chartered Financial Analyst® Program, by Don M. Chance, CFA. Copyright © 2003 by AIMR.

said to be short. This usage is in keeping with the fact that parties who go long in other instruments pay a known amount and receive a claim on an unknown amount. In some swaps, however, both sides are floating or variable, and this terminology breaks down.

1.1 Characteristics of Swap Contracts

Although technically a swap can have a single payment, most swaps involve multiple payments. Thus, we refer to a swap as a *series* of payments. In fact, we have already covered a swap with one payment, which is just a forward contract. Hence, a swap is basically a series of forward contracts. With this idea in mind, we can see that a swap is like an agreement to buy something over a period of time. We might be paying a variable price or a price that has already been fixed; we might be paying an uncertain price, or we might already know the price we shall pay.

When a swap is initiated, neither party pays any amount to the other. Therefore, a swap has zero value at the start of the contract. Although it is not absolutely necessary for this condition to be true, swaps are typically done in this fashion. Neither party pays anything up front. There is, however, a technical exception to this point in regard to currency swaps. Each party pays the notional principal to the other, but the amounts exchanged are equivalent, though denominated in two different currencies.

Each date on which the parties make payments is called a **settlement date**, sometimes called a payment date, and the time between settlement dates is called the **settlement period**. On a given settlement date when payments are due, one party makes a payment to the other, which in turn makes a payment to the first party. With the exception of currency swaps and a few variations associated with other types of swaps, both sets of payments are made in the same currency. Consequently, the parties typically agree to exchange only the net amount owed from one party to the other, a practice called **netting**. In currency swaps and a few other special cases, the payments are not made in the same currency; hence, the parties usually make separate payments without netting. Note the implication that swaps are generally settled in cash. It is quite rare for swaps to call for actual physical delivery of an underlying asset.

A swap always has a **termination date**, the date of the final payment. We can think of this date as its expiration date, as we do with other derivatives. The original time to maturity is sometimes called the **tenor** of a swap.

The swap market is almost exclusively an over-the-counter market, so swaps contracts are customized to the parties' specific needs. Several of the leading futures exchanges have created futures contracts on swaps. These contracts allow participants to hedge and speculate on the rates that will prevail in the swap market at future dates. Of course, these contracts are not swaps themselves but, as derivatives of swaps, they can in some ways serve as substitutes for swaps. These futures contracts have been moderately successful, but their volume is insignificant compared with the over-the-counter market for swaps.

As we have discussed in previous readings, over-the-counter instruments are subject to default risk. Default is possible whenever a payment is due. When a series of payments is made, there is default risk potential throughout the life of the contract, depending on the financial condition of the two parties. But default can be somewhat complicated in swaps. Suppose, for example, that on a settlement date, Party A owes Party B a payment of $50,000 and Party B owes Party A a payment of $12,000. Agreeing to net, Party A owes Party B $38,000 for that particular payment. Party A may be illiquid, or perhaps even bankrupt, and unable to make the payment. But it may be the case that the market value of the swap, which reflects the present value of the remaining payments, could be positive from the perspective of Party A and negative from the perspective of Party B. In that case, Party B owes Party A more for the remaining payments.

The handling of default in swaps can be complicated, depending on the contract specifications and the applicable laws under which the contract was written. In most cases, the above situation would be resolved by having A be in default but possessing an asset, the swap, that can be used to help settle its other liabilities.

1.2 Termination of a Swap

As we noted earlier, a swap has a termination or expiration date. Sometimes, however, a party could want to terminate a swap before its formal expiration. This scenario is much like a party selling a bond before it matures or selling an exchange-traded option or futures contract before its expiration. With swaps, early termination can take place in several ways.

As we mentioned briefly, a swap has a market value that can be calculated during its life. If a party holds a swap with a market value of $125,000, for example, it can settle the swap with the counterparty by having the counterparty pay it $125,000 in cash. This payment terminates the transaction for both parties. From the opposite perspective, a party holding a swap with a negative market value can terminate the swap by paying the market value to the counterparty. Terminating a swap in this manner is possible only if the counterparties specify in advance that such a transaction can be made, or if they reach an agreement to do so without having specified in advance. In other words, this feature is not automatically available and must be agreed to by both parties.

Many swaps are terminated early by entering into a separate and offsetting swap. For example, suppose a corporation is engaged in a swap to make fixed payments of 5 percent and receive floating payments based on LIBOR, with the payments made each 15 January and 15 July. Three years remain on the swap. That corporation can offset the swap by entering into an entirely new swap in which it makes payments based on LIBOR and receives a fixed rate with the payments made each 15 January and 15 July for three years. The swap fixed rate is determined by market conditions at the time the swap is initiated. Thus, the fixed rate on the new swap is not likely to match the fixed rate on the old swap, but the effect of this transaction is simply to have the floating payments offset; the fixed payments will net out to a known amount. Hence, the risk associated with the floating rate is eliminated. The default risk, however, is not eliminated because both swaps remain in effect.

Another way to terminate a swap early is sell the swap to another counterparty. Suppose a corporation holds a swap worth $75,000. If it can obtain the counterparty's permission, it can find another party to take over its payments. In effect, it sells the swap for $75,000 to that party. This procedure, however, is not commonly used.

A final way to terminate a swap early is by using a **swaption**. This instrument is an option to enter into a swap at terms that are established in advance. Thus, a party could use a swaption to enter into an offsetting swap, as described above.

THE STRUCTURE OF GLOBAL SWAP MARKETS

2

The global swaps market is much like the global forward and over-the-counter options markets, which we covered in some detail in the preceding readings. It is made up of dealers, which are banks and investment banking firms. These dealers make markets in swaps, quoting bid and ask prices and rates, thereby offering to take either side of a swap transaction. Upon taking a position in a swap, the dealer generally offsets the risk by making transactions in other markets. The counterparties to swaps are either end users or other dealers. The end users are often corporations with risk management problems that can be solved by engaging in a swap—a corporation or other end user is usually exposed to or needs an exposure to some type of risk that arises from interest rates, exchange rates, stock prices, or commodity prices. The end user contacts a dealer that makes a market in swaps. The two engage in a transaction, at which point the dealer assumes some risk from the end user. The dealer then usually lays off the risk by engaging in a transaction with another party. That transaction could be something as simple as a futures contract, or it could be an over-the-counter transaction with another dealer.

Risk magazine conducts annual surveys of participants in various derivative products. Exhibit 1 presents the results of those surveys for currency and interest rate swaps. One survey provides opinions of banks and investment banks that are swaps dealers. In the other survey, the respondents are end users. The results give a good idea of the major players in this market. It is interesting to note the disagreement between how dealers view themselves and how end users view them. Also, note that the rankings change, sometimes drastically, from year to year.

Exhibit 1	*Risk* Magazine Surveys of Banks, Investment Banks, and Corporate End Users to Determine the Top Three Dealers in Currency and Interest Rate Swaps

	Respondents	
Currencies	**Banks and Investment Banks**	**Corporate End Users**
Currency Swaps		
$/€	UBS Warburg	Citigroup
	JP Morgan Chase	Royal Bank of Scotland
	Deutsche Bank	Bank of America
$/¥	JP Morgan Chase	Citigroup
	UBS Warburg	Bank of America
	Credit Suisse First Boston/Deutsche Bank	JP Morgan Chase
$/£	Royal Bank of Scotland	Royal Bank of Scotland
	JP Morgan Chase	Citigroup
	Goldman Sachs	Deutsche Bank
$/SF	UBS Warburg	UBS Warburg
	Goldman Sachs	Citigroup
	Credit Suisse First Boston	Credit Suisse First Boston
Interest Rate Swaps (2–10 years)		
$	JP Morgan Chase	JP Morgan Chase
	Bank of America	Bank of America
	Morgan Stanley	Royal Bank of Scotland
€	JP Morgan Chase	Royal Bank of Scotland
	Deutsche Bank	Deutsche Bank
	Morgan Stanley	Citigroup
¥	JP Morgan Chase	Royal Bank of Scotland
	Deutsche Bank	Barclays Capital
	Bank of America	Citigroup/JP Morgan Chase
£	Royal Bank of Scotland	Royal Bank of Scotland
	Barclays Capital	Barclays Capital
	UBS Warburg	Deutsche Bank

	Respondents	
Currencies	**Banks and Investment Banks**	**Corporate End Users**
SF	UBS Warburg	UBS Warburg
	Credit Suisse First Boston	Credit Suisse First Boston
	Zürcher Kantonalbank	Zürcher Kantonalbank

Note: $ = U.S. dollar, € = euro, ¥ = Japanese yen, £ = U.K. pound sterling, SF = Swiss franc.
Source: *Risk*, September 2002, pp. 30–67 for banks and investment banking dealer respondents, and June 2002, pp. 24–34 for corporate end user respondents. Ratings for swaps with maturities less than 2 years and greater than 10 years are also provided in the September 2002 issue of *Risk*.

TYPES OF SWAPS

We alluded to the fact that the underlying asset in a swap can be a currency, interest rate, stock, or commodity. We now take a look at these types of swaps in more detail.

3.1 Currency Swaps

In a currency swap, each party makes interest payments to the other in different currencies.[2] Consider this example. The U.S. retailer Target Corporation (NYSE: TGT) does not have an established presence in Europe. Let us say that it has decided to begin opening a few stores in Germany and needs €9 million to fund construction and initial operations. TGT would like to issue a fixed-rate euro-denominated bond with face value of €9 million, but the company is not very well known in Europe. European investment bankers have given it a quote for such a bond. Deutsche Bank, AG (NYSE: DB), however, tells TGT that it should issue the bond in dollars and use a swap to convert it into euros.

Suppose TGT issues a five-year US$10 million bond at a rate of 6 percent. It then enters into a swap with DB in which DB will make payments to TGT in U.S. dollars at a fixed rate of 5.5 percent and TGT will make payments to DB in euros at a fixed rate of 4.9 percent each 15 March and 15 September for five years. The payments are based on a notional principal of 10 million in dollars and 9 million in euros. We assume the swap starts on 15 September of the current year. The swap specifies that the two parties exchange the notional principal at the start of the swap and at the end. Because the payments are made in different currencies, netting is not practical, so each party makes its respective payments.[3]

---

2 It is important at this point to clear up some terminology confusion. Foreign currency is often called *foreign exchange* or sometimes *FX*. There is another transaction called an *FX swap*, which sounds as if it might be referring to a currency swap. In fact, an FX swap is just a long position in a forward contract on a foreign currency and a short position in a forward contract on the same currency with a different expiration. Why this transaction is called a swap is not clear, but this transaction existed before currency swaps were created. In futures markets, the analogous transaction is called a *spread*, reflecting as it does the risk associated with the spread between the prices of futures contracts with different expirations.

3 In this example, we shall assume 180 days between payment dates. In practice, exact day counts are usually used, leading to different fixed payment amounts in one six-month period from those of another. In the example here, we are only illustrating the idea behind swap cash flows, so it is convenient to keep the fixed payments the same. Later in the reading, we shall illustrate situations in which the exact day count is used, leading to fixed payments that vary slightly.

Thus, the swap is composed of the following transactions:15 September:

- DB pays TGT €9 million
- TGT pays DB $10 million

Each 15 March and 15 September for five years:

- DB pays TGT 0.055(180/360)$10 million = $275,000
- TGT pays DB 0.049(180/360) €9 million = €220,500

15 September five years after initiation:

- DB pays TGT $10 million
- TGT pays DB €9 million

Note that we have simplified the interest calculations a little. In this example, we calculated semiannual interest using the fraction 180/360. Some parties might choose to use the exact day count in the six-month period divided by 365 days. LIBOR and Euribor transactions, the predominant rates used in interest rate swaps, nearly always use 360 days, as mentioned in previous readings. Exhibit 2 shows the stream of cash flows from TGT's perspective.

Exhibit 2	**Cash Flows to TGT on Swap with DB**

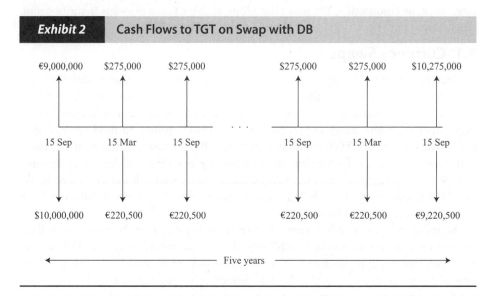

Note that the Target–Deutsche Bank transaction looks just like TGT is issuing a bond with face value of €9 million and that bond is purchased by DB. TGT converts the €9 million to $10 million and buys a dollar-denominated bond issued by DB. Note that TGT, having issued a bond denominated in euros, accordingly makes interest payments to DB in euros. DB, appropriately, makes interest payments in dollars to TGT. At the end, they each pay off the face values of the bonds they have issued. We emphasize that the Target–Deutsche Bank transaction *looks like* what we have just described. In fact, neither TGT nor DB actually issues or purchases a bond. They exchange only a series of cash flows that replicated the issuance and purchase of these bonds.

Exhibit 3 illustrates how such a combined transaction would work. TGT issues a bond in dollars (Exhibit 3, Panel A). It takes the dollars and passes them through to DB, which gives TGT the €9 million it needs. On the interest payment dates, the swap generates $275,000 of the $300,000 in interest TGT needs to pay its bondholders (Panel B). In turn, TGT makes interest payments in euros. Still, small dollar interest payments are necessary because TGT cannot issue a dollar bond at the swap rate. At the end of the transaction, TGT receives $10 million back from DB and passes it through to its bondholders (Panel C). TGT pays DB €9 million, thus effectively paying off a euro-denominated bond.

TGT has effectively issued a dollar-denominated bond and converted it to a euro-denominated bond. In all likelihood, it can save on interest expense by funding its need for euros in this way, because TGT is better known in the United States than in Europe. Its swap dealer, DB, knows TGT well and also obviously has a strong presence in Europe. Thus, DB can pass on its advantage in euro bond markets to TGT. In addition, had TGT issued a euro-denominated bond, it would have assumed no credit risk. By entering into the swap, TGT assumes a remote possibility of DB defaulting. Thus, TGT saves a little money by assuming some credit risk.

Exhibit 3	Issuing a Dollar-Denominated Bond and Using a Currency Swap to Convert a Euro-Denominated Bond

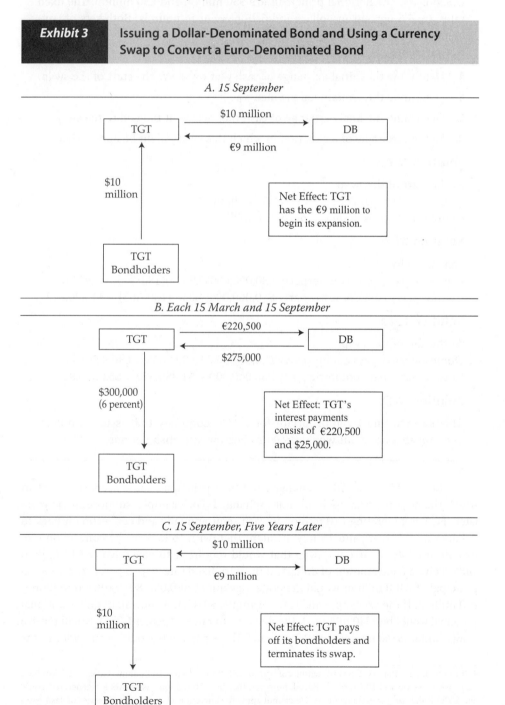

Returning to the Target swap, recall that Target effectively converted a fixed-rate loan in dollars to a fixed-rate loan in euros. Suppose instead that TGT preferred to borrow in euros at a floating rate. It then would have specified that the swap required it to make payments to DB at a floating rate. Had TGT preferred to issue the dollar-denominated bond at a floating rate, it would have specified that DB pay it dollars at a floating rate.

Example 1

Consider a currency swap in which the domestic party pays a fixed rate in the foreign currency, the British pound, and the counterparty pays a fixed rate in U.S. dollars. The notional principals are $50 million and £30 million. The fixed rates are 5.6 percent in dollars and 6.25 percent in pounds. Both sets of payments are made on the basis of 30 days per month and 365 days per year, and the payments are made semiannually.

A. Determine the initial exchange of cash that occurs at the start of the swap.

B. Determine the semiannual payments.

C. Determine the final exchange of cash that occurs at the end of the swap.

D. Give an example of a situation in which this swap might be appropriate.

Solution to A:

At the start of the swap:
Domestic party pays counterparty $50 million
Counterparty pays domestic party £30 million

Solution to B:

Semiannually:
Domestic party pays counterparty £30,000,000(0.0625)(180/365) = £924,658
Counterparty pays domestic party $50,000,000(0.056)(180/365) = $1,380,822

Solution to C:

At the end of the swap:
Domestic party pays counterparty £30,000,000 + £924,658 = £30,924,658
Counterparty pays domestic party $50,000,000 + $1,380,822 = $51,380,822

Solution to D:

This swap would be appropriate for a U.S. company that issues a dollar-denominated bond but would prefer to borrow in British pounds.

Although TGT and DB exchanged notional principal, some scenarios exist in which the notional principals are not exchanged. For example, suppose many years later, TGT is generating €10 million in cash semi-annually and converting it back to dollars on 15 January and 15 July. It might then wish to lock in the conversion rate by entering into a currency swap that would require it to pay a dealer €10 million and receive a fixed amount of dollars. If the euro fixed rate were 5 percent, a notional principal of €400 million would generate a payment of 0.05(180/360)€400 million = €10 million. If the exchange rate is, for example, $0.85, the equivalent dollar notional principal would be $340 million. If the dollar fixed rate is 6 percent, TGT would receive 0.06(180/360)$340 million = $10.2 million.[4] These payments would occur twice a year

---

[4] It might appear that TGT has somehow converted cash flows worth €10 million($0.085) = $8.5 million into cash flows worth $10.2 million. Recall, however, that the €10 million cash flows are generated yearly and $0.85 is the *current* exchange rate. We cannot apply the current exchange rate to a series of cash flows over various future dates. We would apply the respective forward exchange rates, not the spot rate, to the series of future euro cash flows.

for the life of the swap. TGT might then lock in the conversion rate by entering into a currency swap with notional principal amounts that would allow it to receive a fixed amount of dollars on 15 January and 15 July. There would be no reason to specify an exchange of notional principal. As we previously described, there are four types of currency swaps. Using the original Target-Deutsche Bank swap as an example, the semiannual payments would be:

Swap A   TGT pays euros at a fixed rate; DB pays dollars at a fixed rate.

Swap B   TGT pays euros at a fixed rate; DB pays dollars at a floating rate.

Swap C   TGT pays euros at a floating rate; DB pays dollars at a floating rate.

Swap D   TGT pays euros at a floating rate; DB pays dollars at a fixed rate.

Or, reversing the flow, TGT could be the payer of dollars and DB could be the payer of euros:

Swap E   TGT pays dollars at a fixed rate; DB pays euros at a fixed rate.

Swap F   TGT pays dollars at a fixed rate; DB pays euros at a floating rate.

Swap G   TGT pays dollars at a floating rate; DB pays euros at a floating rate.

Swap H   TGT pays dollars at a floating rate; DB pays euros at a fixed rate.

Suppose we combine Swap A with Swap H. With TGT paying euros at a fixed rate and DB paying euros at a fixed rate, the euro payments wash out and the net effect is

Swap I   TGT pays dollars at a floating rate; DB pays dollars at a fixed rate.

Suppose we combine Swap B with Swap E. Similarly, the euro payments again wash out, and the net effect is

Swap J   TGT pays dollars at a fixed rate; DB pays dollars at a floating rate.

Suppose we combine Swap C with Swap F. Likewise, the euro floating payments wash out, and the net effect is

Swap K   TGT pays dollars at a fixed rate; DB pays dollars at a floating rate.

Lastly, suppose we combine Swap D with Swap G. Again, the euro floating payments wash out, and the net effect is

Swap L   TGT pays dollars at a floating rate; DB pays dollars at a fixed rate.

Of course, the net results of I and L are equivalent, and the net results of J and K are equivalent. What we have shown here, however, is that combinations of currency swaps eliminate the currency flows and leave us with transactions in only one currency. A swap in which both sets of interest payments are made in the same currency is an interest rate swap.

3.2 Interest Rate Swaps

As we discovered in the above paragraph, an interest rate swap can be created as a combination of currency swaps. Of course, no one would create an interest rate swap that way; doing so would require two transactions when only one would suffice. Interest rate swaps evolved into their own market. In fact, the interest rate swap market is much bigger than the currency swap market, as we have seen in the notional principal statistics.

As previously noted, one way to look at an interest rate swap is that it is a currency swap in which both currencies are the same. Consider a swap to pay Currency A fixed and Currency B floating. Currency A could be dollars, and B could be euros. But what if A and B are both dollars, or A and B are both euros? The first case is a dollar-denominated plain vanilla swap; the second is a euro denominated plain vanilla swap. A **plain vanilla swap** *is simply an interest rate swap in which one party pays a* *fixed rate and the other pays a floating rate, with both sets of payments in the same currency.* In fact, the plain vanilla swap is probably the most common derivative transaction in the global financial system.

Note that because we are paying in the same currency, there is no need to exchange notional principals at the beginning and at the end of an interest rate swap. In addition, the interest payments can be, and nearly always are, netted. If one party owes $X and the other owes $Y, the party owing the greater amount pays the net difference, which greatly reduces the credit risk. Finally, we note that there is no reason to have both sides pay a fixed rate. The two streams of payments would be identical in that case. So in an interest rate swap, either one side always pays fixed and the other side pays floating, or both sides pay floating, but never do both sides pay fixed.[5]

Thus, in a plain vanilla interest rate swap, one party makes interest payments at a fixed rate and the other makes interest payments at a floating rate. Both sets of payments are on the same notional principal and occur on regularly scheduled dates. For each payment, the interest rate is multiplied by a fraction representing the number of days in the settlement period over the number of days in a year. In some cases, the settlement period is computed assuming 30 days in each month; in others, an exact day count is used. Some cases assume a 360-day year; others use 365 days.

Let us now illustrate an interest rate swap. Suppose that on 15 December, General Electric Company (NYSE: GE) borrows money for one year from a bank such as Bank of America (NYSE: BAC). The loan is for $25 million and specifies that GE will make interest payments on a quarterly basis on the 15th of March, June, September, and December for one year at the rate of LIBOR plus 25 basis points. At the end of the year, it will pay back the principal. On the 15th of December, March, June, and September, LIBOR is observed and sets the rate for that quarter. The interest is then paid at the end of the quarter.[6]

GE believes that it is getting a good rate, but fearing a rise in interest rates, it would prefer a fixed-rate loan. It can easily convert the floating-rate loan to a fixed-rate loan by engaging in a swap. Suppose it approaches JP Morgan Chase (NYSE: JPM), a large dealer bank, and requests a quote on a swap to pay a fixed rate and receive LIBOR, with payments on the dates of its loan payments. The bank prices the swap and quotes a fixed rate of 6.2 percent.[7] The fixed payments will be made based on a day count of 90/365, and the floating payments will be made based on 90/360. Current LIBOR is 5.9 percent. Therefore, the first fixed payment, which GE makes to JPM, is $25,000,000(0.062)(90/365) = $382,192. This is also the amount of each remaining fixed payment.

The first floating payment, which JPM makes to GE, is $25,000,000(0.059) (90/360) = $368,750. Of course, the remaining floating payments will not be known until later. Exhibit 4 shows the pattern of cash flows on the swap from GE's perspective.

---

5 The case of both sides paying floating is called a basis swap.
6 Again, we assume 90 days in each interest payment period for this example. The exact payment dates are not particularly important for illustrative purposes.
7 Typically the rate is quoted as a spread over the rate on a U.S. Treasury security with a comparable maturity. Suppose the yield on a two-year Treasury note is 6 percent. Then the swap would be quoted as 20 basis points over the two-year Treasury rate. By quoting the rate in this manner, GE knows what it is paying over the Treasury rate, a differential called the swap spread. In addition, a quote in this form protects the bank from the rate changing drastically either during the phone conversation or shortly thereafter. Thus, the quote can stay in effect for a reasonable period of time while GE checks out quotes from other dealers.

Exhibit 4	Cash Flow to GE on Swap with JPM

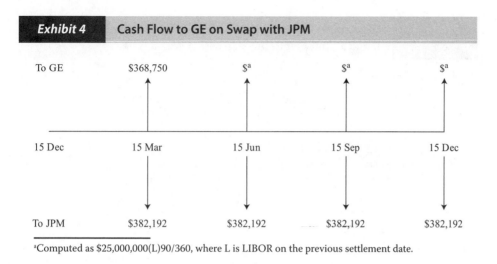

To GE $368,750 $^{a} $^{a} $^{a}

15 Dec   15 Mar   15 Jun   15 Sep   15 Dec

To JPM $382,192 $382,192 $382,192 $382,192

[a]Computed as $25,000,000(L)90/360, where L is LIBOR on the previous settlement date.

Example 2

Determine the upcoming payments in a plain vanilla interest rate swap in which the notional principal is €70 million. The end user makes semiannual fixed payments at the rate of 7 percent, and the dealer makes semiannual floating payments at Euribor, which was 6.25 percent on the last settlement period. The floating payments are made on the basis of 180 days in the settlement period and 360 days in a year. The fixed payments are made on the basis of 180 days in the settlement period and 365 days in a year. Payments are netted, so determine which party pays which and what amount.

Solution:

The fixed payments are €70,000,000(0.07)(180/365) = €2,416,438.
The upcoming floating payment is €70,000,000(0.0625)(180/360) = €2,187,500.
The net payment is that the party paying fixed will pay the party paying floating €2,416,438 − €2,187,500 = €228,938.

Note in Exhibit 4 that we did not show the notional principal, because it was not exchanged. We could implicitly show that GE received $25 million from JPM and paid $25 million to JPM at the start of the swap. We could also show that the same thing happens at the end. If we look at it that way, it appears as if GE has issued a $25 million fixed-rate bond, which was purchased by JPM, which in turn issued a $25 million floating-rate bond, which was in turn purchased by GE. We say that *it appears* as if this is what happened: In fact, neither party actually issued a bond, but they have generated the cash flows that would occur if GE had issued such a fixed-rate bond, JPM had issued such a floating-rate bond, and each purchased the bond of the other. In other words, we could include the principals on both sides to make each set of cash flows look like a bond, yet the overall cash flows would be the same as on the swap.

So let us say that GE enters into this swap. Exhibit 5 shows the net effect of the swap and the loan. GE pays LIBOR plus 25 basis points to Bank of America on its loan, pays 6.2 percent to JPM, and receives LIBOR from JPM. The net effect is that GE pays 6.2 + 0.25 = 6.45 percent fixed.

Exhibit 5	GE's Conversion of a Floating-Rate Loan to a Fixed-Rate Loan Using an Interest Rate Swap with JPM

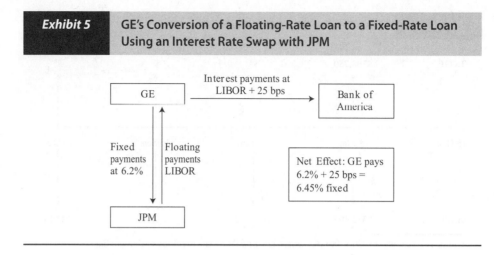

Now, JPM is engaged in a swap to pay LIBOR and receive 6.2 percent. It is exposed to the risk of LIBOR increasing. It would, therefore, probably engage in some other type of transaction to offset this risk. One transaction commonly used in this situation is to sell Eurodollar futures. As discussed in the reading on risk management applications of option strategies, Eurodollar futures prices move $25 in value for each basis point move in LIBOR. JPM will determine how sensitive its position is to a move in LIBOR and sell an appropriate number of futures to offset the risk. Note that Bank of America is exposed to LIBOR as well, but in the banking industry, floating-rate loans are often made because the funding that the bank obtained to make the loan was probably already at LIBOR or a comparable floating rate.

It is possible but unlikely that GE could get a fixed-rate loan at a better rate. The swap involves some credit risk: the possibility, however small, that JPM will default. In return for assuming that risk, GE in all likelihood would get a better rate than it would if it borrowed at a fixed rate. JPM is effectively a wholesaler of risk, using its powerful position as one of the world's leading banks to facilitate the buying and selling of risk for companies such as GE. Dealers profit from the spread between the rates they quote to pay and the rates they quote to receive. The swaps market is, however, extremely competitive and the spreads have been squeezed very tight, which makes it very challenging for dealers to make a profit. Of course, this competition is good for end users, because it gives them more attractive rates.

3.3 Equity Swaps

By now, it should be apparent that a swap requires at least one variable rate or price underlying it. So far, that rate has been an interest rate.[8] In an equity swap, the rate is the return on a stock or stock index. This characteristic gives the equity swap two features that distinguish it from interest rate and currency swaps.

First, the party making the fixed-rate payment could also have to make a variable payment based on the equity return. Suppose the end user pays the equity payment and receives the fixed payment, i.e., it pays the dealer the return on the S&P 500 Index, and the dealer pays the end user a fixed rate. If the S&P 500 increases, the return is positive and the end user pays that return to the dealer. If the S&P 500 goes down, however, its return is obviously negative. In that case, the end user would pay the dealer the *negative return on the S&P 500*, which means that it would receive that return from the dealer. For example, if the S&P 500 falls by 1 percent, the dealer would pay the end user 1 percent, in addition to the fixed payment the dealer makes in any case. So the dealer, or in general the party receiving the equity return, could end up making *both* a fixed-rate payment and an equity payment.

---

8 Currency swaps also have the element that the exchange rate is variable.

The second distinguishing feature of an equity swap is that the payment is not known until the end of the settlement period, at which time the return on the stock is known. In an interest rate or currency swap, the floating interest rate is set at the beginning of the period.[9] Therefore, one always knows the amount of the upcoming floating interest payment.[10]

Another important feature of some equity swaps is that the rate of return is often structured to include both dividends and capital gains. In interest rate and currency swaps, capital gains are not paid.[11] Finally, we note that in some equity swaps, the notional principal is indexed to change with the level of the stock, although we will not explore such swaps in this volume.[12]

Equity swaps are commonly used by asset managers. Let us consider a situation in which an asset manager might use such a swap. Suppose that the Vanguard Asset Allocation Fund (NASDAQ: VAAPX) is authorized to use swaps. On the last day of December, it would like to sell $100 million in U.S. large-cap equities and invest the proceeds at a fixed rate. It believes that a swap allowing it to pay the total return on the S&P 500, while receiving a fixed rate, would achieve this objective. It would like to hold this position for one year, with payments to be made on the last day of March, June, September, and December. It enters into such a swap with Morgan Stanley (NYSE: MWD).

Specifically, the swap covers a notional principal of $100 million and calls for VAAPX to pay MWD the return on the S&P 500 Total Return Index and for MWD to pay VAAPX a fixed rate on the last day of March, June, September, and December for one year. MWD prices the swap at a fixed rate of 6.5 percent. The fixed payments will be made using an actual day count/365 days convention. There are 90 days between 31 December and 31 March, 91 days between 31 March and 30 June, 92 days between 30 June and 30 September, and 92 days between 30 September and 31 December. Thus, the fixed payments will be

31 March:	$100,000,000(0.065)(90/365) = $1,602,740
30 June:	$100,000,000(0.065)(91/365) = $1,620,548
30 September:	$100,000,000(0.065)(92/365) = $1,638,356
31 December:	$100,000,000(0.065)(92/365) = $1,638,356

Exhibit 6 shows the cash flow stream to VAAPX.

| Exhibit 6 | Cash Flows to VAAPX on Equity Swap with MWD |

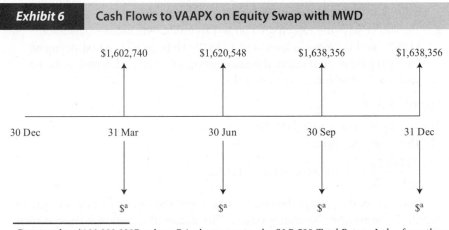

[a]Computed as $100,000,000R, where R is the return on the S&P 500 Total Return Index from the previous settlement date.

---

9 Technically, there are interest rate swaps in which the floating rate is set at the end of the period, at which time the payment is made.

10 In a currency swap, however, one does not know the exchange rate until the settlement date.

11 In some kinds of interest rate swaps, the total return on a bond, which includes dividends and capital gains, is paid. This instrument is called a **total return swap** and is a common variety of a credit derivative.

12 Some interest rate swaps also have a notional principal that changes.

Suppose that on the day the swap is initiated, 31 December, the S&P 500 Total Return Index is at 3,517.76. Now suppose that on 31 March, the index is at 3,579.12. The return on the index is

$$\frac{3{,}579.12}{3{,}517.76} - 1 = 0.0174$$

Thus, the return is 1.74 percent. The equity payment that VAAPX would make to MWD would be $100,000,000(0.0174) = $1,740,000.

Of course, this amount would not be known until 31 March, and only the difference between this amount and the fixed payment would be paid. Then on 31 March, the index value of 3,579.12 would be the base for the following period. Suppose that on 30 June, the index declines to 3,452.78. Then the return for the second quarter would be

$$\frac{3{,}452.78}{3{,}579.12} - 1 = -0.0353$$

Therefore, the loss is 3.53 percent, requiring a payment of $100,000,000(0.0353) = $3,530,000.

Because this amount represents a loss on the S&P 500, MWD would make a payment to VAAPX. In addition, MWD would also owe VAAPX the fixed payment of $1,620,548. It is as though VAAPX sold out of its position in stock, thereby avoiding the loss of about $3.5 million, and moved into a fixed-income position, thereby picking up a gain of about $1.6 million.

Example 3

A mutual fund has arranged an equity swap with a dealer. The swap's notional principal is $100 million, and payments will be made semiannually. The mutual fund agrees to pay the dealer the return on a small-cap stock index, and the dealer agrees to pay the mutual fund based on one of the two specifications given below. The small-cap index starts off at 1,805.20; six months later, it is at 1,796.15.

A. The dealer pays a fixed rate of 6.75 percent to the mutual fund, with payments made on the basis of 182 days in the period and 365 days in a year. Determine the first payment for both parties and, under the assumption of netting, determine the net payment and which party makes it.

B. The dealer pays the return on a large-cap index. The index starts off at 1155.14 and six months later is at 1148.91. Determine the first payment for both parties and, under the assumption of netting, determine the net payment and which party makes it.

Solution to A:

The fixed payment is $100,000,000(0.0675)182/365 = $3,365,753

The equity payment is

$$\left(\frac{1796.15}{1805.20} - 1\right)\$100{,}000{,}000 = -\$501{,}329$$

Because the fund pays the equity return and the equity return is negative, the dealer must pay the equity return. The dealer also pays the fixed return, so the dealer makes both payments, which add up to $3,365,753 + $501,329 = $3,867,082. The net payment is $3,867,082, paid by the dealer to the mutual fund.

Solution to B:

The large-cap equity payment is

$$\left(\frac{1148.91}{1155.14} - 1\right)\$100{,}000{,}000 = -\$539{,}329$$

The fund owes – $501,329, so the dealer owes the fund $501,329. The dealer owes – $539,329, so the fund owes the dealer $539,329. Therefore, the fund pays the dealer the net amount of $539,329 – $501,329 = $38,000.

Exhibit 7 illustrates what VAAPX has accomplished. It is important to note that the conversion of its equity assets into fixed income is not perfect. VAAPX does not hold a portfolio precisely equal to the S&P 500 Total Return Index. To the extent that VAAPX's portfolio generates a return that deviates from the index, some mismatching can occur, which can be a problem. As an alternative, VAAPX can request that MWD give it a swap based on the precise portfolio that VAAPX wishes to sell off. In that case, however, MWD would assess a charge by lowering the fixed rate it pays or raising the rate VAAPX pays to it.[13]

Exhibit 7	VAAPX's Conversion of an Equity Position into a Fixed-Income Position

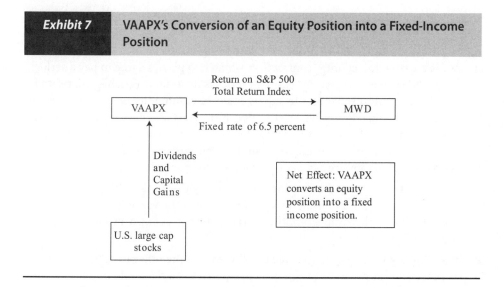

In our previous VAAPX example, the fund wanted to move some money out of a large-cap equity position and invest the proceeds at a fixed rate. Suppose instead that they do not want to move the proceeds into a fixed-rate investment. VAAPX could structure a swap to pay it a floating rate or the return on some other equity index. For example, an asset allocation from U.S. large-cap stocks to U.S. small-cap stocks could be accomplished by having MWD pay the return on the S&P 500 Small Cap 600 Index.

Suppose VAAPX wanted to move out of a position in U.S. stocks and into a position in U.K. large-cap stocks. It could structure the swap to have MWD pay it the return on the FTSE (Financial Times Stock Exchange) 100 Index. Note, however, that this index is based on the prices of U.K. stocks as quoted in pounds sterling. If VAAPX wanted the exposure in pounds—that is, it wanted the currency risk as well as the risk of the U.K. stock market—the payments from MWD to VAAPX would be made in pounds. VAAPX could, however, ask for the payments in dollars. In that case, MWD would hedge the currency risk and make payments in dollars.

Although our focus is on currency, interest rate, and equity products, we shall take a very brief look at some other types of swaps.

---

13 Note, however, that VAAPX is converting not its entire portfolio but simply a $100 million portion of it.

3.4 Commodity and Other Types of Swaps

Just as currencies, interest rates, and equities can be used to structure swaps, so too can commodities and just about anything that has a random outcome and to which a corporation, financial institution, or even an individual is exposed. Commodity swaps are very commonly used. For example, airlines enter into swaps to hedge their future purchases of jet fuel. They agree to make fixed payments to a swap dealer on regularly scheduled dates and receive payments determined by the price of jet fuel. Gold mining companies use swaps to hedge future deliveries of gold. Other parties dealing in such commodities as natural gas and precious metals often use swaps to lock in prices for future purchases and sales. In addition, swaps can be based on non-storable commodities, like electricity and the weather. In the case of the weather, payments are made based on a measure of a particular weather factor, such as amounts of rain, snowfall, or weather related damage.

SUMMARY

- Swaps are over-the-counter contracts in which two parties agree to pay a series of cash flows to each other. At least one series is floating or variable and related to an interest rate, exchange rate, equity price, or commodity price; the other can be fixed or floating. Swaps have zero value at the start and have payments made on scheduled payment or settlement dates and a final termination or expiration date. When swap payments are made in the same currency, the payments are usually netted. Swaps are subject to default on the part of either party.

- Swaps can be terminated by having one party pay the market value of the swap to the other party, by entering into a swap in which the variable payments offset, by selling the swap to another party, or by exercising a swaption to enter into an offsetting swap.

- In a currency swap, each party makes payments to the other in different currencies. A currency swap can have one party pay a fixed rate in one currency and the other pay a fixed rate in the other currency; have both pay a floating rate in their respective currencies; have the first party pay a fixed rate in one currency and the second party pay a floating rate in the other currency; or have the first party pay a floating rate in one currency and the second pay a fixed rate in the other currency. In currency swaps, the notional principal is usually exchanged at the beginning and at the end of the life of the swap, although this exchange is not mandatory.

- The payments on a currency swap are calculated by multiplying the notional principal by the fixed or floating interest rate times a day-count adjustment. This procedure is done in each currency, and the respective parties make their separate payments to each other. The payments are not netted.

- In a plain vanilla interest rate swap, one party makes payments at a fixed rate and the other makes payments at a floating rate, with no exchange of notional principal. A typical plain vanilla swap involves one party paying a fixed rate and the other paying a floating rate such as LIBOR. Swaps are often done by a party borrowing floating at a rate tied to LIBOR; that party then uses a pay-fixed, receive-floating swap to offset the risk of its exposure to LIBOR and effectively convert its loan to a fixed-rate loan.

- The payments on an interest rate swap are calculated by multiplying the notional principal by the fixed or floating interest rate times a day-count adjustment. The respective amounts are netted so that the party owing the greater amount makes a net payment to the other.

■ The three types of equity swaps involve one party paying a fixed rate, a floating rate, or the return on another equity, while the other party pays an equity return. Therefore, an equity swap is a swap in which at least one party pays the return on a stock or stock index.

■ The equity payment (or payments, if both sides of the swap are related to an equity return) on an equity swap is calculated by multiplying the return on the stock over the settlement period by the notional principal. If there is a fixed or floating payment, it is calculated in the same manner as in an interest rate swap. With payments in a single currency, the two sets of payments are netted.

PRACTICE PROBLEMS FOR READING 64

1. A U.S. company enters into a currency swap in which it pays a fixed rate of 5.5 percent in euros and the counterparty pays a fixed rate of 6.75 percent in dollars. The notional principals are $100 million and €116.5 million. Payments are made semiannually and on the basis of 30 days per month and 360 days per year.

   A. Calculate the initial exchange of payments that takes place at the beginning of the swap.

   B. Calculate the semiannual payments.

   C. Calculate the final exchange of payments that takes place at the end of the swap.

2. A British company enters into a currency swap in which it pays a fixed rate of 6 percent in dollars and the counterparty pays a fixed rate of 5 percent in pounds. The notional principals are £75 million and $105 million. Payments are made semiannually and on the basis of 30 days per month and 360 days per year.

   A. Calculate the initial exchange of payments that takes place at the beginning of the swap.

   B. Calculate the semiannual payments.

   C. Calculate the final exchange of payments that takes place at the end of the swap.

3. A U.S. company has entered into an interest rate swap with a dealer in which the notional principal is $50 million. The company will pay a floating rate of LIBOR and receive a fixed rate of 5.75 percent. Interest is paid semiannually, and the current LIBOR is 5.15 percent. Calculate the first payment and indicate which party pays which. Assume that floating-rate payments will be made on the basis of 180/360 and fixed-rate payments will be made on the basis of 180/365.

4. A German company that has issued floating-rate notes now believes that interest rates will rise. It decides to protect itself against this possibility by entering into an interest rate swap with a dealer. In this swap, the notional principal is €25 million and the company will pay a fixed rate of 5.5 percent and receive Euribor. The current Euribor is 5 percent. Calculate the first payment and indicate which party pays which. Assume that floating-rate payments will be made on the basis of 90/360 and fixed-rate payments will be made on the basis of 90/365.

5. An asset manager wishes to reduce his exposure to large-cap stocks and increase his exposure to small-cap stocks. He seeks to do so using an equity swap. He agrees to pay a dealer the return on a large-cap index, and the dealer agrees to pay the manager the return on a small-cap index. For each of the scenarios listed below, calculate the first overall payment and indicate which party makes the payment. Assume that payments are made semiannually. The notional principal is $100 million.

   A. The value of the small-cap index starts off at 689.40, and the large-cap index starts at 1130.20. In six months, the small-cap index is at 625.60 and the large-cap index is at 1251.83.

  B. The value of the small-cap index starts off at 689.40 and the large-cap index starts at 1130.20. In six months, the small-cap index is at 703.23 and the large-cap index is at 1143.56.

6. An asset manager wishes to reduce her exposure to small-cap stocks and increase her exposure to fixed-income securities. She seeks to do so using an equity swap. She agrees to pay a dealer the return on a small-cap index and the dealer agrees to pay the manager a fixed rate of 5.5 percent. For each of the scenarios listed below, calculate the overall payment six months later and indicate which party makes the payment. Assume that payments are made semiannually (180 days per period) and there are 365 days in each year. The notional principal is $50 million.

  A. The value of the small-cap index starts off at 234.10 and six months later is at 238.41.

  B. The value of the small-cap index starts off at 234.10 and six months later is at 241.27.

7. An asset manager wishes to reduce his exposure to fixed-income securities and increase his exposure to large-cap stocks. He seeks to do so using an equity swap. He agrees to pay a dealer a fixed rate of 4.5 percent, and the dealer agrees to pay the manager the return on a large-cap index. For each of the scenarios listed below, calculate the overall payment six months later and indicate which party makes it. Assume that payments are made semiannually (180 days per period) and there are 365 days in a year. The notional principal is $25 million.

  A. The value of the large-cap index starts off at 578.50 and six months later is at 622.54.

  B. The value of the large-cap index starts off at 578.50 and six months later is at 581.35.

8. The party agreeing to make the fixed-rate payment might also be required to make the variable payment in:

  A. an equity swap but not an interest rate swap.

  B. an interest rate swap but not an equity swap.

  C. both an equity swap and an interest rate swap.

9. The formula for calculating the payoff at expiration of a forward rate agreement (FRA) is:

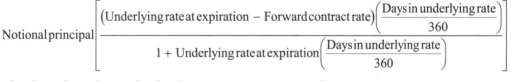

$$\text{Notional principal}\left[\frac{(\text{Underlying rate at expiration} - \text{Forward contract rate})\left(\dfrac{\text{Days in underlying rate}}{360}\right)}{1 + \text{Underlying rate at expiration}\left(\dfrac{\text{Days in underlying rate}}{360}\right)}\right]$$

  Use the above formula to solve for the payment at expiration for an investor who went long a 3 × 9 FRA with a notional principal of $10,000,000 where the 180-day LIBOR rate at expiration is 4.80 percent and the forward contract rate was set at 5.20 percent.

  A. −$588,235.

  B. −$19,531.

  C. $19,493.

10. Agrawal Telecom is considering issuing $10,000,000 of 6.75% fixed-coupon bonds to finance an expansion. Alternatively, Agrawal could borrow the funds in the Eurodollar market using a series of six-month LIBOR contracts. A swap contract matching the maturity of the 6.75% coupon bonds is available.

The swap uses six-month LIBOR as the floating-rate component. Identify the interest rate swap that Agrawal should use to convert the Eurodollar borrowing to the equivalent of issuing fixed-income bonds.

A. Agrawal would use a pay-fixed, receive-floating interest rate swap.

B. Agrawal would use a pay-floating, receive-fixed interest rate swap.

C. Agrawal would use a total return equity payer swaption to evaluate the two borrowing options.

11. Determine the upcoming payments on a swap with a notional principal of $5,000,000 in which the fixed-rate payer makes semiannual fixed payments of 8% and the counterparty makes floating-rate payments at Euribor. The Euribor rate at the last settlement period was 7.25%.

The fixed-rate payments are made on the basis of 180 days in the settlement period and 365 days in a year. The floating-rate payments use a 180/360 day convention.

A. The net payment is $16,010 from the fixed-rate payer to the floating-rate payer.

B. The net payment is $18,750 from the fixed-rate payer to the floating-rate payer.

C. The net payment is $18,750 from the floating-rate payer to the fixed-rate payer.

12. A portfolio manager entered into a swap with a dealer. The swap's notional principal is $100 million, payments are to be made semiannually, and the swap allows netting of payments. The dealer agrees to pay a fixed annual rate of 4 percent while the asset manager agrees to pay the return on a stock index. The index value at initiation of the swap is 280. If the value of the stock index six months after initiation of the swap is 250, the payment from the dealer to the asset manager would be *closest* to:

A. $2 million.

B. $9 million.

C. $13 million.

SOLUTIONS FOR READING 64

1. **A.** The payments at the beginning of the swap are as follows:

    The U.S. company (domestic party) pays the counterparty $100 million.

    The counterparty pays the U.S. company €116.5 million.

   B. The semiannual payments are as follows:

    The U.S. company (domestic party) pays the counterparty €116,500,000(0.055)(180/360) = €3,203,750.

    The counterparty pays the U.S. company $100,000,000(0.0675) × (180/360) = $3,375,000.

   C. The payments at the end of the swap are as follows:

    The U.S. company (domestic party) pays the counterparty €116.5 million + €3,203,750.

    The counterparty pays the U.S. company $100 million +$3,375,000.

2. **A.** The payments at the beginning of the swap are as follows:

    The British company (domestic party) pays the counterparty £75 million.

    The counterparty pays the British company $105 million.

   B. The semiannual payments are as follows:

    The British company (domestic party) pays the counterparty $105,000,000(0.06)(180/360) = $3,150,000.

    The counterparty pays the British company £75,000,000(0.05) × (180/360) = £1,875,000.

   C. The payments at the end of the swap are as follows:

    The British company (domestic party) pays the counterparty $105 million + $3,150,000.

    The counterparty pays the British company £75 million + £1,875,000.

3. The fixed payments are $50,000,000(0.0575)(180/365) = $1,417,808. The floating payments are $50,000,000(0.0515)(180/360) = $1,287,500. The net payment is $130,308, made by the party paying fixed—that is, the dealer pays the company.

4. The fixed payments are €25,000,000(0.055)(90/365) = €339,041. The floating payments are €25,000,000(0.05)(90/360) = €312,500. The net payment is €26,541, made by the party paying fixed—that is, the company pays the dealer.

5. **A.** The small-cap equity payment is $\left(\dfrac{625.60}{689.40} - 1\right)(100,000,000) = -\$9,254,424$.

    The asset manager owes $9,254,424 to the dealer.

    The large-cap equity payment is $\left(\dfrac{1251.83}{1130.20} - 1\right)(100,000,000) = \$10,761,812$.

    The asset manager owes this amount to the dealer.

    The overall payment made by the asset manager to the dealer is $9,254,424 + $10,761,812 = $20,016,236.

   B. The small-cap equity payment is $\left(\dfrac{703.23}{689.40} - 1\right)(100,000,000) = \$2,006,092$.

    The dealer owes the asset manager this amount.

    The large-cap equity payment is $\left(\dfrac{1143.56}{1130.20} - 1\right)(100,000,000) = \$1,182,092$.

    The asset manager owes this amount to the dealer.

    The overall payment made by the dealer to the asset manager is $2,006,092 − $1,182,092 = $824,000.

6. A. The small-cap equity payment is $\left(\dfrac{238.41}{234.10} - 1\right)(50{,}000{,}000) = \$920{,}547.$

   The asset manager owes the dealer this amount.

   The fixed interest payment is $(50{,}000{,}000)(0.055)(180/365) = \$1{,}356{,}164.$

   The dealer owes this amount to the asset manager.

   So the dealer pays to the asset manager $\$1{,}356{,}164 - \$920{,}547 = \$435{,}617.$

B. The small-cap equity payment is $\left(\dfrac{241.27}{234.10} - 1\right)(50{,}000{,}000) = \$1{,}531{,}397.$

   The asset manager owes the dealer this amount.

   The fixed interest payment is $(50{,}000{,}000)(0.055)(180/365) = \$1{,}356{,}164.$

   The dealer owes this amount to the asset manager.

   So the asset manager pays to the dealer $\$1{,}531{,}397 - \$1{,}356{,}164 = \$175{,}233.$

7. A. The large-cap equity payment is $\left(\dfrac{622.54}{578.50} - 1\right)(25{,}000{,}000) = \$1{,}903{,}198.$

   The dealer owes this amount to the asset manager.

   The fixed interest payment is $(25{,}000{,}000)(0.045)(180/365) = \$554{,}795.$

   The asset manager owes this amount to the dealer.

   So the dealer pays to the asset manager $\$1{,}903{,}198 - \$554{,}795 = \$1{,}348{,}403.$

B. The large-cap equity payment is $\left(\dfrac{581.35}{578.50} - 1\right)(25{,}000{,}000) = \$123{,}163.$

   The dealer owes this amount to the asset manager.

   The fixed interest payment is $(25{,}000{,}000)(0.045)(180/365) = \$554{,}795.$

   The asset manager owes this amount to the dealer.

   So the asset manager pays to the dealer $\$554{,}795 - \$123{,}163 = \$431{,}632.$

8. A is correct. If the equity referenced in the equity swap shows a negative return for a settlement date, the "receive-equity, pay-fixed" party would pay both a variable payment based on the negative equity return and the fixed-rate payment. Given that interest rates will not go negative, an analogous situation cannot occur in interest rate swaps.

9. B is correct. A 3 × 9 FRA uses the 180-day LIBOR contract as the underlying rate. Solve $(0.048 - 0.052) \times (180/360) / [1 + 0.048 \times (180/360)] = -0.001953125.$ Multiply by \$10,000,000. The answer is approximately – \$19,531.

10. A is correct. Agrawal would owe floating-rate interest on the LIBOR loans. The "receive-floating" part of the swap would offset those payments, while the "pay-fixed" side of the swap resembles the fixed-coupon payments on the 6.75 percent coupon bonds.

11. A is correct. The calculation is $\$5{,}000{,}000 \times 0.08 \times (180/365) - \$5{,}000{,}000 \times 0.0725 \times (180/360) = \$16{,}010.$

12. C is correct. The loss on the stock index means that the dealer must also pay the negative amount to the asset manager in addition to the fixed rate on the notional principal. The amount that the dealer would pay is approximately \$13 million:

   $(\$100{,}000{,}000)(0.04) / 2 = \$2{,}000{,}000$ for the fixed payment

   The negative return on the stock index computed as follows is $(250/280) - 1 = -0.1071$, for a dollar payment of $-0.1071(100{,}000{,}000) = \$10{,}714{,}286$ for the stock index.

   The dealer must pay roughly \$2 million plus \$11 million.

Risk Management Applications of Option Strategies

by Don M. Chance, CFA

LEARNING OUTCOMES

Mastery	The candidate should be able to:
☐	**a** determine the value at expiration, the profit, maximum profit, maximum loss, breakeven underlying price at expiration, and payoff graph of the strategies of buying and selling calls and puts and determine the potential outcomes for investors using these strategies;
☐	**b** determine the value at expiration, profit, maximum profit, maximum loss, breakeven underlying price at expiration, and payoff graph of a covered call strategy and a protective put strategy, and explain the risk management application of each strategy.

INTRODUCTION

In a previous reading we examined strategies that employ forward and futures contracts. Recall that forward and futures contracts have linear payoffs and do not require an initial outlay. Options, on the other hand, have nonlinear payoffs and require the payment of cash up front. By having nonlinear payoffs, options permit their users to benefit from movements in the underlying in one direction and to not be harmed by movements in the other direction. In many respects, they offer the best of all worlds, a chance to profit if expectations are realized with minimal harm if expectations turn out to be wrong. The price for this opportunity is the cash outlay required to establish the position. From the standpoint of the holder of the short position, options can lead to extremely large losses. Hence, sellers of options must be well compensated in the form of an adequate up-front premium and must skillfully manage the risk they assume.

In this reading, we look at option strategies that are typically used in equity investing, which include standard strategies involving single options and strategies that combine options with the underlying.

Let us begin by reviewing the necessary notation. These symbols are the same ones we have previously used. First recall that time 0 is the time at which the strategy is initiated and time T is the time the option expires, stated as a fraction of a year. Accordingly, the amount of time until expiration is simply T − 0 = T, which is (Days to expiration)/365. The other symbols are

c_0, c_T = price of the call option at time o and time T
p_0, p_T = price of the put option at time 0 and time T[1]
X = exercise price
S_0, S_T = price of the underlying at time 0 and time T
V_0, V_T = value of the position at time 0 and time T
Π = profit from the transaction: V_0, V_T
r = risk free rate

Some additional notation will be introduced when necessary.

Note that we are going to measure the profit from an option transaction, which is simply the final value of the transaction minus the initial value of the transaction. Profit does not take into account the time value of money or the risk. Although a focus on profit is not completely satisfactory from a theoretical point of view, it is nonetheless instructive, simple, and a common approach to examining options. Our primary objective here is to obtain a general picture of the manner in which option strategies perform. With that in mind, discussing profit offers probably the best trade-off in terms of gaining the necessary knowledge with a minimum of complexity.

In this reading, we assume that the option user has a view regarding potential movements of the underlying. In most cases that view is a prediction of the direction of the underlying, but in some cases it is a prediction of the volatility of the underlying. In all cases, we assume this view is specified over a horizon that corresponds to the option's life or that the option expiration can be tailored to the horizon date. Hence, for the most part, these options should be considered customized, over-the-counter options.[2] Every interest rate option is a customized option.

Because the option expiration corresponds to the horizon date for which a particular view is held, there is no reason to use American options. Accordingly, all options in this reading are European options. Moreover, we shall not consider terminating the strategy early. Putting an option in place and closing the position prior to expiration is certainly a legitimate strategy. It could reflect the arrival of new information over the holding period, but it requires an understanding of more complex issues, such as valuation of the option and the rate at which the option loses its time value. Thus, we shall examine the outcome of a particular strategy over a range of possible values of the underlying only on the expiration day.

2   OPTION STRATEGIES FOR EQUITY PORTFOLIOS

Many typical illustrations of option strategies use individual stocks, but we shall use options on a stock index, the NASDAQ 100, referred to simply as the NASDAQ. We shall assume that in addition to buying and selling options on the NASDAQ, we can also buy the index, either through construction of the portfolio itself, through an index mutual fund, or an exchange-traded fund.[3] We shall simply refer to this instrument as a stock. We are given the following numerical data:

S_0 = 2000, value of the NASDAQ 100 when the strategy is initiated

T = 0.0833, the time to expiration (one month = 1/12)

---

1 As in the reading on option markets and contracts, lower case indicates European options, and upper case indicates American options. In this reading, all options are European.

2 If the options discussed were exchange-listed options, it would not significantly alter the material in this reading.

3 Exchange-traded shares on the NASDAQ 100 are called NASDAQ 100 Trust Shares and QQQs, for their ticker symbol. They are commonly referred to as Qubes, trade on the AMEX, and are the most active exchange-traded fund and often the most actively traded of all securities. Options on the NASDAQ 100 are among the most actively traded as well.

The options available will be the following:[4]

Exercise Price	Call Price	Put Price
1950	108.43	56.01
2000	81.75	79.25
2050	59.98	107.39

Let us start by examining an initial strategy that is the simplest of all: to buy or sell short the underlying. Panel A of Exhibit 1 illustrates the profit from the transaction of buying a share of stock. We see the obvious result that if you buy the stock and it goes up, you make a profit; if it goes down, you incur a loss. Panel B shows the case of selling short the stock. Recall that this strategy involves borrowing the shares from a broker, selling them at the current price, and then buying them back at a later date. In this case, if you sell short the stock and it goes down, you make a profit. Conversely, if it goes up, you incur a loss. Now we shall move on to strategies involving options, but we shall use the stock strategies again when we combine options with stock.

In this section we examine option strategies in the context of their use in equity portfolios. Although these strategies are perfectly applicable for fixed-income portfolios, corporate borrowing scenarios, or even commodity risk management situations, they are generally more easily explained and understood in the context of investing in equities or equity indices.

Exhibit 1	Simple Stock Strategies

A. Buy Stock

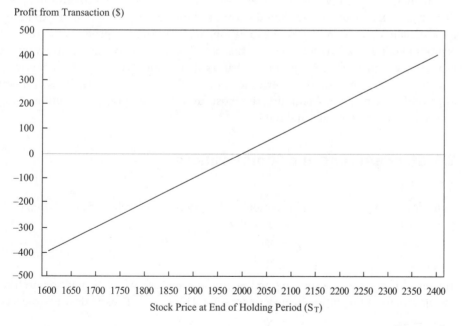

Profit from Transaction ($)

Stock Price at End of Holding Period (S_T)

(continued)

---

4 These values were obtained using the Black–Scholes–Merton model. By using this model, we know we are working with reasonable values that do not permit arbitrage opportunities.

Exhibit 1	Continued

B. Sell Short Stock

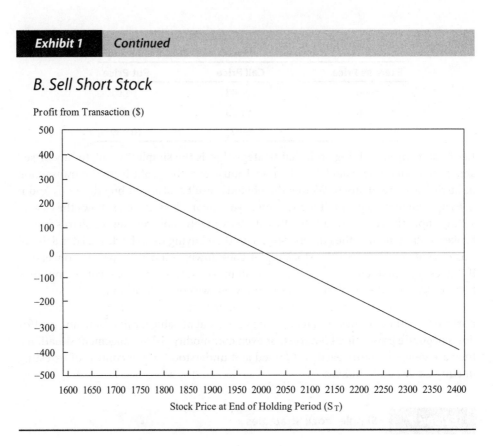

Profit from Transaction ($)

To analyze an equity option strategy, we first assume that we establish the position at the current price. We then determine the value of the option at expiration for a specific value of the index at expiration. We calculate the profit as the value at expiration minus the current price. We then generate a graph to illustrate the value at expiration and profit for a range of index values at expiration. Although the underlying is a stock index, we shall just refer to it as the underlying to keep things as general as possible. We begin by examining the most fundamental option transactions, long and short positions in calls and puts.

2.1 Standard Long and Short Positions

2.1.1 Calls

Consider the purchase of a call option at the price c_0. The value at expiration, c_T, is $c_T = \max(0, S_T - X)$. Broken down into parts,

$$c_T = 0 \qquad\qquad \text{if } S_T \leq X$$
$$c_T = S_T - X \qquad \text{if } S_T > X$$

The profit is obtained by subtracting the option premium, which is paid to purchase the option, from the option value at expiration, $\Pi = c_T - c_0$. Broken down into parts,

$$\Pi = -c_0 \qquad\qquad\quad \text{if } S_T \leq X$$
$$\Pi = S_T - X - c_0 \qquad \text{if } S_T > X$$

Now consider this example. We buy the call with the exercise price of 2000 for 81.75. Consider values of the index at expiration of 1900 and 2100. For $S_T = 1900$,

$$c_T = \max(0, 1900 - 2000) = 0$$
$$\Pi = 0 - 81.75 = -81.75$$

For $S_T = 2100$,

$$c_T = max(0, 2100 - 2000) = 100$$
$$\Pi = 100 - 81.75 = 18.25$$

Exhibit 2 illustrates the value at expiration and profit when S_T, the underlying price at expiration, ranges from 1600 to 2400. We see that buying a call results in a limited loss of the premium, 81.75. For an index value at expiration greater than the exercise price of 2000, the value and profit move up one-for-one with the index value, and there is no upper limit.

It is important to identify the breakeven index value at expiration. Recall that the formula for the profit is $\Pi = max(0, S_T - X) - c_0$. We would like to know the value of S_T for which $\Pi = 0$. We shall call that value S_T^*. It would be nice to be able to solve $\Pi = max(0, S_T^* - X) - c_0 = 0$ for S_T^*, but that is not directly possible. Instead, we observe that there are two ranges of outcomes, one in which $\Pi = S_T^* - X - c_0$ for $S_T^* > X$, the case of the option expiring in-the-money, and the other in which $\Pi = -c_0$ for $S_T \leq X$, the case of the option expiring out-of-the-money. It is obvious from the equation and by observing Exhibit 2 that in the latter case, there is no possibility of breaking even. In the former case, we see that we can solve for S_T^*. Setting $\Pi = S_T^* - X - c_0 = 0$, we obtain $S_T^* = X + c_0$.

Thus, the breakeven is the exercise price plus the option premium. This result should be intuitive: The value of the underlying at expiration must exceed the exercise price by the amount of the premium to recover the cost of the premium. In this problem, the breakeven is $S_T^* = 2000 + 81.75 = 2081.75$. Observe in Exhibit 2 that the profit line crosses the axis at this value.

In summarizing the strategy, we have the following results for the option buyer:

$$c_T = max(0, S_T - X)$$

Value at expiration $= c_T$

Profit : $\Pi = c_T - c_0$

Maximum profit $= \infty$

Maximum loss $= c_0$

Breakeven: $S_T^* = X + c_0$

Exhibit 2	Buy Call

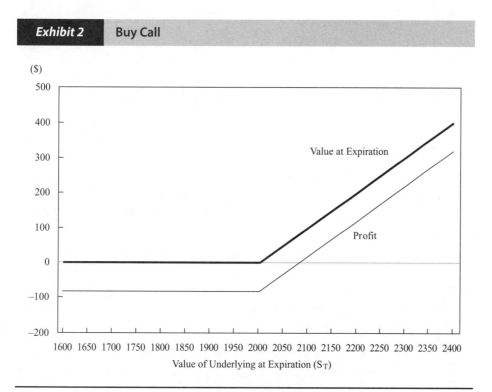

($)

Value of Underlying at Expiration (S_T)

Call options entice naive speculators, but it is important to consider the *likely* gains and losses more than the *potential* gains and losses. For example, in this case, the underlying must go up by about 4.1 percent in one month to cover the cost of the call. This increase equates to an annual rate of almost 50 percent and is an unreasonable expectation by almost any standard. If the underlying does not move at all, the loss is 100 percent of the premium.

For the seller of the call, the results are just the opposite. The sum of the positions of the seller and buyer is zero. Hence, we can take the value and profit results for the buyer and change the signs. The results for the maximum profit and maximum loss are changed accordingly, and the breakeven is the same. Hence, for the option seller,

$$c_T = \max(0, S_T - X)$$

Value at expiration $= -c_T$

Profit : $\Pi = -c_T + c_0$

Maximum profit $= c_0$

Maximum loss $= \infty$

Breakeven: $S_T^* = X + c_0$

Exhibit 3 shows the results for the seller of the call. Note that the value and profit have a fixed maximum. The worst case is an infinite loss. Just as there is no upper limit to the buyer's potential gain, there is no upper limit to how much the seller can lose.

Call options are purchased by investors who are bullish. We now turn to put options, which are purchased by investors who are bearish.

Exhibit 3   **Sell Call**

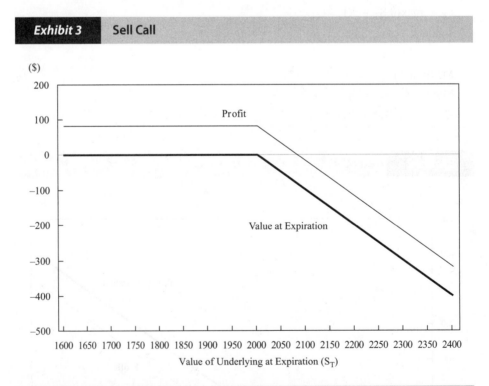

Example 1

Consider a call option selling for $7 in which the exercise price is $100 and the price of the underlying is $98.

A. Determine the value at expiration and the profit for a buyer under the following outcomes:

    i. The price of the underlying at expiration is $102.

    ii. The price of the underlying at expiration is $94.

B. Determine the value at expiration and the profit for a seller under the following outcomes:

    i. The price of the underlying at expiration is $91.

    ii. The price of the underlying at expiration is $101.

C. Determine the following:

    i. The maximum profit to the buyer (maximum loss to the seller).

    ii. The maximum loss to the buyer (maximum profit to the seller).

D. Determine the breakeven price of the underlying at expiration.

Solution to A:

Call buyer

i. Value at expiration = $c_T = \max(0, S_T - X) = \max(0, 102 - 100) = 2$

$$\Pi = c_T - c_0 = 2 - 7 = -5$$

ii. Value at expiration = $c_T = \max(0, S_T - X) = \max(0, 94 - 100) = 0$

$$\Pi = c_T - c_0 = 0 - 7 = -7$$

Solution to B:

Call seller

i. Value at expiration = $-c_T = -\max(0, S_T - X) = -\max(0, 91 - 100) = 0$

$$\Pi = -c_T + c_0 = -0 + 7 = 7$$

ii. Value at expiration = $-c_T = -\max(0, S_T - X) = -\max(0, 101 - 100) = -1$

$$\Pi = -c_T + c_0 = -1 + 7 = 6$$

Solution to C:

Maximum and minimum

i. Maximum profit to buyer (loss to seller) = ∞

ii. Maximum loss to buyer (profit to seller) = $c_0 = 7$

Solution to D:

$$S_T^* = X + c_0 = 100 + 7 = 107$$

2.1.2 *Puts*

The value of a put at expiration is $p_T = \max(0, X - S_T)$. Broken down into parts,

$$p_T = X - S_T \qquad \text{if } S_T < X$$
$$p_T = 0 \qquad \text{if } S_T \geq X$$

The profit is obtained by subtracting the premium on the put from the value at expiration:

$$\Pi = p_T - p_0$$

Broken down into parts,

$$\Pi = X - S_T - p_0 \qquad \text{if } S_T < X$$
$$\Pi = -p_0 \qquad \text{if } S_T \geq X$$

For our example and outcomes of $S_T = 1900$ and 2100, the results are as follows:

$S_T = 1900$:

$\qquad p_T = \max(0, 2000 - 1900) = 100$

$\qquad \Pi = 100 - 79.25 = 20.75$

$S_T = 2100$:

$\qquad p_T = \max(0, 2000 - 2100) = 0$

$\qquad \Pi = 0 - 79.25 = -79.25$

These results are shown in Exhibit 4. We see that the put has a maximum value and profit and a limited loss, the latter of which is the premium. The maximum value is obtained when the underlying goes to zero.[5] In that case, $p_T = X$. So the maximum profit is $X - p_0$. Here that will be $2000 - 79.25 = 1920.75$.

The breakeven is found by breaking up the profit equation into its parts, $\Pi = X - S_T - p_0$ for $S_T < X$ and $\Pi = -p_0$ for $S_T \geq X$. In the latter case, there is no possibility of breaking even. It refers to the range over which the entire premium is lost. In the former case, we denote the breakeven index value as S_T^*, set the equation to zero, and solve for S_T^* to obtain $S_T^* = X - p_0$. In our example, the breakeven is $S_T^* = 2000 - 79.25 = 1920.75$.

Exhibit 4	Buy Put

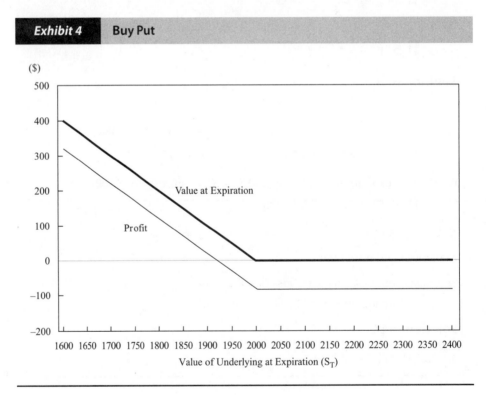

In summary, for the strategy of buying a put we have

$p_T = \max(0, X - S_T)$

Value at expiration $= p_T$

Profit : $\Pi = p_T - p_0$

Maximum profit $= X - p_0$

Maximum loss $= p_0$

Breakeven: $S_T^* = X - p_0$

---

[5] The maximum value and profit are not visible on the graph because we do not show S_T all the way down to zero.

Now consider the *likely* outcomes for the holder of the put. In this case, the underlying must move down by almost 4 percent in one month to cover the premium. One would hardly ever expect the underlying to move down at an annual rate of almost 50 percent. Moreover, if the underlying does not move downward at all (a likely outcome given the positive expected return on most assets), the loss is 100 percent of the premium.

For the sale of a put, we simply change the sign on the value at expiration and profit. The maximum profit for the buyer becomes the maximum loss for the seller and the maximum loss for the buyer becomes the maximum profit for the seller. The breakeven for the seller is the same as for the buyer. So, for the seller,

$$p_T = \max(0, X - S_T)$$
$$\text{Value at expiration} = -p_T$$
$$\text{Profit}: \Pi = -p_T + p_0$$
$$\text{Maximum profit} = p_0$$
$$\text{Maximum loss} = X - p_0$$
$$\text{Breakeven}: S_T{}^* = X - p_0$$

Exhibit 5 graphs the value at expiration and the profit for this transaction.

Exhibit 5	Sell Put

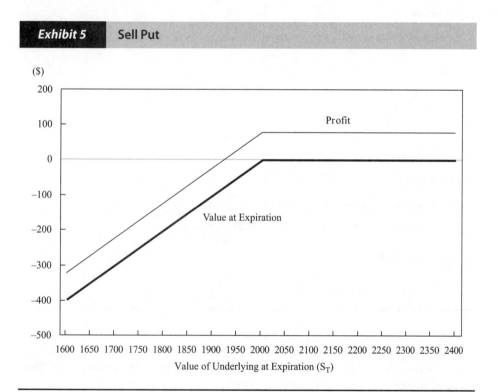

Value of Underlying at Expiration (S_T)

Example 2

Consider a put option selling for $4 in which the exercise price is $60 and the price of the underlying is $62.

A. Determine the value at expiration and the profit for a buyer under the following outcomes:

   i. The price of the underlying at expiration is $62.

   ii. The price of the underlying at expiration is $55.

B. Determine the value at expiration and the profit for a seller under the following outcomes:

  i. The price of the underlying at expiration is $51.

  ii. The price of the underlying at expiration is $68.

C. Determine the following:

  i. The maximum profit to the buyer (maximum loss to the seller).

  ii. The maximum loss to the buyer (maximum profit to the seller).

D. Determine the breakeven price of the underlying at expiration.

Solution to A:

Put buyer

$$\text{Value at expiration} = p_T = \max(0, X - S_T) = \max(0, 60 - 62) = 0$$
$$\Pi = p_T - p_0 = 0 - 4 = -4$$
$$\text{Value at expiration} = p_T = \max(0, X - S_T) = \max(0, 60 - 55) = 5$$
$$\Pi = p_T - p_0 = 5 - 4 = 1$$

Solution to B:

Put seller

i. $\text{Value at expiration} = -p_T = -\max(0, X - S_T) = -\max(0, 60 - 51) = -9$

$$\Pi = -p_T + p_0 = -9 + 4 = -5$$

ii. $\text{Value at expiration} = -p_T = -\max(0, X - S_T) = -\max(0, 60 - 68) = 0$

$$\Pi = -p_T + p_0 = 0 + 4 = 4$$

Solution to C:

Maximum and minimum

i. Maximum profit to buyer (loss to seller) = $X - p_0 = 60 - 4 = 56$

ii. Maximum loss to buyer (profit to seller) = $p_0 = 4$

Solution to D:

$$S_T^* = X - p_0 = 60 - 4 = 56$$

It may be surprising to find that we have now covered all of the information we need to examine all of the other option strategies. We need to learn only a few basic facts. We must know the formula for the value at expiration of a call and a put. Then we need to know how to calculate the profit for the purchase of a call and a put, but that calculation is simple: the value at expiration minus the initial value. If we know these results, we can calculate the value at expiration of the option and the profit for any value of the underlying at expiration. If we can do that, we can graph the results for a range of possible values of the underlying at expiration. Because graphing can take a long time, however, it is probably helpful to learn the basic shapes of the value and profit graphs for calls and puts. Knowing the profit equation and the shapes of the graphs, it is easy to determine the maximum profit and maximum loss. The breakeven can be determined by setting the profit equation to zero for the case in which the profit equation contains S_T. Once we have these results for the long call and put, it is an easy matter to turn them around and obtain the results for the short call and put. Therefore, little if any memorization is required. From there, we can go on to strategies that combine an option with another option and combine options with the underlying.

2.2 Risk Management Strategies with Options and the Underlying

In this section, we examine two of the most widely used option strategies, particularly for holders of the underlying. One way to reduce exposure without selling the underlying is to sell a call on the underlying; the other way is to buy a put.

2.2.1 Covered Calls

A **covered call** is a relatively conservative strategy, but it is also one of the most misunderstood strategies. A covered call is a position in which you own the underlying and sell a call. The value of the position at expiration is easily found as the value of the underlying plus the value of the short call:

$$V_T = S_T - \max(0, S_T - X)$$

Therefore,

$$V_T = S_T \qquad\qquad \text{if } S_T \leq X$$
$$V_T = S_T - (S_T - X) = X \qquad \text{if } S_T > X$$

We obtain the profit for the covered call by computing the change in the value of the position, $V_T - V_0$. First recognize that V_0, the value of the position at the start of the contract, is the initial value of the underlying minus the call premium. We are long the underlying and short the call, so we must subtract the call premium that was received from the sale of the call. The initial investment in the position is what we pay for the underlying less what we receive for the call. Hence, $V_0 = S_0 - c_0$. The profit is thus

$$\Pi = S_T - \max(0, S_T - X) - (S_0 - c_0)$$
$$= S_T - S_0 - \max(0, S_T - X) + c_0$$

With the equation written in this manner, we see that the profit for the covered call is simply the profit from buying the underlying, $S_T - S_0$, plus the profit from selling the call, $-\max(0, S_T - X) + c_0$. Breaking it down into ranges,

$$\Pi = S_T - S_0 + c_0 \qquad\qquad \text{if } S_T \leq X$$
$$\Pi = S_T - S_0 - (S_T - X) + c_0 = X - S_0 + c_0 \qquad \text{if } S_T > X$$

In our example, $S_0 = 2000$. In this section we shall use a call option with the exercise price of 2050. Thus $X = 2050$, and the premium, c_0, is 59.98. Let us now examine two outcomes: $S_T = 2100$ and $S_T = 1900$. The value at expiration when $S_T = 2100$ is $V_T = 2100 - (2100 - 2050) = 2050$, and when $S_T = 1900$, the value of the position is $V_T = 1900$.

In the first case, we hold the underlying worth 2100 but are short a call worth 50. Thus, the net value is 2050. In the second case, we hold the underlying worth 1900 and the option expires out-of-the-money.

In the first case, $S_T = 2100$, the profit is $\Pi = 2050 - 2000 + 59.98 = 109.98$. In the second case, $S_T = 1900$, the profit is $\Pi = 1900 - 2000 + 59.98 = -40.02$. These results are graphed for a range of values of S_T in Exhibit 6. Note that for all values of S_T greater than 2050, the value and profit are maximized. Thus, 2050 is the maximum value and 109.98 is the maximum profit.[6]

---

6 Note in Exhibit 6 that there is a large gap between the value at expiration and profit, especially compared with the graphs of buying and selling calls and puts. This difference occurs because a covered call is mostly a position in the underlying asset. The initial value of the asset, S_0, accounts for most of the difference in the two lines. Note also that because of the put–call parity relationship we covered in the reading on option markets and contracts, a covered call looks very similar to a short put.

As evident in Exhibit 6 and the profit equations, the maximum loss would occur when S_T is zero. Hence, the profit would be $S_T - S_0 + c_0$. The profit is $-S_0 + c_0$ when $S_T =$ 0. This means that the maximum loss is $S_0 - c_0$. In this example, $-S_0 + c_0$ is $-2000 +$ 59.98 $= -1940.02$. Intuitively, this would mean that you purchased the underlying for 2000 and sold the call for 59.98. The underlying value went to zero, resulting in a loss of 2000, but the call expired with no value, so the gain from the option is the option premium. The total loss is 1940.02.

Exhibit 6	Covered Call (Buy Underlying, Sell Call)

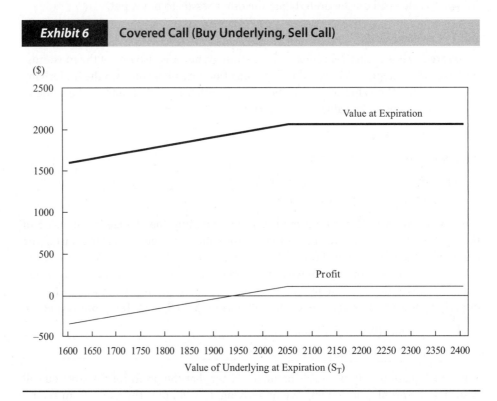

The breakeven underlying price is found by examining the profit equations and focusing on the equation that contains S_T. In equation form, $\Pi = S_T - S_0 + c_0$ when $S_T \leq X$. We let S_T^* denote the breakeven value of S_T, set the equation to zero, and solve for S_T^* to obtain $S_T^* = S_0 - c_0$. The breakeven and the maximum loss are identical. In this example, the breakeven is $S_T^* = 2000 - 59.98 = 1940.02$, which is seen in Exhibit 6.

To summarize the covered call, we have the following:

Value at expiration: $V_T = S_T - \max(0, S_T - X)$

Profit : $\Pi = V_T - S_0 + c_0$

Maximum profit $= X - S_0 + c_0$

Maximum loss $= S_0 - c_0$

Breakeven: $S_T^* = S_0 - c_0$

Because of the importance and widespread use of covered calls, it is worthwhile to discuss this strategy briefly to dispel some misunderstandings. First of all, some investors who do not believe in using options fail to see that selling a call on a position in the underlying reduces the risk of that position. Options do not automatically increase risk. The option part of this strategy alone, viewed in isolation, seems an extremely risky strategy. We noted in Section 2.1.1 that selling a call without owning the stock exposes the investor to unlimited loss potential. But selling a covered call—adding a short call to a long position in a stock—reduces the overall risk. Thus, any investor who holds a stock cannot say he is too conservative to use options.

Following on that theme, however, one should also view selling a covered call as a strategy that reduces not only the risk but also the expected return compared with simply holding the underlying. Hence, one should not expect to make a lot of money writing calls on the underlying. It should be apparent that in fact the covered call writer could miss out on significant gains in a strong bull market. The compensation for this willingness to give up potential upside gains, however, is that in a bear market the losses on the underlying will be cushioned by the option premium.

It may be disconcerting to some investors to look at the profit profile of a covered call. The immediate response is to think that no one in their right mind would invest in a strategy that has significant downside risk but a limited upside. Just owning the underlying has significant downside risk, but at least there is an upside. But it is important to note that the visual depiction of the strategy, as in Exhibit 6, does not tell the whole story. It says nothing about the likelihood of certain outcomes occurring.

For example, consider the covered call example we looked at here. The underlying starts off at 2000. The maximum profit occurs when the option expires with the underlying at 2050 or above, an increase of 2.5 percent over the life of the option. We noted that this option has a one-month life. Thus, the underlying would have to increase at an approximate annual rate of at least 2.5% (12) = 30% for the covered call writer to forgo all of the upside gain. There are not many stocks, indices, or other assets in which an investor would expect the equivalent of an annual move of at least 30 percent. Such movements obviously do occur from time to time, but they are not common. Thus, covered call writers do not often give up large gains.

But suppose the underlying did move to 2050 or higher. As we previously showed, the value of the position would be 2050. Because the initial value of the position is 2000 − 59.98 = 1940.02, the rate of return would be 5.7 percent for one month. Hence, the maximum return is still outstanding by almost anyone's standards.[7]

Many investors believe that the initial value of a covered call should not include the value of the underlying if the underlying had been previously purchased. Suppose, for example, that this asset, currently worth 2000, had been bought several months ago at 1900. It is tempting to ignore the current value of the underlying; there is no current outlay. This view, however, misses the notion of opportunity cost. If an investor currently holding an asset chooses to write a call on it, she has made a conscious decision not to sell the asset. Hence, the current value of the asset should be viewed as an opportunity cost that is just as real as the cost to an investor buying the underlying at this time.

Sellers of covered calls must make a decision about the chosen exercise price. For example, one could sell the call with an exercise price of 1950 for 108.43, or sell the call with an exercise price of 2000 for 81.75, or sell the call with an exercise price of 2050 for 59.98. The higher the exercise price, the less one receives for the call but the more room for gain on the upside. There is no clear-cut solution to deciding which call is best; the choice depends on the risk preferences of the investor.

Finally, we should note that anecdotal evidence suggests that writers of call options make small amounts of money, but make it often. The reason for this phenomenon is generally thought to be that buyers of calls tend to be overly optimistic, but that argument is fallacious. The real reason is that the expected profits come from rare but large payoffs. For example, consider the call with exercise price of 2000 and a premium of 81.75. As we learned in Section 2.1, the breakeven underlying price is 2081.75—a gain of about 4.1 percent in a one-month period, which would be an exceptional return

---

7 Of course, we are not saying that the performance reflects a positive alpha. We are saying only that the upside performance given up reflects improbably high returns, and therefore the limits on the upside potential are not too restrictive.

for almost any asset. These prices were obtained using the Black–Scholes–Merton model, so they are fair prices. Yet the required underlying price movement to profit on the call is exceptional. Obviously someone buys calls, and naturally, someone must be on the other side of the transaction. Sellers of calls tend to be holders of the underlying or other calls, which reduces the enormous risk they would assume if they sold calls without any other position.[8] Hence, it is reasonable to expect that sellers of calls would make money often, because large underlying price movements occur only rarely. Following this line of reasoning, however, it would appear that sellers of calls can consistently take advantage of buyers of calls. That cannot possibly be the case. What happens is that buyers of calls make money less often than sellers, but when they do make money, the leverage inherent in call options amplifies their returns. Therefore, when call writers lose money, they tend to lose big, but most call writers own the underlying or are long other calls to offset the risk.

Example 3

Consider a bond selling for $98 per $100 face value. A call option selling for $8 has an exercise price of $105. Answer the following questions about a covered call.

A. Determine the value of the position at expiration and the profit under the following outcomes:

   i. The price of the bond at expiration is $110.

   ii. The price of the bond at expiration is $88.

B. Determine the following:

   i. The maximum profit.

   ii. The maximum loss.

C. Determine the breakeven bond price at expiration.

Solution to A:

  i. $V_T = S_T - \max(0, S_T - X) = 110 - \max(0, 110 - 105) = 110 - 110 + 105 = 105$

$$\Pi = V_T - V_0 = 105 - (S_0 - c_0) = 105 - (98 - 8) = 15$$

  ii. $V_T = S_T - \max(0, S_T - X) = 88 - \max(0, 88 - 105) = 88 - 0 = 88$

$$\Pi = V_T - V_0 = 88 - (S_0 - c_0) = 88 - (98 - 8) = -2$$

Solution to B:

  i. Maximum profit $= X - S_0 + c_0 = 105 - 98 + 8 = 15$

  ii. Maximum loss $= S_0 - c_0 = 98 - 8 = 90$

Solution to C:

$$S_T^* = S_0 - c_0 = 98 - 8 = 90$$

Covered calls represent one widely used way to protect a position in the underlying. Another popular means of providing protection is to buy a put.

2.2.2 *Protective Puts*

Because selling a call provides some protection to the holder of the underlying against a fall in the price of the underlying, buying a put should also provide protection. A

---

[8] Sellers of calls who hold other calls are engaged in transactions called spreads.

put, after all, is designed to pay off when the price of the underlying moves down. In some ways, buying a put to add to a long stock position is much better than selling a call. As we shall see here, it provides downside protection while retaining the upside potential, but it does so at the expense of requiring the payment of cash up front. In contrast, a covered call generates cash up front but removes some of the upside potential.

Holding an asset and a put on the asset is a strategy known as a **protective put**. The value at expiration and the profit of this strategy are found by combining the value and profit of the two strategies of buying the asset and buying the put. The value is $V_T = S_T + \max(0, X - S_T)$. Thus, the results can be expressed as

$$V_T = S_T + (X - S_T) = X \qquad \text{if } S_T \leq X$$
$$V_T = S_T \qquad \text{if } S_T > X$$

When the underlying price at expiration exceeds the exercise price, the put expires with no value. The position is then worth only the value of the underlying. When the underlying price at expiration is less than the exercise price, the put expires in-the-money and is worth $X - S_T$, while the underlying is worth S_T. The combined value of the two instruments is X. When the underlying is worth less than the exercise price at expiration, the put can be used to sell the underlying for the exercise price.

The initial value of the position is the initial price of the underlying, S_0, plus the premium on the put, p_0. Hence, the profit is $\Pi = S_T + \max(0, X - S_T) - (S_0 + p_0)$. The profit can be broken down as follows:

$$\Pi = X - (S_0 + p_0) \qquad \text{if } S_T \leq X$$
$$\Pi = S_T - (S_0 + p_0) \qquad \text{if } S_T > X$$

In this example, we are going to use the put with an exercise price of 1950. Its premium is 56.01. Recalling that the initial price of the underlying is 2000, the value at expiration and profit for the case of $S_T = 2100$ are

$$V_T = 2100$$
$$\Pi = 2100 - (2100 + 56.01) = 43.99$$

For the case of $S_T = 1900$, the value at expiration and profit are

$$V_T = 1950$$
$$\Pi = 1950 - (2000 + 56.01) = -106.01$$

The results for a range of outcomes are shown in Exhibit 7. Note how the protective put provides a limit on the downside with no limit on the upside.[9] Therefore, we can say that the upper limit is infinite. The lower limit is a loss of 106.01. In the worst possible case, we can sell the underlying for the exercise price, but the up-front cost of the underlying and put are 2056.01, for a maximum loss of 106.01.

Now let us find the breakeven price of the underlying at expiration. Note that the two profit equations are $\Pi = S_T - (S_0 + p_0)$ if $S_T > X$ and $\Pi = X - (S_0 + p_0)$ if $S_T \leq X$. In the latter case, there is no value of the underlying that will allow us to break even. In the former case, $S_T > X$, we change the notation on S_T to S_T^* to denote the breakeven value, set this expression equal to zero, and solve for S_T^*:

$$S_T^* = S_0 + p_0$$

---

[9] Note that the graph for a protective put looks like the graph for a call. This result is due to put–call parity, as covered in the reading on option markets and contracts.

| Exhibit 7 | Protective Put (Buy Underlying, Buy Put) |

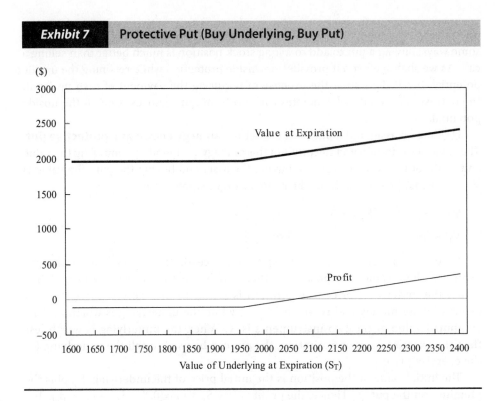

To break even, the underlying must be at least as high as the amount expended up front to establish the position. In this problem, this amount is 2000 + 56.01 = 2056.01.

To summarize the protective put, we have the following:

Value at expiration: $V_T = S_T + \max(0, X - S_T)$

Profit: $\Pi = V_T - S_0 - p_0$

Maximum profit $= \infty$

Maximum loss $= S_0 + p_0 - X$

Breakeven: $S_T{}^* = S_0 + p_0$

A protective put can appear to be a great transaction with no drawbacks. It provides downside protection with upside potential, but let us take a closer look. First recall that this is a one-month transaction and keep in mind that the option has been priced by the Black–Scholes–Merton model and is, therefore, a fair price. The maximum loss of 106.01 is a loss of 106.01/2056.01 = 5.2%. The breakeven of 2056.01 requires an upward move of 2.8 percent, which is an annual rate of about 34 percent. From this angle, the protective put strategy does not look quite as good, but in fact, these figures simply confirm that protection against downside loss is expensive. When the protective put is fairly priced, the protection buyer must give up considerable upside potential that may not be particularly evident from just looking at a graph.

The purchase of a protective put also presents the buyer with some choices. In this example, the buyer bought the put with exercise price of 1950 for 56.01. Had he bought the put with exercise price of 2000, he would have paid 79.25. The put with exercise price of 2050 would have cost 107.39. The higher the price for which the investor wants to be able to sell the underlying, the more expensive the put will be.

The protective put is often viewed as a classic example of insurance. The investor holds a risky asset and wants protection against a loss in value. He then buys insurance in the form of the put, paying a premium to the seller of the insurance, the put writer. The exercise price of the put is like the insurance deductible because the magnitude of the exercise price reflects the risk assumed by the party holding the underlying. The higher the exercise price, the less risk assumed by the holder of the underlying and the more risk assumed by the put seller. The lower the exercise price, the more risk assumed by the holder of the underlying and the less risk assumed by the put seller. In insurance, the higher the deductible, the more risk assumed by the insured party and the less risk assumed by the insurer. Thus, a higher exercise price is analogous to a lower insurance deductible.

Like traditional insurance, this form of insurance provides coverage for a period of time. At the end of the period of time, the insurance expires and either pays off or not. The buyer of the insurance may or may not choose to renew the insurance by buying another put.

Example 4

Consider a currency selling for $0.875. A put option selling for $0.075 has an exercise price of $0.90. Answer the following questions about a protective put.

A. Determine the value at expiration and the profit under the following outcomes:

   i. The price of the currency at expiration is $0.96.

   ii. The price of the currency at expiration is $0.75.

B. Determine the following:

   i. The maximum profit.

   ii. The maximum loss.

C. Determine the breakeven price of the currency at expiration.

Solutions:

A. **i.** $V_T = S_T + \max(0, X - S_T) = 0.96 + \max(0, 0.90 - 0.96) = 0.96$

        $\Pi = V_T - V_0 = 0.96 - (S_0 + p_0) = 0.96 - (0.875 + 0.075) = 0.01$

   ii. $V_T = S_T + \max(0, X - S_T) = 0.75 + \max(0, 0.90 - 0.75) = 0.90$

        $\Pi = V_T - V_0 = 0.90 - (S_0 + p_0) = 0.90 - (0.875 + 0.075) = -0.05$

B. **i.** Maximum profit = ∞

   ii. Maximum loss = $S_0 + p_0 - X = 0.875 + 0.075 - 0.90 = 0.05$

C. $S_T^* = S_0 + p_0 = 0.875 + 0.075 = 0.95$

Finally, we note that a protective put can be modified in a number of ways. One in particular is to sell a call to generate premium income to pay for the purchase of the put. This strategy is known as a collar.

SUMMARY

- The profit from buying a call is the value at expiration, $\max(0, S_T - X)$, minus c_0, the option premium. The maximum profit is infinite, and the maximum loss is the option premium. The breakeven underlying price at expiration is the exercise price plus the option premium. When one sells a call, these results are reversed.

- The profit from buying a put is the value at expiration, $\max(0, X - S_T)$, minus p_0, the option premium. The maximum profit is the exercise price minus the option premium, and the maximum loss is the option premium. The breakeven underlying price at expiration is the exercise price minus the option premium. When one sells a put, these results are reversed.

- The profit from a covered call—the purchase of the underlying and sale of a call—is the value at expiration, $S_T - \max(0, S_T - X)$, minus $S_0 - c_0$, the cost of the underlying minus the option premium. The maximum profit is the exercise price minus the original underlying price plus the option premium, and the maximum loss is the cost of the underlying less the option premium. The breakeven underlying price at expiration is the original price of the underlying minus the option premium.

- The profit from a protective put—the purchase of the underlying and a put—is the value at expiration, $S_T + \max(0, X - S_T)$, minus the cost of the underlying plus the option premium, $S_0 + p_0$. The maximum profit is infinite, and the maximum loss is the cost of the underlying plus the option premium minus the exercise price. The breakeven underlying price at expiration is the original price of the underlying plus the option premium.

PRACTICE PROBLEMS FOR READING 65

1. Consider a call option selling for $4 in which the exercise price is $50.

   A. Determine the value at expiration and the profit for a buyer under the following outcomes:

      i. The price of the underlying at expiration is $55.

      ii. The price of the underlying at expiration is $51.

      iii. The price of the underlying at expiration is $48.

   B. Determine the value at expiration and the profit for a seller under the following outcomes:

      i. The price of the underlying at expiration is $49.

      ii. The price of the underlying at expiration is $52.

      iii. The price of the underlying at expiration is $55.

   C. Determine the following:

      i. The maximum profit to the buyer (maximum loss to the seller).

      ii. The maximum loss to the buyer (maximum profit to the seller).

   D. Determine the breakeven price of the underlying at expiration.

2. Suppose you believe that the price of a particular underlying, currently selling at $99, is going to increase substantially in the next six months. You decide to purchase a call option expiring in six months on this underlying. The call option has an exercise price of $105 and sells for $7.

   A. Determine the profit under the following outcomes for the price of the underlying six months from now:

      i. $99.

      ii. $104.

      iii. $105.

      iv. $109.

      v. $112.

      vi. $115.

   B. Determine the breakeven price of the underlying at expiration. Check that your answer is consistent with the solution to Part A of this problem.

3. Consider a put option on the NASDAQ 100 selling for $106.25 in which the exercise price is 2100.

   A. Determine the value at expiration and the profit for a buyer under the following outcomes:

      i. The price of the underlying at expiration is 2125.

      ii. The price of the underlying at expiration is 2050.

      iii. The price of the underlying at expiration is 1950.

   B. Determine the value at expiration and the profit for a seller under the following outcomes:

      i. The price of the underlying at expiration is 1975.

     ii. The price of the underlying at expiration is 2150.

  C. Determine the following:

     i. The maximum profit to the buyer (maximum loss to the seller).

     ii. The maximum loss to the buyer (maximum profit to the seller).

  D. Determine the breakeven price of the underlying at expiration.

4. Suppose you believe that the price of a particular underlying, currently selling at $99, will decrease considerably in the next six months. You decide to purchase a put option expiring in six months on this underlying. The put option has an exercise price of $95 and sells for $5.

  A. Determine the profit for you under the following outcomes for the price of the underlying six months from now:

     i. $100.

     ii. $95.

     iii. $93.

     iv. $90.

     v. $85.

  B. Determine the breakeven price of the underlying at expiration. Check that your answer is consistent with the solution to Part A of this problem.

  C.   **i.** What is the maximum profit that you can have?

     ii. At what expiration price of the underlying would this profit be realized?

5. You simultaneously purchase an underlying priced at $77 and write a call option on it with an exercise price of $80 and selling at $6.

  A. What is the term commonly used for the position that you have taken?

  B. Determine the value at expiration and the profit for your strategy under the following outcomes:

     i. The price of the underlying at expiration is $70.

     ii. The price of the underlying at expiration is $75.

     iii. The price of the underlying at expiration is $80.

     iv. The price of the underlying at expiration is $85.

  C. Determine the following:

     i. The maximum profit.

     ii. The maximum loss.

     iii. The expiration price of the underlying at which you would realize the maximum profit.

     iv. The expiration price of the underlying at which you would incur the maximum loss.

  D. Determine the breakeven price at expiration.

6. Suppose you simultaneously purchase an underlying priced at $77 and a put option on it, with an exercise price of $75 and selling at $3.

  A. What is the term commonly used for the position that you have taken?

  B. Determine the value at expiration and the profit for your strategy under the following outcomes:

     i. The price of the underlying at expiration is $70.

     ii. The price of the underlying at expiration is $75.

     iii. The price of the underlying at expiration is $80.

     iv. The price of the underlying at expiration is $85.

      v. The price of the underlying at expiration is $90.

   C. Determine the following:

      i. The maximum profit.

      ii. The maximum loss.

      iii. The expiration price of the underlying at which you would incur the maximum loss.

   D. Determine the breakeven price at expiration.

7. The recent price per share of Dragon Vacations, Inc. is $50 per share. Calls with exactly six months left to expiration are available on Dragon with strikes of $45, $50, and $55. The prices of the calls are $8.75, $6.00, and $4.00, respectively. Assume that each call contract is for 100 shares of stock and that at initiation of the strategy the investor purchases 100 shares of Dragon at the current market price. Further assume that the investor will close out the strategy in six months when the options expire, including the sale of any stock not delivered against exercise of a call, whether the stock price goes up or goes down. If the closing price of Dragon stock in six months is exactly $60, the profit to a covered call using the $50 strike call is *closest* to:

   A. $400.

   B. $600.

   C. $1,600.

8. The recent price per share of Win Big, Inc. is €50 per share. Verna Hillsborough buys 100 shares at €50. To protect against a fall in price, Hillsborough buys one put, covering 100 shares of Win Big, with a strike price of €40. The put premium is €1 per share. If Win Big closes at €45 per share at the expiration of the put and Hillsborough sells her shares at €45, Hillsborough's profit from the stay/put is *closest* to:

   A. −€1,100.

   B. −€600.

   C. €900.

SOLUTIONS FOR READING 65

1. **A.** Call buyer

   i. $c_T = \max(0, S_T - X) = \max(0, 55 - 50) = 5$
   $\Pi = c_T - c_0 = 5 \quad 4 = 1$

   ii. $c_T = \max(0, S_T - X) = \max(0, 51 - 50) = 1$
   $\Pi = c_T - c_0 = 1 - 4 = -3$

   iii. $c_T = \max(0, S_T - X) = \max(0, 48 - 50) = 0$
   $\Pi = c_T - c_0 = 0 - 4 = -4$

   B. Call seller

   i. $\text{Value} = -c_T = -\max(0, S_T - X) = -\max(0, 49 - 50) = 0$
   $\Pi = -c_T + c_0 = -0 + 4 = 4$

   ii. $\text{Value} = -c_T = -\max(0, S_T - X) = -\max(0, 52 - 50) = -2$
   $\Pi = -c_T + c_0 = -2 + 4 = 2$

   iii. $\text{Value} = -c_T = -\max(0, S_T - X) = -\max(0, 55 - 50) = -5$
   $\Pi = -c_T + c_0 = -5 + 4 = -1$

   C. Maximum and minimum

   i. Maximum profit to buyer (loss to seller) $= \infty$

   ii. Maximum loss to buyer (profit to seller) $= c_0 = 4$

   D. $S_T{}^* = X + c_0 = 50 + 4 = 54$

2. **A.** **i.** $c_T = \max(0, S_T - X) = \max(0, 99 - 105) = 0$
   $\Pi = c_T - c_0 = 0 - 7 = -7$

   ii. $c_T = \max(0, S_T - X) = \max(0, 104 - 105) = 0$
   $\Pi = c_T - c_0 = 0 - 7 = -7$

   iii. $c_T = \max(0, S_T - X) = \max(0, 105 - 105) = 0$
   $\Pi = c_T - c_0 = 0 - 7 = -7$

   iv. $c_T = \max(0, S_T - X) = \max(0, 109 - 105) = 4$
   $\Pi = c_T - c_0 = 4 - 7 = -3$

   v. $c_T = \max(0, S_T - X) = \max(0, 112 - 105) = 7$
   $\Pi = c_T - c_0 = 7 - 7 = 0$

   vi. $c_T = \max(0, S_T - X) = \max(0, 115 - 105) = 10$
   $\Pi = c_T - c_0 = 10 - 7 = 3$

   B. $S_T{}^* = X + c_0 = 105 + 7 = 112$

   Clearly, this result is consistent with our solution above, where the profit is exactly zero in Part A(v), in which the price at expiration is 112.

3. **A.** Put buyer

   i. $p_T = \max(0, X - S_T) = \max(0, 2100 - 2125) = 0$
   $\Pi = p_T - p_0 = 0 - 106.25 = -106.25$

ii. $p_T = \max(0, X - S_T) = \max(0, 2100 - 2050) = 50$

$\Pi = p_T - p_0 = 50 - 106.25 = -56.25$

iii. $p_T = \max(0, X - S_T) = \max(0, 2100 - 1950) = 150$

$\Pi = p_T - p_0 = 150 - 106.25 = 43.75$

B. Put seller

i. Value $= -p_T = -\max(0, X - S_T) = -\max(0, 2100 - 1975) = -125$

$\Pi = -p_T + p_0 = -125 + 106.25 = -18.75$

ii. Value $= -p_T = -\max(0, X - S_T) = -\max(0, 2100 - 2150) = 0$

$\Pi = -p_T + p_0 = -0 + 106.25 = 106.25$

C. Maximum and minimum

i. Maximum profit to buyer(loss to seller) $= X - p_0 = 2100 - 106.25 = 1993.75$

ii. Maximum loss to buyer(profit to seller) $= p_0 = 106.25$

D. $S_T{}^* = X - p_0 = 2100 - 106.25 = 1993.75$

4. A. i. $p_T = \max(0, X - S_T) = \max(0, 95 - 100) = 0$

$\Pi = p_T - p_0 = 0 - 5 = -5$

ii. $p_T = \max(0, X - S_T) = \max(0, 95 - 95) = 0$

$\Pi = p_T - p_0 = 0 - 5 = -5$

iii. $p_T = \max(0, X - S_T) = \max(0, 95 - 93) = 2$

$\Pi = p_T - p_0 = 2 - 5 = -3$

iv. $p_T = \max(0, X - S_T) = \max(0, 95 - 90) = 5$

$\Pi = p_T - p_0 = 5 - 5 = 0$

v. $p_T = \max(0, X - S_T) = \max(0, 95 - 85) = 10$

$\Pi = p_T - p_0 = 10 - 5 = 5$

B. $S_T{}^* = X - p_0 = 95 - 5 = 90$

Clearly, this result is consistent with our solution above, where the profit is exactly zero in Part A(iv), in which the price at expiration is 90.

C. i. Maximum profit (to put buyer) $= X - p_0 = 95 - 5 = 90$.

ii. This profit would be realized in the unlikely scenario of the price of the underlying falling all the way down to zero.

5. A. This position is commonly called a covered call.

B. i. $V_T = S_T - \max(0, S_T - X) = 70 - \max(0, 70 - 80) = 70 - 0 = 70$

$\Pi = V_T - V_0 = 70 - (S_0 - c_0) = 70 - (77 - 6) = 70 - 71 = -1$

ii. $V_T = S_T - \max(0, S_T - X) = 75 - \max(0, 75 - 80) = 75 - 0 = 75$

$\Pi = V_T - V_0 = 75 - (S_0 - c_0) = 75 - (77 - 6) = 4$

iii. $V_T = S_T - \max(0, S_T - X) = 80 - \max(0, 80 - 80) = 80 - 0 = 80$

$\Pi = V_T - V_0 = 80 - (S_0 - c_0) = 80 - (77 - 6) = 9$

    iv. $V_T = S_T - \max(0, S_T - X) = 85 - \max(0, 85 - 80) = 85 - 5 = 80$

        $\Pi = V_T - V_0 = 80 - (S_0 - c_0) = 80 - (77 - 6) = 9$

  C. **i.** Maximum profit $= X - S_0 + c_0 = 80 - 77 + 6 = 9$

    ii. Maximum loss $= S_0 - c_0 = 77 - 6 = 71$

    iii. The maximum profit would be realized if the expiration price of the underlying is at or above the exercise price of $80.

    iv. The maximum loss would be incurred if the underlying price drops to zero.

  D. $S_T{}^* = S_0 - c_0 = 77 - 6 = 71$

6. **A.** This position is commonly called a protective put.

  B. **i.** $V_T = S_T + \max(0, X - S_T) = 70 + \max(0, 75 - 70) = 70 + 5 = 75$

        $\Pi = V_T - V_0 = 75 - (S_0 + p_0) = 75 - (77 + 3) = 75 - 80 = -5$

    ii. $V_T = S_T + \max(0, X - S_T) = 75 + \max(0, 75 - 75) = 75 + 0 = 75$

        $\Pi = V_T - V_0 = 75 - (S_0 + p_0) = 75 - (77 + 3) = 75 - 80 = -5$

    iii. $V_T = S_T + \max(0, X - S_T) = 80 + \max(0, 75 - 80) = 80 + 0 = 80$

        $\Pi = V_T - V_0 = 80 - (S_0 + p_0) = 80 - (77 + 3) = 80 - 80 = 0$

    iv. $V_T = S_T + \max(0, X - S_T) = 85 + \max(0, 75 - 85) = 85 + 0 = 85$

        $\Pi = V_T - V_0 = 85 - (S_0 + p_0) = 85 - (77 + 3) = 85 - 80 = 5$

    v. $V_T = S_T + \max(0, X - S_T) = 90 + \max(0, 75 - 90) = 90 + 0 = 90$

        $\Pi = V_T - V_0 = 90 - (S_0 + p_0) = 90 - (77 + 3) = 90 - 80 = 10$

  C. **i.** Maximum profit $= \infty$

    ii. Maximum loss $= -(X - S_0 - p_0) = -(75 - 77 - 3) = 5$

    iii. The maximum loss would be incurred if the expiration price of the underlying were at or below the exercise price of $75.

  D. $S_T{}^* = S_0 + p_0 = 77 + 3 = 80$

7. B is correct. Buying the stock at $50 and delivering it against the $50 strike call generates a payoff of zero. The premium is retained by the writer. The net profit is $6.00 per share × 100 shares or $600.

8. B is correct. The loss on her stock is (€45 − €50) × 100 = − €500. She also paid €100 for the put. The put expires worthless, making her total loss €600.

Alternative Investments

TOPIC LEVEL LEARNING OUTCOME

The candidate should be able to demonstrate a working knowledge of the analysis of alternative investments, including hedge funds, private equity, real estate, and commodities.

ALTERNATIVE INVESTMENTS
STUDY SESSION

18

Alternative Investments

Investors are increasingly turning to alternative investments seeking diversification benefits and higher returns. This study session describes the common types of alternative investments, their valuation, their unique risks and opportunities, and their relation to traditional investments.

Although defining "alternative investments" is difficult, certain features (e.g., limited liquidity and specialized legal structures) are typically associated with alternative investments. This study session describes these features and their impact on investment decisions. The first reading provides an overview of major categories of alternative investments, including real estate, private equity, venture capital, hedge funds, closely held companies, distressed securities, and commodities. The second reading explores some issues in commodity investing.

READING ASSIGNMENTS

Reading 66 *Introduction to Alternative Investments*
by Terri Duhon, George Spentzos, CFA and Scott D. Stewart, CFA

Reading 67 *Investing in Commodities*
Global Perspectives on Investment Management: Learning from the Leaders, edited by Rodney N. Sullivan, CFA

66

Introduction to Alternative Investments

by Terri Duhon, George Spentzos, CFA, and Scott D. Stewart, CFA

LEARNING OUTCOMES

Mastery	The candidate should be able to:
☐	**a** compare alternative investments with traditional investments;
☐	**b** describe categories of alternative investments;
☐	**c** describe potential benefits of alternative investments in the context of portfolio management;
☐	**d** describe hedge funds, private equity, real estate, commodities, and other alternative investments, including, as applicable, strategies, sub-categories, potential benefits and risks, fee structures, and due diligence;
☐	**e** describe issues in valuing, and calculating returns on, hedge funds, private equity, real estate, and commodities;
☐	**f** describe, calculate, and interpret management and incentive fees and net-of-fees returns to hedge funds;
☐	**g** describe risk management of alternative investments

INTRODUCTION

Assets under management in vehicles classified as alternative investments have grown rapidly since the mid-1990s. This growth has largely been because of the interest in these investments by institutions, such as endowment and pension funds, and high net worth individuals seeking diversification and return opportunities. Alternative investments are perceived to behave differently from traditional investments. Many investors hope they will provide positive returns throughout the economic cycle; this goal is an absolute return objective. A relative return objective, which is often the objective of portfolios of traditional investments, seeks to achieve a return relative to an equity or fixed income benchmark. However, despite an absolute return objective, alternative investments are not free of risk and may be correlated with other investments, including traditional investments, especially in periods of financial crisis.

This reading is organized as follows. Section 2 describes alternative investments, their basic characteristics and categories; general strategies of alternative investment portfolio managers; the role of alternative investments in a diversified portfolio; and investment structures used to provide access to alternative investments. Sections 3, 4, 5, and 6 describe features of hedge funds, private equity, real estate, and commodities, respectively, along with issues in calculating returns to and valuation of each. Section 7 briefly describes other alternative investments. Section 8 provides an overview of risk management, including due diligence, of alternative investments. A summary and practice problems conclude the reading.

ALTERNATIVE INVESTMENTS

Alternative investments fall outside of the definition of long-only investments in stocks, bonds, and cash (often referred to as traditional investments). In other words, they are alternatives to long-only positions in stocks, bonds, and cash. The usage of the terms traditional and alternatives should not be construed to imply that alternatives are necessarily uncommon and/or relatively recent additions to the investment universe. Alternative investments include investments in assets such as real estate and commodities, which are arguably two of the oldest investment classes.

Alternative investments also include non-traditional approaches to investing within special vehicles, such as private equity funds, hedge funds, and some exchange traded funds (ETFs). These funds typically give the manager flexibility to use derivatives and leverage, make investments in illiquid assets, and take short positions. The assets invested in can include traditional assets (stocks, bonds, and cash) as well as other assets. Management of alternative investments is almost always active. Alternative investments, particularly investments through special vehicles, are often characterized by high fees, low diversification of managers and investments within the alternatives investment portfolio (because of the large size of investments), high use of leverage, and restrictions on fund redemptions.

There are several other characteristics common to many alternative investments. An alternative investment may not be expected to have all these characteristics but will typically be expected to have many of them. These characteristics include the following:

- Illiquidity of underlying investments
- Narrow manager specialization
- Low correlation with traditional investments
- Low level of regulation and less transparency
- Limited and potentially problematic historical risk and return data
- Unique legal and tax considerations

Although assets under management in alternative investments have grown rapidly, they remain a small part of total investable assets, as illustrated in Exhibit 1.

Exhibit 1	Global Assets Under Management, September 2010 (in trillions USD)

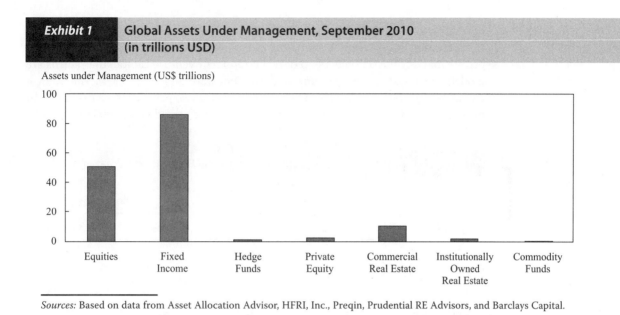

Sources: Based on data from Asset Allocation Advisor, HFRI, Inc., Preqin, Prudential RE Advisors, and Barclays Capital.

Institutions and high net worth individuals have been at the forefront of those investing in alternative investments in the expectation of diversifying their portfolios and enhancing their risk/return profiles. Their hopes that alternative investments will behave differently from traditional investments and will provide positive absolute returns throughout the economic cycle may not be realistic. Alternative investments are not free of risk and may be correlated with other risky investments, especially in periods of financial crisis. Over a long historical time period, the average correlation with traditional investments may be low but, in any particular period, the correlation can differ from the average correlation.

Investors must be careful in evaluating the historical record of alternative investments because reported return data can be problematic. Further, reported returns and standard deviations are averages and may not be representative of sub-periods within the reported period or future periods. Many investments, such as direct real estate and private equity are often valued using estimated values (appraised values) rather than actual market prices for the subject investments; as a result, the volatility of returns, as well as the correlation of returns with the returns of traditional asset classes, will tend to be underestimated. Venture capital market returns may be estimated using the technique proposed by Woodward and Hall (2004) to address data problems with historical published indices, which reflect underlying investments held at cost. [1] The record of manager universes, such as hedge fund indices, may be subject to a variety of biases, including survivorship and backfill biases.[2] Thus, the indices may be inherently biased upwards. Commodity indices can be highly weighted in one particular sector, such as oil and gas. Different weightings and constituents in index construction can significantly affect the indices and their results and comparability.

Exhibit 2 shows the historical returns to various investment classes, as well as the standard deviations of the returns, based on selected indices. The indices were selected for their breadth and data quality but nevertheless may not be fully representative

---

[1] This technique involves statistical estimation of quarterly market returns utilizing published Thomson Reuters VC index returns and NASDAQ market index returns.

[2] Survivorship bias is a bias related to the inclusion of only "live" investment funds. The returns of funds that have been liquidated are excluded. Backfill bias is the bias that results from including previous return data for funds that enter the index. Both biases may result in returns that are artificially high because the survivorship bias most likely results in the index excluding poorly performing funds, and the backfill bias most likely results in the index including high-performing funds.

of returns to the investment class. For example, the return to the Global S&P REIT index may not be representative of returns to equity investment in real estate through private markets (direct ownership of real estate). For venture capital, the returns are modeled using the technique proposed by Woodward and Hall (2004). The average annual returns and standard deviations are shown for two periods: the 20-year period of 1Q1990 to 4Q2009 and the two and a quarter-year period of 4Q2007 to 4Q2009.

Exhibit 2	Alternative Investments Historical Returns and Volatilities			
	1Q1990–4Q2009		4Q2007–4Q2009	
Index	Mean	St. Dev.	Mean	St. Dev.
Global stocks	6.2%	16.8%	−10.8%	24.2%
Global bonds	7.2	6.0	6.7	9.0
Hedge funds	8.2	6.4	−4.9	8.0
Commodities	4.5	23.4	−15.9	32.1
Real estate	9.4	18.5	−17.6	33.8
Private equity	10.8	19.4	−10.0	27.8
Venture capital	12.4	25.9	−9.5	29.9
LIBOR	4.2	0.6	1.9	0.5

Note: Mean and standard deviation are based on annualized U.S. dollar returns.
Sources: Global stocks = MSCI All Country World Index; Global bonds = Barclays Capital Global Aggregate Bond Index; Hedge funds = HFRI Fund of Funds Composite Index; Commodities = S&P GSCI Commodity Index; Real estate = S&P Global REIT Index; Private equity = S&P Listed Private Equity Index; Venture capital = Modeled using Thomson Reuters and NASDAQ indices.

Over the 20-year period, the mean returns to hedge funds, real estate, private equity, and venture capital exceeded the mean returns to global stocks and bonds. The average standard deviation of all but hedge funds also exceeded the average standard deviation of global stocks and bonds. Hedge funds appear to have had a higher average return and lower standard deviation than global stocks over the 20-year period but this may be due, at least partially, to hedge fund indices' reporting biases. Commodities had the lowest mean return over the 20-year period and higher standard deviation than all but venture capital. The higher mean returns of alternative investments, except for commodities, compared with stocks and bonds, may be because of active managers' exploitation of less efficiently priced assets, illiquidity premiums, and/or account leverage. The higher mean returns may also be the result of tax advantages. For example, REITs may not be subject to taxes at the fund level if they meet certain conditions. In a poorly performing economy, the use of leverage and investment in illiquid assets may be reasonably expected to lead to poor results. During 4Q2007 to 4Q2009, the mean returns to alternative investments, other than hedge funds, were similar to or even lower than those to global stocks, and the standard deviations exceeded those of global stocks. Alternative investments did not provide the desired protection during 4Q2007 to 4Q2009, a period categorized as a time of financial crisis. The average returns and standard deviations for the 20-year period of 1Q1990 to 4Q2009 are very different from the average returns and standard deviations for the shorter sub-period of 4Q2007 to 4Q2009. However, it is the long-term potential that attracts many investors.

The 2007 annual report for the Yale University Endowment provides one investor's reasoning behind the attractiveness of investing in alternatives:

"The heavy allocation [70% target allocation] in 2007 to nontraditional asset classes stems from their return potential and diversifying power. Today's actual and target portfolios have significantly higher expected returns and lower volatility than the 1987 portfolio. Alternative assets, by their very nature, tend to be less efficiently priced than traditional marketable securities, providing an opportunity to exploit market inefficiencies through active management. The Endowment's long time horizon is well suited to exploiting illiquid, less efficient markets such as venture capital, leveraged buyouts, oil and gas, timber, and real estate."[3]

The link between the quote above and the expected characteristics of alternative investments is clear: diversifying power (low correlation), higher expected returns (positive absolute return), and illiquid and potentially less efficient markets. This link also highlights the importance of having the ability and willingness to take a long-term prospective. Allocating a portion of an endowment portfolio to alternative investments is not unique to Yale. INSEAD, as of September 2007, had allocated its endowment heavily into alternative investments: 22 percent was in real assets, 24 percent was in hedge funds, and 10 percent was in private equity. The remaining 44 percent was invested evenly in traditional financial assets such as global stocks and bonds.[4] This example is not to imply that every university endowment fund is invested heavily in alternative investments. For example, the London School of Economics and Political Science endowment funds are split into three pools and only one, as of 2006, had a target asset allocation of 10 percent into alternative investments.[5]

High net worth investors have also embraced alternative investments. According to the Spectrem Group's 2010 study of American investors with assets greater than $25 million, more than half have allocations to hedge funds, private equity, and venture capital, with 20 percent of the total portfolio allocated to alternatives investments.[6] The increasing interest by institutions and high net worth individuals in alternative investments has resulted in significant growth in each category since the beginning of 2000. The following are examples of growth in the categories of private equity, real estate, and commodities.

- The Private Equity Council estimated that private equity leveraged buyout deals were approximately $720 billion in 2007 compared with $100 billion in 2000.[7]

- Ernst & Young reported a growth in global real estate investment trusts (REITs) from $608 billion as of 30 June 2006 to $764 billion as of 30 June 2007. In 1990, the market capitalization of the global REITs was less than $10 billion.[8]

- According to calculations published by the U.S. Commodity Futures Trading Commission, assets allocated to commodity index trading strategies have risen from $13 billion in 2003 to $260 billion in March 2008.[9]

The enthusiasm for alternative investments was tested during 2008 when alternative investment assets under management declined as losses were incurred and funds were withdrawn. However, alternative investments continue to represent a significant proportion of the portfolios of pension funds, endowments, foundations, and high net worth individuals.

---

3 www.yale.edu/investments/Yale_Endowment_07.pdf.

4 www.insead.com/campaign/how_contribute/documents/Endowment_FAQ's2007_10_15.doc.

5 www.lse.ac.uk/collections/financeDivision/pdf/2006AnnualAccounts.pdf.

6 See "Ultra-Wealthy Embracing Hedge Funds", *Financial Planning*, 12 November 2010.

7 Private Equity Council, *Public Value: A Primer on Private Equity*, 2007.

8 Ernst & Young, *Global Real Estate Investment Trust Report*, 2007.

9 CIT Supplemental Report, March 2008; CFTC Commitment of Traders Report.

> **EXAMPLE 1**
>
> ## Characteristics of Alternative Investments
>
> Compared with traditional investments, alternative investments are *most likely* to be characterized by high:
>
> **A.** leverage.
>
> **B.** liquidity.
>
> **C.** regulation.
>
> ### Solution:
>
> A is correct. Alternative investments are likely to use more leverage than traditional investments. Alternative investments are likely to be more illiquid and subject to less regulation.

2.1 Categories of Alternative Investments

Considering the variety of characteristics common to many alternative investments, it is not surprising that no consensus exists on a definitive list of these investments. There is even considerable debate as to what represents a category versus a sub-category of alternative investments. For instance, some listings define distressed securities as a separate category whereas other listings consider distressed securities as a sub-category of the hedge funds and/or private equity categories, or even a subset of high yield bond investing. Similarly, managed futures are sometimes defined as a separate category and sometimes as a sub-category of hedge funds and/or commodities. The listing below is one approach to define broad categories of alternative investments. Each of the categories is described in detail later in this reading.

■ **Hedge Funds**: Hedge funds are private investment vehicles that manage portfolios of securities and derivative positions using a variety of strategies. They may employ long and short positions, are often highly leveraged, and aim to deliver positive total performance regardless of broad market performance.

■ **Private Equity Funds**: Private equity funds generally invest in companies (either start-up or established) that are not listed on a public exchange, or in public companies with the intent to take them private. The majority of private equity activity involves **leveraged buyouts** of established profitable and cash generative companies with solid customer bases, proven products, and high quality management. **Venture capital**, which typically involves investing in or providing financing to start-up or young companies with high growth potential, is a small portion of the private equity market.

■ **Real Estate**: Real estate investments may be in buildings and/or land, including timberland and farmland, either directly or indirectly. The growing popularity of securitization structures broadened the definition of real estate investing. It now includes private commercial real estate equity (e.g., ownership of an office building), private commercial real estate debt (e.g., directly issued loans or mortgages on commercial property), public real estate equity (e.g., REITs), and public commercial real estate debt (e.g., commercial mortgage-backed securities) investments.

■ **Commodities**: Commodities investments may be in physical commodity products such as grains, metals, and crude oil, either through owning cash instruments, utilizing derivative products, or investing in businesses engaged in the production of physical commodities. The main vehicles used by investors to gain exposure to commodities are commodity futures contracts and funds benchmarked to commodity indices. Commodity indices are typically based on various underlying commodity futures.

- **Other**: Other alternative investments may include tangible assets (such as fine wine, art, antique furniture and automobiles, stamps, coins, and other collectibles) and intangible assets (such as patents).

2.2 Return: General Strategies

Managers of portfolios invest in one of two basic ways to achieve returns: passively or actively. Passive managers assume that markets are efficient and focus on beta drivers of return. Beta, a measure of sensitivity relative to a particular market index, is a measure of systematic risk.[10] Active managers assume that inefficiencies exist that may be exploited to earn positive return after adjusting for beta risk. This is defined as alpha return. The expected alpha return is zero for passive managers. There are many approaches to managing alternative investment funds, but typically these funds are actively managed and are expected to generate positive alpha return.

Total return = Alpha return + Beta return

Beta-driven portfolios are positioned to efficiently take on market risk. For example, an investment fund that closely tracks the S&P 500 index would be said to be entirely driven by beta. This type of fund seeks to replicate the return on the "market" and thus should be 100 percent correlated to the "market" as represented by the S&P 500 index.

Alpha returns are by definition uncorrelated with beta returns and are presumably the result of managers' special skills in capturing non-systematic opportunities in the market. The fact that these returns, at least in theory, cannot be explained by market risk makes them valuable and sought after. Alpha returns in theory are well suited as performance enhancers and diversifiers in an investment portfolio. In practice, managers' records of delivering unique alpha returns are mixed. Many purported active portfolio exposures, such as style biases and macro positions, are in fact correlated with the markets and as a result largely generate beta returns rather than alpha returns.

Portfolios of real estate investment trusts (REITs) and commodity and infrastructure exchange traded funds (ETFs) may provide beta exposure to a category of alternative investments. However, alternative investments generally claim to offer alpha return opportunities. Alpha-seeking alternative investment strategies reflect several characteristics that differentiate them from long-only passive investments in traditional assets. Basic alpha-seeking strategies (these are not mutually exclusive) can be categorized as follows:

- **Absolute return**: Absolute return strategies seek to generate returns that are independent of market returns; theoretically, betas of funds using absolute return strategies should be close to zero.[11] As a result, with an absolute return strategy, there is typically no market index specified to beat. Instead, the formal performance objective tends to be stated relative to either a cash rate such as LIBOR, a return over the rate of inflation (a real return target), or an absolute, nominal return target such as 10 percent.

- **Market segmentation**: Market segmentation exists when capital cannot migrate effortlessly from lower expected return areas to higher ones. Segmentation typically results from institutional, contractual, or regulatory restrictions on traditional asset managers or from differences across investors

---

10 Systematic risk should not be confused with the term "systemic" risk, which is used in the credit markets to mean highly correlated default risk.
11 In practice, most funds have some market exposure.

in investment objectives or liabilities. Segmentation brought on by investment constraints includes portfolios managed relative to published market indices, limitations on the use of derivatives, and restrictions on the proportion of low quality or foreign securities. These restrictions provide an opportunity for more flexible managers to move into higher returning segments more quickly than more restricted or conservative investors.

- **Concentrated portfolios**: This strategy entails concentrating assets among fewer securities, strategies, and/or managers, which results in less diversification but may enable an investor to achieve higher returns if these concentrated positions outperform the market. Concentrated portfolio strategies are attractive because of high-alpha potential.

Although much of the attraction of alternative investments seems to be based on returns, the risks associated with those returns must also be factored in. Risks can be considered both on a stand-alone basis and within the context of a portfolio (the modern portfolio theory approach). As mentioned earlier, risks for alternative investments include low liquidity, limited redemption availability and transparency, and the challenge of manager diversification.

Returns may be measured relative to stand-alone risk using risk ratios and exploring return distributions. A commonly reported risk ratio is the Sharpe Ratio, which equals an investment's return, net of a risk-free rate, divided by its return standard deviation; it is a common measure among the investment community because of the ease of calculation using historical results. Other risk measures, such as those that emphasize downside risk, are also frequently considered.[12]

Sharpe ratios for traditional and alternative investments, based on the same information used in Exhibit 2, are shown in Panel A of Exhibit 3. It should be noted that the reported or available historical return data used may not be reliable and/or representative of the return data for the investment class.

Many downside risk measures, such as the chance of losing a certain amount of money in a given period, are used in practice. Panel B of Exhibit 3 includes some measures indicative of downside risk: the frequencies of monthly returns less than −1 percent, −5 percent, and −10 percent during 1990–2009, and in the right column, the worst return reported in a month.

Exhibit 3	Sharpe Ratios and Downside Risk Measures, Based on 1990–2009 Returns

Panel A: Sharpe Ratios (using annualized returns)

Index	
Global stocks	0.12
Global bonds	0.50
Hedge funds	0.62
Commodities	0.01
Real estate	0.28
Private equity	0.34
Venture capital	0.32

[12] The Sharpe ratio is discussed in greater detail in the CFA Program Level I Quantitative Methods reading "Statistical Concepts and Market Returns." Other risk measures include Treynor, Jensen, and Sortino ratios and value at risk (VaR), which are also discussed in Level I of the CFA Program.

Exhibit 3	Continued

Panel B: Downside Frequencies

Index	Frequency of Monthly Return Less Than...			Worst Monthly Return
	–1%	–5%	–10%	
Global stocks	32.1%	10.0%	2.1%	–19.8%
Global bonds	15.0	0.0	0.0	–3.8
Hedge funds	12.5	1.3	0.0	–7.5
Commodities	37.1	16.3	4.6	–28.2
Real estate	28.8	5.8	2.5	–30.5
Private equity	29.6	10.8	2.5	–23.4
Venture capital	30.0	16.7	3.8	–24.5

Sharpe ratios (using LIBOR as a proxy for the risk-free rate) indicate that based on reported data, during 1990–2009, hedge funds offered the best risk–return trade-off and commodities the worst. Venture capital displayed a similar downside risk profile as commodities but its higher reported return (see Exhibit 2) results in a higher Sharpe ratio over the period. Hedge funds offered similar downside risk as bonds and a higher Sharpe ratio.

The Sharpe ratio and downside risk measures do not take into account the potentially low level of correlation of alternative investments with traditional investments. A less than perfect correlation between investments reduces the standard deviation of a diversified portfolio below the weighted average of the standard deviations of the investments. Risk in the portfolio context is discussed in the next section.

2.3 Portfolio Context: Integration of Alternative Investments with Traditional Investments

A key motivation cited for investing in alternative investments is their diversifying potential; there is a perceived opportunity to improve the risk/return relationship within the portfolio context. Given the historical return, volatility, and correlation profiles of alternative investments, combining a portfolio of alternative investments with a portfolio of traditional investments potentially improves the risk/return profile of the overall portfolio. The correlation between some categories of alternative investments and traditional investments has historically over long periods been low, or at least less than perfect, providing diversification opportunities. The historically higher returns to most categories of alternative investments compared with traditional investments result in potentially higher returns to a portfolio containing alternative investments, and the less than perfect correlation with traditional investments results in portfolio risk (standard deviation) being less than a weighting of the standard deviations. However, in identifying the appropriate allocation to alternative investments, an investment manager is likely to consider more than mean return and average standard deviation of returns. When considering potential portfolio combinations, historical downside frequencies and worst return in a month for potential portfolio combinations may be included in the analysis.

The purported diversification benefits and improved risk–return contributions of alternative investments to portfolios explains why institutional investors such as pension funds may allocate a portion of their portfolios to alternative investments.

However, there are challenges; these include getting reliable measures of risk and return, identifying the appropriate allocation, and selecting portfolio managers.

2.4 Investment Structures

The most common structure for many alternative investments, such as hedge funds and private equity funds, is a partnership, where the fund is the **general partner** (GP) and investors are **limited partners** (LPs). Limited partnerships are restricted to investors who are expected to understand and to be able to assume the risks associated with the investments. Fund investments, because they are not offered to the general public, may not be regulated or be less regulated than offerings to the general public.[13] The GP runs the business and theoretically bears unlimited liability for anything that might go wrong. Because most individuals are unwilling to bear unlimited liability, the GP is usually a limited liability corporation. Limited partners own a fractional interest in the partnership based on their investment and as agreed to by the partners; an LP's fractional interest is often referred to as his or her share of the partnership. These partnerships are frequently located in tax-efficient locations, which benefit both the GP and the LPs. Funds set up as private investment partnerships typically have a limit on the number of LPs.[14]

Funds are generally structured with a **management fee** based on assets under management (sometimes called the base fee) plus an **incentive fee (or performance fee)** based on realized profits. Sometimes, the fee structure specifies that the incentive fee is only earned after the fund achieves a specified return known as a hurdle rate. Fee calculations also take into account **high water marks**, which reflect the highest cumulative return used to calculate an incentive fee. It is the highest value, net of fees, that the fund has reached. The use of high water marks protects clients from paying twice for the same performance. This basic partnership and fee structure is used by many alternative investment funds, including hedge funds. Fee structures are discussed in more detail later in the reading.

HEDGE FUNDS

In 1949 Alfred Winslow Jones, a sociologist investigating fundamental and technical research to forecast the stock market for *Fortune* magazine, set up an investment fund with himself as general partner. The fund followed three key tenets: (1) always maintain short positions, (2) always use leverage, and (3) only charge an incentive fee of 20 percent of profits with no fixed fees. Jones called his portfolio a "hedged" fund (eventually shortened to "hedge fund") because he had short positions to offset his long positions in the stock market. Theoretically, the overall portfolio was hedged against major market moves.

Although Jones' original three tenets still have some relevance to the hedge fund industry, not all hedge funds maintain short positions and/or use leverage, and most

---

13 In the United States, the U.S. Securities Act of 1933 regulates the process by which investment securities are offered. Most alternatives funds are structured as "private placements," which are defined within Regulation D of the Securities Act and sometimes called "Reg D Offerings."

14 Because of the inherent risk involved in alternative investments, investment is typically restricted to a specified number of investors meeting certain criteria. The number and the criteria can be specified by regulation or set by the fund. In the U.S., the number depends on whether funds target *"Accredited Investors"* or *"Qualified Purchasers"* (as defined by the Investment Company Act of 1940, Sections 3(c) 1 and 7, respectively). A fund can have no more than 100 Accredited Investors (individuals with at least $1 million and institutions with at least $5 million in investable assets) or no more than 500 Qualified Purchasers (individuals with at least $5 million and institutions with at least $25 million in investable assets).

hedge funds have some non-incentive fees. The typical contemporary hedge fund can be characterized as follows:

- It is an aggressively managed portfolio of investments across asset classes and regions that is leveraged, takes long and short positions, and/or uses derivatives.

- It has a goal of generating high returns, either in an absolute sense or over a specified market benchmark and has few, if any, investment restrictions.

- It is set up as a private investment partnership open to a limited number of investors willing and able to make a large initial investment.

- It often imposes restrictions on **redemptions**. Investors may be required to keep their money in the hedge fund for a minimum period (referred to as a **lockup period**) before they are allowed to make withdrawals or redeem shares. Investors may be required to give notice of their intent to redeem; the **notice period** is typically 30 to 90 days in length. Also, investors may be charged a fee to redeem shares.

The willingness of investors to invest in hedge funds, despite the restrictions on redemptions, is largely because of the reported returns of some hedge funds and their perceived low correlation with traditional investments. The positive performance of many funds in the early 2000s when other investments had declined supported the diversification potential of hedge funds in a portfolio. The growth of interest in hedge funds as investments led to the emergence of funds of funds.

Funds of funds are funds that hold a portfolio of hedge funds. They make hedge funds accessible to smaller investors, while allowing them to be diversified to some extent among hedge funds. Also, funds of funds presumably have some expertise in conducting due diligence on hedge funds and may be able to negotiate better redemption terms. Funds of funds invest in numerous hedge funds, diversifying across fund strategies, investment regions, and management styles. The distinction between a single fund and a fund of funds is not necessarily clear-cut because many hedge funds invest in other hedge funds.

Hedge funds are less restricted than traditional investment managers and thus may have the flexibility to invest anywhere they see opportunity. This characteristic is best exemplified in the concept of a side pocket, which allows hedge funds the flexibility to invest a percentage of the assets under management, generally less than 20 percent, how and when they see fit. Most hedge funds do have a broadly stated strategy, and a side pocket allows some deviation from the strategy. A hedge fund can also be structured as one "asset management" business that is "contracted" to manage several different funds (e.g., SuperStar Asset Management might manage SuperStar Credit Fund, SuperStar Commodities Fund, and SuperStar Multi-Strategy Fund).

The growing popularity of hedge funds is illustrated in Exhibit 4, which shows assets under management and net asset flows for the period of 1990 through 2010. Assets under management grew from approximately $39 billion in 1990 to $491 billion in 2000 to $1,868 billion in 2007. Comparing net asset flows to the change in assets under management indicates that much of the growth in assets under management was because of performance. In 2008, assets under management declined because of withdrawals (a negative net asset flow) and a decline in the value of the assets under management. In 2009, a negative net asset flow was offset by an increase in the value of the assets under management. In 2010, assets under management exceeded assets under management in 2007.

Exhibit 4	Growth of Assets Under Management, 1990–2010

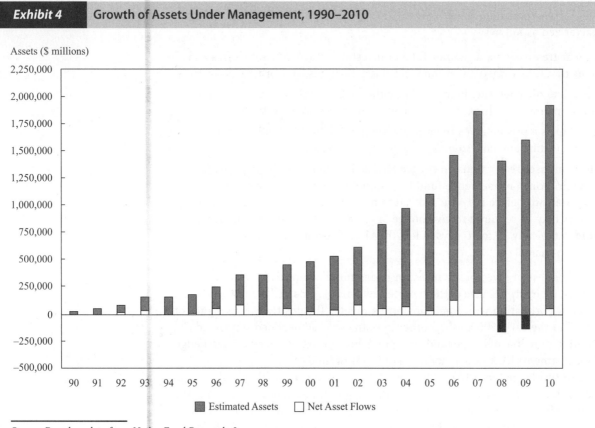

Assets ($ millions)

Source: Based on data from Hedge Fund Research, Inc.

Exhibit 5 illustrates the returns *net of fees* to hedge funds based on data provided by Hedge Fund Research, Inc. (HFRI). The HFRI family of indices includes the HFRI Fund Weighted Composite Index and the HFRI Fund of Funds Index. The HFRI Fund Weighted Composite Index is an equally weighted performance index based on the self-reported data of over 2,000 individual funds included in the HFR database. The HFRI Fund of Funds Index is an equally weighted performance index of funds of funds included in the HFR database. Both indices suffer from issues related to self-reporting, but the HFRI Fund of Funds Index reflects the actual performance of portfolios of hedge funds. This index may show a lower reported return because of the added layer of fees,[15] but it may be a more realistic representation of average hedge fund performance. The cumulative performance of the HFRI Fund of Funds Index exceeds that of the Barclays Capital Global Aggregate Bond Index[16] and the MSCI All Country World Index[17] (a global equity index) over the period of 1990 to 2009.

---

15 A fund of funds has an extra layer of fees. Each hedge fund in which a fund of funds invests is structured to receive a management fee plus a performance fee, and the fund of funds is also structured to receive a management fee plus a performance fee.
16 The Barclays Capital Global Aggregate Bond Index provides a broad-based measure of the global investment grade fixed-rate debt markets.
17 The MSCI All Country World Index is based on equity indices of 45 countries: 24 developed and 21 emerging. It is a free float-adjusted market capitalization weighted index.

Exhibit 5	Performance of Funds of Funds, Global Bonds, and Global Stocks, 1990–2009

1990 = 100

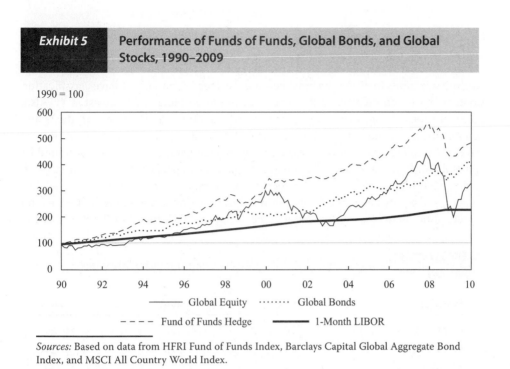

Sources: Based on data from HFRI Fund of Funds Index, Barclays Capital Global Aggregate Bond Index, and MSCI All Country World Index.

Exhibit 6 compares the return and a variety of risk and performance measures of the HFRI Hedge Fund of Funds Index, the MSCI Global Total Return Index, the Barclays Capital Global Aggregate Bond Index, and LIBOR. As shown in Exhibit 5, the "worst drawdown" reflecting the period of largest cumulative negative returns for hedge funds and global equities was over the period that began in 2007 (when each peaked) and ended in 2009. Over the 20-year period, hedge funds had a higher average annualized return and a lower annualized volatility and so appeared to dominate equities in both return and risk. Note that the returns and volatilities (standard deviations) represent an average and are not representative of any single year. Over this period, global bonds appear to have superior returns compared with global stocks. This result is surprising given the expected risk–return relationships. In fact, this outcome is primarily because of the poor performance of stocks over the years 2008 and 2009 (see Exhibit 2).

Exhibit 6	Risk–Return Characteristics of Hedge Funds and Other Investments, 1990–2009

	FoF Hedge	Global Stocks	Global Bonds	1-Mo. LIBOR
Annualized return	8.2%	6.2%	7.2%	4.2%
Annualized volatility	6.4%	16.8%	6.0%	0.6%
Sharpe Ratio	0.62	0.12	0.50	
% Positive months	71.7%	61.3%	63.8%	100.0%
Best month	6.9%	11.9%	6.2%	0.7%
Worst month	−7.5%	−19.8%	−3.8%	0.0%
Worst drawdown	−22.2%	−54.6%	−10.1%	0.0%

Sources: FoF Hedge data are from HFRI Fund of Funds Weighted Composite Index; global stocks data are from MSCI World All Country Total Returns Index; global bonds data are from Barclays Capital Global Aggregate Bond Index.

3.1 Hedge Fund Strategies

Hedge funds are typically classified by strategy, but categorizations vary. Many classifying organizations focus on the most common strategies, but others have classification systems based on different criteria such as the underlying assets invested in. Also, classifications change over time as new strategies, often based on new products and opportunities in the market, are introduced. Classifying hedge funds is important so that investors can review aggregate performance data, select strategies to build a portfolio of funds, and select or construct appropriate performance benchmarks. In 2008, HFRI identified four broad categories of strategies: event-driven, relative value, macro, and equity hedge.[18] Exhibit 7 shows the approximate percentage of hedge fund assets under management by strategy, according to HFRI, for 1990, 2008, and 2010.

Exhibit 7	Percentage of Assets under Management by Strategy		
Strategy	**1990**	**2008**	**2010**
Event-driven	10	25	26
Relative value	14	25	24
Macro	39	16	20
Equity hedge	37	34	30

3.1.1 *Event-Driven Strategies*

Event-driven strategies seek to profit from short-term events, typically involving potential changes in corporate structure such as an acquisition or restructuring, that are expected to affect individual companies. This strategy is considered "bottom up" (company level analysis followed by aggregation and analysis of a larger group, such as an industry) as opposed to "top down" (global macro analysis followed by sectoral/regional analysis followed by company analysis). Investments may include long and short positions in common and preferred stocks, as well as debt securities and options. Further subdivisions of this category by HFRI include the following:

■ Merger Arbitrage: Generally, these strategies involve going long (buying) the stock of the company being acquired and going short (selling) the stock of the acquiring company when the merger/acquisition is announced. The manager expects the acquirer to ultimately overpay for the acquisition and perhaps suffer from an increased debt load. The primary risk in this strategy is that the announced merger or acquisition does not occur, and the hedge fund has not closed its positions on a timely basis.

■ Distressed/Restructuring: These strategies focus on the securities of companies either in bankruptcy or perceived to be near to bankruptcy. There are a variety of ways hedge funds attempt to profit from distressed securities. The hedge fund may simply purchase fixed income securities trading at a significant discount to par. This transaction is done in anticipation of the company restructuring and the fund earning a profit from the subsequent sale of the securities. The hedge fund may also use a more complicated approach and buy senior debt and short junior debt or buy preferred stock and short common stock. This transaction is done in expectation of a profit as the spread between

---

18 The Chartered Alternative Investment Analyst (CAIA) Association classifies hedge funds into four broad categories: corporate restructuring, convergence trading, opportunistic, and market directional. These approximately coincide with event-driven, relative value, macro, and equity hedge, respectively.

the securities widens. The fund may also short sell the company's stock, but this transaction involves considerable risk given the potential for loss if the company's prospects improve.

- Activist: The term activist is a shortened form of "activist shareholder." These strategies focus on the purchase of sufficient equity in order to influence a company's policies or direction. For example, the activist hedge fund may advocate for divestitures, restructuring, capital distributions to shareholders, and/or changes in management and company strategy. These hedge funds are distinct from private equity because they operate in the public equity market.

- Special Situations: These strategies focus on opportunities in the equity of companies that are currently engaged in restructuring activities other than merger/acquisitions and bankruptcy. These activities include security issuance/repurchase, special capital distributions, and asset sales/spin-offs.

3.1.2 *Relative Value Strategies*

Relative value funds seek to profit from a pricing discrepancy (an unusual short-term relationship) between related securities. The expectation is that the pricing discrepancy will be resolved in time. This strategy typically involves buying and selling related securities. Examples of relative value strategies include the following:

- Fixed Income Convertible Arbitrage: These are market neutral (a zero beta portfolio, at least in theory) investment strategies that seek to exploit a perceived mispricing between a convertible bond and its component parts (the underlying bond and the embedded stock option). The strategy typically involves buying convertible debt securities and simultaneously selling the same issuer's common stock.

- Fixed Income Asset Backed: These strategies focus on the relative value between a variety of asset-backed securities (ABS) and mortgage-backed securities (MBS) and seek to take advantage of mispricing across different asset-backed securities.

- Fixed Income General: These strategies focus on the relative value within the fixed income markets. Strategies may incorporate trades between two corporate issuers, between corporate and government issuers, between different parts of the same issuer's capital structure, or between different parts of an issuer's yield curve. Currency dynamics and government yield curve considerations may also come into play when managing these fixed income instruments.

- Volatility: These strategies typically use options to go long or short market volatility either in a specific asset class or across asset classes.

- Multi-Strategy: These strategies trade relative value within and across asset classes or instruments. The strategy does not focus upon one type of trade (e.g., convertible arbitrage), a single basis for trade (e.g., volatility), or a particular asset class (e.g., fixed income) but instead looks for investment opportunities wherever they might exist.

3.1.3 *Macro Strategies*

Macro hedge funds emphasize a "top down" approach to identify economic trends evolving across the world. Trades are made based on expected movements in economic variables. Generally, these funds trade opportunistically in the fixed income, equity, currency, and commodity markets. Macro hedge funds use long and/or short positions to potentially profit from a view on overall market direction as influenced by major economic trends and/or events.

3.1.4 *Equity Hedge Strategies*

Equity hedge strategies can be thought of as the original hedge fund category. They are focused on public equity markets and take long and short positions in equity and equity derivative securities. They are not focused on equity trades categorized as consistent with Event-driven or Macro strategies. Equity hedge strategies use a "bottom up" as opposed to "top down" approach. Others, not structured as hedge funds, may use some similar strategies. Examples of equity hedge strategies include the following:

▪ Market Neutral: These strategies use quantitative (technical) and/or fundamental analysis to identify under- and over-valued equity securities. The hedge fund takes long positions in securities it has identified as undervalued and short positions in securities it has identified as overvalued. The hedge fund tries to maintain a net position that is neutral with respect to market risk. Ideally, the portfolio should have a beta of approximately zero. The intent is to profit from individual securities movements while hedging against market risk.

▪ Fundamental Growth: These strategies use fundamental analysis to identify companies expected to exhibit high growth and capital appreciation. The hedge fund takes long positions in identified companies.

▪ Fundamental Value: These strategies use fundamental analysis to identify companies that are undervalued. The hedge fund takes long positions in identified companies.

▪ Quantitative Directional: These strategies use technical analysis to identify companies that are under- and overvalued and to ascertain relationships between securities. The hedge fund takes long positions in securities identified as undervalued and short positions in securities identified as overvalued. The hedge fund typically varies levels of net long or short exposure depending upon the anticipated direction of the market and stage in the market cycle. Similar long/short approaches exist that are based upon fundamental analysis.

▪ Short Bias: These strategies use quantitative (technical) and/or fundamental analysis to identify overvalued equity securities. The hedge fund takes short positions in securities identified as overvalued. The fund typically varies its net short exposure based upon market expectations, going fully short in declining markets.

▪ Sector Specific: These strategies exploit expertise in a particular sector and use quantitative (technical) and fundamental analysis to identify opportunities in the sector.

Many hedge funds start as a focused operation, specializing in one strategy or asset class and if successful, diversify and over time become multi-strategy funds. Large, multi-strategy funds are an alternative to funds of funds. Although funds of funds may offer advantages (for example, access by smaller investors, diversified hedge fund portfolio, better redemption terms, and/or due diligence expertise) that multi-strategy funds do not have, a primary difference between a multi-strategy hedge fund and a fund of funds is the extra layer of fees associated with a fund of funds. Each hedge fund in which a fund of funds invests is structured to receive a management fee plus an incentive fee, and the fund of funds is also structured to receive a management fee plus an incentive fee.

3.2 Hedge Funds and Diversification Benefits

Given the broad range of strategies across hedge funds, general statements about hedge fund performance are not necessarily meaningful. Further, there is a general lack of performance persistence; hedge fund strategies that generate the highest returns in some years can be the ones to perform the most poorly in subsequent years.

The general premise of hedge funds is that they can make money (in other words, earn absolute returns) regardless of the stock market's direction. Their flexibility and the fact that they are not typically restricted to long only positions gives them the opportunity to respond to market fluctuations. In addition, hedge funds have traditionally been thought of as "arbitrage" players, meaning that they seek to earn returns while hedging against risks. Of course, in efficient markets, it is hard to find true arbitrage opportunities. In fact, one of the benefits some hedge funds provide to the financial marketplace is that they help make the markets more efficient by providing liquidity with contrarian views. As the hedge fund market has grown, many traditional hedge fund strategies have become increasingly crowded, forcing funds to take on more risk to generate competitive returns.

Less than perfect correlation with the stock market may provide diversification benefits. However, the sometimes claim that hedge fund performance is uncorrelated, not just less than perfectly correlated, with stock market performance is unsubstantiated. Looking at Exhibit 8, the claims of lack of correlation with the stock market appear to be supported in the period of 2000 to 2002, but are not supported in the subsequent period of 2003 to 2009. Further, during periods of financial crisis, the correlation between hedge fund and stock market performances may increase.

Exhibit 8	Returns for Hedge Fund, Global Stocks and Bonds, and LIBOR, 2000–2009

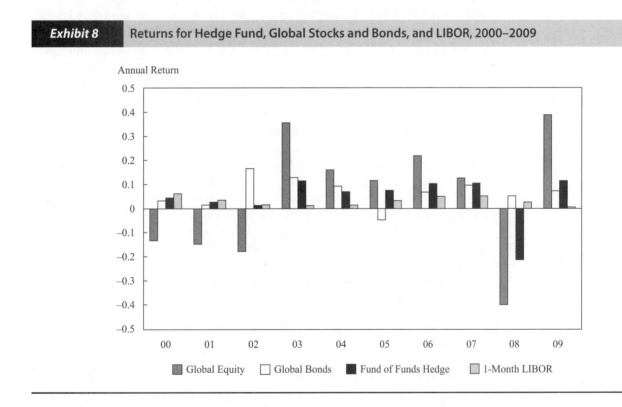

3.3 Hedge Fund Fees and Other Considerations

Hedge fund assets under management have grown over the 10-year period of 2000 through 2009, but they remain a small percentage of the asset management business overall. Hedge funds, however, earn a significantly higher percentage of fees. For example, in 2007 hedge funds managed 3 percent of total managed funds (hedge funds plus mutual funds) but earned 28 percent of managed fund revenue (fees).[19]

---

19 International Financial Services London estimates based on Watson Wyatt, Bridgewell, Merrill Lynch, ICI, SwissRe, and Hennessee Group data.

3.3.1 *Fees and Returns*

It is important to consider a hedge fund's fee structure prior to making an investment. The hedge fund fee structure accounts for the disproportionately high revenues earned relative to mutual funds and affects the returns to investors. A common fee structure in the hedge fund market is "2 and 20," which reflects a 2 percent management fee and a 20 percent incentive fee. Additionally, funds of funds typically charge a 1 percent management fee and a 10 percent incentive fee. The incentive fee may be calculated on profits net of management fees or on profits before management fees (in other words, the incentive fee is calculated independent of management fees).

Sometimes, the fee structure specifies that the incentive fee is only earned after the fund achieves a specified return known as a hurdle rate. The hurdle rate is frequently set based on a risk-free rate proxy (e.g., LIBOR or a specified Treasury bill rate) plus a premium but may be set as an absolute, nominal, or real return target. The incentive fee can be based on returns in excess of the hurdle rate (hard hurdle rate) or on the entire return (soft hurdle rate).

The fee structure may specify that before an incentive fee is paid, following a year in which the fund's value has declined, the fund's value must return to a previous high water mark. Note that the high water mark is typically the highest value reported by the fund; the amount reported is net of fees. High water marks reflect the highest cumulative return used to calculate an incentive fee. In other words, the hedge fund must recover its past losses and return to its high water mark before any additional incentive fee is earned. Clients are not charged an incentive fee if the latest cumulative return does not exceed the prior high water mark. This use of a high water mark protects clients from paying twice for the same performance. Although poorly performing hedge funds may not receive an incentive fee, the management fee is earned irrespective of returns.

Although "2 and 20" and "1 and 10" represent common fee structures for hedge funds and funds of funds, respectively, many fee structure variations exist in the marketplace. Not all hedge funds charge 2 and 20, and different classes of investors may have different fee structures. Hedge funds may be willing to negotiate terms, including fees and notice and lockup periods, with potential investors. A fee structure may differ from 2 and 20 based on the promised length of the investment. In other words, the longer investors agree to keep their money in the hedge fund, the lower the fees. A fee structure may vary from 2 and 20 based on supply and demand and historical performance. Sometimes, rebates or reductions in fees are given to investors or to the placement agent who introduced another investor to the hedge fund.

Fee structures and their effect on the resulting returns to investors are demonstrated in the following example.

Example 2

Fee and Return Calculations

AWJ Capital is a hedge fund with $100 million of initial investment capital. They charge a 2 percent management fee based on assets under management at year-end and a 20 percent incentive fee. In its first year, AWJ Capital has a 30 percent return. Assume management fees are calculated using end-of-period valuation.

1. What are the fees earned by AWJ if the incentive and management fees are calculated independently? What is an investor's effective return given this fee structure?

2. What are the fees earned by AWJ assuming that the incentive fee is calculated based on return net of the management fee? What is an investor's net return given this fee structure?

3. If the fee structure specifies a hurdle rate of 5 percent and the incentive fee is based on returns in excess of the hurdle rate, what are the fees earned by AWJ assuming the performance fee is calculated net of the management fee? What is an investor's net return given this fee structure?

In the second year, the fund value declines to $110 million.

4. The fee structure is as specified for question 1 but also includes the use of a high water mark. What are the fees earned by AWJ in the second year? What is an investor's net return for the second year given this fee structure?

In the third year, the fund value increases to $128 million.

5. The fee structure is as specified in questions 1 and 4. What are the fees earned by AWJ in the third year? What is an investor's net return for the third year given this fee structure?

6. What are the arithmetic and geometric mean annual returns over the three-year period based on the fee structure specified in questions 1, 4, and 5? What is the capital gain to the investor over the three-year period? What are the total fees paid to AWJ over the three-year period?

Solution to 1:

AWJ fees

$130 million × 2% = $2.6 million management fee

($130 − $100) million × 20% = $6 million incentive fee

Total fees to AWJ Capital = $8.6 million

Investor return: ($130 − $100 − $8.6)/$100 = 21.40%

Solution to 2:

$130 million × 2% = $2.6 million management fee

($130 − $100 − $2.6) million × 20% = $5.48 million incentive fee

Total fees to AWJ Capital = $8.08 million

Investor return: ($130 − $100 − $8.08)/$100 = 21.92%

Solution to 3:

$130 million × 2% = $2.6 million management fee

($130 − $100 − $5 − $2.6) million × 20% = $4.48 million incentive fee

Total fees to AWJ Capital = $7.08 million

Investor return: ($130 − $100 − $7.08)/$100 = 22.92%

Solution to 4:

$110 million × 2% = $2.2 million management fee

No incentive fee because the fund has declined in value.

Total fees to AWJ Capital = $2.2 million

Investor return: ($110 − $2.2 − $121.4)/$121.4 = −11.20%. The beginning capital position in the second year for the investors is ($130 − $8.6) million = $121.4 million. The ending capital position at the end of the second year is ($110 − $2.2) million= $107.8 million.

Solution to 5:

$128 million × 2% = $2.56 million management fee

($128 – $121.4) million× 20% = $1.32 million incentive fee. The $121.4 million represents the high-water mark established at the end of Year 1.

Total fees to AWJ Capital = $3.88 million

Investor return: ($128 – $3.88 – $107.8)/$107.8 = 15.14%. The ending capital position at the end of Year 3 is $124.12 million. This is the new high-water mark.

Solution to 6:

Arithmetic mean annual return = (21.4% – 11.20% + 15.14%)/3 = 8.45%

Geometric mean annual return = [cube root of (124.12/100)] – 1 = 7.47%

Capital gain to the investor = ($124.12 – $100) million = $24.12 million

Total fees = ($8.6 + $2.2 + $3.88) million = $14.68 million

As can be seen from the example, the return to an investor in a fund is significantly different from the return to the fund. Hedge fund indices generally report performance net of fees. However, if fee structures vary, the net-of-fees returns may vary among investors and from that included in the index. The multilayered fee structure of funds of funds has the effect of further diluting returns to the investor, but this disadvantage is balanced with several attractive features. Funds of funds may provide a diversified portfolio of hedge funds, may provide access to hedge funds that may otherwise be closed to direct investments, and may offer expertise in and conduct due diligence in selecting the individual hedge funds. Fund-of-funds money is considered "fast" money by hedge fund managers because fund-of-funds managers tend to be the first to redeem their money when hedge funds start to perform poorly, and they may also have negotiated redemption terms that are more favorable (for example, a shorter lockup period and/or notice period).

Example 3

Comparison of Returns—Investment Directly into a Hedge Fund or through a Fund of Funds

An investor is contemplating investing €100 million in either the ABC Hedge Fund (ABC HF) or the XYZ Fund of Funds (XYZ FOF). XYZ FOF has a "1 and 10" fee structure and invests 10 percent of its assets under management in ABC HF. ABC HF has a standard "2 and 20" fee structure with no hurdle rate. Management fees are calculated on an annual basis on assets under management at the beginning of the year. Management fees and incentive fees are calculated independently. ABC HF has a 20 percent return for the year before management and incentive fees.

1. Calculate the return to the investor of investing directly in ABC HF.

2. Calculate the return to the investor of investing in XYZ FOF. Assume that the other investments in the XYZ FOF portfolio generate the same return before management fees as ABC HF and have the same fee structure as ABC HF.

3. Why would the investor choose to invest in an FOF instead of an HF given the effect of the "double fee" as demonstrated in the answers to questions 1 and 2?

Solution to 1:

ABC HF has a profit before fees on a €100 million investment of €20 million (= 100 million × 20%). The management fee is €2 million (= €100 million × 2%) and the incentive fee is €4 million (= 20 million × 20%). The return to the investor is 14 percent [= (20 − 2 − 4)/100].

Solution to 2:

XYZ FOF earns a 14 percent return or €14 million profit after fees on €100 million invested with hedge funds. XYZ FOF charges the investor a management fee of €1 million (= €100 million × 1%) and an incentive fee of €1.4 million (= €14 million × 10%). The return to the investor is 11.6 percent [= (14 − 1 − 1.4)/100].

Solution to 3:

This scenario assumed that returns were the same for all underlying hedge funds. In practice, this result will not likely be the case, and XYZ FOF may provide due diligence expertise and potentially valuable diversification.

The hedge fund business is attractive to portfolio managers because the management fee of 2 percent alone can generate significant revenue if assets under management are large. Throughout the late 1990s and the early 2000s, many new hedge funds were launched. However, not all hedge funds launched remain in business long. One study suggests that more than a quarter of all hedge funds fail within the first three years because of performance problems.[20] This outcome is one of the reasons survivorship bias is such a problem in hedge fund indices. Because of the survivorship and backfill biases, hedge fund indices may not reflect actual average hedge fund performance but rather the performance of hedge funds that are performing well.

3.3.2 *Other Considerations*

Hedge funds may use leverage to seek higher returns on their investments. Leverage has the effect of magnifying gains or losses because the hedge fund can take a large position relative to the capital committed. Hedge funds may leverage their portfolios by borrowing capital and/or using derivatives.

For example, if a hedge fund expects the price of Nestlé SA (SIX Swiss Exchange: NESN) to increase, it can take a number of actions to benefit from the expected price increase. The fund can buy a thousand shares of Nestlé, buy 10 futures contracts on Nestlé on the NYSE Euronext, buy calls on a thousand shares of Nestlé, or sell puts on a thousand shares of Nestlé to profit from the expected price increase. The profit or loss from holding the futures will be similar to the profit or loss from holding the shares, but the capital requirement for the investment in the futures is far lower. If the hedge fund had bought calls on a thousand shares of Nestlé, the fund would have paid a relatively small premium and potentially experienced a significant profit if Nestlé had increased in price. The maximum loss to the fund would have been the premium paid. If the hedge fund had sold puts on a thousand shares of Nestlé expecting the price to rise and the puts to not be exercised, the fund would have a maximum profit equal to the relatively small premium received. However, if Nestlé declined in price, the potential loss is extremely large.

---

20 Brooks and Kat, 2002.

Investors, including hedge funds, may be required to put up some collateral when using derivatives if they are going to be exposed to potential losses on their positions. This collateral requirement helps to protect against default on the position and helps to protect the counterparty (or clearinghouse) on the derivative. The amount of collateral depends on the riskiness of the investment and the creditworthiness of the hedge fund or other investor.

The borrowing of capital also leverages a portfolio. It often takes the form of buying on margin. By borrowing, a hedge fund is able to invest a larger amount than was invested in the fund. Hedge funds normally trade through **prime brokers**, who provide services including custody, administration, lending, short borrowing, and trading. A hedge fund will normally negotiate its margin requirements with its prime broker(s). The prime broker effectively lends the hedge fund money to make investments, and the hedge fund puts money or other collateral into a margin account with the prime broker. The margin account represents the hedge fund's equity in the position. The margin requirement depends on the riskiness of the investment and the creditworthiness of the hedge fund.

The smaller the margin requirement, the more leverage is available to the hedge fund. Leverage is a large part of the reason that hedge funds make either larger than normal returns or significant losses; the leverage magnifies both gains and losses. If the margin account or the hedge fund's equity in a position declines below a certain level, the lender initiates a margin call and requests the hedge fund put up more collateral. Margin calls can have the effect of magnifying losses because in order to meet a margin call, the hedge fund may liquidate (close) the losing position. This liquidation can lead to further losses if the order size is sufficiently large to move the security's market price.

Another factor that can magnify losses for hedge funds is investor redemptions. **Redemptions** frequently occur when a hedge fund is performing poorly. In the hedge fund industry, a **drawdown** is a reduction in net asset value (NAV).[21] When drawdowns occur, investors may decide to exit the fund or redeem at least a portion of their shares. Redemptions may require the hedge fund manager to liquidate some positions and incur transaction costs. As stated above, the liquidation of a position may further magnify the losses on the position. Redemption fees may serve to discourage redemption and to help the hedge fund managers recover transaction costs. Notice periods may allow the hedge fund manager to liquidate a position in an orderly fashion without magnifying the losses. Lockup periods give the hedge fund manager time to implement and potentially realize the expected results of a strategy. If the hedge fund is unlucky enough to experience a drawdown after the fund launch, the lockup period will force investors to stay in the fund rather than withdraw. The ability for a hedge fund to demand a long lockup period and still raise a significant amount of money depends a great deal on the reputation of either the firm or the hedge fund manager. Funds of funds may offer more redemption flexibility than afforded by direct investment in hedge funds because of special redemption arrangements with the underlying hedge fund managers, maintenance of a cash fund, or access to temporary financing.

Whereas hedge funds are not subject to extensive regulation globally, there have been calls for more oversight. Hedge funds in the United Kingdom are required to be registered with the Financial Services Authority (FSA),[22] and some hedge funds in the United States are registered with the Securities and Exchange Commission (SEC). The lack of regulation explains why hedge funds are not transparent to outsiders or proactive in communicating their strategies and reporting their returns. In response to the calls for oversight, the European Union (EU) has adopted the Directive on

---

21 Net asset value is the value of the fund's total assets minus liabilities, divided by the number of shares outstanding.

22 A new regulatory authority is expected to succeed the FSA in the United Kingdom as of 2012.

Alternative Investment Fund Managers (AIFM Directive), which must be implemented by mid-2013 by EU members.

Offshore jurisdictions (for example, the Cayman Islands) are often the locale for registering funds, whether managed in the United States, Europe, or Asia. However, some hedge funds choose to register domestically. The choice to register, for example, in the United States or the United Kingdom, may be because of the added credibility of registering with the SEC or the FSA, respectively. Sometimes, onshore hedge funds set up complementary offshore funds to attract additional capital.

Example 4

Effect of Redemption

A European credit hedge fund has a very short notice period of a week because the fund believes that it invests in highly liquid asset classes and is market neutral. The fund has a small number of holdings that represent a significant portion of the outstanding issue of each holding. The fund's lockup period has expired. Unfortunately, in one particular month, because of the downgrades of two large holdings, the hedge fund has a drawdown (decline in NAV) of over 5 percent. The declines in value of the two holdings result in margin calls from their prime broker, and the drawdown results in requests to redeem 50 percent of total partnership interests. The combined requests are *most likely* to:

A. force the hedge fund to liquidate or unwind 50 percent of its positions in an orderly fashion throughout the week.

B. have little impact on the prices received when liquidating the positions because it has a week before the partnership interests are redeemed.

C. result in a forced liquidation, which will drive prices down further and result in a bigger drawdown, so that the remaining investors will redeem their partnership interests leading to fund liquidation and closure.

Solution:

C is correct. One week may not be enough time to unwind the fund's positions in an orderly fashion so that the unwinding does not further drive down prices. A downgrading is not likely to have a temporary effect, so even if other non-losing positions are liquidated to meet the redemption requests, it is unlikely that the two large holdings will return to previous or higher values. Also, the hedge fund may have a week to satisfy the requests for redemptions, but the margin call must be met immediately. Thus, it is most likely that a forced liquidation will drive down prices, resulting in further drawdowns and redemption requests so that ultimately the fund will liquidate and cease to exist.

3.4 Hedge Fund Valuation Issues

Valuations are important for calculating performance and meeting redemptions. The frequency with which and how hedge funds are valued varies among funds. Hedge funds are generally valued on a daily, weekly, monthly, and/or quarterly basis. The valuation may use market or estimated values of underlying positions. When market prices or quotes are used for valuation, funds may differ in which price or quote they use (for example, bid price, ask price, average quote, and median quote). A common practice is to use the average quote [(bid + ask)/2]. A more conservative and theoretically accurate approach is to use bid prices for longs and ask prices for shorts; these are the prices at which the positions could be closed.

The underlying positions may be in highly illiquid or non-traded investments and therefore, it is necessary to estimate values because there are no reliable market values. Estimated values may be computed using statistical models. Any model should be independently tested, benchmarked, and calibrated to industry-accepted standards to ensure a consistency of approach. Because of the potential for conflicts of interests affecting estimates of value, procedures for in-house valuations should be developed and adhered to.

Liquidity is an important issue for valuation, but becomes particularly so for strategies involving convertible bonds, collateralized debt obligations, distressed debt, and emerging markets fixed income securities, which may be relatively illiquid. If a quoted market price is available, the use of liquidity discounts or "haircuts" is actually inconsistent with valuation guidance under most generally accepted accounting standards. However, many practitioners believe that liquidity discounts are necessary to reflect fair value. This assumption has resulted in some funds having two NAVs—trading and reporting. The trading NAV incorporates liquidity discounts, based on the size of the position held relative to the total amount outstanding in the issue and its trading volume. The reporting NAV is based on quoted market prices.

Example 5

Hedge Fund Valuation

A hedge fund with a market neutral strategy restricts its investment universe to domestic publicly traded equity securities that are actively traded. In calculating net asset value, the fund is most likely to use which of the following to value underlying positions?

A. Average quotes

B. Average quotes adjusted for liquidity

C. Bid price for shorts and ask price for longs

Solution:

A is correct. The fund is most likely to use average quotes. The securities are actively traded so no liquidity adjustment is required. If the fund uses bid/ask prices, the fund would use ask prices for shorts and bid prices for longs; these are the prices at which the positions could be closed.

3.5 Due Diligence for Investing in Hedge Funds

There are many issues to consider when investing in hedge funds. A basic question is whether one wants to rely upon the expertise of a fund of funds to invest in a portfolio of hedge funds or whether one has the expertise to undertake the hedge fund investment selection process. Funds of funds potentially offer the benefits of providing a diversified portfolio of hedge funds, supplying expertise in conducting due diligence, and negotiating favorable redemption terms. These potential benefits come at the cost of an additional layer of fees. Also, although a fund of funds may provide expertise in due diligence, the investor should still conduct due diligence when choosing a fund of funds.

Investors in hedge funds should consider many factors in their decision-making process. This section highlights some of the key due diligence points to consider, but does not provide an exhaustive list of factors to consider. Key factors to consider include investment strategy, investment process, competitive advantage, track record, size and longevity, management style, key-person risk, reputation, investor relations, plans for growth, and systems risk management.

Investment strategy and process are challenging to fully assess because hedge funds may limit disclosure in order to maintain their competitive advantage and to not give away information that is considered proprietary. However, it should be possible to identify in which markets the hedge fund invests, the general investment strategy (for example, long/short, relative arbitrage, etc.) and the basic process to implement this strategy, and the benchmark against which the fund gauges its performance.

Track record is a commonly viewed consideration because it should be readily available and is often assumed to be an indicator of future performance and risk (perhaps incorrectly, based on studies of performance persistence).[23] Investors should establish how the returns are calculated (e.g., based on estimates of value or market prices) and reported (e.g., before or after fees) and how the returns and risks compare with some benchmark. The investor should inquire about the fee structure because this information will have an impact, as demonstrated earlier, on the return to the investor.

Size and longevity are also common items for review.[24] The older a fund, the more likely it has not caused significant losses to its investors (otherwise, it is likely to have experienced redemptions, been unable raise further capital, and been liquidated). As a result, older funds are likely to have experienced growth in assets under management through both capital appreciation and additional investments (capital injections). Many investors require hedge funds to have a minimum track record of two years before they will invest. This requirement makes it particularly difficult for start-up funds to raise money as their managers need capital to invest before they can build a track record. In many cases, start-up funds receive money from seed investors who want a share of the business for their investment.

A hedge fund's size is an important consideration for investors because many investors set a minimum size on their investments and restrict the percentage of a fund's overall assets under management that their investment can represent. For example, if an investor's minimum investment size is $10 million and the investor's maximum percentage of a fund is 10 percent, the minimum hedge fund size the investor can consider is $100 million (= $10 million/0.1).

The hedge fund due diligence process also focuses on many qualitative factors. These include management style, key person risk, reputation, investor relations, and plans for growth. A thorough due diligence process will also include a review of management procedures, including leverage, brokerage, and diversification policies. The use of leverage and counterparty risk can significantly affect a fund's risk and performance. In addition to gathering information about the fund's prime broker and custody arrangements for securities, the investor should identify the auditor of the hedge fund and ensure that the auditor is independent and known for conducting competent audits.

Systems risk management is an important consideration for reviewing a hedge fund. Relevant risk management questions to ask are varied and related to the type of securities in which the hedge fund invests. Ultimately, the answers should provide comfort to investors that the risk management of the fund is performed in a rigorous fashion. In many cases, particularly with smaller funds or those that invest in more unusual or illiquid assets, the answers to these questions may indicate that the systems and processes are simplistic or that the answers may be very complex. Commonly, hedge funds believe that their strategies, systems, and processes are proprietary and are not willing to provide too much information to potential investors. This reluctance means that conducting due diligence can be very challenging. Regulation of hedge funds is likely to increase in the future, which may help with the due diligence process.

---

[23] For a discussion on the record of institutional investors' record at selecting managers, see Stewart, Heisler, Knittel, and Neumann, 2009.

[24] For a discussion of quantitative factors investors use to select investment managers, see Heisler, Knittel, Neumann, and Stewart, 2007.

Example 6

Due Diligence

HF Alpha and HF Beta invest in the same asset class using a similar investment strategy. A potential investor has gathered the following data from the hedge funds:

Characteristic	HF Alpha	HF Beta
Annualized returns	15%	10%
Sharpe Ratio	1.3	1.6
Size (US$ millions)	200	500
Fees	1.5 and 15	2 and 20
Track Record	2 years	5 years

Based on the above information, the investor is *most likely* to:

A. invest in HF Beta because of its higher Sharpe ratio.

B. question how the annualized returns are calculated.

C. invest in HF Alpha because of its higher returns and lower fees.

Solution:

B is correct. It is important to know how returns are calculated and if they are comparable before making any decision. If the returns are both reported net-of-fees, the higher fees on HF Beta may account for most of the difference in returns.

PRIVATE EQUITY

Private equity generally means investing in privately owned companies or in public companies with the intent to take them private. There are different stages and types of private equity investing. The focus of private equity firms may change through time as business conditions and the availability of financing change. A possible categorization of private equity identifies leveraged buyouts, venture capital, development capital, and distressed investing as primary private equity strategies.

Leveraged buyouts (LBOs) or highly leveraged transactions refer to private equity firms establishing buyout funds (or LBO funds) that acquire public companies or established private companies with a significant percentage of the purchase price financed through debt. The assets of the target company typically serve as the collateral for the debt, and the cash flows of the target company are expected to be sufficient to service the debt. The debt becomes part of the capital structure of the target company if the buyout goes through. The target company after the buyout becomes or remains a privately owned company.

Venture capital entails investing in or providing financing to private companies with high growth potential. Typically, these are start-up or young companies, but venture capital can be provided at a variety of stages.

Development capital generally refers to minority equity investments in more mature companies that are looking for capital to expand or restructure operations, enter new markets, or finance major acquisitions.

Distressed investing typically entails buying the debt of mature companies in financial difficulties. These companies may be in bankruptcy proceedings, have defaulted on debt, or seem likely to default on debt. Some investors attempt to identify companies with a temporary cash flow problem but a good business plan that will help the company survive and in the end flourish. These investors buy the company's debt in expectation of the company and its debt increasing in value. Turnaround investors buy debt and plan to be more active in the management and direction of the company. They seek distressed companies to restructure and revive.

The level of activity in private equity is cyclical. The cyclicality is shown visually over a relatively short period in Exhibit 9. It should be noted that detailed information on private equity activity is not always readily available.

Exhibit 9	Private Equity Funds Raised, 1998–2008

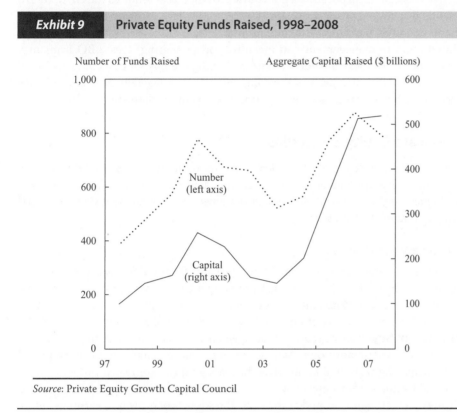

Source: Private Equity Growth Capital Council

4.1 Private Equity Structure and Fees

Like hedge funds, private equity funds are typically structured as partnerships where outside investors are Limited Partners (LPs) and the private equity firm, which may manage a number of funds, is the General Partner (GP). Most private equity firms charge both a management fee and an incentive fee on a fund basis. The management fees generally range from 1 to 3 percent of **committed capital**. Committed capital is the amount that the LPs have agreed to provide to the private equity fund. Private equity funds raise committed capital, and draw down on those commitments over 3 to 5 years when they have a specific investment to make. Until the committed capital is fully drawn down and invested, the management fee is based on committed capital, *not* invested capital. The committed capital basis for management fees is an important distinction from hedge funds where management fees are based on assets under management. After the committed capital is fully invested, the fees are paid only on the funds remaining in the investment vehicle; as investments are exited, capital is paid back to the investors, and they no longer pay fees on that portion of their investment.

For most private equity funds, the GP does not earn an incentive fee until the LPs have received their initial investment back. The GP typically receives 20 percent of the total profit of the private equity fund as an incentive or profit sharing fee.[25] The

---

25 The incentive fee may also be calculated on a deal-by-deal basis.

LPs receive 80 percent of the total profit of the equity fund plus the return of their initial investment. If distributions are made based on profits earned over time rather than at exit from investments of the fund, the distributions may result in receipts by the GP of more than 20 percent of the total profit. Most private equity partnership agreements include policies that protect the LPs from this contingency. These policies include prohibiting distributions of incentive fees to the GP until the LPs have received back their invested capital, setting up an escrow account for a portion of the incentive fees, and incorporating a **clawback** provision that requires the GP to return any funds distributed as incentive fees until the LPs have received back their initial investment and 80 percent of the total profit.

In addition to management and incentive (profit sharing) fees, LBO firms may receive other fees. These include a fee for arranging the buyout of a company based upon the selling (buyout) price of the company, a fee if a deal falls through, and a fee for arranging for divestitures of assets after the buyout is complete.

4.2 Private Equity Strategies

There are many private equity strategies. A common categorization, as indicated earlier, identifies leveraged buyouts, venture capital, development capital, and distressed investing as the primary strategies. However, leveraged buyouts and venture capital are the dominant strategies.

4.2.1 Leveraged Buyouts

LBOs are sometimes referred to as "going private" transactions because, after the acquisition of a publicly traded company, the target company's equity is generally no longer publicly traded. When the target company is an established private company, it is not a "going private" transaction. The LBO may also be of a specific type. In MBOs (**management buyouts**), the current management team is involved in the acquisition, and in MBIs (**management buy-ins**), the current management team is being replaced and the acquiring team will be involved in managing the company. LBO managers seek to add value—from improving company operations and growing revenue and ultimately increasing profits and cash flows. The sources of growth in earnings before interest, taxes, depreciation, and amortization (EBITDA), in order of contribution to growth, include organic revenue growth, cost reduction/restructuring, acquisition, and other.[26] However, the potential returns in this category are to a large extent due to the use of leverage. If debt financing is unavailable or costly, LBOs are less likely to occur.

4.2.1.1 LBO Financing   Debt is central to the structure and feasibility of buyouts in private equity. Target companies are rarely purchased using only the equity of the buyout company. In order to potentially increase equity returns and increase the number of transactions a particular fund can make, private equity firms use debt to finance a significant proportion of each deal (in other words, they use leverage). For example, in a buyout deal, a private equity firm may invest equity representing 30 percent of the purchase price and raise the rest of the purchase price in the debt markets. They may use a combination of bank loans, often called leveraged loans because of the amount of the capital structure of the company they represent, and high yield bonds.

Leveraged loans often carry covenants intended to protect the investors. The covenants may require or restrict certain actions. The covenants may require the company to maintain specified financial ratios within certain limits, submit information so that the bank can monitor performance, or operate within certain parameters. The covenants may restrict the company from further borrowing (in other words, no additional bonds can be issued and no additional funds can be borrowed from banks

---

26 Source: Private Equity Growth Council.

or other sources), or impose limits on paying dividends or making operating decisions. Similarly, bond terms may include covenants intended to protect the bondholders. However, one of the key differences between leveraged loans and the bonds is that leveraged loans are generally senior secured debt and the bonds are unsecured in the case of bankruptcy. Therefore, even given covenants, because of the amount of leverage employed, the bonds issued to finance an LBO are usually high yield bonds that receive low quality ratings and must offer high coupons to attract investors.

A typical LBO capital structure includes equity, bank debt (leveraged loans), and high yield bonds. Leveraged loans often provide a larger amount of capital than either equity or high yield bonds. As an alternative to high yield bonds, **mezzanine financing** may also be used.[27] Mezzanine financing refers to debt or preferred shares with a relationship to common equity due to a feature such as attached warrants or conversion options. Being subordinate to both senior and high yield debt, mezzanine financing typically pays a higher coupon rate. In addition to interest or dividends, this type of financing offers a potential return based on increases in the value of common equity.

The variety of available financing choices provides flexibility for a target company to match its repayment schedules with expected inflows and permits higher levels of leverage compared with traditional bank debt. The optimal capital structure takes into account a variety of factors, including the company's projected cash flows, investor willingness to purchase different types of debt and accept different levels of leverage, the availability of equity, and the required rates of return for equity and different types of debt considering leverage. The optimal capital structure will be different for every deal.

4.2.1.2 Characteristics of Attractive Target Companies for LBOs

Private equity firms invest in companies across many sectors, although an individual private equity firm may specialize in a certain sector or sectors. Whatever the targeted sector(s), there are several characteristics, any one of which may make a company particularly attractive as an LBO target. The characteristics include:

- Undervalued/depressed stock price: The intrinsic value of the company is perceived by the private equity firm to exceed its market price. Private equity firms are therefore willing to pay a premium to the market price to secure shareholder approval. Firms try to buy assets/companies cheaply, and may focus on companies that are out of favor in the public markets and have stock prices that reflect this perception.

- Willing management: Existing management is looking for a deal. Management may have identified opportunities but do not have access to the resources to make substantial investments in new processes, personnel, equipment, etc. to drive long-term growth. Also, private equity may provide management with the time and capital to turn a company around.

- Inefficient companies: Private equity firms seek to generate attractive returns on equity by creating value in the companies they buy. They achieve this goal by identifying companies that are inefficiently managed and that have the potential to perform well if managed better.

- Strong and sustainable cash flow: Companies that generate strong cash flow are attractive because in an LBO transaction, the target company will be taking on a significant portion of debt. Cash flow is necessary to make interest payments on the increased debt load.

- Low leverage: Private equity firms focus on target companies that do not currently have a significant portion of debt on their balance sheets. This characteristic makes it easier to utilize debt to finance a large portion of the purchase price.

---

27 This type of loan is referred to as *mezzanine financing* because of its location on the balance sheet and is a *type* of financing.

■ Assets: Private equity managers like companies that have a significant amount of physical assets. These physical assets can be used as security, and secured debt is cheaper than unsecured debt.

4.2.2 *Venture Capital*

Venture capital (VC) is often categorized by the stage at which the venture capital is provided to the company of interest. The company that is being invested in is often called the **portfolio company** because it will become part of the portfolio of the VC fund. The stages range from inception of an idea for a company to the point when the company is about to make an initial public offering (IPO) or be acquired—most typically, by a strategic buyer. The investment return required varies based on the stage of development of the company. Investors in early stage companies will demand higher expected returns relative to later stage investors. The ultimate returns realized depend on the portfolio company's success in transitioning from a start-up to a going and growing concern.

Venture capitalists are not passive investors. They are actively involved with the companies in which they invest. The VC fund typically gets an equity interest in the company in which it is investing. The VC fund may also provide some debt financing.

1. Formative-stage financing occurs when the company is still in the process of being formed and encompasses several financing steps, which are described as follows:

    a. Angel investing is capital provided at the idea stage. Funds may be used to transform the idea into a business plan and to assess market potential. The amount of financing at this stage is typically small and provided by individuals (often friends and family) rather than by VC funds.

    b. Seed-stage financing or seed capital generally supports product development and/or marketing efforts, including market research. This point is generally the first stage at which VC funds invest.

    c. Early stage financing (early stage venture capital) is provided to companies moving toward operation but before commercial production and sales have occurred. Early stage financing may be provided to initiate commercial production and sales.

2. Later-stage financing (expansion venture capital) is provided after commercial production and sales have begun but before any IPO. Funds may be used for initial expansion of a company already producing and selling a product or for major expansion, such as physical plant expansion, product improvement, or a major marketing campaign.

3. Mezzanine-stage financing[28] (mezzanine venture capital) is provided to prepare to go public and represents the bridge between the expanding company and the IPO.

Formative-stage financing generally is done via ordinary or convertible preferred share transfers to the investor (VC fund), and management retains control of the company. Later-stage financing generally involves management selling control of the company to the venture capital investor; financing is provided through equity and debt (the fund may also use convertible bonds or convertible preferred shares). The debt financing is not intended for income generation to the VC fund but rather, it is for the recovery and control of assets in a bankruptcy situation. Simply put, it provides more protection to the VC fund than equity.

---

28 The term, "mezzanine-stage financing" is used because this financing is provided at the stage between being a private and public company. The focus is on *when* the financing occurs.

In order to make an investment, a venture capitalist needs to be convinced that the management team of the portfolio company is competent and that there is a solid business plan with strong prospects for growth and development. Because these investments are not in mature businesses with years of operational and financial performance history, the complexity involved with venture capital involves accurately estimating company valuation based on future prospects. This estimation is more of an unknown than in LBO investing, which targets mature, underperforming public companies. As the portfolio company matures and moves into later-stage financing, there is more certainty around valuation but less so than with an LBO investment.

4.2.3 *Other Private Equity Strategies*

There are several other specialties for private equity firms. These specialties include development capital, also called minority equity investing, which earns profits from funding business growth or restructuring. Many times, minority equity investing is initiated and sought by management, who are interested in realizing earnings from selling a portion of their shares before they are able to go public. Although this scenario occurs most commonly with private companies, publicly quoted companies sometimes seek private equity capital, in opportunities called PIPEs (private investment in public equities).

Distressed investing by a private equity firm typically involves purchasing the debt of troubled companies (companies that are bankrupt, in default, or likely to default). The distressed debt often trades at prices significantly less than the face value of the debt. If the company can be turned around, the debt may recover its value. The return on investment is a function of the ability of the turnaround investor to restructure the company either operationally or financially. Distressed debt investors may be involved in the turnaround and may assume an active role in the management and direction of the company or in the reorganization of the company. Some distressed investors are passive investors who simply try to identify companies that they expect to increase in value; debt holders will benefit from the increase before equity holders. Distressed debt investors are sometimes referred to as vulture investors.

Other private equity strategies exist. These strategies may involve the provision of specific financing (for example, mezzanine funds) or investing in companies in specific industries. As the financial environment changes and evolves, additional strategies may emerge.

4.2.4 *Exit Strategies*

The ultimate goal for private equity is to improve new or underperforming businesses and exit them at high valuations. Private equity firms buy and hold companies for an average of five years. However, the time to exit can range from less than six months to over 10 years. Before deciding on an exit strategy, private equity managers take into account the dynamics of the industry in which the portfolio company competes, overall economic cycles, interest rates, and company performance.

Below are common exit strategies pursued by private equity portfolio managers:

- Trade sale: This strategy refers to the sale of a company to a strategic buyer such as a competitor. A trade sale can be conducted through an auction process or by private negotiation. Benefits of a trade sale include (a) an immediate cash exit for the private equity fund; (b) potential for high valuation of the asset because strategic buyers may be willing and able to pay more than other potential buyers because of anticipated synergies; (c) fast and simple execution; (d) lower transaction costs than an IPO; and (e) lower levels of disclosure and higher confidentiality because the private equity firm is generally only dealing with one other party. Disadvantages of trade sales include (a) possible opposition by management; (b) lower attractiveness to employees of the portfolio company; (c) a limited number of potential trade buyers; and (d) a possible lower price than in an IPO.

■ IPO: This approach involves the portfolio company selling its shares, including some or all of those held by the private equity firm, to public investors through an IPO. Advantages for an IPO exit include (a) potential for the highest price; (b) management approval since they are retained; (c) publicity for the private equity firm; and (d) potential ability to retain future upside potential as the private equity firm may choose to remain a large shareholder. Disadvantages for an IPO exit include (a) high transaction costs paid to investment banks and lawyers; (b) long lead times; (c) risk of stock market volatility; (d) high disclosure requirements; (e) potential lock-up period, which requires the private equity firm to retain an equity position for a specified period after the IPO; and (f) the fact that an IPO is usually only appropriate for larger companies with attractive growth profiles.

■ Recapitalization: A recapitalization is not a true exit strategy as the private equity firm typically maintains control; however, it does allow the private equity investor to extract money from the company. Recapitalization is a very popular strategy when interest rates are low as the private equity firm re-leverages or introduces leverage to the company and pays itself a dividend. A recapitalization is often a prelude to a later exit.

■ Secondary Sales: This approach represents a sale to another private equity firm or other group of investors.

■ Write-off/Liquidation: A write-off occurs when a transaction has not gone well, and the private equity firm is updating its value of the investment or liquidating the portfolio company to move on to other projects.

The above exit strategies may be pursued individually, combined together, or used for a partial exit strategy. For example, it is not unusual to see a private equity fund sell a portion of a portfolio company to a competitor via a trade sale and then complete a secondary sale to another private equity firm for the remaining portion.

4.3 Private Equity: Diversification Benefits, Performance, and Risk

Private equity funds may provide higher return opportunities relative to traditional investments through their ability to invest in private companies, their influence on portfolio companies' management and operations, and/or their use of leverage. Investments in private equity funds can add diversity to a portfolio comprised of publicly traded stocks and bonds because they may have less than perfect correlation with those investments.

Exhibit 10 shows the mean annual returns for the Thomson Reuters U.S. Private Equity Performance Index (PEPI) and the NASDAQ and S&P 500 indices for a variety of periods ending 31 March 2010. Over the 3-, 5-, 10-, and 20-year periods ending 31 March 2010, U.S. private equity funds, based on the PEPI, on average outperformed stocks based on the NASDAQ and S&P 500 indices. The returns to the PEPI were less than the returns to the NASDAQ and S&P 500 indices for the 1-year period ending 31 March 2010.

Exhibit 10	Comparison of Annual Returns with U.S. Private Equity and U.S. Stocks				
	1 year	**3 years**	**5 years**	**10 years**	**20 years**
All private equity	21.9	0.6	5.8	2.8	11.3
NASDAQ	51.5	−0.3	3.6	−6.2	9.1
S&P 500	42.3	−6.1	−0.2	−2.4	6.5

Note: All periods end 31 March 2010.
Source: Thomson Reuters' 10 August 2010 Press Release, "U.S. Private Equity Short-Term Performance Turns Sharply Positive."

However, the PEPI may not be a reliable measure of performance because of challenges in measuring the historical performance of private equity investing. As with hedge funds, private equity return indices rely on self-reporting and are subject to survivorship, backfill, and other biases. These characteristics typically lead to overstatement of published returns. Moreover, in the absence of a liquidity event, private equity firms may not regularly mark to market their investments. This failure to mark to market leads to understatement of measures of volatility and correlations with other investments. Thus, data adjustments are required to more reliably measure the benefits of private equity investing.

Exhibit 11 lists annualized standard deviations of published quarterly and annual returns of private equity investments for the period of 1981 to 2009. The volatility based on published quarterly returns reflects few liquidity events and results in much lower volatility estimates than using annual returns. Note that the difference between the two measures (quarterly and annual) using MSCI World is insignificant because the stocks in the index are marked to market on a regular basis. In July 2009, private equity firms began reporting investments at their estimated fair values; these estimates are frequently based on market multiples. This change in valuation methodology is reflected in the new International Private Equity and Venture Capital Valuation Guidelines.

Exhibit 11	Annualized Standard Deviations of Returns to Private Equity Investments, 1981–2009	
	Quarterly	**Annual**
Venture capital*	23.0	40.4
Private equity*	15.6	25.9
MSCI World	19.0	19.8

*Thomson Venture Economics, June 1981 to June 2009

According to the historical, standard deviations of annual returns shown in Exhibit 11, private equity investments, including venture capital, are riskier than investing in common stocks. Investors should require a higher return from accepting a higher risk, including illiquidity and leverage risks.

Recognizing its higher risk, private equity, including venture capital investing, may provide benefits to a diversified portfolio. If investors believe they can identify skillful private equity fund managers (managers who can identify attractive portfolio companies and invest in them at reasonable valuations, as well as improve their operations and profitability), investors may benefit from superior returns (returns in excess of those expected given the additional leverage, market, and liquidity risks). Kaplan and Schoar (2005) find significant differences in the returns to the top quartile of funds compared with the bottom quartile of funds for the period; the cash flow internal rate of return (IRR) is 22 percent per year for the top quartile compared with 3 percent per year for the bottom quartile. Further, Kaplan and Schoar find evidence of performance persistence. Identifying top performing funds appears to be critical.

4.4 Portfolio Company Valuation

In order to identify and invest in attractive portfolio companies, private equity professionals must be able to value those companies. There are three common approaches used in the private equity industry to value a company: market or comparable, discounted cash flow (DCF), and asset-based.

A market or comparables approach values a company or its equity using multiples of different measures. For example, an earnings before interest, taxes, depreciation, and amortization (EBITDA) multiple is commonly used in valuing large, mature private companies. For other types of companies, multiples of measures based on net income or revenue may be more appropriate. The EBITDA multiple may be determined by looking at the market value of a similar publicly traded company or the price recently paid for a comparable business, divided by EBITDA. Net income and revenue multiples may be based on the multiples from transactions in comparable companies but are frequently based on heuristics.[29]

Example 7

Portfolio Company Valuation

A private equity fund is considering purchasing a radio broadcaster that had an EBITDA of $200 million. In the past year, three radio broadcasting companies were sold for 8x EBITDA, 10x EBITDA, and 9x EBITDA. Based on this information, the maximum value the private equity fund is most likely to assign to the broadcaster is:

A. $1,600 million.

B. $1,800 million.

C. $2,000 million.

Solution:

C is correct. The maximum value the private equity fund is most likely to assign is that using the highest multiple (10 × $200 million = $2,000 million). The minimum value the seller may be willing to accept is that using the lowest multiple. Of course, in negotiations, growth prospects, risk, size, current market conditions, etc. will be considered.

A discounted cash flow (DCF) approach values a company or its equity as the present value of the relevant expected future cash flows. Future free cash flow projections may be discounted to compute a present value of the portfolio company or its equity. Free cash flow to the firm and the weighted average cost of capital may be used to estimate the value of the company. Free cash flow to equity and the cost of equity may

---

[29] Heuristics are mental shortcuts based on experience and knowledge that simplify decision making. They are sometimes called "rules of thumb."

be used to estimate the value of the company's equity. One simple approach takes a measure such as income or cash flow and divides it by a capitalization rate to arrive at an estimate of value. This is conceptually different but practically similar to using an income or cash-based multiple. If the value estimated using a DCF approach is higher than the current price of the investment, the opportunity may be an attractive one.

An asset-based approach values a company based on the values of its underlying assets less the value of any related liabilities. In effect, this approach arrives at the value of the company to the equity holders. This approach assumes that the value of a company is equal to the sum of the values of a company's assets minus its liabilities. The valuations can be arrived at using market (fair) values or other values such as liquidation values. Fair values assume an orderly transaction, whereas liquidation values assume a distressed transaction. The liquidation value is an estimate of how much money could be raised if a company's assets were sold in a liquidation scenario. Liquidation value is the net amount that will be realized if the business is terminated, the assets are sold, and the liabilities are satisfied. In a weak economic environment, liquidation values will most likely be far lower than the immediately previous fair values because there will tend to be many assets for sale and fewer potential buyers.

4.5 Private Equity: Investment Considerations and Due Diligence

Current and anticipated economic conditions, including interest rate and capital availability expectations, are critical factors to consider when evaluating an investment in private equity. Refinancing risk must also be evaluated. If refinancing becomes unavailable, a lack of financing can result in default. The extent to which there is undrawn but committed capital can also affect the private equity sector and the returns to investors.

Investing in private equity firms requires patience. Investors who are comfortable with long-term commitment of funds and illiquidity are best suited to considering private equity investing. Private equity typically requires a long-term commitment on the part of an LP because of the long time lag between investments in and exits from portfolio companies. Once a commitment has been made and an investor becomes an LP, the investor has very limited liquidity options. As many investors are averse to illiquidity, there should be a liquidity risk premium for private equity investors.

Assuming these characteristics are acceptable, the investor must consider the choice of GP. In this regard, many of the due diligence questions for hedge fund selection are relevant to private equity. Some of the important issues to investigate are the GP's experience and knowledge—financial and operating, the valuation methodology used, the alignment of the GP's incentives with the interests of the LPs, the plan to draw on committed capital, and the planned exit strategies.

REAL ESTATE

Real estate investing is often thought of as direct or indirect ownership (equity investing) in real estate property such as land and buildings. However, real estate investing also includes lending (debt investing) against real estate property (for example, providing a mortgage loan or purchasing mortgage-backed securities). The property generally serves as collateral for the lending.

Key reasons for investing in real estate include the following:

■ Potential for competitive long-term total returns driven by both income generation and capital appreciation.

- Prospect that multiple-year leases with fixed rents for some property types may lessen cash flow impact from economic shocks.
- Likelihood that diversification benefits may be provided by less than perfect correlation with other asset classes.
- Potential to provide an inflation hedge if rents can be adjusted quickly for inflation.

Real estate property ownership is represented by a title and may reflect access to air rights, mineral rights, and surface rights in addition to the rights of use of buildings and land. Titles can be purchased, leased, sold, mortgaged, or transferred together or separately, in whole or in part. Real estate investments may also be in the form of partnerships, equity, or debt. Much real estate is residential, but if it is owned with the intention to let, lease, or rent it in order to generate income, it is classified as commercial (i.e., income producing) real estate. In addition to residential real estate classified as commercial, commercial real estate includes other types of real estate properties such as office and retail properties. Some real estate properties may be farmed, provide forest products, or have natural resources that can be obtained by extraction to generate income; the resulting products, such as wheat, timber, gold, and oil, are considered commodities. As a result, some investors include timberland and farmland in their commodities portfolio rather than in their real estate portfolio. Other investors simply treat farmland and timberland as a separate category.

Institutional ownership of commercial property totaled over $2 trillion as of 2008, as shown in Exhibit 12.

Exhibit 12	Institutionally Owned Global Real Estate Property Assets Under Management (US$ millions)
Europe	1,135,881
North America	710,994
Australasia	143,280
Asia	94,440
Latin America	10,075
Middle East	190
Africa	164
Total	**2,095,024**

Source: Based on data from Property Funds Research, 2008.

Real estate property exhibits unique features compared with other investment asset classes. The basic indivisibility, unique characteristics (i.e., no two properties are identical), and the fixed location of real estate property has implications for investors. For example, the size of investment may have to be large and may be relatively illiquid. Also, real estate property typically requires operational management. Real estate may be subject to government regulations affecting what can be done to modify the existing land or property, to whom and how ownership can be transferred, and to other restrictions on ownership. Local or regional markets and real estate property values can be independent of country-wide or global price movements as local factors may override wider market trends. Cross-border investment in real estate is increasingly common and requires knowledge of country, regional, and local markets.

5.1 Forms of Real Estate Investment

Real estate investing may take a variety of forms. Real estate investments may be classified along two dimensions: debt or equity based, and in private or public markets. Equity investments in real estate that occur in the private markets are often referred to as direct investments in real estate. The money to finance real estate property purchases comes from many sources. A well known form of debt financing of real estate purchases is mortgages. Private investors—institutional and individual, real estate corporations, and real estate investment trusts (REITs)—may provide the equity financing for the purchase.

REITs sell shares to raise funds to make property purchases. The shares of REITs are typically publicly traded and represent an indirect investment in real estate property. Similarly, mortgages may be packaged and securitized into asset-backed securitized debt obligations (mortgage-backed securities) that represent rights to receive cash flows from portfolios of mortgage loans. Exhibit 13 shows some examples of the basic forms of real estate investments.

Exhibit 13	Basic Forms of Real Estate Investments and Examples	
	Debt	**Equity**
Private	■ Mortgages ■ Construction lending	■ Direct ownership of real estate. Ownership can be through, sole ownership, joint ventures, real estate limited partnerships, or other commingled funds.
Public	■ Mortgage-backed securities (residential and commercial) ■ Collateralized mortgage obligations	■ Shares in real estate corporations ■ Shares of real estate investment trusts

Within the basic forms, there can be many variations.

■ Direct ownership can be free and clear, where the title to the property is transferred to the owner unencumbered by any financing lien, such as from a mortgage. Initial purchase costs associated with direct ownership may include legal expenses, survey costs, engineering/environmental studies, and valuation (appraisal) fees. Of course, ongoing maintenance and refurbishment charges are also incurred. The property must be managed, which has related costs. The owner may manage the property or may employ a local managing agent.

■ Leveraged ownership occurs where the property title is obtained through an equity purchase combined with mortgage financing. In addition to the initial purchase costs above, there are mortgage arrangement fees. A mortgage is secured by the property and in the event of a breach of lending terms, the creditor can petition for the title. Any appreciation (depreciation) of the value of the property plus the net operating income in excess of the debt servicing costs provides investors with a leveraged gain (loss) on their equity.

■ Financing provided to leveraged owners is frequently in the form of stand-alone mortgage loans. These loans represent passive investments where the lender expects to receive a predefined stream of payments over the finite life of the mortgage. The loan may become a form of property ownership if the borrower defaults. Investments may be in the form of "whole" loans based on specific properties (typically, direct investment through private markets) or through participation in a pool of mortgage loans (typically, indirect investment in real estate through publicly traded securities such as mortgage-backed securities).

■ Real estate equity investors may utilize different types of pooled vehicles arranged by an intermediary. These vehicles include the following:

● Real estate limited partnerships offer exposure to real estate projects while preserving limited liability (to the amount of the initial investment) and leaving management and liability to general partners who specialize in real estate management.

● REITs issue shares that are typically publicly traded. REITs invest in various types of real estate and provide retail investors with access to a diversified real estate property portfolio and professional management. REITs are required to distribute most of their taxable income to their shareholders.

■ Securitization of residential and commercial mortgages provides retail and institutional investors with access to a diversified portfolio of mortgages and allows the original lenders to alter their portfolio of investments. Mortgages are combined into pools and then into slices (called tranches) by investment banks. The tranches, each having different payment characteristics, are then sold to investors. These securities are generally not considered alternative investments but are held as part of the fixed income (or credit) portfolio.

REITs and partnerships have fees for managing the assets embedded in their valuations. Fee structures for investment funds can be similar to those in private equity, with investment management fees based on committed capital or invested capital. These fees typically range from 1 to 2 percent of capital per annum. Funds also charge performance-based fees, similar to a private equity fund.

5.2 Real Estate Investment Categories

The majority of real estate property may be classified as either commercial or residential. In this reading, residential properties are defined narrowly to include only owner-occupied, single residences (often referred to as single-family residential property). Residential properties owned with the intention to let, lease, or rent them are classified as commercial. Commercial properties also include office, retail, industrial and warehouse, and hospitality (e.g., hotels and motels) properties. Commercial properties may also have mixed uses. Commercial properties generate returns from income (e.g., rent) and capital appreciation. Opportunities for capital appreciation will be affected by several factors, including development strategies, market conditions, and property-specific features.

5.2.1 *Residential Property*

For many individuals and families, real estate investment takes the form of direct equity investment (i.e., ownership) in a residence with the intent to occupy.[30] In other words, a home is purchased. Given the price of homes, most purchasers cannot provide the entire financing (i.e., pay cash) and must borrow funds to make the purchase. Any appreciation (depreciation) in the value of the home increases (decreases) the owner's equity in the home.

Financial institutions are the main providers (originators) of debt financing (typically, through mortgages) for home ownership. The originators of single-family residential mortgages are making a direct, debt investment in the home. Before offering a mortgage, the due diligence process should include ensuring that the borrower is

---

30 Residential properties (single or multi-family) are considered commercial property if they are maintained as rental properties.

making an appropriate equity investment in the home (in other words, paying an adequate proportion of the purchase price), conducting a credit review of the borrower, establishing that the borrower has sufficient cash flows to make the required payments on the mortgage and to maintain the home, appraising (estimating the value of) the home, and ensuring that adequate and appropriate insurance is in place on the home. Home loans may be held on the originator's balance sheet or securitized and offered to the financial markets. Securitization provides indirect, debt investment opportunities in residential property via securitized debt products, such as residential mortgage-backed securities (RMBS), to other investors.

5.2.2 *Commercial Real Estate*

Commercial property has traditionally been considered an appropriate direct investment—equity and debt—for institutional funds or high-net-worth individuals with long time horizons and limited liquidity needs. This perception of appropriateness for only certain types of investors was primarily because of the complexity of the investments, the large investments required, and the relative illiquidity of the investments. Direct, equity investing (i.e., ownership) is further complicated because commercial property requires active and experienced, professional management. The success of the equity investment is a function of a variety of factors, including how well the property is managed, general economic and specific real estate market conditions, and the extent of and terms of any debt financing.

In order to provide direct debt financing, the lender (investor) will conduct financial analyses to establish the creditworthiness of the borrower, to ensure that the property will generate cash flows sufficient to service the debt, to estimate the value of the property, and to evaluate economic conditions. The estimate of the value of the property is critical because the loan-to-value ratio is a critical factor in the lending decision. The borrower's equity in the property is an indicator of commitment to the success of the project and provides a cushion to the lender because the property is generally used as collateral for the loan.

Indirect investment vehicles provide individual investors with the opportunity to invest in real estate. For example, shares of REITs provide indirect, equity investment opportunities in real estate and commercial mortgage-backed securities (CMBS) provide indirect, debt investment opportunities in real estate.

5.2.3 *REIT Investing*

The risk and return characteristics of REITs depend on the type of investment they make. Mortgage REITs, which invest primarily in mortgages, are similar to fixed income investments. Equity REITs, which invest primarily in commercial or residential properties and employ leverage, are similar to direct equity investments in leveraged real estate.

Gross income from rents represents a relatively predictable income stream and, after servicing the debt, is a source of return to equity REITs. Although the regulations with respect to REITs vary among countries, in general, equity REITs have an obligation to distribute the majority of their income to shareholders to retain their regulatory tax-advantaged status. At least 90 percent of revenue (including rent and realized capital gains), net of expenses, must often be distributed in the form of dividends.

The business strategy for equity REITs is simple: maximize property occupancy rates and rents in order to maximize income and dividends. Equity REITs, like other public companies, must report earnings per share based on net income as defined by generally accepted accounting principles (GAAP).

5.2.4 *Mortgage-Backed Securities (MBS)*

The MBS structure is based on the securitization model of buying a pool of assets and assigning the income and principal returns into individual security tranches, as illustrated in Exhibit 14 for commercial mortgage-backed securities (CMBS). On the right hand side of the exhibit, the ranking of losses is indicative of the priority of claims against the real estate property. MBS may be issued privately or publicly. These securities are often included in broad fixed income indices and in indices that are used to indicate the performance of real estate investments.

Exhibit 14	**CMBS Security Structure**

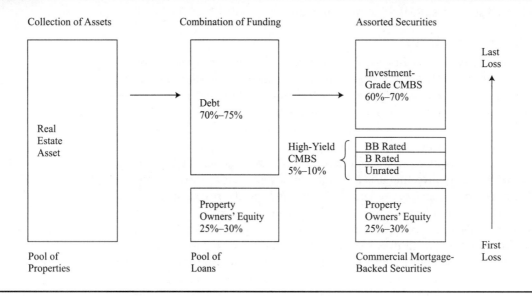

5.2.5 *Timberland and Farmland*

Timberland offers an income stream based on the sale of timber products as a component of total return and has historically provided a return that is not highly correlated with other asset classes. Timberland functions as both a factory and a warehouse. Timber can be grown and easily stored by not harvesting. This feature offers the flexibility of harvesting more trees when timber prices are up, and delaying harvests when prices are down. Timberland has three primary return drivers: biological growth, commodity price changes, and land price changes.

Farmland is often perceived to provide a hedge against inflation. Its returns include an income component related to harvest quantities and agricultural commodity prices. Farmland consists of two main property types: row crops that are planted and harvested annually (i.e., more than one planting and harvesting can occur in a year depending upon the crop and the climate) and permanent crops that grow on trees or vines. Unlike with timberland, there is little flexibility in harvesting, and farm products must be harvested when ripe. Farmland may also be used as pastureland for livestock. Similar to timberland, farmland has three primary return drivers: harvest quantities, commodity prices, and land price changes.

5.3 Real Estate Performance and Diversification Benefits

There are a variety of indices globally that are intended to measure returns to real estate. However, these indices vary in the selection and valuation of components and longevity. A real estate index can generally be categorized as an appraisal index, a repeat sales (transactions-based) index, or a REIT index. Appraisal indices use estimates of value (appraisals) as inputs to the indices. These appraisals, which are conducted by experts, rely on comparable sales and cash flow analysis techniques. Even though the appraisals are done by experts, they are still subjective. The appraisals are done periodically, often annually, but some appraised values included in an index may be from more than one year earlier. This factor, and the way appraisals are done, may result in indices that understate volatility.

Repeat sales indices use repeat sales of properties to construct the indices. The change in prices of properties with repeat sales are measured and used to construct the index. These indices suffer from a sample selection bias because the properties that sell in each period vary and may not be representative. Also, the properties that transact are not a random sample and may be biased towards those that have increased in value or decreased in value depending on current economic conditions. The higher the number of sales, the more reliable and relevant is the index.

REIT indices use the prices of publicly traded shares of REITs to construct the indices. The more frequently the shares trade, the more reliable is the index. However, the index is not necessarily representative of the properties of interest to the investor.

An investor will find a variety of indices to choose from and may find one that seems representative of the market of interest to them. However, the investor should be aware of how the index is constructed and the inherent limitations resulting from the construction method. Investors should also be aware that the apparent low correlation of real estate with other asset classes may be because of limitations in the real estate index construction.

A comparison of returns on U.S. real estate based on different indices is provided in Exhibit 15. The National Council of Real Estate Investment Fiduciaries (NCREIF) constructs a variety of appraisal-based indices. The National Association of Real Estate Investment Trusts (NAREIT) constructs a variety of indices based on the prices of shares of REITs. The NAREIT returns based on REIT share prices are clearly more volatile—displaying higher standard deviations and a lower worst calendar year return—than the NCREIF returns based on appraisals. The NCREIF Farmland index shows the least reported volatility. The lowest annualized return shown is that of commercial property based on appraisals (NCREIF Property index).

Exhibit 15	Historical Returns of U.S. Real Estate Indices, 1992–3Q2010			
	NCREIF Data			**NAREIT**
	Property*	**Timber**	**Farmland**	**All REITs**
Annualized return	7.6%	10.9%	10.9%	10.1%
Ann. standard deviation	8.2%	11.4%	7.6%	18.6%
Worst calendar year	−16.9%	−5.2%	2.0%	−37.3%

*Commercial real estate property

Global and regional REIT returns are displayed in Exhibit 16. The table shows the disparity among regional returns and demonstrates the importance of knowledge of country, local, and regional markets. However, a cursory examination indicates a significant degree of correlation among the regional returns.

| Exhibit 16 | Historical Returns of Global REITs |

	Global Composite Return Components			North America Return Components			Asia Return Components			Europe Return Components		
Year	Total	Price	Income	Total	Price	Income	Total	Price	Income	Total	Price	Income
1998	−8.2	−12.5	4.4	−17.7	−22.7	5.0	−3.2	−6.9	3.7	5.0	1.5	3.5
1999	8.9	3.7	5.2	−4.4	−11.3	6.9	32.2	28.2	3.9	−3.2	−6.9	3.7
2000	13.2	7.9	5.3	31.2	22.7	8.6	1.2	−1.9	3.1	8.1	4.2	3.9
2001	−3.8	−7.9	4.0	10.0	4.1	5.9	−17.2	−19.6	2.3	−6.1	−9.4	3.3
2002	2.8	−2.4	5.2	2.4	−3.8	6.2	−7.2	−10.6	3.4	21.7	16.8	4.9
2003	40.7	33.5	7.2	37.7	29.7	8.1	44.8	38.5	6.4	44.7	38.7	6.0
2004	38.0	32.0	6.0	33.5	26.9	6.6	36.9	32.2	4.6	52.7	47.0	5.8
2005	15.4	10.7	4.7	13.2	8.1	5.1	23.4	18.6	4.7	9.4	6.0	3.4
2006	42.4	37.5	4.9	36.3	30.9	5.4	36.5	32.2	4.3	67.0	62.8	4.2
2007	−7.0	−10.0	3.0	−14.9	−18.3	3.3	14.8	11.7	3.1	−24.5	−26.6	2.1
2008	−55.0	−56.9	1.9	−51.0	−53.3	2.3	−58.1	−59.6	1.5	−56.0	−57.9	1.9

Note: Data are as of 3 December 2008.
Source: Based on data from NAREIT.

During 1990–2009, the correlations of global REITs (NAREIT Global composite) and global stocks (MSCI All Country World Index) and global REITs and global bonds (Barclays Capital Global Aggregate Bond Index) were 0.597 and 0.068, respectively. Correlations of global real estate and equity returns are relatively high, and correlation of global real estate and bond returns are relatively low. The returns from investing in REITs and investing in equities are more highly correlated with each other than with bonds because both are affected similarly by the business cycle.

5.4 Real Estate Valuation

Until a property is actually sold, real estate values need to be estimated. This process is often referred to as appraising the property. There are a variety of approaches used to value real estate property. Common techniques for appraising real estate property include comparable sales, income, and cost approaches.

▪ Comparable sales approach: This approach involves determining an approximate value based on recent sales of similar properties. Adjustments are made for differences in key characteristics of the property being appraised and the sold properties identified as similar. Key characteristics include condition, age, location, and size. Adjustments are also made for price changes in the relevant real estate market between dates of sales.

▪ Income approach: Direct capitalization and discounted cash flow approaches are two income-based approaches to appraisal of an income-producing property.

The direct capitalization approach estimates the value of an income-producing property based upon the level and quality of its net operating income (NOI). NOI is similar to EBITDA and represents the income to the property after deducting operating expenses, including property taxes, insurance, maintenance, utilities, and repairs but before depreciation, financing costs, and income taxes. NOI is a proxy for property level operating cash flow. The expected annual NOI is divided by a capitalization rate (or cap rate) to estimate the value of the property. A cap rate is a discount rate less a growth rate. The reciprocal of the cap rate is a multiple that can be applied to NOI. The cap rate is estimated for a given property based on relevant information, including cap rates on sales of comparable properties, general business conditions, property quality, and assesment of management. The analysis might include assessing the strength of tenants, the level of landlord involvement, the extent and adequacy of repairs and improvements, the vacancy rate, management and operating costs, and expected inflation of costs and rent.

The discounted cash flow approach discounts future projected cash flows to arrive at a present value of the property. Typically, the analysis involves projections of annual operating cash flows for a finite number of periods and a resale or reversion value at the end of that total period. The projected resale value is often estimated using a direct capitalization approach.

■ Cost approach: This approach evaluates the replacement cost of the property by estimating the value of the land and the costs of rebuilding using current construction costs and standards. Costs include building materials, labour to build, tenant improvements, and various "soft" costs, including architectural and engineering costs, legal, insurance and brokerage fees, and environmental assessment costs. The cost of rebuilding is the replacement cost of the building(s) in new condition and is adjusted to take into account the location and condition of the existing building(s).

A combination and reconciliation of these approaches may be used to increase confidence in the appraisal.

5.4.1 *REIT Valuations*

REITs are composed of a portfolio of real estate properties or mortgages and as a result, a REIT security's valuation depends on the characteristics of the entire pool. There are two basic approaches to estimating the intrinsic value of a REIT: income-based and asset-based. The estimates of value can be compared with the observed market price of the REIT.

Income-based approaches for REITs are typically similar to the direct capitalization approach. A measure of income, which is a cash flow proxy, is capitalized into a value indication by using a cap rate (an alternative calculation could multiply the income measure by the reciprocal of the cap rate). Two common measures used are funds from operations (FFO) and adjusted funds from operations (AFFO). FFO, in its most basic form, equals net income plus depreciation charges on real estate property less gains from sales of real estate property plus losses on sales of real estate property. These adjustments to net income effectively exclude depreciation and the gains and losses from sales of real estate property from the FFO. Depreciation is excluded because it represents a non-cash charge and is often unrelated to changes in the value of the property. Gains and losses from sales are excluded because these are assumed to be non-recurring. AFFO adjusts the FFO for recurring capital expenditures. It is similar to a free cash flow measure.

The cap rate and its reciprocal multiple are estimated based on a variety of factors, including market cap rates and multiples of recent transactions, current market and economic conditions, expectations for growth in the relevant measure, risks associated with the REIT's underlying properties, and the financial leverage of the REIT.

Asset-based approaches calculate a REIT's NAV. Generally, a REIT's NAV is calculated as the estimated market value of a REIT's total assets minus the value of its total liabilities. REIT shares frequently trade at prices that differ from its NAV per share. Both premiums and discounts to the NAV are observed in the market.

5.5 Real Estate Investment Risks

Real estate investments, like any investment, may fail to perform in accordance with expectations. Property values are subject to variability based on national and global economic conditions, local real estate conditions, and interest rate levels. Other risks inherent to real estate investments include the ability of fund management to select, finance, and manage real properties, and changes in government regulations. Management of the underlying properties includes handling rentals or leasing of the property, controlling expenses, directing maintenance and improvements, and ultimately disposing of the property. Expenses may increase because of circumstances beyond the control of management. Returns to both debt and equity investors in real estate depend to a large extent on the ability of the owners or their agents to successfully operate the underlying properties.

Investments in distressed properties and property development are subject to greater risks than investments in properties with stable operations and/or sound financial condition. Property development is subject to special risks, including regulatory issues, construction delays, and cost overruns. Regulatory issues include the failure to receive zoning, occupancy and other approvals and permits, and the impact of environmental regulation. Economic conditions can also change over the development and disposition period, which can be very lengthy. Acquisitions and developments may be financed with lines of credit or other forms of temporary financing rather than long-term debt financing. There is a risk that long-term financing with acceptable terms might not be available when desired. Financing problems with one property may cause further activity by the same owner to be curtailed.

It is important to recognize that many equity investment real estate funds pursue leverage to potentially increase returns to their investors. Leverage magnifies the impact of gains and losses, because of operations and changes in property value, on the equity investors. Leverage increases the risk to equity investors and also increases the risk to debt investors. Leverage increases the risk that there will be insufficient funds to make expected interest payments and that principal will be not be recovered in its entirety. As the loan-to-value ratio increases, the latter risk increases.

6   COMMODITIES

Commodities are physical products. Returns on commodity investments are based on changes in price rather than on an income stream such as interest, dividends, or rent. In fact, holding commodities (i.e., the physical products) incurs costs for transportation and storage. Thus, most commodity investors do not trade actual physical commodities, but rather trade commodity derivatives. The underlying for a commodity derivative may be a single commodity or an index of commodities.

Trading in physical commodities is primarily limited to a smaller group of entities that are part of the physical supply chain. Some investors that are not part of the supply chain may invest in physical commodities, but the commodities are typically those that are non-perishable, of high value relative to weight and volume, and easily stored at relatively low cost. Most investors invest in commodities using commodity derivatives. However, because the prices of commodity derivatives are, to a significant extent, a function of the underlying commodity prices, it is important to understand the physical supply chain and general supply–demand dynamics of a commodity. The supply chain consists of entities that actually produce the commodities, users of the commodities, and participants in between. These entities may trade commodity derivatives for hedging purposes. Other investors, sometimes referred to as speculators, trade commodity derivatives in search of profit based largely on changes or expected changes in the price of the underlying commodities. Non-hedging investors include retail and institutional investors, hedge funds, proprietary desks within financial institutions, and trading desks operating within the physical supply chain.

Commodities include precious and base (i.e., industrial) metals, energy products, and agricultural products. Some examples of each type are shown in Exhibit 17. The relative importance, amount, and price of individual commodities evolve with society's preferences and needs. The increasing industrialization of China, India, and other emerging markets has driven strong global demand for commodities. Developing markets need increasing amounts of oil, steel, and other materials to support manufacturing, infrastructure development, and consumption demands of their populations. Emerging technologies, such as advanced cell phones and electric vehicles, may create demand for new materials to meet manufacturing needs. Thus, commodities of interest evolve over time.

Exhibit 17	Examples of Commodities
Sector	**Sample Commodities**
Energy	Oil, natural gas, electricity, coal
Base Metals	Copper, aluminum, zinc, lead, tin, nickel
Precious Metals	Gold, silver, platinum
Agriculture	Grains, livestock, coffee
Other	Carbon credits, freight, forest products

Commodities may be further classified based on a variety of factors, including physical location and grade or quality. For example, there are many grades and locations of oil. Similarly, there are many grades and locations of wheat. Commodity derivative contracts specify terms such as quantity, quality, maturity date, and delivery location.

Commodity derivatives may be attractive to investors not only for the potential profits but also because of the perceptions that commodities are effective hedges against inflation (i.e., commodity prices historically have been correlated with inflation) and that commodities are effective for portfolio diversification (i.e., commodity returns have historically low correlations with returns of other investments in the portfolio). Institutional investors, particularly endowments, foundations, and increasingly corporate and public pension funds and sovereign wealth funds are allocating more of their portfolios to investments in commodities and commodity derivatives. There were $354 billion of commodity investments under management in 2010, compared with less than $20 billion in 2001.[31]

6.1 Commodity Derivatives and Indices

The majority of commodities investing is implemented through derivatives, and commodity index futures are a popular derivative.[32] Commodity derivatives include futures, forwards, options, and swaps. These contracts may trade on exchanges (exchange-traded products, or ETPs) or over the counter (OTC). They are described as follows:

- Futures and forward contracts are obligations to buy or sell a specific amount of a given commodity at a fixed price, location, and date in the future. Futures contracts are ETPs, marked to market daily, and generally are not settled with delivery and receipt of the physical commodity. Forward contracts trade OTC,

31 Barclays Capital, November 2010.
32 Stoll & Whaley (2009) report commodities indexing totaling $174 billion as of July 2009.

and the expectation is that delivery and receipt of the physical commodity will occur. Counterparty risk is higher for forward contracts.

■ Options contracts for commodities give their holders the right, but not the obligation, to buy or sell a specific amount of a given commodity at a specified price and delivery location on or before a specified date in the future. Options can be ETPs or OTC traded.

■ Swaps contracts are agreements to exchange streams of cash flows between two parties based on future commodity or commodity index prices. One party typically makes fixed payments in exchange for payments that depend on a specified commodity or commodity index price.

Commodity indices typically use the price of futures contracts on the commodities included in them rather than the prices of the commodities themselves. As a result, the performance of a commodity index can be quite different from the performance of the underlying commodities. Commodity indices also vary in the commodities included in them and the weighting methods used. Thus, they vary in their exposures to specific commodities or commodity sectors.

6.2 Other Commodity Investment Vehicles

Commodity exposure can be achieved through other means than direct investment in commodities or commodity derivatives. Although commodity exposure is most commonly accessed via commodity derivatives, either directly or through an investment manager, alternative means are becoming increasingly popular. Alternative means of achieving commodity exposure include the following:

■ Exchange traded funds (ETFs) may be suitable for investors who can only buy equity shares or seek the simplicity of trading them. ETFs may invest in commodities or futures of commodities (often, specializing in a particular sector) seeking to track the performance of the commodities. For example, the SPDR Gold Trust ETF (NYSE: GLD) attempts to track the price of gold and owned over $50 billion in gold bullion as of November 2010. There are also commodity index-linked ETFs. ETFs may use leverage. Like mutual funds or unit trusts, ETFs charge fees that are included in their expense ratios, although the ETF expense ratios are generally lower than those of most mutual funds.

■ Common stock of companies exposed to a particular commodity, such as Royal Dutch Shell, which is exposed to oil, may be purchased. Investors may consider owning shares in a few commodity-exposed companies in order to have a small exposure to commodities. However, it is unclear that the performance of these stocks closely tracks the performance of the underlying commodity(ies).

■ Managed futures funds are actively managed investment funds. Professional money managers invest in the futures market (and forwards market sometimes) on behalf of the funds. These funds historically focused on commodity futures, but today they may invest in other futures contracts as well. The funds may concentrate on specific commodity sectors or may be broadly diversified. They are similar to hedge funds in that each fund has a general partner, and fees typically follow a 2 and 20 structure. The funds may operate similarly to mutual funds with shares that are available to the general public, or they may operate like hedge funds and restrict sales to high net worth and institutional investors. The former may be appealing to retail investors because of the professional management, low minimum investment, and relatively high liquidity.

■ Individual managed accounts are managed by chosen professional money managers with expertise in commodities and futures on behalf of high net worth individuals or institutional investors.

- Funds exist that specialize in specific commodity sectors. For example, private energy partnerships, like private equity funds, are a popular way for institutions to gain exposure to the energy sector. Management fees can range from 1 to 3 percent of committed capital with a lockup period of 10 years and extensions of 1- and 2-year periods. Publicly available energy mutual funds and unit trusts typically focus on the oil and gas sector. They may focus on upstream (drilling), midstream (refineries), or downstream (chemicals). Management fees for these funds are in line with those of other public equity managers and range from 0.4 to 1 percent.

6.3 Commodity Performance and Diversification Benefits

The arguments for investing in commodities include the potential for returns, portfolio diversification, and inflation protection. Investors may invest in commodities if they believe prices will increase in the short or intermediate terms. If commodity prices determine inflation index levels, then over time, on average, commodities should yield a zero real return. Commodity futures contracts may offer liquidity or other premiums, creating the opportunity for a real return different from zero.

The portfolio diversification argument is based on the observation that commodities historically have behaved differently during the business cycle from stocks and bonds. Panel A of Exhibit 18 shows the correlation between selected commodities, global equity, and global bond indices. Panel B shows returns, standard deviations, and Sharpe ratios for different investments. In the 20-year period of 1990–2009, commodities exhibited a low correlation with traditional assets; the correlations of commodities with global stocks and global bonds were 0.160 and 0.133, respectively. The correlations of stocks, bonds, and commodities are expected to be positive because each of the assets has some exposure to the global business cycle. Note that the selected commodity index (S&P GSCI Commodity Index) is heavily weighted toward the energy sector and that each commodity may exhibit unique behavior.

Exhibit 18	Commodities Return Correlations and Volatility

Panel A: Monthly Return Correlations, 1990–2009

	Global Stocks	Global Bonds	Commodities	1-mo. LIBOR	U.S. CPI
Global stocks	1.000	0.274	0.160	−0.057	−0.016
Global bonds		1.000	0.133	−0.020	−0.054
Commodities			1.000	0.025	0.336
1-mo. LIBOR				1.000	0.116

Panel B: Annualized Risk and Return, 1990–2009

	Global Stocks	Global Bonds	Commodities	1-mo. LIBOR	U.S. CPI
Return	6.2%	7.2%	4.5%	4.2%	2.7%
Volatility	16.8%	6.0%	23.4%	0.6%	1.2%
Sharpe ratio	0.12	0.50	0.01	0.00	NA

Sources: Global stocks = MSCI All Country World Index; Global bonds = Barclays Capital Global Aggregate Bond Index; Commodities = S&P GSCI Commodity Index.

The argument for commodities as a hedge against inflation is related to the fact that commodity prices affect inflation calculations. Commodities, especially energy and food, impact the cost of living for consumers. The positive correlation of 0.336 between monthly commodity price changes and monthly changes in the U.S. CPI supports this assertion. The correlations between the U.S. CPI and global stocks and global bonds are negative. The volatility of commodity prices, especially energy and food, is much higher than that of reported consumer inflation. Consumer inflation is computed from many products used by consumers, including housing, that change more slowly than commodity prices. Commodity investments, especially when combined with leverage, exhibit high volatility, and have led to many well-publicized losses among commodity players. A sample of these losses is provided in Exhibit 19.

Exhibit 19	Large Commodity Investor Losses
Affected Company	**Loss**
Bank of Montreal (2007)	Wrong-way bets on natural gas led to a pre-tax loss of C$680 million (US$663 million)
Amaranth Advisors LLC (2006)	Bad bets on natural gas triggered US$6.6 billion of losses
China Aviation Oil (Singapore) Corp. (2004)	Loss of US$550 million on speculative oil futures trades, forcing debt restructuring

Source: "The 20 Biggest Trading Disasters," The Telegraph, January 2008.

6.4 Commodity Prices and Investments

Commodity spot prices are a function of supply and demand, costs of production and storage, value to users, and global economic conditions. Non-hedging investors with positions in physical commodities may be accumulating or divesting a particular commodity. Supplies of commodities are determined by production and inventory levels and the actions of non-hedging investors. Demand for commodities is determined by the needs of end users and the actions of non-hedging investors.

Supplies of commodities cannot be altered quickly by producers because extended lead times may exist and affect production levels. For example, agricultural output may be altered by planting more and changing farming techniques, but at least a growing cycle is required before the actual output occurs. However, for agricultural products, at least one factor, which is outside of the control of the producer, the weather, will have a significant effect on output. Increased oil and mining production may require a number of years. Weather can also have significant effect on oil production in parts of the world. For commodities, the inability of suppliers to quickly respond to changes in demand levels may result in supply levels that are too low in times of economic growth and too high in times of economic slowing. In addition, despite advancing technology, the cost of new supply may grow over time. For example, the cost of new energy and mineral exploration tends to exceed that of past finds because easy discoveries tend to be exploited first. If the costs of production are high, the producers are unlikely to produce more than what is needed to meet anticipated demand and to maintain more than modest levels of inventory.

Overall demand levels are influenced by global manufacturing dynamics and economic growth. Manufacturing needs can change in a period of months as orders and inventories vary. Investors seek to anticipate these changes by monitoring economic events, including government policy, inventory levels, and forecasts for growth. When demand levels and investors' orders to buy and sell over a given period of time change quickly, the resulting mismatch of supply and demand may lead to price volatility.

6.4.1 *Pricing of Commodity Futures Contracts*

It is important to understand futures contracts and the sources of return for each commodity futures contract because commodity investments often involve the use of futures contracts. These contracts trade on exchanges. The buyer (i.e., the long side) of a futures contract is obligated to take delivery of the commodity or its cash equivalent based on the spot price at expiration and will pay a settlement price. The settlement price is an amount specified in the contract or the previous mark-to-market price if the contract has been marked to market. In other words, the long side is obligated to buy the commodity at the settlement price. The long side of a futures contract increases in value when the value of the underlying commodity increases in value. The seller of a futures contract (i.e., the short side) is obligated to deliver the commodity or its cash equivalent based on the spot price at expiration and will receive the settlement price.

Futures positions are often closed over the life of the contract by taking the opposite position to that originally entered into. In other words, the long side will sell an identical futures contract, and the short side will buy an identical futures contract. If a contract is outstanding at expiration, it is typically not settled by delivery and receipt of the physical commodity but rather, it is settled by cash equal to the difference between the cash equivalent and settlement price. If a contract is physically settled, there are specific rules defining the characteristics of acceptable delivery, such as the quality of the commodity and the location of the delivery.

Parties to a futures contract are required to make an initial margin payment on the contract; each party has a separate margin account. Futures contracts and margin accounts are typically marked to market daily. On a daily basis, the futures exchange calculates price changes in the contract and the values of the margin accounts given the new price. If the value in a margin account declines sufficiently, the investor will receive a margin call and will be required to make an additional payment into the margin account. If the investor is unable or unwilling to do so, the investor's position will be closed.

Given the characteristics of a commodity, the price of a futures contract (futures price) may be approximated by the following formula:[33]

Futures price ≈ Spot price (1+r) + Storage costs − Convenience yield

where r is the period's short-term risk-free interest rate. Arbitrage opportunities would exist if the futures price differs from the spot price compounded at the risk-free rate. For example, if the spot price of a commodity is 100 and the risk-free interest rate is 5 percent and the 1-year futures price is 107 as opposed to 105, an arbitrageur can buy the commodity for 100 and sell a futures contract for 107. Assuming no storage costs, when the commodity is delivered for 107, the arbitrageur earns 2 in excess of that earned investing in the risk-free asset. However, commodities typically incur a storage cost. The buyer of a futures contract, in effect, gains access to the commodity in the future without buying it now and incurring storage costs. The futures price includes an amount for storage costs of the underlying commodity over the life of the contract. The storage and interest costs together are sometimes referred to as "the cost of carry" or "the carry." Finally, the buyer of the futures contract does not have immediate access to the commodity but will receive it in the future. The buyer has given up the convenience of having physical possession of the commodity and having it immediately available for use. The futures price is adjusted for the loss of convenience; the convenience yield is subtracted to arrive at the futures price. The value

---

33 Futures pricing is discussed in greater detail in Level II of the CFA Program curriculum.

of convenience may vary over time and across users. For example, the convenience yield to having heating oil in January in Canada is higher than the convenience yield to having heating oil in Canada in July or to having heating oil in Australia in January.

Futures prices may be higher or lower than spot prices depending upon the convenience yield. When futures prices are higher than the spot price, the commodity forward curve is upward sloping, and the prices are referred to as being in contango. *Contango* occurs when there is little or no convenience yield. When futures prices are lower than the spot price, the commodity forward curve is downward sloping, and the prices are referred to as being in backwardation. *Backwardation* occurs when the convenience yield is high.

There are three sources of return for each commodity futures contract: the roll yield, the collateral yield, and the change in spot prices for the underlying commodity.

Roll Yield: The term "roll yield" refers to the difference between the spot price of a commodity and the price specified by its futures contract (or the difference between two futures contracts with different expiration dates). The formula shows that, with a convenience yield high enough to position the futures price below the spot price, the price of the futures contract generally rolls up to the spot price as the expiry date of the futures contract approaches. This price convergence earns the bearer of the futures contract a positive roll yield. This explanation is called the *theory of storage*. An alternative theory, called the *hedging pressure hypothesis*, suggests the difference between the spot and futures price is determined by user preferences and risk premiums.

Collateral Yield: The collateral yield component of the commodity index returns is the interest earned on the collateral (plus invested cash up to the value of the underlying asset) posted as a good-faith deposit for the futures contracts. In measuring this component of return, index managers typically assume that futures contracts are fully collateralized and that the collateral is invested in risk-free assets. Thus, the returns on a passive investment in commodity futures are expected to equal the return on the collateral plus a risk premium (i.e., the hedging pressure hypothesis) or the convenience yield net of storage costs (i.e., the theory of storage).

Spot Prices: The primary determinant of spot (or current) prices is the relationship between current supply and demand, as discussed earlier.

7   OTHER ALTERNATIVE INVESTMENTS

There are numerous other investments that do not fit within the definition of traditional investments (i.e., long-only investments in stocks, bonds, and cash) and may be considered alternative investments. Many of these other investments are categorized as collectibles.

Collectibles are tangible assets such as antiques and fine art, fine wine, rare stamps and coins, jewelry and watches, and sports memorabilia. Collectibles do not provide current income, but they can potentially provide long-term capital appreciation, diversify a portfolio, and be a source of enjoyment while held. However, there is no guarantee that any of these benefits will be realized. Collectibles can fluctuate dramatically in value and be highly illiquid with potential difficulty in realizing gains. Transactions can occur in a number of ways and settings, including through professional auctioneers; in local flea markets, online auctions, garage sales, and antique stores; or directly with personal collectors. Investors must have a degree of expertise, otherwise one may be vulnerable to fads, fakes, and fraud. Also, some collectibles must be stored in appropriate conditions to preserve their condition and avoid declines in value because of deterioration of the asset. Wine should be cellared, art should be kept in a humidity- and temperature-controlled environment, and coins and stamps must be handled with care to preserve their values. Although some collectibles (e.g., some great wines; fine art; and rare stamps, coins, and trading cards) have experienced great appreciation, this result is by no means the norm.

There are a number of indices that provide information about returns to these investments. Any of these indices are not necessarily reliable or representative of performance of a collectibles asset class as a whole. The Stanley Gibbons' SG 100 Stamp Index measures the performance, using retail and auction prices, of the 100 most traded stamps in the world. This index has increased from 291.50 at the end of 2000 to 475.78 at the end of 2010. This increase equals a 5 percent return per year over the 10-year period. This return, however, does not represent the return to the overall population of traded stamps.

The popularity of art as an investment has led to the creation of a number of art price indices. For example, Artprice provides statistics, econometric data, and indices to help measure returns on artworks. Another company that develops indices, Art Market Research, does not restrict itself to art but has over 500 indices in three broad categories: Painting; Antiques, Collectibles, Etc.; and Other Markets. The indices range from very broad [e.g., Painting (General) and Antiques (General)] to more specific [e.g., Chinese Ceramics (General) and Ancient Coins (General)] to very specific (e.g., Wrist-Watches Patek Philippe, Continental Flint-lock Pistols 1700–1800, and in wine, Château Lafite 1961). Subscribers are even able to specify parameters and create their own indices. Christie's first published an index of wine auction prices (listed by château) in 1972.

Collectors have no doubt been trading sports memorabilia since sporting events began to take place. One can only imagine the market for a piece of equipment or a keepsake of a martial artist in ancient China, an Olympian in ancient Greece, or a gladiator in ancient Rome. Trading cards—sports and other—have been swapped and sold in the United States since the early 1900s and are increasing in popularity elsewhere.[34] As is the case with any collectible, considerable expertise and perhaps a little luck are required to invest successfully in sports memorabilia.

RISK MANAGEMENT OVERVIEW

Alternative investments pose unusual challenges for investors seeking to manage risk. They are often characterized by asymmetric risk and return profiles, limited portfolio transparency, and illiquidity. Because of the active use of derivatives by many alternatives managers, operational risk, financial risk, counterparty risk, and liquidity risk are key considerations for prospective investors. The returns to some types of alternatives, such as private equity, may rely to a great extent on manager skill rather than on general asset class performance. For these reasons, traditional risk and return measures (such as mean return, standard deviation of returns, and beta) may not provide an adequate picture of characteristics of alternative investments. Moreover, these measures may not be reliable or representative of specific investments.

8.1 Investment and Risk Management Process

Investment risk management is not solely the responsibility of either the investor or the manager of an investment portfolio. The investor, possibly in consultation with others, decides on an allocation to alternative investments. The investor then needs to decide the vehicles and managers of the investments and the amounts that will be allocated

---

34 The most valuable baseball card in history, T206 Honus Wagner, was sold in 2007 for $2.35 million.

to each alternative investment class and manager. Risk has to be taken into account and due diligence conducted in making these decisions. The manager of an investment portfolio makes investment decisions consistent with the portfolio's established investment policies, taking risk into account. Investor due diligence should be used to ensure portfolio risk is effectively managed by the portfolio manager. Pension consultants, wealth managers, and individual investors all recognize that risk management processes can differ substantially between different alternative investment categories.

8.1.1 Risk Management Issues

Risks vary across alternative investments. The risks associated with investing in private markets (e.g., private equity funds and real estate ownership) differ from the risks associated with investing in publicly traded markets (e.g., commodity futures and REITs). Private equity and direct real estate ownership may involve selecting companies or properties, managing them, and then selling them years later. Private equity and hedge funds may have long lockup periods. As a result, investors' funds may be tied up for years. Intermediate valuations are challenging. As a result, any malfeasance or mismanagement may go undetected for years, so due diligence on the part of the investor is critical. The illiquid nature of alternative investments also means that poor manager selection can create a lingering drag on the portfolio. Limited partnership vehicles may limit the visibility of underlying holdings and liquidity to investor assets.

Portfolios of publicly traded securities are more liquid, with prices that are more timely and observable. For those who seek liquidity, publicly traded securities, such as shares of REITs, ETFs, and publicly traded private equity firms, may serve as the means for investing in alternatives.

8.1.2 Risk Issues for Implementation

For allocation purposes, the investor should recognize that historical returns and the standard deviation of those returns using indices may not be representative of the returns and volatility of alternative investments. Further, the reported correlations of those investments with other investments may vary from the actual correlations. As is always the case, even if these are relevant and representative measures of historical performance, past performance is not necessarily representative of future performance. The performance of alternative investments can be highly correlated with the business cycle, especially commodities and real estate investments, and may be susceptible to bubbles (i.e., much higher prices than justified by fundamentals). Investors should consider valuation before making allocation changes.

When selecting managers or funds, the investor should recognize that there may be significant differences in returns and risks among individual managers or funds and the overall investment class. Large institutional investors deal with this challenge by diversifying across managers or funds, but this approach may not be practical for smaller investors. As a result, these smaller investors may invest in (publicly traded) or with (private) a few large, diversified funds.

There are several risks of which alternative investment portfolio managers need to be mindful. In the case of illiquid investments, most notably in private equity or venture capital, there is a real possibility of 100 percent loss of equity on individual investments. As a result, portfolios should be diversified sufficiently to reduce the possibility of this outcome happening to all investments. At the same time, the manager should avoid diluting the opportunity for making substantial returns by arbitrarily identifying a target number of investments and, in the process, selecting inferior investments. Managers should consider and manage the risk associated with the use of leverage.

Performance fee structures, while high, may encourage alignment of interests between investors and managers. However, established portfolio managers may seek to attract large amounts of capital and to profit from the management fees based on assets under management or committed capital without seeking superior performance. Performance fees may also encourage hedge fund managers who experience a large loss to liquidate their funds instead of working them back to par.

8.1.3 *Due Diligence Issues Regarding Risk*

Due diligence of alternative investment managers necessitates special procedures, over and above the process required for a manager of a portfolio of publicly traded securities. Historical measures of performance may not be reliable or representative as a result of intermediate valuation estimates and narrow portfolio diversification. With limited transparency and long horizons, the honesty of the company's staff needs to be carefully reviewed.

Hedge funds will have trading desks much like long-only investment firms, but private equity and real estate companies usually make investment decisions via an investment committee of partners. These may or may not include external non-executive directors or subject matter experts. The committee votes on the rationale, analysis, and suitability of every investment and requires a majority in favour before investor funds are committed. This committee may also oversee and vote on exit strategies of investments, including timing and realization price.

Independent valuation of illiquid underlying assets should be performed on a regular basis. Often, this analysis is done in conjunction with a portfolio review explaining the performance of every transaction in detail, its status, and future strategy for the portfolio. Limits on security type, leverage, sector, geography, and individual positions should be well defined in the offering memorandum, and the positions should be carefully monitored by the manager and regularly reported to clients.

Hedge fund risk is often monitored by a chief risk officer, who should be separated from the investment process. As part of the risk management process, a hedge fund needs to establish and maintain limits on leverage, sector, and individual positions. Investments in commodities may be subject to counterparty risks as well as leverage risks. The exposure to counterparty risk and leverage risk should be regularly monitored and reported. Policies limiting leverage, positions, and sectors as well as counterparty exposures may be adopted.

One issue for investors is that hedge and commodity funds may seek to keep their positions and strategies private. This lack of transparency makes it difficult for the investor to effectively manage diversification across funds and to conduct adequate due diligence.

8.2 Risk–Return Measures

The Sharpe ratio is a risk–return measure frequently reported because of its ease of calculation and understandability. The Sharpe ratio may not be the appropriate risk–return measure for alternative investments because measures of return and standard deviation may not be relevant and reliable given the illiquid nature of the assets. The illiquid nature of the assets means that estimates, rather than observable transaction prices, may be used for valuation purposes. As a result, returns may be smoothed and/or overstated and the volatility of returns understated. Also, the use of standard deviation as the measure of risk ignores the diversification impact for a broad portfolio of managers and alternative investments.

Many alternative investments do not exhibit close-to-normal distributions of returns, which is a crucial assumption for the validity of a standard deviation as a comprehensive risk measure. Alternative investment returns tend to be leptokurtic, negatively skewed (i.e., they have fat tails characterized by positive average returns and long-tails downside characterized by potential extreme losses). For this reason, a measure of downside risk, ideally non-normal, would be useful. Downside risk measures focus on the left side of the return distribution curve where losses occur. For example, value at risk (VaR) is a measure of the minimum amount of loss expected over a given time period at a given level of probability. In other words, this measure answers a question such as, "What is the minimum amount expected to be lost in a year with a 5 percent probability?" However, this measure, if it is calculated using standard deviation, will underestimate the VaR for a negatively skewed distribution. Shortfall or safety-first risk measures the probability that the portfolio value will fall below some minimum acceptable level over a given time period. In other words, this measure answers a question such as, "What is the probability of losing 20 percent of principal in any given year?" This measure also uses standard deviation as the measure of risk. The Sortino ratio, another measure of downside risk, uses downside deviation rather than standard deviation as a measure of risk. Assuming normal probability distributions when calculating these measures will lead to an underestimation of downside risk for a negatively skewed distribution.

Understanding and evaluating "tail events"—low probability, high severity instances of stress—is an important, yet extraordinarily difficult aspect of the risk management process. Stress testing/scenario analysis is often used as a complement to VaR to develop a better understanding of the potential loss of a portfolio under both normal and stressed market conditions. Stress testing involves estimating losses under extremely unfavourable conditions.

8.3 Due Diligence Overview

Manager selection is a critical factor in portfolio performance. A manager should have a verifiable track record and display a high level of expertise and experience with the asset type. The asset management team should be assigned an appropriate workload and provided sufficient resources. Moreover, they should be rewarded with an effective compensation package to ensure alignment of interest, continuity, motivation, and thoughtful oversight of assets.

Fraud, while infrequent, is always a possibility. The investor should be sceptical of unusually good and overly consistent reported performance. Third-party custody of assets and independent verification of results can help reduce the chance of an investor being defrauded. Diversification across mangers is also wise.

For a new investor, a proper due diligence process should be carried out to ensure that the targeted investment is in compliance with its prospectus and that it will meet his/her investment strategy, risk and return objectives, and restrictions. Existing investors should monitor results and fund holdings to determine whether a fund has performed in line with expectations and continues to comply with its prospectus.

Exhibit 20 lists key items that should be considered in a typical due diligence process.

Exhibit 20	A Typical Due Diligence Process

Organization:
- Experience and quality of management team, compensation, and staffing
- Analysis of prior and current funds
- Track record/alignment of interests
- Reputation and quality of third-party service providers, e.g., lawyers, auditors, prime brokers

Exhibit 20	**Continued**

Portfolio Management:	■ Investment process
	■ Target markets/asset types/strategies
	■ Sourcing of investments
	■ Role of operating partners
	■ Underwriting
	■ Environmental and engineering review process
	■ Integration of asset management/acquisitions/ dispositions
	■ Disposition process, including how initiated and executed
Operations and Controls:	■ Reporting and accounting methodology
	■ Audited financial statements and other internal controls
	■ Valuations—frequency and approach(es)
	■ Insurance and contingency plans
Risk Management:	■ Fund policies and limits
	■ Risk management policy
	■ Portfolio risk and key risk factors
	■ Leverage and currency—risks/constraints/hedging
Legal Review:	■ Fund structure
	■ Registrations
	■ Existing/prior litigation
Fund Terms:	■ Fees (management and performance) and expenses
	■ Contractual terms
	■ Investment period and fund term and extensions
	■ Carried interest
	■ Distributions
	■ Conflicts
	■ Limited partners' rights
	■ "Key Person" and/or other termination procedures

Alternative investing may add value to an investor's portfolio. However, to be effective, alternative investing requires thoughtful implementation, including consideration of the amount to allocate to alternative investments and of diversification among alternative investments. Valuation issues, manager selection, and risk management are other items to be considered.

SUMMARY

This reading has provided an overview of the characteristics, potential benefits, and risks of alternative investments. Features of some categories of alternative investments were described. Including alternative investments in an investor's portfolio may result in benefits, such as diversification benefits. However, these benefits do not come without associated risks. It is important that investors understand these risks before including alternative investments in their portfolios. Some key points of the reading are summarized below:

▪ Alternative investments are alternatives to long-only positions in stocks, bonds, and cash. Alternative investments include investments in assets such as real estate and commodities and investments in special vehicles such as private equity and hedge funds.

▪ Characteristics, common to many alternative investments compared with traditional investments, include lower liquidity, less regulation, lower transparency; higher fees; and limited and potentially problematic historical risk and return data.

▪ Alternative investments often have unique legal and tax considerations and may be highly leveraged.

▪ Alternative investments are attractive to investors because of potential for diversification and higher returns when added to a portfolio of traditional investments.

▪ The risks associated with alternative investments must be factored into the decision-making process.

▪ Many alternative investments are valued for performance reporting purposes, including reporting to index providers, using estimated values rather than actual market prices. As a result, the volatility of returns and correlation of returns with the returns to traditional investments will tend to be underestimated. It is important to identify and understand how alternative investments are valued.

▪ Indices for alternative investments may be subject to a variety of biases, including survivorship and backfill biases.

▪ Alternative investment strategies are typically active, alpha-seeking strategies.

▪ Many alternative investments, such as hedge and private equity funds, use a partnership structure with a general partner (the fund) that manages the business and bears unlimited liability and limited partners (investors) who own fractional interests in the partnership.

▪ The general partner (the fund) typically receives a management fee based on assets under management or committed capital (the former is common to hedge funds and the latter is common to private equity funds) and an incentive fee based on realized profits.

▪ Hurdle rates, high water marks, lockup and notice periods, side pockets, and clawback provisions may also be specified in a partnership agreement.

▪ The fee structure affects the returns to investors (limited partners) in alternative investments such as hedge and private equity funds.

▪ Hedge funds are typically classified by strategy. One such classification includes four broad categories of strategies: event-driven, relative value, macro, and equity hedge.

▪ Primary private equity fund strategies include leveraged buyouts, venture capital, development capital, and distressed investing. Leveraged buyouts and venture capital are the dominant strategies.

▪ Real estate investing includes direct and indirect ownership of real estate property and lending against real estate properties.

▪ Real estate property has some unique features, including basic indivisibility, heterogeneity (no two properties are identical), and fixed location.

- The required amount to directly invest in real estate may be large, and the investment may be relatively illiquid. Different investment forms, such as REITs and mortgage securitizations, partially accommodate these issues.

- Commodity investments may involve investing in actual physical commodities or in producers of commodities, but more typically, commodity investing is done using commodity derivatives.

- Returns to commodity investing are based on changes in price and do not include an income stream such as dividends, interest, or rent.

- Managing risks associated with alternative investments can be challenging because these investments are often characterized by asymmetric risk and return profiles, limited portfolio transparency, and illiquidity.

- Traditional risk and return measures (such as mean return, standard deviation of returns, and beta) may not provide an adequate picture of characteristics of alternative investments. Moreover, these measures may not be reliable or representative of specific investments.

- Operational, financial, counterparty, and liquidity risks may be key considerations for those investing in alternative investments.

- It is critical to do due diligence to assess whether (a) a potential investment is in compliance with its prospectus; (b) the appropriate organizational structure and policies for managing investments, operations, risk, and compliance are in place; and (c) the fund terms appear reasonable.

- The inclusion of alternative investments in a portfolio, including the amounts to allocate, should be considered in the context of an investor's risk–return objectives, constraints, and preferences.

REFERENCES

Brooks, C., and H. Kat. 2002. "The Statistical Properties of Hedge Fund Index Returns and Their Implications for Investors." *Journal of Alternative Investments*, vol. 5, no. 25 : 44.

Hall, Robert, and Susan Woodward. 2004. "Benchmarking the Returns to Venture." National Bureau of Economic Research. January, 2004.

Heisler, J., C. Knittel, J. Neumann, and S. Stewart. 2007. "Why do Institutional Plan Sponsors Hire and Fire Their Investment Managers?" *Journal of Business and Economic Studies*, vol. 13, no. 1 : 88–118.

Kaplan, Steven N., and Antoinette Schoar. 2005. "Private Equity Performance, Returns, Persistence, and Capital Flows." *Journal of Finance*, vol. 60, no. 4 : 1791–1823.

Stewart, S., J. Heisler, C. Knittel, and J. Neumann. 2009. "Absence of Value: an Analysis of Investment Allocation Decisions by Institutional Plan Sponsors." *Financial Analysts Journal*, vol. 65, no. 6 : 34–51.

Stoll, Hans R. and Robert E. Whaley. 2009. "Commodity Index Investing and Commodity Futures Prices." Working paper, Vanderbilt University.

PRACTICE PROBLEMS[1] FOR READING 66

1. Which of the following is *least likely* to be considered an alternative investment?

   A. Real estate

   B. Commodities

   C. Long-only equity funds

2. An investor is seeking an investment that can take long and short positions, may use multi-strategies, and historically exhibits low correlation with a traditional investment portfolio. The investor's goals will be *best* satisfied with an investment in:

   A. real estate.

   B. a hedge fund.

   C. a private equity fund.

3. Relative to traditional investments, alternative investments are *least likely* to be characterized by:

   A. high levels of transparency.

   B. limited historical return data.

   C. significant restrictions on redemptions.

4. Alternative investment funds are typically managed:

   A. actively.

   B. to generate positive beta return.

   C. assuming that markets are efficient.

5. An investor is most likely to consider adding alternative investments to a traditional investment portfolio because:

   A. of their historically higher returns.

   B. of their historically lower standard deviation of returns.

   C. their inclusion is expected to reduce the portfolio's Sharpe ratio.

6. An investor may prefer a single hedge fund to a fund of funds if he seeks:

   A. due diligence expertise.

   B. better redemption terms.

   C. a less complex fee structure.

7. Hedge funds are similar to private equity funds in that both:

   A. are typically structured as partnerships.

   B. assess management fees based on assets under management.

   C. do not earn an incentive fee until the initial investment is repaid.

8. An investor seeks a current income stream as a component of total return, and desires an investment that historically has low correlation with other asset classes. The investment *most likely* to achieve the investor's goals is:

   A. timberland.

   B. collectibles.

   C. commodities.

1 Developed by Jennie I. Sanders, CFA (Austin, TX, USA).

9. A hedge fund invests primarily in distressed debt. Quoted market prices are available for the underlying holdings but they trade infrequently. Which of the following will the hedge fund *most likely* use in calculating net asset value for trading purposes?

   A. Average quotes

   B. Average quotes adjusted for liquidity

   C. Bid prices for short positions and ask prices for long positions

10. Angel investing capital is typically provided in which stage of financing?

   A. Later-stage.

   B. Formative-stage.

   C. Mezzanine-stage.

11. If a commodity's forward curve is in contango, the component of a commodities futures return *most likely* to reflect this is:

   A. spot prices.

   B. the roll yield.

   C. the collateral yield.

12. United Capital is a hedge fund with $250 million of initial capital. United charges a 2% management fee based on assets under management at year end, and a 20% incentive fee based on returns in excess of an 8% hurdle rate. In its first year, United appreciates 16%. Assume management fees are calculated using end-of-period valuation. The investor's net return assuming the performance fee is calculated net of the management fee is *closest* to:

   A. 11.58%.

   B. 12.54%.

   C. 12.80%.

13. Capricorn Fund of Funds invests GBP 100 million in each of Alpha Hedge Fund and ABC Hedge Fund. Capricorn FOF has a "1 and 10" fee structure. Management fees and incentive fees are calculated independently at the end of each year. After one year, net of their respective management and incentive fees, the investment in Alpha is valued at GBP80 million and the investment in ABC is valued at GBP140 million. The annual return to an investor in Capricorn, net of fees assessed at the fund of funds level, is *closest* to:

   A. 7.9%.

   B. 8.0%.

   C. 8.1%.

14. An analyst wanting to assess the downside risk of an alternative investment is *least likely* to use the investment's:

   A. Sortino ratio.

   B. value at risk (VaR).

   C. standard deviation of returns.

SOLUTIONS FOR READING 66

1. C is correct. Long-only equity funds are typically considered traditional investments and real estate and commodities are typically classified as alternative investments.

2. B is correct. Hedge funds may use a variety of strategies (event-driven, relative value, macro and equity hedge), generally have a low correlation with traditional investments, and may take long and short positions.

3. A is correct. Alternative investments are characterized as typically having low levels of transparency.

4. A is correct. There are many approaches to managing alternative investment funds but typically these funds are actively managed and aim to generate positive alpha return.

5. A is correct. The historically higher returns to most categories of alternative investments compared with traditional investments result in potentially higher returns to a portfolio containing alternative investments. The less than perfect correlation with traditional investments results in portfolio risk (standard deviation) being less than the weighted average of the standard deviations of the investments. This has potential to increase the Sharpe ratio in spite of the historically higher standard deviation of returns of most categories of alternative investments.

6. C is correct. Hedge funds of funds have multi-layered fee structures, while the fee structure for a single hedge fund is less complex. Funds of funds presumably have some expertise in conducting due diligence on hedge funds and may be able to negotiate more favorable redemption terms than could an individual investor in a single hedge fund.

7. A is correct. Private equity funds and hedge funds are typically structured as partnerships where investors are limited partners (LP) and the fund is the general partner (GP). The management fee for private equity funds is based on committed capital whereas for hedge funds the management fees are based on assets under management. For most private equity funds, the general partner does not earn an incentive fee until the limited partners have received their initial investment back.

8. A is correct. Timberland offers an income stream based on the sale of timber products as a component of total return and has historically generated returns not highly correlated with other asset classes.

9. B is correct. Many practitioners believe that liquidity discounts are necessary to reflect fair value. This has resulted in some funds having two NAVs—for trading and reporting. The fund may use average quotes for reporting purposes but apply liquidity discounts for trading purposes.

10. B is correct. Formative-stage financing occurs when the company is still in the process of being formed and encompasses several financing steps. Angel investing capital is typically raised in this early stage of financing.

11. B is correct. Roll yield refers to the difference between the spot price of a commodity and the price specified by its futures contract (or the difference between two futures contracts with different expiration dates). When futures prices are higher than the spot price, the commodity forward curve is upward sloping, and the prices are referred to as being in contango. Contango occurs when there is little or no convenience yield.

12. B is correct. The net investor return is 12.54%, calculated as:

      End of year capital = $250 million x 1.16 = $290 million

      Management fee = $290 million x 2% = $5.8 million

      Hurdle amount = 8% of $250 million = $20 million;

      Incentive fee = ($290 – $250 – $20 – $5.8) million x 20% = $2.84 million

      Total fees to United Capital = ($5.8 + $2.84) million = $8.64 million

      Investor net return: ($290 – $250 – $8.64) / $250 = 12.54%

13. A is correct because the net investor return is 7.9%, calculated as:

    First, note that "1 and 10" refers to a 1% management fee, and a 10% incentive fee.

      End of year capital = GBP140 million + GBP80 million = GBP220 million

      Management fee = GBP220 million x 1% = GBP2.2 million

      Incentive fee = (GBP220 – GBP200) million x 10% = GBP2 million

      Total fees to Capricorn = (GBP2.2 + GBP2) million = GBP4.2 million

      Investor net return: (GBP220 – GBP200 – GBP4.2) / GBP200 = 7.9%

14. C is correct. Downside risk measures focus on the left side of the return distribution curve where losses occur. The standard deviation of returns assumes that returns are normally distributed. Many alternative investments do not exhibit close-to-normal distribution of returns, which is a crucial assumption for the validity of a standard deviation as a comprehensive risk measure. Assuming normal probability distributions when calculating these measures will lead to an underestimation of downside risk for a negatively skewed distribution. Both the Sortino ratio and the value-at-risk measure are both measures of downside risk.

67

Investing in Commodities

by Ronald G. Layard-Liesching

LEARNING OUTCOMES	
Mastery	**The candidate should be able to:**
☐	**a** explain the relationship between spot prices and expected future prices in terms of contango and backwardation;
☐	**b** describe the sources of return and risk for a commodity investment and the effect on a portfolio of adding an allocation to commodities;
☐	**c** explain why a commodity index strategy is generally considered an active investment.

Investing in commodities remains controversial. But a long-only allocation to commodities brings risk reduction and inflation protection to a traditional portfolio asset mix. As more public and private pension funds are searching for higher-returning and liability-matching assets, interest in commodity investment is rising rapidly. Currently, the majority of institutional investment in commodities is index based, and trading to maintain index exposure makes this an active strategy. And although institutional commodity investment is in its infancy, newer strategies, such as index plus and active long-only, are increasing in popularity.

Commodities are now capturing the interest of institutional investors because, to put it simply, the math works. The average U.S. public pension fund has a return target of 8 percent, but the prospect over the next few years for the basic 60 percent/40 percent equity/fixed-income mix is dim. With the estimated return for bonds around 5 percent, a gross equity return of nearly 11 percent a year is needed to make up the difference. Few investors believe this type of return is achievable. Thus, plan sponsors are seeking new uncorrelated sources of return, such as commodities, to introduce into the traditional portfolio mix.

Funds are also increasingly concerned with managing liability-relative risks and are turning to liability-driven investment strategies. The United States has a huge problem with underfunded retirement benefits, but in many other countries, the situation is even worse. Hence, around the globe, pension fund chief investment officers are trying to find the asset class with an expected risk–return profile that improves upon that of more traditional investments and more closely matches their funds' growing liabilities. This quest is driving managers to alternative investments, in general, and to commodities, in particular.

> **NOTE:** Commodity index strategies, unlike U.S. equity index strategies, are active strategies because of the high turnover.

This presentation comes from the 2006 Financial Analysts Seminar held in Evanston, Illinois, on 16–21 July 2006.

Global Perspectives on Investment Management: Learning from the Leaders, edited by Rodney N. Sullivan, CFA. Copyright © 2006 by CFA Institute.

This reading will begin with a basic introduction to commodities before proceeding to a discussion of the controversies surrounding the commodity markets. Then, I will explain how commodities fit into a portfolio and will suggest a lens other than mean–variance analysis with which to view their contribution. Through that lens, commodity investment appears rather attractive. The existence of a commodity return premium is currently actively debated mainly because the asset class does not produce cash flow. So, I will outline the sources of commodity returns. Finally, I will explain the alternatives for institutions seeking to implement commodity investment programs.

COMMODITY BASICS

Commodity strategies require investing cash collateral to support derivatives exposure. The principal derivatives are forwards and futures contracts. Note that a relationship exists between the spot (current) price of the commodity and the expected spot price of the commodity at the maturity date of the derivative contract. If the future price is above the spot price, this is referred to as "contango." If the future price is below the spot price, this is referred to as "backwardation."

Contango

When a commodity market is in contango, as illustrated in Figure 1, futures prices are higher than the spot price because market participants believe the spot price will be higher in the future. Contango often occurs when a commodity's price is high and volatile, as is the case currently with oil. For example, the oil consumer, such as an airline, drives the price of the futures higher than the spot price as it attempts to hedge against the risk of higher spot prices, which could ultimately cause it to go out of business.

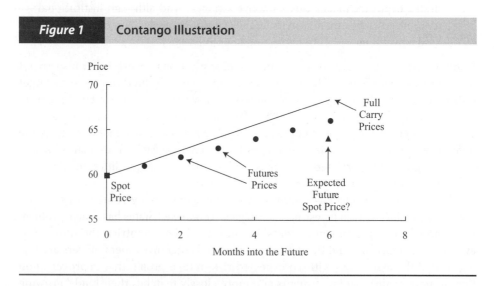

| Figure 1 | Contango Illustration |

The amount by which the relative price of the futures can rise is limited, however, by a classic arbitrage trade. If the futures price goes too high, an investor can buy the commodity at the spot price, store it, insure it, and sell it forward. This "carry trade" is a pure financing activity and theoretically limits the futures price to a level called "full carry." A commodity like gold can be easily borrowed in large size, and the borrowing cost of gold is usually below dollar cash interest rates. Hence, this arbitrage means that gold will often be at full carry in the forward market. But different commodities have unique features that affect this relationship.

For example, there may be limitations on storing commodities for future delivery. Hogs, for instance, cannot be stored indefinitely because they have finite lives. There also may be physical limits on available storage for delivery. In these cases, the classic carry trade does not apply. So, forward prices can rise far above the spot price, reflecting a future supply shortage.

For most commodities, the investor buys a futures contract with a set maturity date. When the futures contract is purchased, the investor deposits cash as collateral for the contract with the exchange. This cash generates an additional return called the "collateral yield." But the investor wishes to maintain long-only commodity exposure. So, when the contract matures, it is closed out and another one is bought with a longer maturity. This trade is called "rolling the contract." This contract rolling creates a small profit or loss that is unrelated to the spot price movement. In this way, the investor maintains long exposure to the commodity. For most commodities, exceptions being precious metals, such as silver and gold, it would not be practical to actually hold the physical commodity.

Backwardation

The opposite of contango is when the forward price or futures price of a commodity is below its spot price. This situation is referred to as "backwardation" and is illustrated in Figure 2. Backwardation used to be common in the oil market. When the price of oil was low, producers wanted to hedge their risk of further price declines. Lower prices threatened their ability to stay in business. Backwardation actually used to be the norm in most commodities because a potential price fall had a proportionally bigger impact on the few large producers than on the many small consumers. This feature was analyzed by John Maynard Keynes, who referred to it as "natural backwardation." Commodity producers were willing to sell their commodity below the price they expected it to be in the future to protect against business risk. There was substantial disutility to this large group of producers if the price fell. So, long-only speculators gained by taking over this price risk from the producers. This natural backwardation may be changing, however, because derivatives trading and institutional investing make for greater symmetry. When prices are low and volatile, producers hedge and the market enters backwardation. When prices are high and volatile, consumers hedge. At the same time, investors are attempting to hedge inflation risk. The combination of these two actions creates contango.

Figure 2	Backwardation Illustration

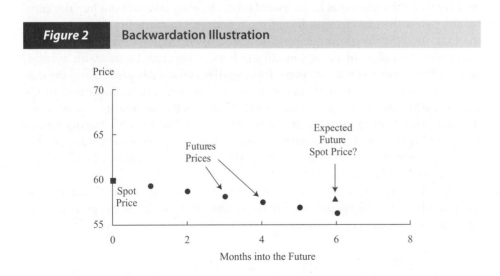

Sources of Return

Long-only investment in commodities is usually obtained via collateralized long positions in commodity futures, forwards, or swaps. The institutional investor receives three distinct sources of return: collateral yield, roll or convenience yield, and the spot price return. Figure 3 plots the three yield components of a commodity index investment. The collateral yield is the return on cash used as margin to take long derivatives exposure. Generally, this is a T-bill return. Active collateral management can enhance this return.

Figure 3	Yield Components of Commodities, January 1986– December 2004

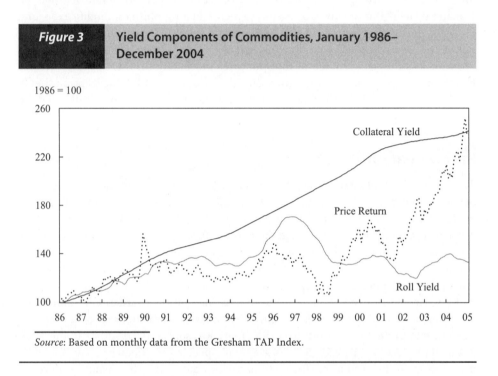

Source: Based on monthly data from the Gresham TAP Index.

The roll yield (also known as "convenience yield") is the return from rolling forward the maturity of the derivatives position. During the period shown in Figure 3, the roll yield was both positive and negative. The return to the long investor is positive when the market is in backwardation; the long investor can buy the commodity below the current spot level from a hedger. On maturity, the hedger pays the long investor the convergence in price between the forward and spot rates. Currently, the roll yield on commodity indices is negative because, on average, commodity markets are in contango. This negative roll yield is particularly the case for oil, which has a large weight in the major commodity indices. Because of future expected oil supply shortages, speculators have driven the futures price of oil above the spot price. For the majority of commodities, long investors are buying futures at a price higher than the spot price. Hence, if the spot price moves sideways, the long position will be closed out at a loss. That difference in price is lost, and as a result, the roll yield is negative.

The price return can obviously be positive or negative based on fluctuations in its spot price caused by supply and demand. Over the past 25 years, price returns, although volatile, have been strong.

COMMODITY CONTROVERSIES

Much controversy exists about whether commodities are an asset class. Fueling the debate over the classification of commodities as an asset class are the arguments that commodity prices decline in the very long run, roll yield may disappear, rolling costs may reduce returns, and the return premium may result from rebalancing. Of course, the argument that commodities cannot be an asset class because they do not generate cash flow is frequently heard, but I will address that later in the reading.

Commodity Prices

Some argue that commodity prices decline in the long run (and hence are not an asset class). Over the last century, spot commodity prices have fallen by some 1.5 percent a year. The time horizons of most portfolios, however, are much shorter than 100 years. Figure 3 shows that from 1989 to 2000, the spot price basically moved sideways, generating minimal price return, but took off like a rocket in early 2001. Investors who bought the argument against holding commodities missed out on this spectacular run-up in price.

Commodity prices decline because of the introduction of new supplies and new production technology (such as the Alaska oil sands and coal gasification), substitution of one commodity for another when prices rise (such as aluminum for copper in power lines), and reduction in the use of certain commodities in technological processes (such as optical fibers for copper).

Offsetting these effects are the facts that global supplies are finite for many commodities, demand for storable commodities is rising, and the engagement in the global economy of the postemergent economies of China and India fundamentally alters global demand and supply.

Most of the fluctuation in commodity prices comes from the demand side of the equation. The supply-side shifts are usually smaller and slower to respond than are demand fluctuations (note that this is not true of electricity, for example, where supply disruptions can cause dramatic price moves). So, as demand rises for a finite supply of a commodity, the price of the commodity is bound to rise.

The demand for storable commodities, which can be held as hard assets, is also increasing. The lack of cash flow from these commodities is irrelevant: Investors hold U.S. dollar balances because of their usefulness as a store of value. The same dynamic is affecting the demand for commodities. Commodities are perceived as a good store of value in an increasingly risky and unstable world.

The prices of commodities will also rise because they are denominated in units of paper currency. As the value of a currency falls, prices of commodities denominated in that currency rise. In other words, the price of commodities operates as an exchange rate. It is the exchange rate between the commodity and the value of a paper currency—the U.S. dollar. So, if the dollar depreciates or loses its purchasing power, the value of commodities will appreciate. The existence of truly massive unfunded U.S. dollar deficits explains one component of the long-term return premium to long commodity investing.

Roll Yield

The roll yield is the yield that has historically existed in situations when the forward price is below the spot price. Producers sell commodities at prices lower than the expected future price to hedge their business risk, which benefits long investors and speculators. But the rapid growth in institutional long-only investors and growing worldwide demand for commodities may have created permanent structural change in the marketplace. It is raising fears that the roll yield may disappear. At the moment, it is indeed negative, but this has been seen before.

When Keynes formulated his theory of natural backwardation, developed futures markets did not exist and the preponderance of market participants were hedgers. The bottom line was that long investors won and hedgers lost. Today's market is no longer dominated by participants with a single motive, so the market can move both ways. Opportunities to add value have thus increased because of the disassociation between the price of the futures and the expected future price.

Rolling Costs

Investing in indices requires that the investor roll his or her exposure. In other words, at the maturity date of the futures contract, the investor can either take physical delivery of the commodity or roll the futures contract, which means buying another contract with a new maturity date. The rolling cost is the cost to sell the maturing contract and buy a new one.

The indices, such as the Goldman Sachs Commodity Index (GSCI) and the Dow Jones-AIG Commodity Index (DJ-AIG), roll on specified dates over five business days. During this period, a very high volume of contracts trades because of the tremendous size of the indices' long holdings. The market makers know which contracts are involved, so the roll, not surprisingly, becomes more expensive. Thus, the dynamics of the roll inflict a hidden, but significant, cost on long-only investors that definitely reduces returns. Roll costs, however, can be reduced or avoided through active roll maturity and timing management.

Return Premium

An academic debate is stirring about the commodity return premium. The debate basically revolves around the fact that over the same time period, the long-term geometric return of the average commodity was close to zero but the geometric return of the commodity index was strong. How can the commodity basket have a higher geometric return than the components? The answer is that index volatility is lower than the average volatility of its constituents (29 percent). Rebalancing occurs when the weights of holdings in different commodities need to be adjusted back to the index weights after large price moves. So, if the oil price rises sharply, oil must be sold and the other commodities purchased. Rebalancing can thus add value. Therefore, the geometric return of a rebalanced portfolio is higher than the average return of its constituents. The approximate relationship, according to Booth and Fama (1992), is

$$G = M - \frac{\sigma^2}{2},$$

where G is the geometric return, M is the arithmetic return, and σ is the volatility. Erb and Harvey (2006) argued that this rebalancing return provides essentially all the return to commodity investing. Gorton and Rouwenhorst (2006) countered this argument, showing that rebalancing interacts with return seriality. The crucial point is that the primary driver of return in commodities is not simply the rebalancing process.

COMMODITIES IN A PORTFOLIO

Long-term commodity investment offers several positives to a portfolio. The risk–return profile of commodities over the past 25 years is similar to that of U.S. equities. Commodities also provide a reduction in portfolio risk, which is the primary argument for adding commodities to traditional portfolios. Return-timing diversification as well as inflation shock and liability matching are other reasons for adding commodities to a portfolio.

Long-Term Return

Figure 4 shows long-term bond, stock, and commodity futures returns. All three returns were positive over the period. From January 1991 to April 2006, the volatilities of the two major commodity indices—the DJ-AIG (12.1 percent) and the GSCI (18.6 percent)—and the volatility of equities as measured by the S&P 500 Index (14.2 percent) were quite similar, as shown in Table 1. As one would assume, the volatility of bonds as measured by the Lehman Brothers U.S. Aggregate Index (3.8 percent) was much lower than that for either equities or commodities. Note that the volatility of the DJ-AIG was lower than that of the GSCI because it is a much more evenly weighted basket of commodities; the GSCI is currently 73 percent energy weighted versus 33 percent for the DJ-AIG. A mean–variance optimizer loves commodities because of their negative correlation with other markets and their interesting risk–return characteristics. As a result, it will allocate a higher percentage of the portfolio to commodities than prudence dictates is wise. There is a better way to analyze the commodity allocation.

Figure 4	Inflation-Adjusted Performance of Stocks, Bonds, and Commodity Futures, July 1959–December 2004

July 1959 = 100

Source: Gorton and Rouwenhorst (2006).

Table 1	Return and Volatility, January 1991–April 2006

Index	Return	Volatility
S&P 500	11.2%	14.2%
DJ-AIG	4.2	12.1
GSCI	7.8	18.6
Lehman Brothers U.S. Aggregate	7.0	3.8

Note: Data are monthly.
Sources: Based on data from Standard & Poor's, Lehman Brothers, and Goldman, Sachs & Co.

Portfolio Risk

A. D. Roy, who published a paper in 1952 at about the same time Harry M. Markowitz was writing his Nobel Prize–winning paper on modern portfolio theory, said that investors do not want to know the long-run average expected rate of return on their portfolios. They want to know what will happen next year. Roy's point was that to be a long-term investor, you have to be able to survive the short run. As an alternative to mean–variance portfolio selection, Roy developed "safety-first" investing—choosing the highest-returning portfolio subject to the worst-case short-run outcome being acceptable.

Table 2 illustrates the portfolio impact of commodities during the period from January 1991 to April 2006. The first row shows the return, volatility, and worst-case return for a portfolio of 60 percent U.S. equities and 40 percent U.S. bonds. Hedge funds, alternatives, and international investing could also be included without changing the results. The annualized return was 11.3 percent, which easily exceeds the current 8.0–8.5 percent target return of most U.S. funds. Annualized volatility for this 60/40 portfolio was 8.6 percent. The return for the 60/40 portfolio over the worst 12 months of the period was −12.3 percent.

Table 2	Portfolio Impact of Commodities, January 1991–April 2006						
Portfolio	Equities	Bonds	GSCI	DJ-AIG	Return	Volatility	Worst 12 Months
1	60%	40%	—	—	11.3%	8.6%	−12.3%
2	55	40	5%	—	11.3	8.0	−11.7
3	50	40	10	—	11.2	7.5	−11.2
4	55	40	—	5%	11.0	8.0	−11.2
5	50	40	—	10	10.6	7.4	−10.1

Note: Data are monthly.
Sources: Based on data from Standard & Poor's, Lehman Brothers, AIG, and Goldman, Sachs & Co.

Note one caveat to this analysis: It assesses only the asset side of the fund, not the fund surplus over liabilities. A typical U.S. corporate pension plan has a liability duration of 14 years, which is equivalent to being short a 14-year-duration bond. Analyzing the surplus for this period would mean the worst-case 12-month return would be −24 percent because liabilities rose at the same time asset prices fell in the perfect storm of 2000 through 2002. The proper analysis should thus always consider assets in relationship to liabilities. If the analysis outlined in Table 2 included the liability side of the equation, then the outcome—that adding commodities to a portfolio improves the worst-case return scenario—would be even more strikingly positive.

When 5 percent of the equity allocation is moved to the GSCI, the worst-case return is reduced by 60 bps, and with a 10 percent allocation to the GSCI, the reduction is more than 1 percentage point. The improvement is a result of the fact that when paper assets fall in value, the value of commodities tends to rise.

In the case of a 10.0 percent allocation to the DJ-AIG, the worst-case return is reduced to −10.1 percent, an improvement of more than 100 bps versus the 10.0 percent allocation to the GSCI. The GSCI does not produce as large an improvement as the DJ-AIG because of the dominant presence of oil in the GSCI. The price of oil is highly volatile and pushes the total index value up and down as the price of oil fluctuates; the DJ-AIG, in contrast, is influenced by the broader trend in commodities and demonstrates greater persistence. The bottom line is that in terms of risk reduction, the more diversified DJ-AIG historically has provided a more potent impact than the GSCI.

Return-Timing Diversification

Long-term returns of any asset class are concentrated in brief periods of time. If the past 20 years of equity returns were sorted from the highest-returning months to the lowest-returning months and then 7 percent of the highest-returning months were removed, the result would be a return equal to bonds. If 10 percent of the highest-returning months were removed, equities would have zero return. If daily returns are used, the return pattern is even more concentrated. Additionally, these periods of high excess return performance vary for different asset classes. So, not only are asset returns concentrated over time, but the periods of outperformance also vary for different asset classes.

Financial assets tend to perform weakly in the late stages of economic recovery, when there are inflation shocks and also when monetary policy becomes restrictive. These are the times when commodities tend to have strong returns because investors perceive that global capacity utilization is high, a shortage of raw commodities is at hand, and inflation is lurking around the corner. Ultimately, rising commodity prices will trigger further monetary tightening, which is not good news for bonds or equities. Clearly, the commodity markets are a natural complement to traditional markets and provide the element of time diversification of returns that is so beneficial in controlling portfolio risk.

The prices of commodities react much more to current supply–demand conditions than do the prices of equities and bonds, which respond more closely to the longer-term outlook. This deviation between time horizons of the two markets provides another interesting aspect of time diversification. Commodity investment also provides diversification across economic environments, which is an excellent corollary to time diversification. Some argue that energy cost is a core source of inflation and thus favor concentrated investment in, for example, the GSCI, which has a high energy weight. As good a solution as that might appear to be as a counterbalance to inflationary pressures, an equally important consideration is the diversification of risk, which argues for investment in a more equally weighted basket of commodities.

Inflation-Liability Matching

Long-term liabilities, whether they are pension payments from pension funds or grants from foundations and endowments, are exposed to erosion from inflation. In order to match the long-term inflation exposure in liabilities, long-only commodity investing provides a natural hedge. Of course, commodities do not match the U.S. Consumer Price Index definition of inflation, but they do match components of the index. Thus, not only does adding commodities to a portfolio reduce risk in the short run, but it also reduces the risk of longer-term inflation exposure.

IMPLEMENTATION OF COMMODITY STRATEGIES

Commodity index strategies, unlike U.S. equity index strategies, are active strategies because of the high turnover. For example, the constituent weights change, which is driven by changes in the weighting formula of the respective benchmark index. Second, a rolling methodology is implied by the index and largely determines the roll frequency of the portfolio. And last, the cash collateral position is continually reinvested as short-term cash equivalents mature and are replaced. Thus, my view is that all commodity investment is active.

Unlike in conventional investment indices, the return correlations between the commodity index constituents in different subcategories are close to zero. Obviously, heating oil correlates with West Texas Intermediate—a type of crude oil used as a benchmark—which correlates with unleaded gasoline. But the average correlation between pork belly futures and gasoline is zero. Within some of the clusters, such as the energy complex and base metals, correlations are high, but between the blocks, correlations are, in essence, zero, which maximizes the rebalance yield.

Commodity indices differ dramatically in their investability, their exposures, and their risk and return characteristics. Although new indices are created all the time, I will focus on just two of them: the GSCI and DJ-AIG. Started in December 1992, the GSCI includes 24 commodities, is production weighted, and gives oil a direct weight of 73.5 percent. The DJ-AIG began in July 1998, includes 19 commodities, and is weighted one-third to production and two-thirds to trading. Individual commodities are limited to 15 percent of the index, and concentration constraints limit energy to a 33 percent weight.

The current estimate of institutional investment in long-only commodity strategies is $120 billion. Of this amount, about $50 billion is invested in the GSCI. Another $30 billion is invested in the DJ-AIG and is expected to increase with the introduction of a new exchange-traded fund (ETF).

Note that a separate, but also growing, activity is institutional investment in active commodity trading. This trading includes the activities of managers of global macro strategies as well as those of long–short commodity trading advisers (CTAs). These long–short strategies, however, are an entirely different beast from long only and have absolute return targets.

The commodity trading industry has a notoriously poor information ratio. Furiously trading long and short commodity positions will not hedge the risk in a pension portfolio. Diversification provided by CTA strategies is beneficial, but allocations are too small for this to be relevant: A 0.5 percent CTA allocation having a correlation with the S&P 500 of −0.1 has minimal impact on portfolio return if the market drops 20 percent. For a CTA strategy to affirmatively impact portfolio-level risk, an allocation of at least 5 percent is required. That allocation would be very hard to sell to investment committees. So, although a CTA strategy is definitely an interesting component in a portfolio and earns its place in the alternative investments pool, that is where it belongs.

Core Commodity Investment Approaches

Commodity investment approaches range from pure index exposure to a CTA long–short strategy. To play a core role in a portfolio, commodity investment can be made by using one of three structures: an index fund, an index-plus strategy, or an active long-only strategy.

Index Fund

An index fund strategy can be implemented simply by purchasing an ETF as well as an index swap or note directly from a dealer.

Index Plus

The goal of an index-plus strategy is to provide an incremental return over the index. About a dozen firms currently offer this type of strategy. Four common ways to enhance the return of the index are through high-collateral return, roll management, rebalancing, and maturity management. In a high-collateral-return strategy, the cash held as margin collateral is worked as hard as possible to pick up any available return and often means moving into short-dated notes and weaker credits. Roll management involves a tactical approach to the timing of the roll on commodity futures contracts. The $80 billion invested in the GSCI and DJ-AIG indices roll on the prespecified five days in each contract settlement month. Deviating from this pattern and rolling earlier than the rest of the market or managing the maturities on forward contracts can result in a positive incremental return over the index. Rebalancing to the index can also be done more or less frequently to add value.

Active Long-Only

Active long-only strategies are a new and developing market. At present, they stand roughly equivalent in development to the currency strategies of the early 1990s. These strategies are usually built around several unique characteristics of commodities markets. These characteristics include the short-run seriality of commodity returns and the long-run reversion of commodity prices driven by market fundamentals. Another active strategy is broader diversification, which, as with any portfolio, improves risk-adjusted performance. For example, the quest for new reserves or alternative energy sources is being diligently pursued by many, and sooner or later, the price of energy will drop because someone will be successful. Portfolio diversification among commodities will protect against this eventuality.

The structural dynamics of commodities argue for active investing. The following quote is from a recent article by Kat and Oomen (2006):

> We have shown that commodity futures returns and volatility may vary considerably over different phases of the business cycle, under different monetary conditions as well as with the shape of the futures curve. This suggests that a purely passive investment in commodities may not be optimal and, given the differences in behavior of different commodities, that some commodities will be better at diversifying equity and bond portfolios than others. (p. 18)

Basically, Kat and Oomen argue that there are real reasons to believe the commodity markets are less than entirely efficient.

Impact of Institutional Investment

The commodity markets are being profoundly changed by the influx of institutional money. Backwardation, when the forward price is below the spot price, has become less stable. Because larger numbers of investors are putting on the same trades, rolls are becoming more expensive and dynamic, which is similar to what has happened to the cost of swapping between small-cap and large-cap U.S. equities.

Because of the influx of institutional money into the market, value is diverging from fundamentals. Copper is an excellent example; its price has risen 300 percent in two years. The situation is similar to what occurred in the currency market as institutional investors became involved. Thirty years ago, currency was primarily used to finance international exports and imports. There was minimal international portfolio investment by institutions in the 1970s, and so, there were minimal currency transactions by institutional investors. Today, institutional investor flows totally dominate currency markets; only some 1.6 percent of daily currency market activity is related to exports and imports. As institutional investor participation builds in commodities, prices will detach from fundamentals. But a commodity's price cannot detach indefinitely from fundamentals because supply will adjust to meet demand. A massive supply response in both the energy and copper markets is in progress and will reverse the dramatic price appreciation of the past few years for these commodities.

More extreme price moves will occur in commodity markets as demand and supply become more frequently misaligned, thus creating forced sales or purchases. In most commodities, a spectacular squeeze occurs as a result of a large market participant's exploitation of structural supply–demand imbalances in a certain commodity. More position squeezes are on the horizon as this market changes.

5 CONCLUSION

Commodity investment improves portfolios. The improvement comes not just from return but from reducing the risk of losing money when stressful market environments occur. An equally important point is that all commodity investment is active; even a so-called passive program involves very high turnover and management of cash. But the real source of added value from active management is utility arbitrage, which is based on the premise that different investors have different objectives and thus accept a cost for transferring risk. Note, however, that institutional investing is altering, and will continue to alter at an escalating pace, the dynamics of the commodity markets. Institutional commodity investment is truly in its infancy.

REFERENCES

Booth, David G., and Eugene F. Fama. 1992. "Diversification Returns and Asset Contributions." *Financial Analysts Journal*, vol. 48, no. 3 (May/June): 26–32.

Erb, Claude B., and Campbell R. Harvey. 2006. "The Strategic and Tactical Value of Commodity Futures." *Financial Analysts Journal*, vol. 62, no. 2 (March/April): 69–97.

Gorton, Gary, and K. Geert Rouwenhorst. 2006. "Facts and Fantasies about Commodity Futures." *Financial Analysts Journal*, vol. 62, no. 2 (March/April): 47–68.

Kat, Harry, and Roel Oomen. 2006. "What Every Investor Should Know about Commodities, Part 1: Univariate Return Analysis." Alternative Investment Research Centre Working Paper No. 29 (January).

Roy, A. D. 1952. "Safety First and Holding of Assets." *Econometrica*, vol. 20, no. 3 (July): 431–449.

APPENDIX

More From Ronald G. Layard-Liesching

This section presents the speaker's lively question and answer session with the conference audience.

Question: How would you characterize the commodity markets today?

Layard-Liesching: Some commodities are experiencing a price bubble—copper, for example. When a commodity trades at a multiple of its marginal extraction cost, it is without a doubt in the midst of a bubble. In my view, this does not preclude a strategic portfolio exposure to commodities.

The driver of the rise in commodity prices is the growth of the global middle class, not growth in China and India per se. Take sugar, for example. Poor people cannot afford it, but when formerly poor people migrate into the middle class and can afford it, they want it. The Chinese government estimates that the size of its middle class is now equal to the population of the United Kingdom, Germany, and France combined. And India, which is expected to overtake China in population, is experiencing a similar dynamic in its rapidly expanding middle class. This is why as an investor you want to be long commodities from a purely strategic point of view.

Individual commodities have always experienced price bubbles, and now, these bubbles will be even bigger as demographic change creates demand spikes.

Question: Can commodities offer protection against inflationary pressures in the cost of services, such as medical care?

Layard-Liesching: No. Obviously, service inflation is a big risk at the moment, but I don't think any investment can really hedge such steeply rising costs.

Question: Could you expand on your comment that commodity prices react more to current supply and demand conditions whereas financial asset prices respond to a longer-term outlook?

Layard-Liesching: The classic formula for the P/E multiple, which is commonly used in equity valuation, incorporates discounted future earnings. In today's stock market, if you eliminated the next three years' estimated earnings, 90 percent of the share-price valuation would still remain. So clearly, the price of shares is determined by long-term expectations of earnings. Commodities, however, have price dynamics that are related to a short-run storage component that in situations of excess causes the price to plummet, and vice versa.

A good example is the electricity market in the United States. When the market has excess electricity, the price plummets because electricity cannot be stored, and when electricity is in short supply, the price goes through the roof because stored capacity does not exist to relieve the demand. In contrast, an equity investment in a utility operates with a much longer time horizon so that the shares of the commodity producer and the commodity itself represent two extremes in time horizon with corresponding implications for the pricing of each.

Question: Can investors get exposure to commodities through commodity producers and extractors?

Layard-Liesching: When you invest in a commodity-producing or extracting company, you are also buying exposure to labor costs and political risk. Because of this, the bottom line is that commodities do better than commodity companies, and in the long run, commodities are also a better inflation hedge than the commodity companies.

Some very interesting opportunities present themselves, however, when commodity companies are severely underpriced in the market. In these instances, the companies will outperform commodities, and when the companies become overpriced, the opposite will be true. So in a portfolio, the two strategies would complement each other nicely.

Glossary

A priori probability   A probability based on logical analysis rather than on observation or personal judgment.

Abnormal profit   Equal to accounting profit less the implicit opportunity costs not included in total accounting costs; the difference between total revenue (TR) and total cost (TC).

Abnormal return   The amount by which a security's actual return differs from its expected return, given the security's risk and the market's return.

Absolute dispersion   The amount of variability present without comparison to any reference point or benchmark.

Absolute frequency   The number of observations in a given interval (for grouped data).

Accelerated book build   An offering of securities by an investment bank acting as principal that is accomplished in only one or two days.

Accelerated methods   Depreciation methods that allocate a relatively large proportion of the cost of an asset to the early years of the asset's useful life.

Account   With the accounting systems, a formal record of increases and decreases in a specific asset, liability, component of owners' equity, revenue, or expense.

Accounting (or explicit) costs   Payments to non-owner parties for services or resources they supply to the firm.

Accounting loss   When accounting profit is negative.

Accounting profit   (income before taxes or pretax income) Income as reported on the income statement, in accordance with prevailing accounting standards, before the provisions for income tax expense.

Accounts payable   Amounts that a business owes to its vendors for goods and services that were purchased from them but which have not yet been paid.

Accounts receivable   (commercial receivables or trade receivables) Amounts customers owe the company for products that have been sold as well as amounts that may be due from suppliers (such as for returns of merchandise).

Accounts receivable turnover   Ratio of sales on credit to the average balance in accounts receivable.

Accrued expenses   (accrued liabilities) Liabilities related to expenses that have been incurred but not yet paid as of the end of an accounting period—an example of an accrued expense is rent that has been incurred but not yet paid, resulting in a liability "rent payable."

Accrued interest   Interest earned but not yet paid.

Accrued revenue   Revenue that has been earned but not yet billed to customers as of the end of an accounting period.

Accumulated depreciation   An offset to property, plant, and equipment (PPE) reflecting the amount of the cost of PPE that has been allocated to current and previous accounting periods.

Acid-test ratio   A stringent measure of liquidity that indicates a company's ability to satisfy current liabilities with its most liquid assets, calculated as (cash + short-term marketable investments + receivables) divided by current liabilities.

Acquisition method   A method of accounting for a business combination where the acquirer is required to measure each identifiable asset and liability at fair value. This method was the result of a joint project of the IASB and FASB aiming at convergence in standards for the accounting of business combinations.

Action lag   Delay from policy decisions to implementation.

Active investment   An approach to investing in which the investor seeks to outperform a given benchmark.

Active return   The return on a portfolio minus the return on the portfolio's benchmark.

Active strategy   In reference to short-term cash management, an investment strategy characterized by monitoring and attempting to capitalize on market conditions to optimize the risk and return relationship of short-term investments.

Activity ratio   (or participation ratio) The ratio of the labor force to total population of working age.

Activity ratios   (asset utilization or operating efficiency ratios) Ratios that measure how efficiently a company performs day-to-day tasks, such as the collection of receivables and management of inventory.

Add-on interest   A procedure for determining the interest on a bond or loan in which the interest is added onto the face value of a contract.

Addition rule for probabilities   A principle stating that the probability that A or B occurs (both occur) equals the probability that A occurs, plus the probability that B occurs, minus the probability that both A and B occur.

Aggregate demand   The quantity of goods and services that households, businesses, government, and foreign customers want to buy at any given level of prices.

Aggregate demand curve   Inverse relationship between the price level and real output.

Aggregate income   The value of all the payments earned by the suppliers of factors used in the production of goods and services.

Aggregate output   The value of all the goods and services produced in a specified period of time.

Aggregate supply   The quantity of goods and services producers are willing to supply at any given level of price.

Aggregate supply curve   The level of domestic output that companies will produce at each price level.

Aging schedule   A breakdown of accounts into categories of days outstanding.

All-or-nothing (AON) orders   An order that includes the instruction to trade only if the trade fills the entire quantity (size) specified.

Allocationally efficient   Said of a market, a financial system, or an economy that promotes the allocation of resources to their highest value uses.

Allowance for bad debts   An offset to accounts receivable for the amount of accounts receivable that are estimated to be uncollectible.

Alternative investment markets   Market for investments other than traditional securities investments (i.e., traditional common and preferred shares and traditional fixed income instruments). The term usually encompasses direct and indirect investment in real estate (including timberland and farmland) and commodities (including precious metals); hedge funds, private equity, and other investments requiring specialized due diligence.

Alternative trading systems   (**electronic communications networks** or **multilateral trading facilities**) Trading venues that function like exchanges but that do not exercise regulatory authority over their subscribers except with respect to the conduct of the subscribers' trading in their trading systems.

American depository receipt   A U.S. dollar-denominated security that trades like a common share on U.S. exchanges.

American depository share   The underlying shares on which American depository receipts are based. They trade in the issuing company's domestic market.

American option   An option that can be exercised at any time until its expiration date.

American-style contracts   An option that can be exercised at any time until its expiration date.

Amortisation   The process of allocating the cost of intangible long-term assets having a finite useful life to accounting periods; the allocation of the amount of a bond premium or discount to the periods remaining until bond maturity.

Amortised cost   The historical cost (initially recognised cost) of an asset, adjusted for amortisation and impairment.

Amortization   The process of allocating the cost of intangible longterm assets having a finite useful life to accounting periods; the allocation of the amount of a bond premium or discount to the periods remaining until bond maturity.

Annual percentage rate   The cost of borrowing expressed as a yearly rate.

Annuity   A finite set of level sequential cash flows.

Annuity due   An annuity having a first cash flow that is paid immediately.

Anticipation stock   Excess inventory that is held in anticipation of increased demand, often because of seasonal patterns of demand.

Antidilutive   With reference to a transaction or a security, one that would increase earnings per share (EPS) or result in EPS higher than the company's basic EPS—antidilutive securities are not included in the calculation of diluted EPS.

Arbitrage   1) The simultaneous purchase of an undervalued asset or portfolio and sale of an overvalued but equivalent asset or portfolio, in order to obtain a riskless profit on the price differential. Taking advantage of a market inefficiency in a risk-free manner. 2) The condition in a financial market in which equivalent assets or combinations of assets sell for two different prices, creating an opportunity to profit at no risk with no commitment of money. In a well-functioning financial market, few arbitrage opportunities are possible. 3) A risk-free operation that earns an expected positive net profit but requires no net investment of money.

Arbitrageurs   Traders who engage in arbitrage (see *arbitrage*).

Arithmetic mean   The sum of the observations divided by the number of observations.

Arms index   A flow of funds indicator applied to a broad stock market index to measure the relative extent to which money is moving into or out of rising and declining stocks.

Asian call option   A European-style option with a value at maturity equal to the difference between the stock price at maturity and the average stock price during the life of the option, or $0, whichever is greater.

Ask   (offer) The price at which a dealer or trader is willing to sell an asset, typically qualified by a maximum quantity (ask size).

Ask size   The maximum quantity of an asset that pertains to a specific ask price from a trader. For example, if the ask for a share issue is $30 for a size of 1,000 shares, the trader is offering to sell at $30 up to 1,000 shares.

Asset allocation   The process of determining how investment funds should be distributed among asset classes.

Asset beta   The unlevered beta; reflects the business risk of the assets; the asset's systematic risk.

Asset class   A group of assets that have similar characteristics, attributes, and risk/return relationships.

Asset utilization ratios   Ratios that measure how efficiently a company performs day-to-day tasks, such as the collection of receivables and management of inventory.

Asset-based loan   A loan that is secured with company assets.

Asset-based valuation models   Valuation based on estimates of the market value of a company's assets.

Assets   Resources controlled by an enterprise as a result of past events and from which future economic benefits to the enterprise are expected to flow.

Assignment of accounts receivable   The use of accounts receivable as collateral for a loan.

At-the-money   An option in which the underlying value equals the exercise price.

Automated Clearing House (ACH)   An electronic payment network available to businesses, individuals, and financial institutions in the United States, U.S. Territories, and Canada.

Automatic stabilizer   A countercyclical factor that automatically comes into play as an economy slows and unemployment rises.

Available-for-sale   Debt and equity securities not classified as either held-to-maturity or held-for-trading securities. The investor is willing to sell but not actively planning to sell. In general, available-for-sale securities are reported at fair value on the balance sheet.

Available-for-sale securities   Debt and equity securities not classified as either held-to-maturity or held-for-trading securities. The investor is willing to sell but not actively planning to sell. In general, available-for-sale securities are reported at fair value on the balance sheet.

Average fixed cost   Total fixed cost divided by quantity.

Average product   Measures the productivity of inputs on average and is calculated by dividing total product by the total number of units for a given input that is used to generate that output.

Average revenue   Quantity sold divided into total revenue.

Average total cost   Total costs divided by quantity.

Average variable cost   Total variable cost divided by quantity.

Back simulation   Another term for the historical method of estimating VAR. This term is somewhat misleading in that the method involves not a *simulation* of the past but rather what *actually happened* in the past, sometimes adjusted to reflect the fact that a different portfolio may have existed in the past than is planned for the future.

Balance of trade deficit   When the domestic economy is spending more on foreign goods and services than foreign economies are spending on domestic goods and services.

Balance sheet (statement of financial position or statement of financial condition) The financial statement that presents an entity's current financial position by disclosing resources the entity controls (its assets) and the claims on those resources (its liabilities and equity claims), as of a particular point in time (the date of the balance sheet).

Balance sheet ratios Financial ratios involving balance sheet items only.

Balanced With respect to a government budget, one in which spending and revenues (taxes) are equal.

Bank discount basis A quoting convention that annualizes, on a 360-day year, the discount as a percentage of face value.

Bar chart A price chart with four bits of data for each time interval—the high, low, opening, and closing prices. A vertical line connects the high and low. A cross-hatch left indicates the opening price and a cross-hatch right indicates the close.

Barter economy An economy where economic agents as house-holds, corporations, and governments "pay" for goods and services with another good or service.

Base rates The reference rate on which a bank bases lending rates to all other customers.

Basic EPS Net earnings available to common shareholders (i.e., net income minus preferred dividends) divided by the weighted average number of common shares outstanding.

Basket of listed depository receipts An exchange-traded fund (ETF) that represents a portfolio of depository receipts.

Behavioral finance A field of finance that examines the psychological variables that affect and often distort the investment decision making of investors, analysts, and portfolio managers.

Behind the market Said of prices specified in orders that are worse than the best current price; e.g., for a limit buy order, a limit price below the best bid.

Bernoulli random variable A random variable having the outcomes 0 and 1.

Bernoulli trial An experiment that can produce one of two outcomes.

Best bid The highest bid in the market.

Best efforts offering An offering of a security using an investment bank in which the investment bank, as agent for the issuer, promises to use its best efforts to sell the offering but does not guarantee that a specific amount will be sold.

Best offer The lowest offer (ask price) in the market.

Beta A measure of systematic risk that is based on the covariance of an asset's or portfolio's return with the return of the overall market.

Bid The price at which a dealer or trader is willing to buy an asset, typically qualified by a maximum quantity.

Bid size The maximum quantity of an asset that pertains to a specific bid price from a trader.

Binomial model A model for pricing options in which the underlying price can move to only one of two possible new prices.

Binomial random variable The number of successes in n Bernoulli trials for which the probability of success is constant for all trials and the trials are independent.

Binomial tree The graphical representation of a model of asset price dynamics in which, at each period, the asset moves up with probability p or down with probability $(1 - p)$.

Block brokers A broker (agent) that provides brokerage services for large-size trades.

Blue chip Widely held large market capitalization companies that are considered financially sound and are leaders in their respective industry or local stock market.

Bollinger Bands A price-based technical analysis indicator consisting of a moving average plus a higher line representing the moving average plus a set number of standard deviations from average price (for the same number of periods as used to calculate the moving average) and a lower line that is a moving average minus the same number of standard deviations.

Bond equivalent yield A calculation of yield that is annualized using the ratio of 365 to the number of days to maturity. Bond equivalent yield allows for the restatement and comparison of securities with different compounding periods.

Bond indenture The governing legal credit agreement, typically incorporated by reference in the prospectus.

Bond market vigilantes Bond market participants who might reduce their demand for long-term bonds, thus pushing up their yields.

Bond option An option in which the underlying is a bond; primarily traded in over-the-counter markets.

Bond yield plus risk premium approach An estimate of the cost of common equity that is produced by summing the before-tax cost of debt and a risk premium that captures the additional yield on a company's stock relative to its bonds. The additional yield is often estimated using historical spreads between bond yields and stock yields.

Bond-equivalent basis A basis for stating an annual yield that annualizes a semiannual yield by doubling it.

Bond-equivalent yield The yield to maturity on a basis that ignores compounding.

Bonus issue of shares A type of dividend in which a company distributes additional shares of its common stock to shareholders instead of cash.

Book building Investment bankers' process of compiling a "book" or list of indications of interest to buy part of an offering.

Book value (or carrying value) The net amount shown for an asset or liability on the balance sheet; book value may also refer to the company's excess of total assets over total liabilities.

Boom An expansionary phase characterized by economic growth "testing the limits" of the economy.

Bottom-up analysis With reference to investment selection processes, an approach that involves selection from all securities within a specified investment universe, i.e., without prior narrowing of the universe on the basis of macroeconomic or overall market considerations.

Break point In the context of the weighted average cost of capital (WACC), a break point is the amount of capital at which the cost of one or more of the sources of capital changes, leading to a change in the WACC.

Breakeven point The number of units produced and sold at which the company's net income is zero (revenues = total costs); in the case of perfect competition, the quantity where price, average revenue, and marginal revenue equal average total cost.

Broad money Encompasses narrow money plus the entire range of liquid assets that can be used to make purchases.

Broker 1) An agent who executes orders to buy or sell securities on behalf of a client in exchange for a commission. 2) *See* Futures commission merchants.

Brokered market A market in which brokers arrange trades among their clients.

Broker–dealer A financial intermediary (often a company) that may function as a principal (dealer) or as an agent (broker) depending on the type of trade.

Budget constraint   A constraint on spending or investment imposed by wealth or income.

Budget surplus/deficit   The difference between government revenue and expenditure for a stated fixed period of time.

Business risk   The risk associated with operating earnings. Operating earnings are uncertain because total revenues and many of the expenditures contributed to produce those revenues are uncertain.

Buy-side firm   An investment management company or other investor that uses the services of brokers or dealers (i.e., the client of the sell side firms).

Buyback   A transaction in which a company buys back its own shares. Unlike stock dividends and stock splits, share repurchases use corporate cash.

Buyout fund   A fund that buys all the shares of a public company so that, in effect, the company becomes private.

CBOE Volatility Index   A measure of near-term market volatility as conveyed by S&P 500 stock index option prices.

CD equivalent yield   A yield on a basis comparable to the quoted yield on an interest-bearing money market instrument that pays interest on a 360-day basis; the annualized holding period yield, assuming a 360-day year.

Call   An option that gives the holder the right to buy an underlying asset from another party at a fixed price over a specific period of time.

Call market   A market in which trades occur only at a particular time and place (i.e., when the market is called).

Call money rate   The interest rate that buyers pay for their margin loan.

Call option   An option that gives the holder the right to buy an underlying asset from another party at a fixed price over a specific period of time.

Callable common shares   Shares that give the issuing company the option (or right), but not the obligation, to buy back the shares from investors at a call price that is specified when the shares are originally issued.

Candlestick chart   A price chart with four bits of data for each time interval. A candle indicates the opening and closing price for the interval. The body of the candle is shaded if the opening price was higher than the closing price, and the body is clear if the opening price was lower than the closing price. Vertical lines known as wicks or shadows extend from the top and bottom of the candle to indicate the high and the low prices for the interval.

Cannibalization   Cannibalization occurs when an investment takes customers and sales away from another part of the company.

Cap   1) A contract on an interest rate, whereby at periodic payment dates, the writer of the cap pays the difference between the market interest rate and a specified cap rate if, and only if, this difference is positive. This is equivalent to a stream of call options on the interest rate. 2) A combination of interest rate call options designed to hedge a borrower against rate increases on a floating-rate loan.

Capacity   The ability of the borrower to make its debt payments on time.

Capital allocation line   (CAL) A graph line that describes the combinations of expected return and standard deviation of return available to an investor from combining the optimal portfolio of risky assets with the risk-free asset.

Capital asset pricing model   (also CAPM) An equation describing the expected return on any asset (or portfolio) as a linear function of its beta relative to the market portfolio.

Capital budgeting   The allocation of funds to relatively long-range projects or investments.

Capital consumption allowance   A measure of the wear and tear (depreciation) of the capital stock that occurs in the production of goods and services.

Capital deepening investment   Increases the stock of capital relative to labor.

Capital expenditure   Expenditure on physical capital (fixed assets).

Capital market expectations   An investor's expectations concerning the risk and return prospects of asset classes.

Capital market line   (CML) The line with an intercept point equal to the risk-free rate that is tangent to the efficient frontier of risky assets; represents the efficient frontier when a risk-free asset is available for investment.

Capital markets   Financial markets that trade securities of longer duration, such as bonds and equities.

Capital rationing   A capital rationing environment assumes that the company has a fixed amount of funds to invest.

Capital stock   The accumulated amount of buildings, machinery, and equipment used to produce goods and services.

Capital structure   The mix of debt and equity that a company uses to finance its business; a company's specific mixture of long-term financing.

Caplet   Each component call option in a cap.

Captive finance subsidiary   A wholly-owned subsidiary of a company that is established to provide financing of the sales of the parent company.

Carrying amount   The amount at which an asset or liability is valued according to accounting principles.

Carrying value   The net amount shown for an asset or liability on the balance sheet; book value may also refer to the company's excess of total assets over total liabilities.

Cartel   Participants in collusive agreements that are made openly and formally.

Cash   In accounting contexts, cash on hand (e.g., petty cash and cash not yet deposited to the bank) and demand deposits held in banks and similar accounts that can be used in payment of obligations.

Cash conversion cycle   (net operating cycle) A financial metric that measures the length of time required for a company to convert cash invested in its operations to cash received as a result of its operations; equal to days of inventory on hand + days of sales outstanding − number of days of payables.

Cash equivalents   Very liquid short-term investments, usually maturing in 90 days or less.

Cash flow additivity principle   The principle that dollar amounts indexed at the same point in time are additive.

Cash flow from operating activities   The net amount of cash provided from operating activities.

Cash flow from operations   The net amount of cash provided from operating activities.

Cash price   The price for immediate purchase of the underlying asset.

Cash settlement   A procedure used in certain derivative transactions that specifies that the long and short parties engage in the equivalent cash value of a delivery transaction.

Central banks   The dominant bank in a country, usually with official or semi-official governmental status.

Change in polarity principle   A tenet of technical analysis that once a support level is breached, it becomes a resistance level. The same holds true for resistance levels; once breached, they become support levels.

Change of control put   A covenant giving bondholders the right to require the issuer to buy back their debt, often at par or at some small premium to par value, in the event that the borrower is acquired.

Character   The quality of a debt issuer's management.

Chart of accounts   A list of accounts used in an entity's accounting system.

Cheapest-to-deliver bond   A bond in which the amount received for delivering the bond is largest compared with the amount paid in the market for the bond.

Classified balance sheet   A balance sheet organized so as to group together the various assets and liabilities into subcategories (e.g., current and noncurrent).

Clawback   A requirement that the GP return any funds distributed as incentive fees until the LPs have received back their initial investment and a percentage of the total profit.

Clearing instructions   Instructions that indicate how to arrange the final settlement ("clearing") of a trade.

Clearinghouse   An entity associated with a futures market that acts as middleman between the contracting parties and guarantees to each party the performance of the other.

Closed-end fund   A mutual fund in which no new investment money is accepted. New investors invest by buying existing shares, and investors in the fund liquidate by selling their shares to other investors.

Coefficient of variation   (CV) The ratio of a set of observations' standard deviation to the observations' mean value.

Coincident economic indicators   Turning points that are usually close to those of the overall economy; they are believed to have value for identifying the economy's present state.

Collateral   The quality and value of the assets supporting an issuer's indebtedness.

Combination   A listing in which the order of the listed items does not matter.

Commercial paper   Unsecured short-term corporate debt that is characterized by a single payment at maturity.

Commercial receivables   **(Trade receivables or accounts receivable)** Amounts customers owe the company for products that have been sold as well as amounts that may be due from suppliers (such as for returns of merchandise).

Committed capital   The amount that the limited partners have agreed to provide to the private equity fund.

Committed lines of credit   A bank commitment to extend credit up to a pre-specified amount; the commitment is considered a short-term liability and is usually in effect for 364 days (one day short of a full year).

Commodity swap   A swap in which the underlying is a commodity such as oil, gold, or an agricultural product.

Common shares   A type of security that represent an ownership interest in a company.

Common stock   See *common shares*.

Common-size analysis   The restatement of financial statement items using a common denominator or reference item that allows one to identify trends and major differences; an example is an income statement in which all items are expressed as a percent of revenue.

Company analysis   Analysis of an individual company.

Comparable company   A company that has similar business risk; usually in the same industry and preferably with a single line of business.

Competitive strategy   A company's plans for responding to the threats and opportunities presented by the external environment.

Complements   Said of goods which tend to be used together; technically, two goods whose cross-price elasticity of demand is negative.

Complete markets   Informally, markets in which the variety of distinct securities traded is so broad that any desired payoff in a future state-of-the-world is achievable.

Complete preferences   The assumption that a consumer is able to make a comparison between any two possible bundles of goods.

Completed contract   A method of revenue recognition in which the company does not recognize any revenue until the contract is completed; used particularly in long-term construction contracts.

Component cost of capital   The rate of return required by suppliers of capital for an individual source of a company's funding, such as debt or equity.

Compounding   The process of accumulating interest on interest.

Comprehensive income   The change in equity of a business enterprise during a period from nonowner sources; includes all changes in equity during a period except those resulting from investments by owners and distributions to owners; comprehensive income equals net income plus other comprehensive income.

Conditional expected value   The expected value of a stated event given that another event has occurred.

Conditional probability   The probability of an event given (conditioned on) another event.

Conditional variances   The variance of one variable, given the outcome of another.

Consistent   With reference to estimators, describes an estimator for which the probability of estimates close to the value of the population parameter increases as sample size increases.

Conspicuous consumption   Consumption of high status goods, such as a luxury automobile or a very expensive piece of jewelry.

Constant maturity treasury   (or CMT) A hypothetical U.S. Treasury note with a constant maturity. A CMT exists for various years in the range of 2 to 10.

Constant returns to scale   The characteristic of constant per-unit costs in the presence of increased production.

Constant-cost industry   When firms in the industry experience no change in resource costs and output prices over the long run.

Constituent securities   With respect to an index, the individual securities within an index.

Consumer choice theory   The theory relating consumer demand curves to consumer preferences.

Consumer surplus   The difference between the value that a consumer places on units purchased and the amount of money that was required to pay for them.

Consumption basket   A specific combination of the goods and services that a consumer wants to consume.

Consumption bundle   A specific combination of the goods and services that a consumer wants to consume.

Continuation patterns   A type of pattern used in technical analysis to predict the resumption of a market trend that was in place prior to the formation of a pattern.

Continuous random variable   A random variable for which the range of possible outcomes is the real line (all real numbers between $-\infty$ and $+\infty$ or some subset of the real line).

Continuous time   Time thought of as advancing in extremely small increments.

Continuous trading market   A market in which trades can be arranged and executed any time the market is open.

Continuously compounded return   The natural logarithm of 1 plus the holding period return, or equivalently, the natural logarithm of the ending price over the beginning price.

Contra account   An account that offsets another account.

Contraction   The period of a business cycle after the peak and before the trough; often called a *recession* or, if exceptionally severe, called a *depression*.

Contractionary   Tending to cause the real economy to contract.

Contractionary fiscal policy   A fiscal policy that has the objective to make the real economy contract.

Contribution margin   The amount available for fixed costs and profit after paying variable costs; revenue minus variable costs.

Conventional cash flow   A conventional cash flow pattern is one with an initial outflow followed by a series of inflows.

Convergence   The tendency for differences in output per capita across countries to diminish over time; in technical analysis, a term that describes the case when an indicator moves in the same manner as the security being analyzed.

Conversion factor   An adjustment used to facilitate delivery on bond futures contracts in which any of a number of bonds with different characteristics are eligible for delivery.

Convertible preference shares   A type of equity security that entitles shareholders to convert their shares into a specified number of common shares.

Core inflation   The inflation rate calculated based on a price index of goods and services except food and energy.

Correlation   A number between −1 and +1 that measures the comovement (linear association) between two random variables.

Correlation coefficient   A number between −1 and +1 that measures the consistency or tendency for two investments to act in a similar way. It is used to determine the effect on portfolio risk when two assets are combined.

Cost averaging   The periodic investment of a fixed amount of money.

Cost of capital   The rate of return that suppliers of capital require as compensation for their contribution of capital.

Cost of debt   The cost of debt financing to a company, such as when it issues a bond or takes out a bank loan.

Cost of goods sold   For a given period, equal to beginning inventory minus ending inventory plus the cost of goods acquired or produced during the period.

Cost of preferred stock   The cost to a company of issuing preferred stock; the dividend yield that a company must commit to pay preferred stockholders.

Cost recovery method   A method of revenue recognition in which the seller does not report any profit until the cash amounts paid by the buyer—including principal and interest on any financing from the seller—are greater than all the seller's costs for the merchandise sold.

Cost structure   The mix of a company's variable costs and fixed costs.

Cost-push   Type of inflation in which rising costs, usually wages, compel businesses to raise prices generally.

Counterparty risk   The risk that the other party to a contract will fail to honor the terms of the contract.

Cournot assumption   Assumption in which each firm determines its profit-maximizing production level assuming that the other firms' output will not change.

Covariance   A measure of the co-movement (linear association) between two random variables.

Covariance matrix   A matrix or square array whose entries are covariances; also known as a variance–covariance matrix.

Covenants   The terms and conditions of lending agreements that the issuer must comply with.

Covered call   An option strategy involving the holding of an asset and sale of a call on the asset.

Credit   With respect to double-entry accounting, a credit records increases in liability, owners' equity, and revenue accounts or decreases in asset accounts; with respect to borrowing, the willingness and ability of the borrower to make promised payments on the borrowing.

Credit analysis   The evaluation of credit risk; the evaluation of the creditworthiness of a borrower or counterparty.

Credit curve   A curve showing the relationship between time to maturity and yield spread for an issuer with comparable bonds of various maturities outstanding, usually upward sloping.

Credit migration risk   (or downgrade risk) The risk that a bond issuer's creditworthiness deteriorates, or migrates lower, leading investors to believe the risk of default is higher.

Credit risk   (or default risk) The risk of loss caused by a counterparty's or debtor's failure to make a promised payment.

Credit scoring model   A statistical model used to classify borrowers according to creditworthiness.

Credit-worthiness   The perceived ability of the borrower to pay what is owed on the borrowing in a timely manner; it represents the ability of a company to withstand adverse impacts on its cash flows.

Cross-default provisions   Provisions whereby events of default such as non-payment of interest on one bond trigger default on all outstanding debt; implies the same default probability for all issues.

Cross-price elasticity of demand   The percent change in quantity demanded for a given small change in the price of another good; the responsiveness of the demand for Product A that is associated with the change in price of Product B.

Cross-sectional analysis   Analysis that involves comparisons across individuals in a group over a given time period or at a given point in time.

Cross-sectional data   Observations over individual units at a point in time, as opposed to time-series data.

Crossing networks   Trading systems that match buyers and sellers who are willing to trade at prices obtained from other markets.

Crowding out   The thesis that government borrowing may divert private sector investment from taking place.

Cumulative distribution function   A function giving the probability that a random variable is less than or equal to a specified value.

Cumulative preference shares   Preference shares for which any dividends that are not paid accrue and must be paid in full before dividends on common shares can be paid.

Cumulative relative frequency   For data grouped into intervals, the fraction of total observations that are less than the value of the upper limit of a stated interval.

Cumulative voting   Voting that allows shareholders to direct their total voting rights to specific candidates, as opposed to having to allocate their voting rights evenly among all candidates.

Currencies   Monies issued by national monetary authorities.

Currency option   An option that allows the holder to buy (if a call) or sell (if a put) an underlying currency at a fixed exercise rate, expressed as an exchange rate.

Currency swap   A swap in which each party makes interest payments to the other in different currencies.

Current assets   (or liquid assets) Assets that are expected to be consumed or converted into cash in the near future, typically one year or less.

Current cost   With reference to assets, the amount of cash or cash equivalents that would have to be paid to buy the same or an equivalent asset today; with reference to liabilities, the undiscounted amount of cash or cash equivalents that would be required to settle the obligation today.

Current government spending   With respect to government expenditures, spending on goods and services that are provided on a regular, recurring basis including health, education, and defense.

Current liabilities   Short-term obligations, such as accounts payable, wages payable, or accrued liabilities, that are expected to be settled in the near future, typically one year or less.

Current ratio   A liquidity ratio calculated as current assets divided by current liabilities.

Cyclical   See *Cyclical companies.*

Cyclical companies   Companies with sales and profits that regularly expand and contract with the business cycle or state of economy.

Daily settlement   See *Marking to market.*

Dark pools   Alternative trading systems that do not display the orders that their clients send to them.

Data mining   (or data snooping) The practice of determining a model by extensive searching through a dataset for statistically significant patterns.

Data snooping   See *Data mining.*

Date of book closure   The date that a shareholder listed on the corporation's books will be deemed to have ownership of the shares for purposes of receiving an upcoming dividend; two business days after the ex-dividend date.

Date of record   The date that a shareholder listed on the corporation's books will be deemed to have ownership of the shares for purposes of receiving an upcoming dividend; two business days after the ex-dividend date.

Day order   An order that is good for the day on which it is submitted. If it has not been filled by the close of business, the order expires unfilled.

Day trader   A trader holding a position open somewhat longer than a scalper but closing all positions at the end of the day.

Days in receivables   Estimate of the average number of days it takes to collect on credit accounts.

Days of inventory on hand (DOH)   An activity ratio equal to the number of days in the period divided by inventory turnover over the period.

Day's sales outstanding   Estimate of the average number of days it takes to collect on credit accounts.

Dead cross   A technical analysis term that describes a situation where a short-term moving average crosses from above a longer-term moving average to below it; this movement is considered bearish.

Dealers   A financial intermediary that acts as a principal in trades.

Dealing securities   Securities held by banks or other financial intermediaries for trading purposes.

Debit   With respect to double-entry accounting, a debit records increases of asset and expense accounts or decreases in liability and owners' equity accounts.

Debt incurrence test   A financial covenant made in conjunction with existing debt that restricts a company's ability to incur additional debt at the same seniority based on one or more financial tests or conditions.

Debt-rating approach   A method for estimating a company's before-tax cost of debt based upon the yield on comparably rated bonds for maturities that closely match that of the company's existing debt.

Debt-to-assets ratio   A solvency ratio calculated as total debt divided by total assets.

Debt-to-capital ratio   A solvency ratio calculated as total debt divided by total debt plus total shareholders' equity.

Debt-to-equity ratio   A solvency ratio calculated as total debt divided by total shareholders' equity.

Declaration date   The day that the corporation issues a statement declaring a specific dividend.

Decreasing returns to scale   Increase in cost per unit resulting from increased production.

Decreasing-cost industry   An industry in which per-unit costs and output prices are lower when industry output is increased in the long run.

Deductible temporary differences   Temporary differences that result in a reduction of or deduction from taxable income in a future period when the balance sheet item is recovered or settled.

Deep-in-the-money   Options that are far in-the-money.

Deep-out-of-the-money   Options that are far out-of-the-money.

Default risk   (or default probability): The probability that a borrower defaults or fails to meet its obligation to make full and timely payments of principal and interest, according to the terms of the debt security.

Default risk premium   An extra return that compensates investors for the possibility that the borrower will fail to make a promised payment at the contracted time and in the contracted amount.

Defensive companies   Companies with sales and profits that have little sensitivity to the business cycle or state of the economy.

Defensive interval ratio   A liquidity ratio that estimates the number of days that an entity could meet cash needs from liquid assets; calculated as (cash + short-term marketable investments + receivables) divided by daily cash expenditures.

Deferred income   A liability account for money that has been collected for goods or services that have not yet been delivered; payment received in advance of providing a good or service.

Deferred revenue   A liability account for money that has been collected for goods or services that have not yet been delivered; payment received in advance of providing a good or service.

Deferred tax assets   A balance sheet asset that arises when an excess amount is paid for income taxes relative to accounting profit. The taxable income is higher than accounting profit and income tax payable exceeds tax expense. The company expects to recover the difference during the course of future operations when tax expense exceeds income tax payable.

Deferred tax liabilities   A balance sheet liability that arises when a deficit amount is paid for income taxes relative to accounting profit. The taxable income is less than the accounting profit and income tax payable is less than tax expense. The company expects to eliminate the liability over the course of future operations when income tax payable exceeds tax expense.

Defined benefit pension plans   Plan in which the company promises to pay a certain annual amount (defined benefit) to the employee after retirement. The company bears the investment risk of the plan assets.

Defined contribution pension plans Individual accounts to which an employee and typically the employer makes contributions, generally on a tax-advantaged basis. The amounts of contributions are defined at the outset, but the future value of the benefit is unknown. The employee bears the investment risk of the plan assets.

Deflation Negative inflation.

Degree of confidence The probability that a confidence interval includes the unknown population parameter.

Degree of financial leverage (DFL) The ratio of the percentage change in net income to the percentage change in operating income; the sensitivity of the cash flows available to owners when operating income changes.

Degree of operating leverage (DOL) The ratio of the percentage change in operating income to the percentage change in units sold; the sensitivity of operating income to changes in units sold.

Degree of total leverage The ratio of the percentage change in net income to the percentage change in units sold; the sensitivity of the cash flows to owners to changes in the number of units produced and sold.

Degrees of freedom (df) The number of independent observations used.

Delivery A process used in a deliverable forward contract in which the long pays the agreed-upon price to the short, which in turn delivers the underlying asset to the long.

Delivery option The feature of a futures contract giving the short the right to make decisions about what, when, and where to deliver.

Delta The relationship between the option price and the underlying price, which reflects the sensitivity of the price of the option to changes in the price of the underlying.

Demand shock A typically unexpected disturbance to demand, such as an unexpected interruption in trade or transportation.

Demand-pull Type of inflation in which increasing demand raises prices generally, which then are reflected in a business's costs as workers demand wage hikes to catch up with the rising cost of living.

Dependent With reference to events, the property that the probability of one event occurring depends on (is related to) the occurrence of another event.

Depository bank A bank that raises funds from depositors and other investors and lends it to borrowers.

Depository institutions Commercial banks, savings and loan banks, credit unions, and similar institutions that raise funds from depositors and other investors and lend it to borrowers.

Depository receipt A security that trades like an ordinary share on a local exchange and represents an economic interest in a foreign company.

Depreciation The process of systematically allocating the cost of long-lived (tangible) assets to the periods during which the assets are expected to provide economic benefits.

Depression See *contraction*.

Derivative A financial instrument whose value depends on the value of some underlying asset or factor (e.g., a stock price, an interest rate, or exchange rate).

Derivative pricing rule A pricing rule used by crossing networks in which a price is taken (derived) from the price that is current in the asset's primary market.

Derivatives dealers Commercial and investment banks that make markets in derivatives.

Descriptive statistics The study of how data can be summarized effectively.

Development capital Minority equity investments in more mature companies that are looking for capital to expand or restructure operations, enter new markets, or finance major acquisitions.

Diffuse prior The assumption of equal prior probabilities.

Diffusion index Reflects the proportion of the index's components that are moving in a pattern consistent with the overall index.

Diluted EPS The EPS that would result if all dilutive securities were converted into common shares.

Diluted shares The number of shares that would be outstanding if all potentially dilutive claims on common shares (e.g., convertible debt, convertible preferred stock, and employee stock options) were exercised.

Diminishing balance method An accelerated depreciation method, i.e., one that allocates a relatively large proportion of the cost of an asset to the early years of the asset's useful life.

Diminishing marginal productivity Describes a state in which each additional unit of input produces less output than previously.

Direct debit program An arrangement whereby a customer authorizes a debit to a demand account; typically used by companies to collect routine payments for services.

Direct format (direct method) With reference to the cash flow statement, a format for the presentation of the statement in which cash flow from operating activities is shown as operating cash receipts less operating cash disbursements.

Direct method See *direct format*.

Direct taxes Taxes levied directly on income, wealth, and corporate profits.

Direct write-off method An approach to recognizing credit losses on customer receivables in which the company waits until such time as a customer has defaulted and only then recognizes the loss.

Disbursement float The amount of time between check issuance and a check's clearing back against the company's account.

Discount To reduce the value of a future payment in allowance for how far away it is in time; to calculate the present value of some future amount. Also, the amount by which an instrument is priced below its face value.

Discount interest A procedure for determining the interest on a loan or bond in which the interest is deducted from the face value in advance.

Discount rate With reference to U.S. banking, the rate for member banks borrowing directly from the U.S. Federal Reserve System.

Discounted cash flow models Valuation models that estimate the intrinsic value of a security as the present value of the future benefits expected to be received from the security.

Discouraged worker A person who has stopped looking for a job or has given up seeking employment.

Discrete random variable A random variable that can take on at most a countable number of possible values.

Discriminatory pricing rule A pricing rule used in continuous markets in which the limit price of the order or quote that first arrived determines the trade price.

Diseconomies of scale Increase in cost per unit resulting from increased production.

Dispersion The variability around the central tendency.

Display size   The size of an order displayed to public view.

Distressed investing   Investing in securities of companies in financial difficulties. Private equity funds typically buy the debt of mature companies in financial difficulties.

Divergence   In technical analysis, a term that describes the case when an indicator moves differently from the security being analyzed.

Diversification ratio   The ratio of the standard deviation of an equally weighted portfolio to the standard deviation of a randomly selected security.

Dividend   A distribution paid to shareholders based on the number of shares owned.

Dividend discount model   (DDM) A present value model that estimates the intrinsic value of an equity share based on the present value of its expected future dividends.

Dividend discount model based approach   An approach for estimating a country's equity risk premium. The market rate of return is estimated as the sum of the dividend yield and the growth rate in dividends for a market index. Subtracting the risk-free rate of return from the estimated market return produces an estimate for the equity risk premium.

Dividend payout ratio   The ratio of cash dividends paid to earnings for a period.

Dividend yield   Annual dividends per share divided by share price.

Divisor   A number (denominator) used to determine the value of a price return index. It is initially chosen at the inception of an index and subsequently adjusted by the index provider, as necessary, to avoid changes in the index value that are unrelated to changes in the prices of its constituent securities.

Double bottoms   In technical analysis, a reversal pattern that is formed when the price reaches a low, rebounds, and then sells off back to the first low level; used to predict a change from a downtrend to an uptrend.

Double coincidence of wants   A prerequisite to barter trades, in particular that both economic agents in the transaction want what the other is selling.

Double declining balance depreciation   An accelerated depreciation method that involves depreciating the asset at double the straight-line rate. This rate is multiplied by the book value of the asset at the beginning of the period (a declining balance) to calculate depreciation expense.

Double top   In technical analysis, a reversal pattern that is formed when an uptrend reverses twice at roughly the same high price level; used to predict a change from an uptrend to a downtrend.

Double-entry accounting   The accounting system of recording transactions in which every recorded transaction affects at least two accounts so as to keep the basic accounting equation (assets = liabilities + owners' equity) in balance.

Down transition probability   The probability that an asset's value moves down in a model of asset price dynamics.

Drag on liquidity   When receipts lag, creating pressure from the decreased available funds.

Drawdown   A reduction in net asset value (NAV).

DuPont analysis   An approach to decomposing return on investment, e.g., return on equity, as the product of other financial ratios.

Duration   A measure of an option-free bond's average maturity. Specifically, the weighted average maturity of all future cash flows paid by a security, in which the weights are the present value of these cash flows as a fraction of the bond's price. A measure of a bond's price sensitivity to interest rate movements.

Dutch Book theorem   A result in probability theory stating that inconsistent probabilities create profit opportunities.

Earnings per share   The amount of income earned during a period per share of common stock.

Earnings surprise   The portion of a company's earnings that is unanticipated by investors and, according to the efficient market hypothesis, merits a price adjustment.

Economic costs   All the remuneration needed to keep a productive resource in its current employment or to acquire the resource for productive use; the sum of total accounting costs and implicit opportunity costs.

Economic indicator   A variable that provides information on the state of the overall economy.

Economic loss   The amount by which accounting profit is less than normal profit.

Economic order quantity–reorder point (EOQ–ROP)   An approach to managing inventory based on expected demand and the predictability of demand; the ordering point for new inventory is determined based on the costs of ordering and carrying inventory, such that the total cost associated with inventory is minimized.

Economic profit   (abnormal or supernormal profit) Equal to accounting profit less the implicit opportunity costs not included in total accounting costs; the difference between total revenue (TR) and total cost (TC).

Economic rent   The surplus value that results when a particular resource or good is fixed in supply and market price is higher than what is required to bring the resource or good onto the market and sustain its use.

Economic stabilization   Reduction of the magnitude of economic fluctuations.

Economies of scale   Reduction in cost per unit resulting from increased production.

Effective annual rate   The amount by which a unit of currency will grow in a year with interest on interest included.

Effective annual yield (EAY)   An annualized return that accounts for the effect of interest on interest; EAY is computed by compounding 1 plus the holding period yield forward to one year, then subtracting 1.

Efficient market   A market in which asset prices reflect new information quickly and rationally.

Elasticity   The percentage change in one variable for a percentage change in another variable; a measure of how sensitive one variable is to a change in the value of another variable.

Elasticity of supply   A measure of the sensitivity of quantity supplied to a change in price.

Electronic communications networks   See *Alternative trading systems*.

Electronic funds transfer (EFT)   The use of computer networks to conduct financial transactions electronically.

Elliott wave theory   A technical analysis theory that claims that the market follows regular, repeated waves or cycles.

Empirical probability   The probability of an event estimated as a relative frequency of occurrence.

Employed   The number of people with a job.

Enterprise value   A measure of a company's total market value from which the value of cash and short-term investments have been subtracted.

Equal weighting   An index weighting method in which an equal weight is assigned to each constituent security at inception.

Equity Assets less liabilities; the residual interest in the assets after subtracting the liabilities.

Equity forward A contract calling for the purchase of an individual stock, a stock portfolio, or a stock index at a later date at an agreed-upon price.

Equity options Options on individual stocks; also known as stock options.

Equity risk premium The expected return on equities minus the risk-free rate; the premium that investors demand for investing in equities.

Equity swap A swap transaction in which at least one cash flow is tied to the return to an equity portfolio position, often an equity index.

Estimate The particular value calculated from sample observations using an estimator.

Estimation With reference to statistical inference, the subdivision dealing with estimating the value of a population parameter.

Estimator An estimation formula; the formula used to compute the sample mean and other sample statistics are examples of estimators.

Eurodollar A dollar deposited outside the United States.

European option An option that can only be exercised on its expiration date.

European-style contracts An option that can only be exercised on its expiration date.

European-style option (or European option) An option that can only be exercised on its expiration date.

Event Any outcome or specified set of outcomes of a random variable.

Ex-date The first date that a share trades without (i.e. "ex") the dividend.

Ex-dividend date The first date that a share trades without (i.e. "ex") the dividend.

Excess kurtosis Degree of peakedness (fatness of tails) in excess of the peakedness of the normal distribution.

Exchange for physicals (EFP) A permissible delivery procedure used by futures market participants, in which the long and short arrange a delivery procedure other than the normal procedures stipulated by the futures exchange.

Exchanges Places where traders can meet to arrange their trades.

Execution instructions Instructions that indicate how to fill an order.

Exercise The process of using an option to buy or sell the underlying.

Exercise price The fixed price at which an option holder can buy or sell the underlying.

Exercise rate The fixed rate at which the holder of an interest rate option can buy or sell the underlying.

Exercise value The value obtained if an option is exercised based on current conditions.

Exercising the option The process of using an option to buy or sell the underlying.

Exhaustive Covering or containing all possible outcomes.

Expansion The period of a business cycle after its lowest point and before its highest point.

Expansionary Tending to cause the real economy to grow.

Expansionary fiscal policy Fiscal policy aimed at achieving real economic growth.

Expected inflation The level of inflation that economic agents expect in the future.

Expected loss Default probability times loss severity given default.

Expected value The probability-weighted average of the possible outcomes of a random variable.

Expenses Outflows of economic resources or increases in liabilities that result in decreases in equity (other than decreases because of distributions to owners); reductions in net assets associated with the creation of revenues.

Experience curve A curve that shows the direct cost per unit of good or service produced or delivered as a typically declining function of cumulative output.

Externality An effect of a market transaction that is borne by parties other than those who transacted.

Extra dividend A dividend paid by a company that does not pay dividends on a regular schedule, or a dividend that supplements regular cash dividends with an extra payment.

FIFO method The first in, first out, method of accounting for inventory, which matches sales against the costs of items of inventory in the order in which they were placed in inventory.

FX swap The combination of a spot and a forward FX transaction.

Face value The amount of cash payable by a company to the bondholders when the bonds mature; the promised payment at maturity separate from any coupon payment.

Factor A common or underlying element with which several variables are correlated.

Fair value The amount at which an asset could be exchanged, or a liability settled, between knowledgeable, willing parties in an arm's-length transaction; the price that would be received to sell an asset or paid to transfer a liability in an orderly transaction between market participants.

Fed funds rate The U.S. interbank lending rate on overnight borrowings of reserves.

Federal funds rate The U.S. interbank lending rate on overnight borrowings of reserves.

Fiat money Money that is not convertible into any other commodity.

Fibonacci sequence A sequence of numbers starting with 0 and 1, and then each subsequent number in the sequence is the sum of the two preceding numbers. In Elliott Wave Theory, it is believed that market waves follow patterns that are the ratios of the numbers in the Fibonacci sequence.

Fiduciary call A combination of a European call and a risk-free bond that matures on the option expiration day and has a face value equal to the exercise price of the call.

Fill or kill See *Immediate or cancel order.*

Financial flexibility The ability to react and adapt to financial adversities and opportunities.

Financial leverage The extent to which a company can effect, through the use of debt, a proportional change in the return on common equity that is greater than a given proportional change in operating income; also, short for the financial leverage ratio.

Financial leverage ratio A measure of financial leverage calculated as average total assets divided by average total equity.

Financial risk The risk that environmental, social, or governance risk factors will result in significant costs or other losses to a company and its shareholders; the risk arising from a company's obligation to meet required payments under its financing agreements.

Financing activities Activities related to obtaining or repaying capital to be used in the business (e.g., equity and long-term debt).

First lien debt   Debt secured by a pledge of certain assets that could include buildings, but may also include property and equipment, licenses, patents, brands, etc.

First mortgage debt   Debt secured by a pledge of a specific property.

First-degree price discrimination   Where a monopolist is able to charge each customer the highest price the customer is willing to pay.

Fiscal multiplier   The ratio of a change in national income to a change in government spending.

Fiscal policy   The use of taxes and government spending to affect the level of aggregate expenditures.

Fisher effect   The thesis that the real rate of interest in an economy is stable over time so that changes in nominal interest rates are the result of changes in expected inflation.

Fisher index   The geometric mean of the Laspeyres index.

Fixed charge coverage   A solvency ratio measuring the number of times interest and lease payments are covered by operating income, calculated as (EBIT + lease payments) divided by (interest payments + lease payments).

Fixed costs   Costs that remain at the same level regardless of a company's level of production and sales.

Fixed price tender offer   Offer made by a company to repurchase a specific number of shares at a fixed price that is typically at a premium to the current market price.

Fixed rate perpetual preferred stock   Nonconvertible, non-callable preferred stock that has a fixed dividend rate and no maturity date.

Flags   A technical analysis continuation pattern formed by parallel trendlines, typically over a short period.

Float   In the context of customer receipts, the amount of money that is in transit between payments made by customers and the funds that are usable by the company.

Float factor   An estimate of the average number of days it takes deposited checks to clear; average daily float divided by average daily deposit.

Float-adjusted market-capitalization weighting   An index weighting method in which the weight assigned to each constituent security is determined by adjusting its market capitalization for its market float.

Floor   A series of put options on an interest rate, with each option expiring at the date on which the floating loan rate will be reset, and with each option having the same exercise rate. A floor in general can have an underlying other than the interest rate.

Floor traders   Market makers that buy and sell by quoting a bid and an ask price. They are the primary providers of liquidity to the market.

Floorlet   Each component put option in a floor.

Flotation cost   Fees charged to companies by investment bankers and other costs associated with raising new capital.

Foreign currency reserves   Holding by the central bank of non-domestic currency deposits and non-domestic bonds.

Foreign exchange gains   (or losses) Gains (or losses) that occur when the exchange rate changes between the investor's currency and the currency that foreign securities are denominated in.

Forward contract   An agreement between two parties in which one party, the buyer, agrees to buy from the other party, the seller, an underlying asset at a later date for a price established at the start of the contract.

Forward rate   The fixed price or rate at which the transaction scheduled to occur at the expiration of a forward contract will take place. This price is agreed on at the initiation date of the contract.

Forward rate agreement   (FRA) A forward contract calling for one party to make a fixed interest payment and the other to make an interest payment at a rate to be determined at the contract expiration.

Fractile   A value at or below which a stated fraction of the data lies.

Fractional reserve banking   Banking in which reserves constitute a fraction of deposits.

Free cash flow   The actual cash that would be available to the company's investors after making all investments necessary to maintain the company as an ongoing enterprise (also referred to as free cash flow to the firm); the internally generated funds that can be distributed to the company's investors (e.g., shareholders and bondholders) without impairing the value of the company.

Free cash flow to equity (FCFE)   The cash flow available to a company's common shareholders after all operating expenses, interest, and principal payments have been made, and necessary investments in working and fixed capital have been made.

Free cash flow to the firm (FCFF)   The cash flow available to the company's suppliers of capital after all operating expenses have been paid and necessary investments in working capital and fixed capital have been made.

Free float   The number of shares that are readily and freely tradable in the secondary market.

Free-cash-flow-to-equity models   Valuation models based on discounting expected future free cash flow to equity.

Frequency distribution   A tabular display of data summarized into a relatively small number of intervals.

Frequency polygon   A graph of a frequency distribution obtained by drawing straight lines joining successive points representing the class frequencies.

Full price   The price of a security with accrued interest.

Fundamental analysis   The examination of publicly available information and the formulation of forecasts to estimate the intrinsic value of assets.

Fundamental value   (also **intrinsic value**) The underlying or true value of an asset based on an analysis of its qualitative and quantitative characteristics.

Fundamental weighting   An index weighting method in which the weight assigned to each constituent security is based on its underlying company's size. It attempts to address the disadvantages of market-capitalization weighting by using measures that are independent of the constituent security's price.

Funds of funds   Funds that hold a portfolio of hedge funds.

Future value (FV)   The amount to which a payment or series of payments will grow by a stated future date.

Futures commission merchants (FCMs)   Individuals or companies that execute futures transactions for other parties off the exchange.

Futures contract   A variation of a forward contract that has essentially the same basic definition but with some additional features, such as a clearinghouse guarantee against credit losses, a daily settlement of gains and losses, and an organized electronic or floor trading facility.

GDP deflator   A gauge of prices and inflation that measures the aggregate changes in prices across the overall economy.

Gains   Asset inflows not directly related to the ordinary activities of the business.

Game theory   The set of tools decision makers use to incorporate responses by rival decision makers into their strategies.

Gamma   A numerical measure of how sensitive an option's delta is to a change in the underlying.

General partner   The partner that runs the business and theoretically bears unlimited liability.

Geometric mean   A measure of central tendency computed by taking the nth root of the product of n non-negative values.

Giffen good   A good that is consumed more as the price of the good rises.

Gilts   Bonds issued by the U.K. government.

Giro system   An electronic payment system used widely in Europe and Japan.

Global depository receipt   A depository receipt that is issued outside of the company's home country and outside of the United States.

Global minimum-variance portfolio   The portfolio on the minimum-variance frontier with the smallest variance of return.

Global registered share   A common share that is traded on different stock exchanges around the world in different currencies.

Gold standard   With respect to a currency, if a currency is on the gold standard a given amount can be converted into a prespecified amount of gold.

Golden cross   A technical analysis term that describes a situation where a short-term moving average crosses from below a longer-term moving average to above it; this movement is considered bullish.

Good-on-close   (market on close) An execution instruction specifying that an order can only be filled at the close of trading.

Good-on-open   An execution instruction specifying that an order can only be filled at the opening of trading.

Good-till-cancelled order   An order specifying that it is valid until the entity placing the order has cancelled it (or, commonly, until some specified amount of time such as 60 days has elapsed, whichever comes sooner).

Goodwill   An intangible asset that represents the excess of the purchase price of an acquired company over the value of the net assets acquired.

Greenmail   The purchase of the accumulated shares of a hostile investor by a company that is targeted for takeover by that investor, usually at a substantial premium over market price.

Gross domestic product   The market value of all final goods and services produced within the economy in a given period of time (output definition) or, equivalently, the aggregate income earned by all households, all companies, and the government within the economy in a given period of time (income definition).

Gross margin   Sales minus the cost of sales (i.e., the cost of goods sold for a manufacturing company).

Gross profit   Sales minus the cost of sales (i.e., the cost of goods sold for a manufacturing company).

Gross profit margin   The ratio of gross profit to revenues.

Grouping by function   With reference to the presentation of expenses in an income statement, the grouping together of expenses serving the same function, e.g. all items that are costs of goods sold.

Grouping by nature   With reference to the presentation of expenses in an income statement, the grouping together of expenses by similar nature, e.g., all depreciation expenses.

Growth cyclical   A term sometimes used to describe companies that are growing rapidly on a long-term basis but that still experience above-average fluctuation in their revenues and profits over the course of a business cycle.

Harmonic mean   A type of weighted mean computed by averaging the reciprocals of the observations, then taking the reciprocal of that average.

Head and shoulders pattern   In technical analysis, a reversal pattern that is formed in three parts: a left shoulder, head, and right shoulder; used to predict a change from an uptrend to a downtrend.

Headline inflation   The inflation rate calculated based on the price index that includes all goods and services in an economy.

Hedge funds   Private investment vehicles that typically use leverage, derivatives, and long and short investment strategies.

Held for trading   (trading securities) Debt or equity financial assets bought with the intention to sell them in the near term, usually less than three months; securities that a company intends to trade.

Held-to-maturity   Debt (fixed-income) securities that a company intends to hold to maturity; these are presented at their original cost, updated for any amortization of discounts or premiums.

Herding   Clustered trading that may or may not be based on information.

Hidden order   An order that is exposed not to the public but only to the brokers or exchanges that receive it.

High water marks   The highest value, net of fees, which a fund has reached. It reflects the highest cumulative return used to calculate an incentive fee.

Histogram   A bar chart of data that have been grouped into a frequency distribution.

Historical cost   In reference to assets, the amount paid to purchase an asset, including any costs of acquisition and/or preparation; with reference to liabilities, the amount of proceeds received in exchange in issuing the liability.

Historical equity risk premium approach   An estimate of a country's equity risk premium that is based upon the historical averages of the risk-free rate and the rate of return on the market portfolio.

Historical simulation   Another term for the historical method of estimating VAR. This term is somewhat misleading in that the method involves not a *simulation* of the past but rather what *actually happened* in the past, sometimes adjusted to reflect the fact that a different portfolio may have existed in the past than is planned for the future.

Holder-of-record date   The date that a shareholder listed on the corporation's books will be deemed to have ownership of the shares for purposes of receiving an upcoming dividend; two business days after the ex-dividend date.

Holding period return   The return that an investor earns during a specified holding period; a synonym for total return.

Holding period return (HPR)   The return that an investor earns during a specified holding period; a synonym for total return.

Holding period yield (HPY)   The return that an investor earns during a specified holding period; holding period return with reference to a fixed-income instrument.

Homogeneity of expectations   The assumption that all investors have the same economic expectations and thus have the same expectations of prices, cash flows, and other investment characteristics.

Horizontal analysis   Common-size analysis that involves comparing a specific financial statement with that statement in prior or future time periods; also, cross-sectional analysis of one company with another.

Horizontal demand schedule   Implies that at a given price, the response in the quantity demanded is infinite.

Household   A person or a group of people living in the same residence, taken as a basic unit in economic analysis.

Hurdle rate   The rate of return that must be met for a project to be accepted.

Hypothesis   With reference to statistical inference, a statement about one or more populations.

Hypothesis testing   With reference to statistical inference, the subdivision dealing with the testing of hypotheses about one or more populations.

IRR rule   An investment decision rule that accepts projects or investments for which the IRR is greater than the opportunity cost of capital.

Iceberg order   An order in which the display size is less than the order's full size.

If-converted method   A method for accounting for the effect of convertible securities on earnings per share (EPS) that specifies what EPS would have been if the convertible securities had been converted at the beginning of the period, taking account of the effects of conversion on net income and the weighted average number of shares outstanding.

Immediate or cancel order   (fill or kill) An order that is valid only upon receipt by the broker or exchange. If such an order cannot be filled in part or in whole upon receipt, it cancels immediately.

Impact lag   The lag associated with the result of actions affecting the economy with delay.

Imperfect competition   A market structure in which an individual firm has enough share of the market (or can control a certain segment of the market) such that it is able to exert some influence over price.

Implicit price deflator for GDP   A gauge of prices and inflation that measures the aggregate changes in prices across the overall economy.

In-the-money   Options that, if exercised, would result in the value received being worth more than the payment required to exercise.

Incentive fee (or performance fee)   Funds distributed by the general partner to the limited partner(s) based on realized profits.

Income   Increases in economic benefits in the form of inflows or enhancements of assets, or decreases of liabilities that result in an increase in equity (other than increases resulting from contributions by owners).

Income constraint   The constraint on a consumer to spend, in total, no more than his income.

Income elasticity of demand   A measure of the responsiveness of demand to changes in income, defined as the percentage change in quantity demanded divided by the percentage change in income.

Income statement   (statement of operations or profit and loss statement) A financial statement that provides information about a company's profitability over a stated period of time.

Income tax paid   The actual amount paid for income taxes in the period; not a provision, but the actual cash outflow.

Income tax payable   The income tax owed by the company on the basis of taxable income.

Income trust   A type of equity ownership vehicle established as a trust issuing ownership shares known as units.

Increasing marginal returns   Where the marginal product of a resource increases as additional units of that input are employed.

Increasing returns to scale   Reduction in cost per unit resulting from increased production.

Increasing-cost industry   An industry in which per-unit costs and output prices are higher when industry output is increased in the long run.

Incremental cash flow   The cash flow that is realized because of a decision; the changes or increments to cash flows resulting from a decision or action.

Independent   With reference to events, the property that the occurrence of one event does not affect the probability of another event occurring.

Independent and identically distributed (IID)   With respect to random variables, the property of random variables that are independent of each other but follow the identical probability distribution.

Independent projects   Independent projects are projects whose cash flows are independent of each other.

Index of Leading Economic Indicators   A composite of economic variables used by analysts to predict future economic conditions.

Indexing   An investment strategy in which an investor constructs a portfolio to mirror the performance of a specified index.

Indifference curve   A curve representing all the combinations of two goods or attributes such that the consumer is entirely indifferent among them.

Indifference curve map   A group or family of indifference curves, representing a consumer's entire utility function.

Indirect format   (indirect method) With reference to cash flow statements, a format for the presentation of the statement which, in the operating cash flow section, begins with net income then shows additions and subtractions to arrive at operating cash flow.

Indirect format   With reference to cash flow statements, a format for the presentation of the statement which, in the operating cash flow section, begins with net income then shows additions and subtractions to arrive at operating cash flow.

Indirect method   See *indirect format*.

Indirect taxes   Taxes such as taxes on spending, as opposed to direct taxes.

Industry   A group of companies offering similar products and/or services.

Industry analysis   The analysis of a specific branch of manufacturing, service, or trade.

Inelastic   Insensitive to price changes.

Inelastic supply   Said of supply that is insensitive to the price of goods sold.

Inflation   The percentage increase in the general price level from one period to the next; a sustained rise in the overall level of prices in an economy.

Inflation Reports   A type of economic publication put out by many central banks.

Inflation premium   An extra return that compensates investors for expected inflation.

Inflation rate   The percentage change in a price index—that is, the speed of overall price level movements.

Inflation uncertainty   The degree to which economic agents view future rates of inflation as difficult to forecast.

Information cascade The transmission of information from those participants who act first and whose decisions influence the decisions of others.

Information-motivated traders Traders that trade to profit from information that they believe allows them to predict future prices.

Informationally efficient A market in which asset prices reflect new information quickly and rationally.

Informationally efficient market A market in which asset prices reflect new information quickly and rationally.

Initial margin The amount that must be deposited in a clearinghouse account when entering into a futures contract.

Initial margin requirement The margin requirement on the first day of a transaction as well as on any day in which additional margin funds must be deposited.

Initial public offering (IPO) The first issuance of common shares to the public by a formerly private corporation.

Installment method With respect to revenue recognition, a method that specifies that the portion of the total profit of the sale that is recognized in each period is determined by the percentage of the total sales price for which the seller has received cash.

Installment sales With respect to revenue recognition, a method that specifies that the portion of the total profit of the sale that is recognized in each period is determined by the percentage of the total sales price for which the seller has received cash.

Intangible assets Assets lacking physical substance, such as patents and trademarks.

Interest Payment for lending funds.

Interest coverage A solvency ratio calculated as EBIT divided by interest payments.

Interest rate A rate of return that reflects the relationship between differently dated cash flows; a discount rate.

Interest rate call An option in which the holder has the right to make a known interest payment and receive an unknown interest payment.

Interest rate cap A series of call options on an interest rate, with each option expiring at the date on which the floating loan rate will be reset, and with each option having the same exercise rate. A cap in general can have an underlying other than an interest rate.

Interest rate collar A combination of a long cap and a short floor, or a short cap and a long floor. A collar in general can have an underlying other than an interest rate.

Interest rate floor A series of put options on an interest rate, with each option expiring at the date on which the floating loan rate will be reset, and with each option having the same exercise rate. A floor in general can have an underlying other than the interest rate.

Interest rate forward See *Forward rate agreement.*

Interest rate option An option in which the underlying is an interest rate.

Interest rate put An option in which the holder has the right to make an unknown interest payment and receive a known interest payment.

Interest rate swap A swap in which the underlying is an interest rate. Can be viewed as a currency swap in which both currencies are the same and can be created as a combination of currency swaps.

Intergenerational data mining A form of data mining that applies information developed by previous researchers using a dataset to guide current research using the same or a related dataset.

Intermarket analysis A field within technical analysis that combines analysis of major categories of securities—namely, equities, bonds, currencies, and commodities—to identify market trends and possible inflections in a trend.

Internal rate of return (IRR) The discount rate that makes net present value equal 0; the discount rate that makes the present value of an investment's costs (outflows) equal to the present value of the investment's benefits (inflows).

Interquartile range The difference between the third and first quartiles of a dataset.

Interval With reference to grouped data, a set of values within which an observation falls.

Interval scale A measurement scale that not only ranks data but also gives assurance that the differences between scale values are equal.

Intrinsic value See *Fundamental value.*

Inventory The unsold units of product on hand.

Inventory blanket lien The use of inventory as collateral for a loan. Though the lender has claim to some or all of the company's inventory, the company may still sell or use the inventory in the ordinary course of business.

Inventory investment Net change in business inventory.

Inventory turnover An activity ratio calculated as cost of goods sold divided by average inventory.

Investing activities Activities which are associated with the acquisition and disposal of property, plant, and equipment; intangible assets; other long-term assets; and both long-term and short-term investments in the equity and debt (bonds and loans) issued by other companies.

Investment banks Financial intermediaries that provide advice to their mostly corporate clients and help them arrange transactions such as initial and seasoned securities offerings.

Investment opportunity schedule A graphical depiction of a company's investment opportunities ordered from highest to lowest expected return. A company's optimal capital budget is found where the investment opportunity schedule intersects with the company's marginal cost of capital.

Investment policy statement (IPS) A written planning document that describes a client's investment objectives and risk tolerance over a relevant time horizon, along with constraints that apply to the client's portfolio.

Investment property Property used to earn rental income or capital appreciation (or both).

January effect (also turn-of-the-year effect) Calendar anomaly that stock market returns in January are significantly higher compared to the rest of the months of the year, with most of the abnormal returns reported during the first five trading days in January.

Joint probability The probability of the joint occurrence of stated events.

Joint probability function A function giving the probability of joint occurrences of values of stated random variables.

Just-in-time (JIT) method Method of managing inventory that minimizes in-process inventory stocks.

Keynesians Economists who believe that fiscal policy can have powerful effects on aggregate demand, output, and employment when there is substantial spare capacity in an economy.

Kondratieff wave A 54-year long economic cycle postulated by Nikolai Kondratieff.

Kurtosis The statistical measure that indicates the peakedness of a distribution.

LIFO layer liquidation (LIFO liquidation) With respect to the application of the LIFO inventory method, the liquidation of old, relatively low-priced inventory; happens when the volume of sales rises above the volume of recent purchases so that some sales are made from relatively old, low-priced inventory.

LIFO method The last in, first out, method of accounting for inventory, which matches sales against the costs of items of inventory in the reverse order the items were placed in inventory (i.e., inventory produced or acquired last are assumed to be sold first).

Labor force The portion of the working age population (over the age of 16) that is employed or is available for work but not working (unemployed).

Labor productivity The quantity of goods and services (real GDP) that a worker can produce in one hour of work.

Laddering strategy A form of active strategy which entails scheduling maturities on a systematic basis within the investment portfolio such that investments are spread out equally over the term of the ladder.

Lagging economic indicators Turning points that take place later than those of the overall economy; they are believed to have value in identifying the economy's past condition.

Laspeyres index A price index created by holding the composition of the consumption basket constant.

Law of diminishing returns The smallest output that a firm can produce such that its long run average costs are minimized.

Law of one price The condition in a financial market in which two equivalent financial instruments or combinations of financial instruments can sell for only one price. Equivalent to the principle that no arbitrage opportunities are possible.

Lead underwriter The lead investment bank in a syndicate of investment banks and broker–dealers involved in a securities underwriting.

Leading economic indicators Turning points that usually precede those of the overall economy; they are believed to have value for predicting the economy's future state, usually near-term.

Legal tender Something that must be accepted when offered in exchange for goods and services.

Lender of last resort An entity willing to lend money when no other entity is ready to do so.

Leptokurtic Describes a distribution that is more peaked than a normal distribution.

Level of significance The probability of a Type I error in testing a hypothesis.

Leverage In the context of corporate finance, leverage refers to the use of fixed costs within a company's cost structure. Fixed costs that are operating costs (such as depreciation or rent) create operating leverage. Fixed costs that are financial costs (such as interest expense) create financial leverage.

Leveraged buyout (LBO) A transaction whereby the target company management team converts the target to a privately held company by using heavy borrowing to finance the purchase of the target company's outstanding shares.

Liabilities Present obligations of an enterprise arising from past events, the settlement of which is expected to result in an outflow of resources embodying economic benefits; creditors' claims on the resources of a company.

Life-cycle stage The stage of the life cycle: embryonic, growth, shakeout, mature, declining.

Likelihood The probability of an observation, given a particular set of conditions.

Limit down A limit move in the futures market in which the price at which a transaction would be made is at or below the lower limit.

Limit move A condition in the futures markets in which the price at which a transaction would be made is at or beyond the price limits.

Limit order Instructions to a broker or exchange to obtain the best price immediately available when filling an order, but in no event accept a price higher than a specified (limit) price when buying or accept a price lower than a specified (limit) price when selling.

Limit order book The book or list of limit orders to buy and sell that pertains to a security.

Limit up A limit move in the futures market in which the price at which a transaction would be made is at or above the upper limit.

Limitations on liens Meant to put limits on how much secured debt an issuer can have.

Limited partners Partners with limited liability. Limited partnerships in hedge and private equity funds are typically restricted to investors who are expected to understand and to be able to assume the risks associated with the investments

Line chart In technical analysis, a plot of price data, typically closing prices, with a line connecting the points.

Linear interpolation The estimation of an unknown value on the basis of two known values that bracket it, using a straight line between the two known values.

Linear scale (or arithmetic scale) A scale in which equal distances correspond to equal absolute amounts.

Liquid market Said of a market in which traders can buy or sell with low total transaction costs when they want to trade.

Liquidating dividend A dividend that is a return of capital rather than a distribution from earnings or retained earnings.

Liquidation To sell the assets of a company, division, or subsidiary piecemeal, typically because of bankruptcy; the form of bankruptcy that allows for the orderly satisfaction of creditors' claims after which the company ceases to exist.

Liquidity The ability to purchase or sell an asset quickly and easily at a price close to fair market value. The ability to meet short-term obligations using assets that are the most readily converted into cash.

Liquidity premium An extra return that compensates investors for the risk of loss relative to an investment's fair value if the investment needs to be converted to cash quickly.

Liquidity ratios Financial ratios measuring the company's ability to meet its short-term obligations.

Liquidity risk The risk that a financial instrument cannot be purchased or sold without a significant concession in price due to the size of the market.

Liquidity trap A condition in which the demand for money becomes infinitely elastic (horizontal demand curve) so that injections of money into the economy will not lower interest rates or affect real activity.

Load fund A mutual fund in which, in addition to the annual fee, a percentage fee is charged to invest in the fund and/or for redemptions from the fund.

Locals Market makers that buy and sell by quoting a bid and an ask price. They are the primary providers of liquidity to the market.

Lockbox system A payment system in which customer payments are mailed to a post office box and the banking institution retrieves and deposits these payments several times a day, enabling the company to have use of the fund sooner than in a centralized system in which customer payments are sent to the company.

Locked limit A condition in the futures markets in which a transaction cannot take place because the price would be beyond the limits.

Lockup period The minimum period before investors are allowed to make withdrawals or redeem shares from a fund.

Logarithmic scale A scale in which equal distances represent equal proportional changes in the underlying quantity.

London Interbank Offered Rate (LIBOR) The Eurodollar rate at which London banks lend dollars to other London banks; considered to be the best representative rate on a dollar borrowed by a private, high-quality borrower.

Long The buyer of a derivative contract. Also refers to the position of owning a derivative.

Long position A position in an asset or contract in which one owns the asset or has an exercisable right under the contract.

Long-lived assets (or long-term assets) Assets that are expected to provide economic benefits over a future period of time, typically greater than one year.

Long-run average total cost curve The curve describing average total costs when no costs are considered fixed.

Long-run industry supply curve A curve describing the relationship between quantity supplied and output prices when no costs are considered fixed.

Long-term contract A contract that spans a number of accounting periods.

Long-term equity anticipatory securities (also LEAPS) Options originally created with expirations of several years.

Longitudinal data Observations on characteristic(s) of the same observational unit through time.

Look-ahead bias A bias caused by using information that was unavailable on the test date.

Loss severity Portion of a bond's value (including unpaid interest) an investor loses in the event of default.

Losses Asset outflows not directly related to the ordinary activities of the business.

Lower bound The lowest possible value of an option.

M^2 A measure of what a portfolio would have returned if it had taken on the same total risk as the market index.

Macaulay duration The duration without dividing by 1 plus the bond's yield to maturity. The term, named for one of the economists who first derived it, is used to distinguish the calculation from modified duration. (See also *modified duration*.)

Maintenance covenants Covenants in bank loan agreements that require the borrower to satisfy certain financial ratio tests while the loan is outstanding.

Maintenance margin The minimum amount that is required by a futures clearinghouse to maintain a margin account and to protect against default. Participants whose margin balances drop below the required maintenance margin must replenish their accounts.

Maintenance margin requirement The margin requirement on any day other than the first day of a transaction.

Management buy-ins Leveraged buyout in which the current management team is being replaced and the acquiring team will be involved in managing the company.

Management buyout (MBO) An event in which a group of investors consisting primarily of the company's existing management purchase all of its outstanding shares and take the company private.

Management fee (or base fee) A fee based on assets under management or committed capital, as applicable.

Manufacturing resource planning (MRP) The incorporation of production planning into inventory management. A MRP analysis provides both a materials acquisition schedule and a production schedule.

Margin call A notice to deposit additional cash or securities in a margin account.

Margin loan Money borrowed from a broker to purchase securities.

Marginal cost The cost of producing an additional unit of a good.

Marginal probability The probability of an event *not* conditioned on another event.

Marginal product Measures the productivity of each unit of input and is calculated by taking the difference in total product from adding another unit of input (assuming other resource quantities are held constant).

Marginal propensity to consume The proportion of an additional unit of disposable income that is consumed or spent; the change in consumption for a small change in income.

Marginal propensity to save The proportion of an additional unit of disposable income that is saved (not spent).

Marginal rate of substitution The rate at which one is willing to give up one good to obtain more of another.

Marginal revenue The change in total revenue divided by the change in quantity sold; simply, the additional revenue from selling one more unit.

Marginal revenue product The amount of additional revenue received from employing an additional unit of an input.

Marginal value curve A curve describing the highest price consumers are willing to pay for each additional unit of a good.

Mark-to-market The revaluation of a financial asset or liability to its current market value or fair value.

Market A means of bringing buyers and sellers together to exchange goods and services.

Market anomaly Change in the price or return of a security that cannot directly be linked to current relevant information known in the market or to the release of new information into the market.

Market bid–ask spread The difference between the best bid and the best offer.

Market float The number of shares that are available to the investing public.

Market liquidity risk The risk that the price at which investors can actually transact—buying or selling—may differ from the price indicated in the market.

Market model A regression equation that specifies a linear relationship between the return on a security (or portfolio) and the return on a broad market index.

Market multiple models Valuation models based on share price multiples or enterprise value multiples.

Market order Instructions to a broker or exchange to obtain the best price immediately available when filling an order.

Market structure The competitive environment (perfect competition, monopolistic competition, oligopoly, and monopoly).

Market value The price at which an asset or security can currently be bought or sold in an open market.

Market-capitalization weighting (or value weighting) An index weighting method in which the weight assigned to each constituent security is determined by dividing its market capitalization by the total market capitalization (sum of the market capitalization) of all securities in the index.

Market-on-close   An execution instruction specifying that an order can only be filled at the close of trading.

Marketable limit order   A buy limit order in which the limit price is placed above the best offer, or a sell limit order in which the limit price is placed below the best bid. Such orders generally will partially or completely fill right away.

Marking to market   A procedure used primarily in futures markets in which the parties to a contract settle the amount owed daily. Also known as the *daily settlement*.

Markowitz efficient frontier   The graph of the set of portfolios offering the maximum expected return for their level of risk (standard deviation of return).

Matching principle   The accounting principle that expenses should be recognized when the associated revenue is recognized.

Matching strategy   An active investment strategy that includes intentional matching of the timing of cash outflows with investment maturities.

Matrix pricing   In the fixed income markets, to price a security on the basis of valuation-relevant characteristics (e.g. debt-rating approach).

Maturity premium   An extra return that compensates investors for the increased sensitivity of the market value of debt to a change in market interest rates as maturity is extended.

Maturity value   The amount of cash payable by a company to the bondholders when the bonds mature; the promised payment at maturity separate from any coupon payment.

Mean absolute deviation   With reference to a sample, the mean of the absolute values of deviations from the sample mean.

Mean excess return   The average rate of return in excess of the risk-free rate.

Mean–variance analysis   An approach to portfolio analysis using expected means, variances, and covariances of asset returns.

Measure of central tendency   A quantitative measure that specifies where data are centered.

Measure of location   A quantitative measure that describes the location or distribution of data; includes not only measures of central tendency but also other measures such as percentiles.

Measure of value   A standard for measuring value; a function of money.

Measurement scales   A scheme of measuring differences. The four types of measurement scales are nominal, ordinal, interval, and ratio.

Median   The value of the middle item of a set of items that has been sorted into ascending or descending order; the 50th percentile.

Medium of exchange   Any asset that can be used to purchase goods and services or to repay debts; a function of money.

Menu costs   A cost of inflation in which businesses constantly have to incur the costs of changing the advertised prices of their goods and services.

Mesokurtic   Describes a distribution with kurtosis identical to that of the normal distribution.

Mezzanine financing   Debt or preferred shares with a relationship to common equity due to a feature such as attached warrants or conversion options and that is subordinate to both senior and high yield debt. It is referred to as mezzanine because of its location on the balance sheet.

Minimum efficient scale   The smallest output that a firm can produce such that its long run average cost is minimized.

Minimum-variance portfolio   The portfolio with the minimum variance for each given level of expected return.

Minsky moment   Named for Hyman Minksy: A point in a business cycle when, after individuals become overextended in borrowing to finance speculative investments, people start realizing that something is likely to go wrong and a panic ensues leading to asset sell-offs.

Mismatching strategy   An active investment strategy whereby the timing of cash outflows is not matched with investment maturities.

Modal interval   With reference to grouped data, the most frequently occurring interval.

Mode   The most frequently occurring value in a set of observations.

Model risk   The use of an inaccurate pricing model for a particular investment, or the improper use of the right model.

Modern portfolio theory   (MPT) The analysis of rational portfolio choices based on the efficient use of risk.

Modified duration   A measure of a bond's price sensitivity to interest rate movements. Equal to the Macaulay duration of a bond divided by one plus its yield to maturity.

Momentum oscillators   A graphical representation of market sentiment that is constructed from price data and calculated so that it oscillates either between a high and a low or around some number.

Monetarists   Economists who believe that the rate of growth of the money supply is the primary determinant of the rate of inflation.

Monetary policy   Actions taken by a nation's central bank to affect aggregate output and prices through changes in bank reserves, reserve requirements, or its target interest rate.

Monetary transmission mechanism   The process whereby a central bank's interest rate gets transmitted through the economy and ultimately affects the rate of increase of prices.

Money   A generally accepted medium of exchange and unit of account.

Money creation   The process by which changes in bank reserves translate into changes in the money supply.

Money market   The market for short-term debt instruments (oneyear maturity or less).

Money market   The market for short-term debt instruments (one-year maturity or less).

Money market yield   A yield on a basis comparable to the quoted yield on an interest-bearing money market instrument that pays interest on a 360-day basis; the annualized holding period yield, assuming a 360-day year.

Money multiplier   Describes how a change in reserves is expected to affect the money supply; in its simplest form, 1 divided by the reserve requirement.

Money neutrality   The thesis that an increase in the money supply leads in the long-run to an increase in the price level, while leaving real variables like output and employment unaffected.

Money-weighted rate of return   The internal rate of return on a portfolio, taking account of all cash flows.

Moneyness   The relationship between the price of the underlying and an option's exercise price.

Monopolist   Said of an entity that is the only seller in its market.

Monopolistic competition   Highly competitive form of imperfect competition; the competitive characteristic is a notably large number of firms, while the monopoly aspect is the result of product differentiation.

Monopoly   In pure monopoly markets, there are no substitutes for the given product or service. There is a single seller, which exercises considerable power over pricing and output decisions.

Monte Carlo simulation   An approach to estimating a probability distribution of outcomes to examine what might happen if particular risks are faced. This method is widely used in the sciences as well as in business to study a variety of problems.

Moving average   The average of the closing price of a security over a specified number of periods. With each new period, the average is recalculated.

Moving-average convergence/divergence oscillator   (MACD) A momentum oscillator that is constructed based on the difference between short-term and long-term moving averages of a security's price.

Multi-factor model   A model that explains a variable in terms of the values of a set of factors.

Multi-market indices   Comprised of indices from different countries, designed to represent multiple security markets.

Multi-step format   With respect to the format of the income statement, a format that presents a subtotal for gross profit (revenue minus cost of goods sold).

Multilateral trading facilities   See *Alternative trading systems*.

Multiplication rule for probabilities   The rule that the joint probability of events A and B equals the probability of A given B times the probability of B.

Multiplier models   Valuation models based on share price multiples or enterprise value multiples.

Multivariate distribution   A probability distribution that specifies the probabilities for a group of related random variables.

Multivariate normal distribution   A probability distribution for a group of random variables that is completely defined by the means and variances of the variables plus all the correlations between pairs of the variables.

Mutual fund   A professionally managed investment pool in which investors in the fund typically each have a pro-rata claim on the income and value of the fund.

Mutually exclusive projects   Mutually exclusive projects compete directly with each other. For example, if Projects A and B are mutually exclusive, you can choose A or B, but you cannot choose both.

n Factorial   For a positive integer n, the product of the first n positive integers; 0 factorial equals 1 by definition. n factorial is written as $n!$.

NDFs   See *Nondeliverable forwards*.

NPV rule   An investment decision rule that states that an investment should be undertaken if its NPV is positive but not undertaken if its NPV is negative.

Narrow money   The notes and coins in circulation in an economy, plus other very highly liquid deposits.

Nash equilibrium   When two or more participants in a non-coop-erative game have no incentive to deviate from their respective equilibrium strategies given their opponent's strategies.

National income   The income received by all factors of production used in the generation of final output. National income equals gross domestic product (or, in some countries, gross national product) minus the capital consumption allowance and a statistical discrepancy.

Natural rate of unemployment   Effective unemployment rate, below which pressure emerges in labor markets.

Neo-Keynesians   A group of dynamic general equilibrium models that assume slow-to-adjust prices and wages.

Net book value   The remaining (undepreciated) balance of an asset's purchase cost. For liabilities, the face value of a bond minus any unamortized discount, or plus any unamortized premium.

Net income   The difference between revenue and expenses; what remains after subtracting all expenses (including depreciation, interest, and taxes) from revenue.

Net operating cycle   An estimate of the average time that elapses between paying suppliers for materials and collecting cash from the subsequent sale of goods produced.

Net present value   (NPV) The present value of an investment's cash inflows (benefits) minus the present value of its cash outflows (costs).

Net profit margin   (**profit margin** or **return on sales**)An indicator of profitability, calculated as net income divided by revenue; indicates how much of each dollar of revenues is left after all costs and expenses.

Net realizable value   Estimated selling price in the ordinary course of business less the estimated costs necessary to make the sale.

Net revenue   Revenue after adjustments (e.g., for estimated returns or for amounts unlikely to be collected).

Net tax rate   The tax rate net of transfer payments.

Netting   When parties agree to exchange only the net amount owed from one party to the other.

Neutral rate of interest   The rate of interest that neither spurs on nor slows down the underlying economy.

New Keynesians   A group of dynamic general equilibrium models that assume slow-to-adjust prices and wages.

New classical macroeconomics   An approach to macroeconomics that seeks the macroeconomic conclusions of individuals maximizing utility on the basis of rational expectations and companies maximizing profits.

New-issue DRP   Dividend reinvestment plan in which the company meets the need for additional shares by issuing them instead of purchasing them.

No-load fund   A mutual fund in which there is no fee for investing in the fund or for redeeming fund shares, although there is an annual fee based on a percentage of the fund's net asset value.

Node   Each value on a binomial tree from which successive moves or outcomes branch.

Nominal GDP   The value of goods and services measured at current prices.

Nominal rate   A rate of interest based on the security's face value.

Nominal risk-free interest rate   The sum of the real risk-free interest rate and the inflation premium.

Nominal scale   A measurement scale that categorizes data but does not rank them.

Non-accelerating inflation rate of unemployment   Effective unemployment rate, below which pressure emerges in labor markets.

Non-cumulative preference shares   Preference shares for which dividends that are not paid in the current or subsequent periods are forfeited permanently (instead of being accrued and paid at a later date).

Non-current assets   Assets that are expected to benefit the company over an extended period of time (usually more than one year).

Non-current liability   An obligation that broadly represents a probable sacrifice of economic benefits in periods generally greater than one year in the future.

Non-cyclical   A company whose performance is largely independent of the business cycle.

Non-participating preference shares   Preference shares that do not entitle shareholders to share in the profits of the company. Instead, shareholders are only entitled to receive a fixed dividend payment and the par value of the shares in the event of liquidation.

Non-renewable resources   Finite resources that are depleted once they are consumed, such as oil and coal.

Non-satiation   The assumption that the consumer could never have so much of a preferred good that she would refuse any more, even if it were free; sometimes referred to as the "more is better" assumption.

Nonconventional cash flow   In a nonconventional cash flow pattern, the initial outflow is not followed by inflows only, but the cash flows can flip from positive (inflows) to negative (outflows) again (or even change signs several times).

Noncurrent assets   Assets that are expected to benefit the company over an extended period of time (usually more than one year).

Nondeliverable forwards   Cash-settled forward contracts, used predominately with respect to foreign exchange forwards.

Nonparametric test   A test that is not concerned with a parameter, or that makes minimal assumptions about the population from which a sample comes.

Nonsystematic risk   Unique risk that is local or limited to a particular asset or industry that need not affect assets outside of that asset class.

Normal distribution   A continuous, symmetric probability distribution that is completely described by its mean and its variance.

Normal profit   The level of accounting profit needed to just cover the implicit opportunity costs ignored in accounting costs.

Notching   Ratings adjustment methodology where specific issues from the same borrower may be assigned different credit ratings.

Notes payable   Amounts owed by a business to creditors as a result of borrowings that are evidenced by (short-term) loan agreements.

Notice period   The length of time (typically 30 to 90 days) in advance that investors may be required to notify a fund of their intent to redeem.

Number of days of inventory   An activity ratio equal to the number of days in a period divided by the inventory ratio for the period; an indication of the number of days a company ties up funds in inventory.

Number of days of payables   An activity ratio equal to the number of days in a period divided by the payables turnover ratio for the period; an estimate of the average number of days it takes a company to pay its suppliers.

Number of days of receivables   Estimate of the average number of days it takes to collect on credit accounts.

Objective probabilities   Probabilities that generally do not vary from person to person; includes a priori and objective probabilities.

Offer   The price at which a dealer or trader is willing to sell an asset, typically qualified by a maximum quantity (ask size).

Official interest rate   (or official policy rate, policy rate) An interest rate that a central bank sets and announces publicly; normally the rate at which it is willing to lend money to the commercial banks.

Official policy rate   An interest rate that a central bank sets and announces publicly; normally the rate at which it is willing to lend money to the commercial banks.

Offsetting   A transaction in exchange-listed derivative markets in which a party re-enters the market to close out a position.

Oligopoly   Market structure with a relatively small number of firms supplying the market.

One-sided hypothesis test   A test in which the null hypothesis is rejected only if the evidence indicates that the population parameter is greater than (smaller than) θ_0. The alternative hypothesis also has one side.

One-tailed hypothesis test   A test in which the null hypothesis is rejected only if the evidence indicates that the population parameter is greater than (smaller than) θ_0. The alternative hypothesis also has one side.

Open market operations   Activities that involve the purchase and sale of government bonds from and to commercial banks and/or designated market makers.

Open-end fund   A mutual fund that accepts new investment money and issues additional shares at a value equal to the net asset value of the fund at the time of investment.

Open-market DRP   Dividend reinvestment plan in which the company purchases shares in the open market to acquire the additional shares credited to plan participants.

Operating activities   Activities that are part of the day-to-day business functioning of an entity, such as selling inventory and providing services.

Operating breakeven   The number of units produced and sold at which the company's operating profit is zero (revenues = operating costs).

Operating cash flow   The net amount of cash provided from operating activities.

Operating cycle   A measure of the time needed to convert raw materials into cash from a sale; it consists of the number of days of inventory and the number of days of receivables.

Operating efficiency ratios   Ratios that measure how efficiently a company performs day-to-day tasks, such as the collection of receivables and management of inventory.

Operating leverage   The use of fixed costs in operations.

Operating profit   (operating income) A company's profits on its usual business activities before deducting taxes.

Operating profit margin   (operating margin) A profitability ratio calculated as operating income (i.e., income before interest and taxes) divided by revenue.

Operating risk   The risk attributed to the operating cost structure, in particular the use of fixed costs in operations; the risk arising from the mix of fixed and variable costs; the risk that a company's operations may be severely affected by environmental, social, and governance risk factors.

Operational independence   A bank's ability to execute monetary policy and set interest rates in the way it thought would best meet the inflation target.

Operationally efficient   Said of a market, a financial system, or an economy that has relatively low transaction costs.

Opportunity cost   The value that investors forgo by choosing a particular course of action; the value of something in its best alternative use.

Option   (option contract) A financial instrument that gives one party the right, but not the obligation, to buy or sell an underlying asset from or to another party at a fixed price over a specific period of time. Also referred to as contingent claims.

Option contract   See *option*.

Option premium   The amount of money a buyer pays and seller receives to engage in an option transaction.

Option price   The amount of money a buyer pays and seller receives to engage in an option transaction.

Order   A specification of what instrument to trade, how much to trade, and whether to buy or sell.

Order precedence hierarchy   With respect to the execution of orders to trade, a set of rules that determines which orders execute before other orders.

Order-driven markets   A market (generally an auction market) that uses rules to arrange trades based on the orders that traders submit; in their pure form, such markets do not make use of dealers.

Ordinal scale   A measurement scale that sorts data into categories that are ordered (ranked) with respect to some characteristic.

Ordinary annuity   An annuity with a first cash flow that is paid one period from the present.

Ordinary shares   (common stock or common shares) Equity shares that are subordinate to all other types of equity (e.g., preferred equity).

Other comprehensive income   Items of comprehensive income that are not reported on the income statement; comprehensive income minus net income.

Other receivables   Amounts owed to the company from parties other than customers.

Out-of-sample test   A test of a strategy or model using a sample outside the time period on which the strategy or model was developed.

Out-of-the-money   Options that, if exercised, would require the payment of more money than the value received and therefore would not be currently exercised.

Outcome   A possible value of a random variable.

Overbought   A market condition in which market sentiment is thought to be unsustainably bullish.

Oversold   A market condition in which market sentiment is thought to be unsustainably bearish.

Owner-of-record date   The date that a shareholder listed on the corporation's books will be deemed to have ownership of the shares for purposes of receiving an upcoming dividend; two business days after the ex-dividend date.

Owners' equity   (shareholders' equity) The excess of assets over liabilities; the residual interest of shareholders in the assets of an entity after deducting the entity's liabilities.

Paasche index   An index formula using the current composition of a basket of products.

Paired comparisons test   A statistical test for differences based on paired observations drawn from samples that are dependent on each other.

Paired observations   Observations that are dependent on each other.

Pairs arbitrage trade   A trade in two closely related stocks involving the short sale of one and the purchase of the other.

Panel data   Observations through time on a single characteristic of multiple observational units.

Parameter   A descriptive measure computed from or used to describe a population of data, conventionally represented by Greek letters.

Parametric test   Any test (or procedure) concerned with parameters or whose validity depends on assumptions concerning the population generating the sample.

Pari passu   On an equal footing.

Participating preference shares   Preference shares that entitle shareholders to receive the standard preferred dividend plus the opportunity to receive an additional dividend if the company's profits exceed a pre-specified level.

Passive investment   A buy and hold approach in which an investor does not make portfolio changes based on short-term expectations of changing market or security performance.

Passive strategy   In reference to short-term cash management, it is an investment strategy characterized by simple decision rules for making daily investments.

Payable date   The day that the company actually mails out (or electronically transfers) a dividend payment.

Payment date   The day that the company actually mails out (or electronically transfers) a dividend payment.

Payments system   The system for the transfer of money.

Payoff   The value of an option at expiration.

Payout   Cash dividends and the value of shares repurchased in any given year.

Payout policy   A company's set of principles guiding payouts.

Peak   The highest point of a business cycle.

Peer group   A group of companies engaged in similar business activities whose economics and valuation are influenced by closely related factors.

Pennants   A technical analysis continuation pattern formed by trendlines that converge to form a triangle, typically over a short period.

Per capita real GDP   Real GDP divided by the size of the population, often used as a measure of the average standard of living in a country.

Per unit contribution margin   The amount that each unit sold contributes to covering fixed costs—that is, the difference between the price per unit and the variable cost per unit.

Percentage-of-completion   A method of revenue recognition in which, in each accounting period, the company estimates what percentage of the contract is complete and then reports that percentage of the total contract revenue in its income statement.

Percentiles   Quantiles that divide a distribution into 100 equal parts.

Perfect competition   (also price taker) A market structure in which the individual firm has virtually no impact on market price, because it is assumed to be a very small seller among a very large number of firms selling essentially identical products.

Performance appraisal   The evaluation of risk-adjusted performance; the evaluation of investment skill.

Performance evaluation   The measurement and assessment of the outcomes of investment management decisions.

Performance measurement   The calculation of returns in a logical and consistent manner.

Period costs   Costs (e.g., executives' salaries) that cannot be directly matched with the timing of revenues and which are thus expensed immediately.

Permanent differences   Differences between tax and financial reporting of revenue (expenses) that will not be reversed at some future date. These result in a difference between the company's effective tax rate and statutory tax rate and do not result in a deferred tax item.

Permutation   An ordered listing.

Perpetuity   A perpetual annuity, or a set of never-ending level sequential cash flows, with the first cash flow occurring one period from now.

Personal consumption expenditures   All domestic personal consumption; the basis for a price index for such consumption called the PCE price index.

Personal disposable income   Equal to personal income less personal taxes.

Personal income   A broad measure of household income that includes all income received by households, whether earned or unearned; measures the ability of consumers to make purchases.

Plain vanilla swap   An interest rate swap in which one party pays a fixed rate and the other pays a floating rate, with both sets of payments in the same currency.

Planning horizon   A time period in which all factors of production are variable, including technology, physical capital, and plant size.

Platykurtic   Describes a distribution that is less peaked than the normal distribution.

Point and figure chart   A technical analysis chart that is constructed with columns of X's alternating with columns of O's such that the horizontal axis represents only the number of changes in price without reference to time or volume.

Point estimate   A single numerical estimate of an unknown quantity, such as a population parameter.

Point of sale (POS)   Systems that capture transaction data at the physical location in which the sale is made.

Policy rate   An interest rate that a central bank sets and announces publicly; normally the rate at which it is willing to lend money to the commercial banks.

Population   All members of a specified group.

Population mean   The arithmetic mean value of a population; the arithmetic mean of all the observations or values in the population.

Population standard deviation   A measure of dispersion relating to a population in the same unit of measurement as the observations, calculated as the positive square root of the population variance.

Population variance   A measure of dispersion relating to a population, calculated as the mean of the squared deviations around the population mean.

Portfolio company   In private equity, the company that is being invested in.

Portfolio demand for money   The demand to hold speculative money balances based on the potential opportunities or risks that are inherent in other financial instruments.

Portfolio planning   The process of creating a plan for building a portfolio that is expected to satisfy a client's investment objectives.

Position   The quantity of an asset that an entity owns or owes.

Position trader   A trader who typically holds positions open overnight.

Posterior probability   An updated probability that reflects or comes after new information.

Potential GDP   The level of real GDP that can be produced at full employment; measures the productive capacity of the economy.

Power of a test   The probability of correctly rejecting the null—that is, rejecting the null hypothesis when it is false.

Precautionary money balances   Money held to provide a buffer against unforeseen events that might require money.

Precautionary stocks   A level of inventory beyond anticipated needs that provides a cushion in the event that it takes longer to replenish inventory than expected or in the case of greater than expected demand.

Preference shares   (or preferred stock) A type of equity interest which ranks above common shares with respect to the payment of dividends and the distribution of the company's net assets upon liquidation. They have characteristics of both debt and equity securities.

Preferred stock   See *Preference shares*.

Premium   The amount of money a buyer pays and seller receives to engage in an option transaction.

Prepaid expense   A normal operating expense that has been paid in advance of when it is due.

Present value   (PV) The present discounted value of future cash flows: For assets, the present discounted value of the future net cash inflows that the asset is expected to generate; for liabilities, the present discounted value of the future net cash outflows that are expected to be required to settle the liabilities.

Present value models   (or discounted cash flow models) Valuation models that estimate the intrinsic value of a security as the present value of the future benefits expected to be received from the security.

Pretax margin   A profitability ratio calculated as earnings before taxes divided by revenue.

Price   The market price as established by the interactions of the market demand and supply factors.

Price discovery   A feature of futures markets in which futures prices provide valuable information about the price of the underlying asset.

Price elasticity of demand   Measures the percentage change in the quantity demanded, given a percentage change in the price of a given product.

Price index   Represents the average prices of a basket of goods and services.

Price limits   Limits imposed by a futures exchange on the price change that can occur from one day to the next.

Price multiple   A ratio that compares the share price with some sort of monetary flow or value to allow evaluation of the relative worth of a company's stock.

Price priority   The principle that the highest priced buy orders and the lowest priced sell orders execute first.

Price relative   A ratio of an ending price over a beginning price; it is equal to 1 plus the holding period return on the asset.

Price return   Measures *only* the price appreciation or percentage change in price of the securities in an index or portfolio.

Price return index   (or price index) An index that reflects *only* the price appreciation or percentage change in price of the constituent securities.

Price stability   In economics, refers to an inflation rate that is low on average and not subject to wide fluctuation.

Price takers   Producers that must accept whatever price the market dictates.

Price to book value   A valuation ratio calculated as price per share divided by book value per share.

Price to cash flow   A valuation ratio calculated as price per share divided by cash flow per share.

Price to earnings ratio   (P/E ratio) The ratio of share price to earnings per share.

Price to sales   A valuation ratio calculated as price per share divided by sales per share.

Price weighting   An index weighting method in which the weight assigned to each constituent security is determined by dividing its price by the sum of all the prices of the constituent securities.

Price-to-earnings ratio   (also P/E) The ratio of share price to earnings per share.

Priced risk   Risk for which investors demand compensation for bearing (e.g. equity risk, company-specific factors, macroeconomic factors).

Primary capital markets (primary markets)   The market where securities are first sold and the issuers receive the proceeds.

Primary market   The market where securities are first sold and the issuers receive the proceeds.

Prime brokers   Brokers that provide services including custody, administration, lending, short borrowing, and trading.

Principal   The amount of funds originally invested in a project or instrument; the face value to be paid at maturity.

Principal business activity   The business activity from which a company derives a majority of its revenues and/or earnings.

Principal value   The amount of cash payable by a company to the bondholders when the bonds mature; the promised payment at maturity separate from any coupon payment.

Prior probabilities   Probabilities reflecting beliefs prior to the arrival of new information.

Priority of claims   Priority of payment, with the most senior or highest ranking debt having the first claim on the cash flows and assets of the issuer.

Private equity securities   Securities that are not listed on public exchanges and have no active secondary market. They are issued primarily to institutional investors via non-public offerings, such as private placements.

Private investment in public equity   An investment in the equity of a publicly traded firm that is made at a discount to the market value of the firm's shares.

Private placement   When corporations sell securities directly to a small group of qualified investors, usually with the assistance of an investment bank.

Probability   A number between 0 and 1 describing the chance that a stated event will occur.

Probability density function   A function with non-negative values such that probability can be described by areas under the curve graphing the function.

Probability distribution   A distribution that specifies the probabilities of a random variable's possible outcomes.

Probability function   A function that specifies the probability that the random variable takes on a specific value.

Producer price index   Reflects the price changes experienced by domestic producers in a country.

Production function   Provides the quantitative link between the level of output that the economy can produce and the inputs used in the production process.

Production opportunity frontier   Curve describing the maximum number of units of one good a company can produce, for any given number of the other good that it chooses to manufacture.

Productivity   The amount of output produced by workers in a given period of time—for example, output per hour worked; measures the efficiency of labor.

Profit   The return that owners of a company receive for the use of their capital and the assumption of financial risk when making their investments.

Profit and loss (P&L) statement   A financial statement that provides information about a company's profitability over a stated period of time.

Profit margin   An indicator of profitability, calculated as net income divided by revenue; indicates how much of each dollar of revenues is left after all costs and expenses.

Profitability ratios   Ratios that measure a company's ability to generate profitable sales from its resources (assets).

Project sequencing   To defer the decision to invest in a future project until the outcome of some or all of a current project is known. Projects are sequenced through time, so that investing in a project creates the option to invest in future projects.

Promissory note   A written promise to pay a certain amount of money on demand.

Property, plant, and equipment   Tangible assets that are expected to be used for more than one period in either the production or supply of goods or services, or for administrative purposes.

Prospectus   The document that describes the terms of a new bond issue and helps investors perform their analysis on the issue.

Protective put   An option strategy in which a long position in an asset is combined with a long position in a put.

Pseudo-random numbers   Numbers produced by random number generators.

Pull on liquidity   When disbursements are paid too quickly or trade credit availability is limited, requiring companies to expend funds before they receive funds from sales that could cover the liability.

Pure discount instruments   Instruments that pay interest as the difference between the amount borrowed and the amount paid back.

Pure-play method   A method for estimating the beta for a company or project; it requires using a comparable company's beta and adjusting it for financial leverage differences.

Put   An option that gives the holder the right to sell an underlying asset to another party at a fixed price over a specific period of time.

Put/call ratio   A technical analysis indicator that evaluates market sentiment based upon the volume of put options traded divided by the volume of call options traded for a particular financial instrument.

Putable common shares   Common shares that give investors the option (or right) to sell their shares (i.e., "put" them) back to the issuing company at a price that is specified when the shares are originally issued.

Put–call parity   An equation expressing the equivalence (parity) of a portfolio of a call and a bond with a portfolio of a put and the underlying, which leads to the relationship between put and call prices.

Quantile   (or fractile) A value at or below which a stated fraction of the data lies.

Quantitative easing   An expansionary monetary policy based on aggressive open market purchase operations.

Quantity   The amount of a product that consumers are willing and able to buy at each price level.

Quantity demanded   The amount of a product that consumers are willing and able to buy at each price level.

Quantity equation of exchange   An expression that over a given period, the amount of money used to purchase all goods and services in an economy, $M \times V$, is equal to monetary value of this output, $P \times Y$.

Quantity theory of money   Asserts that total spending (in money terms) is proportional to the quantity of money.

Quartiles   Quantiles that divide a distribution into four equal parts.

Quasi-fixed cost   A cost that stays the same over a range of production but can change to another constant level when production moves outside of that range.

Quick assets   Assets that can be most readily converted to cash (e.g., cash, short-term marketable investments, receivables).

Quick ratio   A stringent measure of liquidity that indicates a company's ability to satisfy current liabilities with its most liquid assets, calculated as (cash + short-term marketable investments + receivables) divided by current liabilities.

Quintiles   Quantiles that divide a distribution into five equal parts.

Quote-driven market   A market in which dealers acting as principals facilitate trading.

Quoted interest rate   (also stated annual interest rate) A quoted interest rate that does not account for compounding within the year.

Random number   An observation drawn from a uniform distribution.

Random number generator   An algorithm that produces uniformly distributed random numbers between 0 and 1.

Random variable   A quantity whose future outcomes are uncertain.

Range   The difference between the maximum and minimum values in a dataset.

Ratio scales   A measurement scale that has all the characteristics of interval measurement scales as well as a true zero point as the origin.

Real GDP   The value of goods and services produced, measured at base year prices.

Real income   Income adjusted for the effect of inflation on the purchasing power of money.

Real interest rate   Nominal interest rate minus the expected rate of inflation.

Real risk-free interest rate   The single-period interest rate for a completely risk-free security if no inflation were expected.

Realizable (settlement) value   With reference to assets, the amount of cash or cash equivalents that could currently be obtained by selling the asset in an orderly disposal; with reference to liabilities, the undiscounted amount of cash or cash equivalents expected to be paid to satisfy the liabilities in the normal course of business.

Rebalancing   Adjusting the weights of the constituent securities in an index.

Rebalancing policy   The set of rules that guide the process of restoring a portfolio's asset class weights to those specified in the strategic asset allocation.

Recession   A period during which real GDP decreases (i.e., negative growth) for at least two successive quarters, or a period of significant decline in total output, income, employment, and sales usually lasting from six months to a year.

Recognition lag   The lag in government response to an economic problem resulting from the delay in confirming a change in the state of the economy.

Record date   The date that a shareholder listed on the corporation's books will be deemed to have ownership of the shares for purposes of receiving an upcoming dividend; two business days after the ex-dividend date.

Redemptions   Withdrawals of funds by investors.

Refinancing rate   A type of central bank policy rate.

Regulatory risk   The risk associated with the uncertainty of how derivative transactions will be regulated or with changes in regulations.

Relative dispersion   The amount of dispersion relative to a reference value or benchmark.

Relative frequency   With reference to an interval of grouped data, the number of observations in the interval divided by the total number of observations in the sample.

Relative price   The price of a specific good or service in comparison with those of other goods and services.

Relative strength analysis   A comparison of the performance of one asset with the performance of another asset or a benchmark based on changes in the ratio of the securities' respective prices over time.

Relative strength index   A technical analysis momentum oscillator that compares a security's gains with its losses over a set period.

Renewable resources   Resources that can be replenished, such as a forest.

Rent   Payment for the use of property.

Reorganization   Agreements made by a company in bankruptcy under which a company's capital structure is altered and/or alternative arrangements are made for debt repayment; U.S. Chapter 11 bankruptcy. The company emerges from bankruptcy as a going concern.

Repo rates   Short-term collateralized lending rates.

Repurchase agreement   The sale of securities together with an agreement for the seller to buy back the securities at a later date at a higher price; often called a repo. Typically a short-term agreement; if long term, called a term repo.

Reserve requirement   The requirement for banks to hold reserves in proportion to the size of deposits.

Residual claim   The owners' remaining claim on the company's assets after the liabilities are deducted.

Resistance   In technical analysis, a price range in which selling activity is sufficient to stop the rise in the price of a security.

Restricted payments   A bond covenant meant to protect creditors by limiting how much cash can be paid out to shareholders over time.

Retail method   An inventory accounting method in which the sales value of an item is reduced by the gross margin to calculate the item's cost.

Retracement   In technical analysis, a reversal in the movement of a security's price such that it is counter to the prevailing longterm price trend.

Return on assets (ROA)   A profitability ratio calculated as net income divided by average total assets; indicates a company's net profit generated per dollar invested in total assets.

Return on equity (ROE)   A profitability ratio calculated as net income divided by average shareholders' equity.

Return on sales   An indicator of profitability, calculated as net income divided by revenue; indicates how much of each dollar of revenues is left after all costs and expenses.

Return on total capital   A profitability ratio calculated as EBIT divided by the sum of short- and long-term debt and equity.

Return-generating model   A model that can provide an estimate of the expected return of a security given certain parameters and estimates of the values of the independent variables in the model.

Revaluation model   The process of valuing long-lived assets at fair value, rather than at cost less accumulated depreciation. Any resulting profit or loss is either reported on the income statement and/or through equity under revaluation surplus.

Revenue   The amount charged for the delivery of goods or services in the ordinary activities of a business over a stated period; the inflows of economic resources to a company over a stated period.

Reversal patterns   A type of pattern used in technical analysis to predict the end of a trend and a change in direction of the security's price.

Reverse stock split   A reduction in the number of shares outstanding with a corresponding increase in share price, but no change to the company's underlying fundamentals.

Revolving credit agreements   The strongest form of short-term bank borrowing facilities; they are in effect for multiple years (e.g., 3–5 years) and may have optional medium-term loan features.

Rho   The sensitivity of the option price to the risk-free rate.

Ricardian equivalence   An economic theory that implies that it makes no difference whether a government finances a deficit by increasing taxes or issuing debt.

Risk averse   The assumption that an investor will choose the least risky alternative.

Risk aversion The degree of an investor's inability and unwillingness to take risk.

Risk budgeting The establishment of objectives for individuals, groups, or divisions of an organization that takes into account the allocation of an acceptable level of risk.

Risk management The process of identifying the level of risk an entity wants, measuring the level of risk the entity currently has, taking actions that bring the actual level of risk to the desired level of risk, and monitoring the new actual level of risk so that it continues to be aligned with the desired level of risk.

Risk premium An extra return expected by investors for bearing some specified risk.

Risk tolerance The amount of risk an investor is willing and able to bear to achieve an investment goal.

Robust The quality of being relatively unaffected by a violation of assumptions.

Rule of 72 The principle that the approximate number of years necessary for an investment to double is 72 divided by the stated interest rate.

Safety stock A level of inventory beyond anticipated needs that provides a cushion in the event that it takes longer to replenish inventory than expected or in the case of greater than expected demand.

Safety-first rules Rules for portfolio selection that focus on the risk that portfolio value will fall below some minimum acceptable level over some time horizon.

Sales Generally, a synonym for revenue; "sales" is generally understood to refer to the sale of goods, whereas "revenue" is understood to include the sale of goods or services.

Sales returns and allowances An offset to revenue reflecting any cash refunds, credits on account, and discounts from sales prices given to customers who purchased defective or unsatisfactory items.

Sales risk Uncertainty with respect to the quantity of goods and services that a company is able to sell and the price it is able to achieve; the risk related to the uncertainty of revenues.

Salvage value (or residual value) The amount the company estimates that it can sell the asset for at the end of its useful life.

Sample A subset of a population.

Sample excess kurtosis A sample measure of the degree of a distribution's peakedness in excess of the normal distribution's peakedness.

Sample kurtosis A sample measure of the degree of a distribution's peakedness.

Sample mean The sum of the sample observations, divided by the sample size.

Sample selection bias Bias introduced by systematically excluding some members of the population according to a particular attribute—for example, the bias introduced when data availability leads to certain observations being excluded from the analysis.

Sample skewness A sample measure of degree of asymmetry of a distribution.

Sample standard deviation The positive square root of the sample variance.

Sample statistic A quantity computed from or used to describe a sample.

Sample variance A sample measure of the degree of dispersion of a distribution, calculated by dividing the sum of the squared deviations from the sample mean by the sample size minus 1.

Sampling The process of obtaining a sample.

Sampling distribution The distribution of all distinct possible values that a statistic can assume when computed from samples of the same size randomly drawn from the same population.

Sampling error The difference between the observed value of a statistic and the quantity it is intended to estimate.

Sampling plan The set of rules used to select a sample.

Say's law Named for French economist J.B. Say: All that is produced will be sold because supply creates its own demand.

Scalper A trader who offers to buy or sell futures contracts, holding the position for only a brief period of time. Scalpers attempt to profit by buying at the bid price and selling at the higher ask price.

Scenario analysis Analysis that shows the changes in key financial quantities that result from given (economic) events, such as the loss of customers, the loss of a supply source, or a catastrophic event; a risk management technique involving examination of the performance of a portfolio under specified situations. Closely related to stress testing.

Scrip dividend schemes Dividend reinvestment plan in which the company meets the need for additional shares by issuing them instead of purchasing them.

Seasoned offering An offering in which an issuer sells additional units of a previously issued security.

Seats Memberships in a derivatives exchange.

Second lien A secured interest in the pledged assets that ranks below first lien debt in both collateral protection and priority of payment.

Second-degree price discrimination When the monopolist charges different per-unit prices using the quantity purchased as an indicator of how highly the customer values the product.

Secondary market The market where securities are traded among investors.

Secondary precedence rules Rules that determine how to rank orders placed at the same time.

Sector A group of related industries.

Sector indices Indices that represent and track different economic sectors—such as consumer goods, energy, finance, health care, and technology—on either a national, regional, or global basis.

Secured debt Debt in which the debtholder has a direct claim—a pledge from the issuer—on certain assets and their associated cash flows.

Security characteristic line A plot of the excess return of a security on the excess return of the market.

Security market index A portfolio of securities representing a given security market, market segment, or asset class.

Security market line (also SML) The graph of the capital asset pricing model.

Security selection The process of selecting individual securities; typically, security selection has the objective of generating superior risk-adjusted returns relative to a portfolio's benchmark.

Self-investment limits With respect to investment limitations applying to pension plans, restrictions on the percentage of assets that can be invested in securities issued by the pension plan sponsor.

Sell-side firm A broker or dealer that sells securities to and provides independent investment research and recommendations to investment management companies.

Semi-strong-form efficient market A market in which security prices reflect all publicly known and available information.

Semideviation   The positive square root of semivariance (sometimes called semistandard deviation).

Semilogarithmic   Describes a scale constructed so that equal intervals on the vertical scale represent equal rates of change, and equal intervals on the horizontal scale represent equal amounts of change.

Semivariance   The average squared deviation below the mean.

Seniority ranking   Priority of payment of various debt obligations.

Sensitivity analysis   Analysis that shows the range of possible outcomes as specific assumptions are changed.

Separately managed account   (SMA) An investment portfolio managed exclusively for the benefit of an individual or institution.

Settlement date   The date on which the parties to a swap make payments.

Settlement period   The time between settlement dates.

Settlement price   The official price, designated by the clearinghouse, from which daily gains and losses will be determined and marked to market.

Share repurchase   A transaction in which a company buys back its own shares. Unlike stock dividends and stock splits, share repurchases use corporate cash.

Shareholder wealth maximization   To maximize the market value of shareholders' equity.

Shareholder-of-record date   The date that a shareholder listed on the corporation's books will be deemed to have ownership of the shares for purposes of receiving an upcoming dividend; two business days after the ex-dividend date.

Shareholders' equity   Assets less liabilities; the residual interest in the assets after subtracting the liabilities.

Sharpe ratio   The average return in excess of the risk-free rate divided by the standard deviation of return; a measure of the average excess return earned per unit of standard deviation of return.

Shelf registration   A registration of an offering well in advance of the offering; the issuer may not sell all shares registered in a single transaction.

Short   The seller of a derivative contract. Also refers to the position of being short a derivative.

Short position   A position in an asset or contract in which one has sold an asset one does not own, or in which a right under a contract can be exercised against oneself.

Short selling   A transaction in which borrowed securities are sold with the intention to repurchase them at a lower price at a later date and return them to the lender.

Short-run average total cost curve   The curve describing average total costs when some costs are considered fixed.

Short-run supply curve   The section of the marginal cost curve that lies above the minimum point on the average variable cost curve.

Shortfall risk   The risk that portfolio value will fall below some minimum acceptable level over some time horizon.

Shutdown point   The point at which average revenue is less than average variable cost.

Simple interest   The interest earned each period on the original investment; interest calculated on the principal only.

Simple random sample   A subset of a larger population created in such a way that each element of the population has an equal probability of being selected to the subset.

Simple random sampling   The procedure of drawing a sample to satisfy the definition of a simple random sample.

Simulation   Computer-generated sensitivity or scenario analysis that is based on probability models for the factors that drive outcomes.

Simulation trial   A complete pass through the steps of a simulation.

Single-step format   With respect to the format of the income statement, a format that does not subtotal for gross profit (revenue minus cost of goods sold).

Skewed   Not symmetrical.

Skewness   A quantitative measure of skew (lack of symmetry); a synonym of skew.

Solvency   With respect to financial statement analysis, the ability of a company to fulfill its long-term obligations.

Solvency ratios   Ratios that measure a company's ability to meet its long-term obligations.

Sovereign yield spread   An estimate of the country spread (country equity premium) for a developing nation that is based on a comparison of bonds yields in country being analyzed and a developed country. The sovereign yield spread is the difference between a government bond yield in the country being analyzed, denominated in the currency of the developed country, and the Treasury bond yield on a similar maturity bond in the developed country.

Spearman rank correlation coefficient   A measure of correlation applied to ranked data.

Special dividend   A dividend paid by a company that does not pay dividends on a regular schedule, or a dividend that supplements regular cash dividends with an extra payment.

Special purpose entity   (special purpose vehicle or variable interest entity) A non-operating entity created to carry out a specified purpose, such as leasing assets or securitizing receivables; can be a corporation, partnership, trust, limited liability, or partnership formed to facilitate a specific type of business activity.

Special purpose vehicle   See *Special purpose entity*.

Specific identification method   An inventory accounting method that identifies which specific inventory items were sold and which remained in inventory to be carried over to later periods.

Speculative demand for money   (or portfolio demand for money) The demand to hold speculative money balances based on the potential opportunities or risks that are inherent in other financial instruments.

Speculative money balances   Monies held in anticipation that other assets will decline in value.

Speculative value   The difference between the market price of the option and its intrinsic value, determined by the uncertainty of the underlying over the remaining life of the option.

Sponsored   A type of depository receipt in which the foreign company whose shares are held by the depository has a direct involvement in the issuance of the receipts.

Spot markets   Markets that trade assets for immediate delivery.

Spot price   The price for immediate purchase of the underlying asset.

Spread risk   Bond price risk arising from changes in the yield spread on credit-risky bonds; reflects changes in the market's assessment and/or pricing of credit migration (or downgrade) risk and market liquidity risk.

Stackelberg model   A prominent model of strategic decision-making in which firms are assumed to make their decisions sequentially.

Stagflation   When a high inflation rate is combined with a high level of unemployment and a slowdown of the economy.

Standard cost   With respect to inventory accounting, the planned or target unit cost of inventory items or services.

Standard deviation   The positive square root of the variance; a measure of dispersion in the same units as the original data.

Standard normal distribution   The normal density with mean (μ) equal to 0 and standard deviation (σ) equal to 1.

Standardizing   A transformation that involves subtracting the mean and dividing the result by the standard deviation.

Standing limit orders   A limit order at a price below market and which therefore is waiting to trade.

Stated annual interest rate   (also quoted interest rate) A quoted interest rate that does not account for compounding within the year.

Statement of cash flows   (cash flow statement) A financial statement that reconciles beginning-of-period and end-of-period balance sheet values of cash; provides information about an entity's cash inflows and cash outflows as they pertain to operating, investing, and financing activities.

Statement of changes in equity   (statement of owners' equity) A financial statement that reconciles the beginning-of-period and end-of-period balance sheet values of shareholders' equity; provides information about all factors affecting shareholders' equity.

Statement of financial condition   The financial statement that presents an entity's current financial position by disclosing resources the entity controls (its assets) and the claims on those resources (its liabilities and equity claims), as of a particular point in time (the date of the balance sheet).

Statement of financial position   The financial statement that presents an entity's current financial position by disclosing resources the entity controls (its assets) and the claims on those resources (its liabilities and equity claims), as of a particular point in time (the date of the balance sheet).

Statement of operations   A financial statement that provides information about a company's profitability over a stated period of time.

Statement of owners' equity   (Statement of changes in shareholders' equity) A financial statement that reconciles the beginning of-period and end-of-period balance sheet values of shareholders' equity; provides information about all factors affecting shareholders' equity.

Statement of retained earnings   A financial statement that reconciles beginning-of-period and end-of-period balance sheet values of retained income; shows the linkage between the balance sheet and income statement.

Statistic   A quantity computed from or used to describe a sample of data.

Statistical inference   Making forecasts, estimates, or judgments about a larger group from a smaller group actually observed; using a sample statistic to infer the value of an unknown population parameter.

Statistically significant   A result indicating that the null hypothesis can be rejected; with reference to an estimated regression coefficient, frequently understood to mean a result indicating that the corresponding population regression coefficient is different from 0.

Statutory voting   A common method of voting where each share represents one vote.

Stock dividend   A type of dividend in which a company distributes additional shares of its common stock to shareholders instead of cash.

Stock-out losses   Profits lost from not having sufficient inventory on hand to satisfy demand.

Stop order   (or stop-loss order) An order in which a trader has specified a stop price condition.

Stop-loss order   See *Stop order*.

Store of value   The quality of tending to preserve value.

Store of wealth   Goods that depend on the fact that they do not perish physically over time, and on the belief that others would always value the good.

Straight-line method   A depreciation method that allocates evenly the cost of a long-lived asset less its estimated residual value over the estimated useful life of the asset.

Strategic analysis   Analysis of the competitive environment with an emphasis on the implications of the environment for corporate strategy.

Strategic asset allocation   The set of exposures to IPS-permissible asset classes that is expected to achieve the client's long-term objectives given the client's investment constraints.

Strategic groups   Groups sharing distinct business models or catering to specific market segments in an industry.

Stress testing   A set of techniques for estimating losses in extremely unfavorable combinations of events or scenarios.

Strike   The fixed price at which an option holder can buy or sell the underlying.

Strike price   The fixed price at which an option holder can buy or sell the underlying.

Strike rate   The fixed rate at which the holder of an interest rate option can buy or sell the underlying.

Striking price   The fixed price at which an option holder can buy or sell the underlying.

Strong-form efficient market   A market in which security prices reflect all public and private information.

Structural (or cyclically adjusted) budget deficit   The deficit that would exist if the economy was at full employment (or full potential output).

Structural subordination   Arises in a holding company structure when the debt of operating subsidiaries is serviced by the cash flow and assets of the subsidiaries before funds can be passed to the holding company to service debt at the parent level.

Structured note   A variation of a floating-rate note that has some type of unusual characteristic such as a leverage factor or in which the rate moves opposite to interest rates.

Subjective probability   A probability drawing on personal or subjective judgment.

Subordinated debt   A class of unsecured debt that ranks below a firm's senior unsecured obligations.

Substitutes   Said of two goods or services such that if the price of one increases the demand for the other tends to increase, holding all other things equal (e.g., butter and margarine).

Sunk cost   A cost that has already been incurred.

Supernormal profit   Equal to accounting profit less the implicit opportunity costs not included in total accounting costs; the difference between total revenue (TR) and total cost (TC).

Supply shock   A typically unexpected disturbance to supply.

Support   In technical analysis, a price range in which buying activity is sufficient to stop the decline in the price of a security.

Survey approach   An estimate of the equity risk premium that is based upon estimates provided by a panel of finance experts.

Survivorship bias   The bias resulting from a test design that fails to account for companies that have gone bankrupt, merged, or are otherwise no longer reported in a database.

Sustainable growth rate The rate of dividend (and earnings) growth that can be sustained over time for a given level of return on equity, keeping the capital structure constant and without issuing additional common stock.

Sustainable rate of economic growth The rate of increase in the economy's productive capacity or potential GDP.

Swap An agreement between two parties to exchange a series of future cash flows.

Swap contract An agreement between two parties to exchange a series of future cash flows.

Swap spread The difference between the fixed rate on an interest rate swap and the rate on a Treasury note with equivalent maturity; it reflects the general level of credit risk in the market.

Swaption An option to enter into a swap.

Synthetic call The combination of puts, the underlying, and riskfree bonds that replicates a call option.

Synthetic put The combination of calls, the underlying, and riskfree bonds that replicates a put option.

Systematic risk Risk that affects the entire market or economy; it cannot be avoided and is inherent in the overall market. Systematic risk is also known as non diversifiable or market risk.

Systematic sampling A procedure of selecting every kth member until reaching a sample of the desired size. The sample that results from this procedure should be approximately random.

t-Test A hypothesis test using a statistic (t-statistic) that follows a t-distribution.

TRIN A flow of funds indicator applied to a broad stock market index to measure the relative extent to which money is moving into or out of rising and declining stocks.

Tactical asset allocation The decision to deliberately deviate from the strategic asset allocation in an attempt to add value based on forecasts of the near-term relative performance of asset classes.

Target balance A minimum level of cash to be held available— estimated in advance and adjusted for known funds transfers, seasonality, or other factors.

Target capital structure A company's chosen proportions of debt and equity.

Target independent A bank's ability to determine the definition of inflation that they target, the rate of inflation that they target, and the horizon over which the target is to be achieved.

Target semideviation The positive square root of target semivariance.

Target semivariance The average squared deviation below a target value.

Tax base The amount at which an asset or liability is valued for tax purposes.

Tax expense An aggregate of an entity's income tax payable (or recoverable in the case of a tax benefit) and any changes in deferred tax assets and liabilities. It is essentially the income tax payable or recoverable if these had been determined based on accounting profit rather than taxable income.

Tax loss carry forward A taxable loss in the current period that may be used to reduce future taxable income.

Taxable income The portion of an entity's income that is subject to income taxes under the tax laws of its jurisdiction.

Taxable temporary differences Temporary differences that result in a taxable amount in a future period when determining the taxable profit as the balance sheet item is recovered or settled.

Technical analysis A form of security analysis that uses price and volume data, which is often displayed graphically, in decision making.

Technology The process a company uses to transform inputs into outputs.

Tenor The original time to maturity on a swap.

Terminal stock value (or terminal value) The expected value of a share at the end of the investment horizon—in effect, the expected selling price.

Terminal value The expected value of a share at the end of the investment horizon—in effect, the expected selling price.

Termination date The date of the final payment on a swap; also, the swap's expiration date.

Theory of the consumer The branch of microeconomics that deals with consumption—the demand for goods and services—by utility-maximizing individuals.

Theory of the firm The branch of microeconomics that deals with the supply of goods and services by profit-maximizing firms.

Theta The rate at which an option's time value decays.

Third-degree price discrimination When the monopolist segregates customers into groups based on demographic or other characteristics and offers different pricing to each group.

Time to expiration The time remaining in the life of a derivative, typically expressed in years.

Time value The difference between the market price of the option and its intrinsic value, determined by the uncertainty of the underlying over the remaining life of the option.

Time value of money The principles governing equivalence relationships between cash flows with different dates.

Time-period bias The possibility that when we use a time-series sample, our statistical conclusion may be sensitive to the starting and ending dates of the sample.

Time-series data Observations of a variable over time.

Time-weighted rate of return The compound rate of growth of one unit of currency invested in a portfolio during a stated measurement period; a measure of investment performance that is not sensitive to the timing and amount of withdrawals or additions to the portfolio.

Top-down analysis With reference to investment selection processes, an approach that starts with macro selection (i.e., identifying attractive geographic segments and/or industry segments) and then addresses selection of the most attractive investments within those segments.

Total comprehensive income The change in equity during a period resulting from transaction and other events, other than those changes resulting from transactions with owners in their capacity as owners.

Total costs The summation of all costs, where costs are classified according to fixed or variable.

Total factor productivity A scale factor that reflects the portion of growth that is not accounted for by explicit factor inputs (e.g. capital and labor).

Total fixed cost The summation of all expenses that do not change when production varies.

Total probability rule A rule explaining the unconditional probability of an event in terms of probabilities of the event conditional on mutually exclusive and exhaustive scenarios.

Total probability rule for expected value A rule explaining the expected value of a random variable in terms of expected values of the random variable conditional on mutually exclusive and exhaustive scenarios.

Total product   The aggregate sum of production for the firm during a time period.

Total return   Measures the price appreciation, or percentage change in price of the securities in an index or portfolio, plus any income received over the period.

Total return index   An index that reflects the price appreciation or percentage change in price of the constituent securities plus any income received since inception.

Total return swap   A swap in which one party agrees to pay the total return on a security. Often used as a credit derivative, in which the underlying is a bond.

Total revenue   Price times the quantity of units sold.

Total variable cost   The summation of all variable expenses.

Tracking error   The standard deviation of the differences between a portfolio's returns and its benchmark's returns; a synonym of active risk.

Tracking risk   (tracking error) The standard deviation of the differences between a portfolio's returns and its benchmark's returns; a synonym of active risk.

Trade credit   A spontaneous form of credit in which a purchaser of the goods or service is financing its purchase by delaying the date on which payment is made.

Trade payables   Amounts that a business owes to its vendors for goods and services that were purchased from them but which have not yet been paid.

Trade receivables   (**commercial receivables or accounts receivable**) Amounts customers owe the company for products that have been sold as well as amounts that may be due from suppliers (such as for returns of merchandise).

Trading securities   (held-for-trading securities) Securities held by a company with the intent to trade them.

Traditional investment markets   Markets for traditional investments, which include all publicly traded debts and equities and shares in pooled investment vehicles that hold publicly traded debts and/or equities.

Transactions money balances   Money balances that are held to finance transactions.

Transactions motive   In the context of inventory management, the need for inventory as part of the routine production–sales cycle.

Transfer payments   Welfare payments made through the social security system that exist to provide a basic minimum level of income for low-income households.

Transitive preferences   The assumption that when comparing any three distinct bundles, A, B, and C, if A is preferred to B and simultaneously B is preferred to C, then it must be true that A is preferred to C.

Treasury Inflation-Protected Securities   A bond issued by the United States Treasury Department that is designed to protect the investor from inflation by adjusting the principal of the bond for changes in inflation.

Treasury shares   Shares that were issued and subsequently repurchased by the company.

Treasury stock   Shares that were issued and subsequently repurchased by the company.

Treasury stock method   A method for accounting for the effect of options (and warrants) on earnings per share (EPS) that specifies what EPS would have been if the options and warrants had been exercised and the company had used the proceeds to repurchase common stock.

Tree diagram   A diagram with branches emanating from nodes representing either mutually exclusive chance events or mutually exclusive decisions.

Trend   A long-term pattern of movement in a particular direction.

Treynor ratio   A measure of risk-adjusted performance that relates a portfolio's excess returns to the portfolio's beta.

Triangle patterns   In technical analysis, a continuation chart pattern that forms as the range between high and low prices narrows, visually forming a triangle.

Trimmed mean   A mean computed after excluding a stated small percentage of the lowest and highest observations.

Triple bottoms   In technical analysis, a reversal pattern that is formed when the price forms three troughs at roughly the same price level; used to predict a change from a downtrend to an uptrend.

Triple tops   In technical analysis, a reversal pattern that is formed when the price forms three peaks at roughly the same price level; used to predict a change from an uptrend to a downtrend.

Trough   The lowest point of a business cycle.

Trust receipt arrangement   The use of inventory as collateral for a loan. The inventory is segregated and held in trust, and the proceeds of any sale must be remitted to the lender immediately.

Turn-of-the-year effect   Calendar anomaly that stock market returns in January are significantly higher compared to the rest of the months of the year, with most of the abnormal returns reported during the first five trading days in January.

Two-fund separation theorem   The theory that all investors regardless of taste, risk preferences, and initial wealth will hold a combination of two portfolios or funds: a risk-free asset and an optimal portfolio of risky assets.

Two-sided hypothesis test   A test in which the null hypothesis is rejected in favor of the alternative hypothesis if the evidence indicates that the population parameter is either smaller or larger than a hypothesized value.

Two-tailed hypothesis test   A test in which the null hypothesis is rejected in favor of the alternative hypothesis if the evidence indicates that the population parameter is either smaller or larger than a hypothesized value.

Two-week repo rate   The interest rate on a two-week repurchase agreement; may be used as a policy rate by a central bank.

Type I error   The error of rejecting a true null hypothesis.

Type II error   The error of not rejecting a false null hypothesis.

Unanticipated (unexpected) inflation   The component of inflation that is a surprise.

Unbilled revenue   (accrued revenue) Revenue that has been earned but not yet billed to customers as of the end of an accounting period.

Unclassified balance sheet   A balance sheet that does not show subtotals for current assets and current liabilities.

Unconditional probability   The probability of an event *not* conditioned on another event.

Underemployed   A person who has a job but has the qualifications to work a significantly higher-paying job.

Underlying   An asset that trades in a market in which buyers and sellers meet, decide on a price, and the seller then delivers the asset to the buyer and receives payment. The underlying is the asset or other derivative on which a particular derivative is based. The market for the underlying is also referred to as the spot market.

Underwritten offering   An offering in which the (lead) investment bank guarantees the sale of the issue at an offering price that it negotiates with the issuer.

Unearned fees   Unearned fees are recognized when a company receives cash payment for fees prior to earning them.

Unearned revenue (**deferred revenue** or **deferred income**) A liability account for money that has been collected for goods or services that have not yet been delivered; payment received in advance of providing a good or service.

Unemployed People who are actively seeking employment but are currently without a job.

Unemployment rate The ratio of unemployed to the labor force.

Unexpected inflation The component of inflation that is a surprise.

Unit labor cost The average labor cost to produce one unit of output.

Unit normal distribution The normal density with mean (μ) equal to 0 and standard deviation (σ) equal to 1.

Units-of-production method A depreciation method that allocates the cost of a long-lived asset based on actual usage during the period.

Univariate distribution A distribution that specifies the probabilities for a single random variable.

Unlimited funds An unlimited funds environment assumes that the company can raise the funds it wants for all profitable projects simply by paying the required rate of return.

Unsecured debt Debt which gives the debtholder only a general claim on an issuer's assets and cash flow.

Unsponsored A type of depository receipt in which the foreign company whose shares are held by the depository has no involvement in the issuance of the receipts.

Up transition probability The probability that an asset's value moves up.

Utility function A mathematical representation of the satisfaction derived from a consumption basket.

Utils A unit of utility.

Validity instructions Instructions which indicate when the order may be filled.

Valuation The process of determining the value of an asset or service.

Valuation allowance A reserve created against deferred tax assets, based on the likelihood of realizing the deferred tax assets in future accounting periods.

Valuation ratios Ratios that measure the quantity of an asset or flow (e.g., earnings) in relation to the price associated with a specified claim (e.g., a share or ownership of the enterprise).

Value at risk (VAR) A money measure of the minimum value of losses expected during a specified time period at a given level of probability.

Variable costs Costs that fluctuate with the level of production and sales.

Variance The expected value (the probability-weighted average) of squared deviations from a random variable's expected value.

Variation margin Additional margin that must be deposited in an amount sufficient to bring the balance up to the initial margin requirement.

Veblen good A good that increases in desirability with price.

Vega The relationship between option price and volatility.

Venture capital Investments that provide "seed" or start-up capital, early-stage financing, or mezzanine financing to companies that are in the early stages of development and require additional capital for expansion.

Venture capital fund A fund for private equity investors that provides financing for development-stage companies.

Vertical analysis Common-size analysis using only one reporting period or one base financial statement; for example, an income statement in which all items are stated as percentages of sales.

Vertical demand schedule Implies that some fixed quantity is demanded, regardless of price.

Volatility As used in option pricing, the standard deviation of the continuously compounded returns on the underlying asset.

Voluntarily unemployed A person voluntarily outside the labor force, such as a jobless worker refusing an available vacancy.

Vote by proxy A mechanism that allows a designated party—such as another shareholder, a shareholder representative, or management—to vote on the shareholder's behalf.

Warehouse receipt arrangement The use of inventory as collateral for a loan; similar to a trust receipt arrangement except there is a third party (i.e., a warehouse company) that supervises the inventory.

Weak-form efficient market hypothesis The belief that security prices fully reflect all past market data, which refers to all historical price and volume trading information.

Wealth effect An increase (decrease) in household wealth increases (decreases) consumer spending out of a given level of current income.

Weighted average cost method An inventory accounting method that averages the total cost of available inventory items over the total units available for sale.

Weighted average cost of capital A weighted average of the aftertax required rates of return on a company's common stock, preferred stock, and long-term debt, where the weights are the fraction of each source of financing in the company's target capital structure.

Weighted mean An average in which each observation is weighted by an index of its relative importance.

Weighted-average cost of capital A weighted average of the aftertax required rates of return on a company's common stock, preferred stock, and long-term debt, where the weights are the fraction of each source of financing in the company's target capital structure.

Wholesale price index Reflects the price changes experienced by domestic producers in a country.

Winsorized mean A mean computed after assigning a stated percent of the lowest values equal to one specified low value, and a stated percent of the highest values equal to one specified high value.

Working capital The difference between current assets and current liabilities.

Working capital management The management of a company's short-term assets (such as inventory) and short-term liabilities (such as money owed to suppliers).

Yield The actual return on a debt security if it is held to maturity.

Yield spread The difference between the yield on a bond and the yield on a default-free security, usually a government note, of the same maturity. The yield spread is primarily determined by the market's perception of the credit risk on the bond.

Yield to maturity The annual return that an investor earns on a bond if the investor purchases the bond today and holds it until maturity.

Zero-cost collar A transaction in which a position in the underlying is protected by buying a put and selling a call with the premium from the sale of the call offsetting the premium from the purchase of the put. It can also be used to protect a floating-rate borrower against interest rate increases with the premium on a long cap offsetting the premium on a short floor.

Index